Fundamental social rights:

Case law of the European Social Charter

BUNKERS
7 THE DRIVE, HOVE
EAST SUSSEX BN3 3JS

Council of Europe Publishing

French edition:
*Droits sociaux fondamentaux – Jurisprudence
de la Charte sociale européenne*
ISBN 92-871-3189-9

›

Cover design : Atelier de création graphique, Council of Europe
Council of Europe Publishing
F-67075 Strasbourg Cedex

ISBN 92-871-3190-2
© Council of Europe, 1997
Printed in France

Contents

Appendix I

Appendix II

Appendix III

Note to readers

By taking part in the work of the Governmental Committee of the European Social Charter and studying the case law of the Committee of Independent Experts I came to appreciate the great potential of the Charter as an instrument of social and economic progress even today, thirty-five years after its adoption.

This appreciation led to the writing of this book which is dedicated to all those across all the continents who believe that the fight for human rights and human dignity is the noblest of all.

I wish to acknowledge my indebtedness to the Council of Europe and in particular to the Director of Human Rights, Mr Pierre-Henri Imbert.

I also wish to express my gratitude to Mr Régis Brillat, Head of the Social Charter Section, who not only encouraged me in writing this book but also offered me his support and prepared the index. Sincere thanks are due to the Social Charter Section of the Directorate of Human Rights of the Council of Europe, who have read and checked the manuscript and made valuable comments, as a result of which the case law is presented as comprehensively and accurately as possible.

I take full responsibility for any errors or omissions.

This book presents, Article by Article and paragraph by paragraph, the case law of the Committee of Independent Experts of the European Social Charter.

This body is the first to intervene in the control mechanism of the Charter: its task is to decide whether Contracting Parties fulfil their obligations under the Charter (see the presentation of the system of supervision in Appendix I; see also membership of the Committee in Appendix II).

The study covers information up to Conclusions XIII-3 (published in February 1996).

Nicosia, September 1996

Lenia Samuel

Foreword

The European Social Charter is both little known and imperfectly understood:

– little known since the few writings on it to date have usually been published in specialised journals;

– imperfectly understood in that although commentators are quick to point out how complex its supervisory machinery is, how outdated some of the standards it guarantees are and how scant the results achieved through its implementation have been, they mostly fail to mention that it contains a huge body of rules pertaining not only to labour law and protection of workers but also to other spheres and other categories of individuals outside the world of work. They also omit to say that the supervisory machinery, which is based on a governmental reporting system, allows a regular, systematic, comprehensive review of all aspects of national legislation and practice in respect of each provision of the Charter accepted by a state and even of those not accepted.

Lenia Samuel's book is a major contribution to making the Charter more widely known and better understood.

It is written in a clear style which keeps technicality to a minimum without sacrificing scientific accuracy and is aimed at a wide general readership and not just legal specialists. It will enable all those who are interested in the social and economic aspects of human rights to familiarise themselves effortlessly with the most important and comprehensive European treaty in this field.

The author, Principal Administrative Officer responsible for International Affairs in the Ministry of Labour and Social Insurance of Cyprus, has chosen to present the European Social Charter from the angle of the case law of the Committee of Independent Experts, which is the first body involved in the supervisory machinery and which carries out a legal appraisal of the conformity of the situation with the Charter in a given country.

Using her experience as Vice-Chairperson of the Governmental Committee (1995-97), former chairperson of the Governmental Committee (1985-87) and of the Charte-Rel Committee (1992-94), Lenia Samuel presents for each right secured in the Charter the substantive rules and the interpretation of them in the course of the supervision cycles. With its practical examples, the book makes it easy to understand the real scope of the Charter's provisions and at the same time draws a picture of the situations prevailing in the twenty states that have now ratified this instrument.

The reader is thus led to conclude that the Charter has achieved far more wide-ranging results than is generally recognised.

Lenia Samuel's book fills a regrettable vacuum and comes at a turning point in the Charter's existence.

This binding instrument was adopted in 1961 and came into force in 1965. It was supplemented in 1988 by an additional protocol, and from 1991 to 1995 an extensive process of reform was undertaken relating to both the supervisory machinery and the rights secured:

– the 1991 Turin Protocol amending the European Social Charter clarified the functions of the various supervisory bodies and expedited the procedure. It also made it easier, and thus practicable, for the Committee of Ministers to issue recommendations to states which fail to comply fully with their obligations;

- a further protocol, the 1995 Additional Protocol providing for a system of collective complaints, allows trade unions and employer's organisations as wells as certain non-governmental organisations to refer alleged breaches of the Charter to the Committee of Independent Experts. It supplements the traditional supervisory machinery with a new procedure which will help to strengthen protection of human rights in the social and economic field;

- lastly, the revised European Social Charter, which was opened for signature on 3 May 1996, updates and complements the list of rights secured in the Charter.

The time was therefore ripe to take stock of the case law of the Committee, which for the past thirty years has defined the content and scope of the rights set forth in the Charter.

Wider understanding of the Charter's subject-matter and scope is important for ensuring its effectiveness, which, however, is also contingent on the commitment of all concerned: experts, governments, the Parliamentary Assembly, management and labour, and non-governmental organisations. The variety of fields covered in the Charter and broadened in the revised Charter amply justifies a combined effort by all concerned to make the Council of Europe truly the reference organisation in all spheres of human rights, civil, political, economic, social and cultural alike.

Pierre-Henri IMBERT
Director of Human Rights
Council of Europe

Article 1 – The right to work

General

The right to work is the first right protected by the European Social Charter. As the Committee pointed out in the first supervision cycle, "It is of fundamental importance within the context of the Charter, for the effective exercise of several essential rights set forth in the Charter is inconceivable unless the right to work is guaranteed first" (Conclusions I, p. 13). Examples are the right to just conditions of work (Article 2), and the right to fair remuneration (Article 4).

The right to work cannot however mean what it appears to mean: that a state must guarantee a job to every person who desires one, which is evidently impossible to fulfil, as the availability of work depends on the situation of the labour market and on whether the skills of job-seekers correspond to the demands of the market. Accordingly, Article 1 does not aim to provide employment to all those in search of it: instead, it consists of four specific undertakings which will improve job opportunities. The Committee stated this clearly in its first Conclusions:

"This Article aims to ensure the effective exercise of the right to work. Its four paragraphs deal with various aspects of employment policy. Moreover, Article 1 does not merely state a principle: it also specifies the means whereby the Contracting Parties must apply it:

- full employment;

- free choice of occupation;

- free employment agencies;

- vocational guidance training and rehabilitation" (Conclusions I, p. 13).

Paragraph 1 – Full employment

Under the first paragraph of Article 1 of the Charter, the Contracting Parties undertake:

> "to accept as one of their primary aims and responsibilities the achievement and maintenance of as high and stable a level of employment as possible, with a view to the attainment of full employment."

According to the case law of the Committee, the Contracting Parties must prove that they adhere to a coherent economic policy specifically aimed at achieving the ultimate goal of this provision. In addition to proving the existence of appropriate employment policies, the Contracting Parties are expected to take measures in view of its implementation and to supply sufficient information to permit the Committee to evaluate its effects.

The Committee has stated that this policy should:

- concern situations of short, medium and long-term unemployment;

- aim at avoiding, combating or reducing regional imbalance;

- seek to maintain or improve the situation of all groups of workers within society, especially women, young people, the middle-aged and the elderly;

- cover all sectors of the economy, including agriculture (in Conclusions II, p. 179, for instance, the Committee asked the Government of Cyprus to provide information on the measures taken to meet with underemployment in agriculture).

The Committee "interpreted this provision as imposing an obligation as to means rather than an obligation as to results. It recognised that in order to decide whether a country is really fulfilling its obligations, it is necessary to adopt a dynamic standpoint, to assess the situation existing at a given moment, having regard to the continuous action pursued." (Conclusions I, p. 13).

Paragraph 1 of Article 1 has been characterised as a dynamic provision. Its dynamic nature is inherent in the fact that it provides for the progressive attainment of full employment. Commenting generally on provisions of a similar character, the Committee stated that: "These provisions impose an obligation to adopt over the years a course of conduct so as to achieve a development in a stated direction. This makes it incumbent on every government concerned to inform the Committee of such changes as have occurred between the date of the coming into force of the Charter (or that of the preceding report) and the date to which a given report refers. Consequently, a purely static description of a state of affairs at a given moment does not suffice. It is necessary to specify that developments are taking place so as to enable the Committee to assess the progress each country has made in the particular context" (Conclusions I, p. 9).

The Contracting Parties must take measures to improve upon the employment situation which existed at the beginning of the period of reference. Again, actual improvement is not asked for as this may often only be revealed in the long term; what is needed is proof of the adoption of measures contributing towards the attainment of full employment. This was made very clear in the third supervision cycle when the Committee stated that the "decline of unemployment alone is not a sufficient indication of efforts towards the achievement of full employment when, for example, unemployment still affects 5% of the active population. On the other hand, a large increase in the rate of unemployment would not prevent the Committee from concluding that the Charter was being satisfied, as long as a substantial effort is made to improve the labour market situation" (Conclusions III, p. 3).

During the fourth cycle of supervision, covering the years 1972-73, it became patent that in order to deal with growing inflation or economic recession resulting from the oil shocks, the Contracting Parties had introduced a number of measures which had the effect of increasing unemployment in the short term, but which were eventually destined to reduce it. Considering the consistency of this action with the requirements of the first paragraph of Article 1, the Committee stressed that: "Measures to sustain employment should be taken, in pursuance of Article 1 para. 1, to offset the side-effects of action such as anti-inflation measures, made necessary by the current crisis, in order to avoid an excessive rise in unemployment", and that: "special measures should be taken to help those persons who are at a disadvantage in seeking work either because of regional imbalance or disparities based on sex or because of age, since older workers, like the young, run a greater risk of unemployment." (Conclusions IV, p. XIV).

Similarly, in the sixth supervision cycle, the Committee indicated that when the economic situation was such that the prospects of a substantial reduction of employment did not seem very high, Article 1 para. 1 required Contracting Parties to "intensify their efforts, as a priority objective, with a view to reducing unemployment especially among the groups mostly affected by it through the implementation of appropriate economic and social policies" (Conclusions VI, p. 12).

Assessment of compliance

In the first supervision cycle, the Committee stated that: "If a state at any time abandoned the objective of full employment in favour of an economic system providing for a permanent pool of unemployed, it would be infringing the Social Charter" (Conclusions I, p. 14).

In the light of the above-mentioned developments, the Committee decided during the eighth supervision cycle that it would not adopt conclusions under this paragraph. Instead, the Committee has reviewed the policies pursued and the measures taken. Even Spain, when in the thirteenth supervision cycle (third part), the Committee ascertained that the unemployment rate had reached 16.2% and that of women 23.8%, was not found in breach of this provision: likewise Ireland, with a 15.8% level of unemployment.

Several factors account for the absence of conclusions. As has already been suggested, the upward trends in unemployment, characteristic of many countries in the last years, do not necessarily denote failure of employment policies, but reflect economic crises; figures nonetheless could be taken to imply a lack of action towards full employment, whereas facts demonstrate the opposite. Furthermore, the results of many measures against unemployment cannot be foreseen and may take effect long after their implementation; therefore decisions on their efficiency are impossible.

In the last cycle of supervision (XIII-3 – reference period 1992-93), overall unemployment levels rose in almost all Contracting Parties.

The Committee shows great concern for the unemployment of certain categories of workers, asking for measures aimed at improving their situation: those over the age of forty-five, young workers, the long-term unemployed (for more than twelve months), women, in respect of whom unemployment rates are higher and increase more rapidly than those for men, thus widening disparities, and the disabled. Again in the latest cycle, evidence appeared of increases in levels of unemployment for:

– older workers in the case of Austria;

– young people in Finland, France, Greece (where 45.5% of the total unemployed were fifteen to twenty-four year-olds), Ireland, Italy, Luxembourg, the Netherlands, Portugal, Spain, Sweden, Turkey (mainly persons in the fifteen to twenty-four age group with a high education level living in urban areas: 30.2% in 1993) and the United Kingdom;

– the long-term unemployed, especially in Austria, France, Greece,

Ireland, Luxembourg, Malta (53%), the Netherlands, Norway and Portugal;

– women in Cyprus, France, Greece, Italy, Luxembourg and Portugal; Sweden showed a rise in rates for the disabled.

Over the last years a new trend has taken on increasing importance: part-time work, mainly concerning women (Ireland, the Netherlands, Portugal and the United Kingdom). The Committee has devoted much attention to this trend and to that of the increase in temporary employment (Spain and the United Kingdom) and work under fixed-term contracts (France, where these contracts constituted 70% of recruitments in 1993).

The Committee also shows concern for the position of young aliens, nationals of other Contracting Parties to the Charter. In Conclusions XIII-1 (p. 41), the Committee noted an increase in the number of foreign unemployed workers in Sweden. More specifically it asks questions on the requirements for foreign workers: for Austria, for example, it wished to know whether when these persons apply for a work permit for the first time, they were treated on an equal footing with unemployed nationals and aliens (Conclusions X-2, p. 33).

Some positive results have however been noted: measures to reintegrate long-term job-seekers had some effect in the Netherlands, Norway and the United Kingdom, where levels of unemployment remained unchanged over the first part of the thirteenth supervision cycle; the reduction in the gap between unemployment rates for women and those for men in Austria and Denmark; the creation of new jobs in certain sectors which reversed the upward trend in unemployment for those sectors.

Paragraph 2 – The right of the worker to earn his living in an occupation freely entered upon

Under this paragraph, the Contracting Parties undertake:

"to protect effectively the right of the worker [1] to earn his living in an occupation freely entered upon".

Appendix[2] to Article 1 para. 2

"This provision shall not be interpreted as prohibiting or authorising any union security clause or practice".

The Committee recognised in the first cycle of supervision that "this provision was closely bound up with two particularly important problems, viz:

- the prohibition of forced labour; and

- the eradication of all forms of discrimination in employment" (Conclusions I, p. 15).

It can, therefore, be said that this provision requires Contracting States to provide protection A. against forced labour and B. against discrimination in employment practices.

---

1 Generally speaking, the term "worker" takes on the broadest possible meaning in the Charter and also includes women workers and the self-employed, except when the text of the Charter or a specific context impose a different interpretation (such as the appendix to Article 19 para. 6 for women workers, which concerns only the wife of a worker and thus excludes women workers; in respect of the self-employed, Article 4 para. 4 on notice of termination of employment can only apply to salaried employees; and Article 8 which is expressly aimed only at protecting employed women).

2 As a rule the Appendix to the Charter contains important interpretations to be given to some of the Articles as well as a definition of the scope of the Charter in terms of persons protected. The appendix to Article 1 para. 2 stipulates that it is neutral to union security clauses, which means that a closed shop arrangement whereby a worker must be a member of a trade union or a particular trade union is not discrimination which a Contracting Party must take steps to prevent. Thus, Article 1 para. 2 of the Charter, like Article 11 of the European Convention on Human rights and ILO Convention No. 87 (Freedom of Association and Protection of the Right to Organise), takes no stand on the legality of closed shops. However, this appendix only applies to Article 1 para. 2 and the Committee stated its opinion on closed shops under Article 5 (the right to organise), which it considers are against the freedom of organisation (see Article 5).

A. Prohibition of forced labour

The guarantee against forced labour results from the phrase "freely entered upon" of the Article. In the third cycle of supervision, the Committee expressed the view that "the coercion of any worker to carry out work against his wishes, and without his freely expressed consent, is contrary to the Charter. The same applied to the coercion of any worker to carry out work he had previously freely agreed to do, but which he subsequently no longer wanted to carry out" (Conclusions III, p. 5).

The Committee regarded as constituting coercion within the latter meaning and, therefore, as incompatible with the Charter, legislation providing criminal penalties against merchant seamen failing to return to their ship or to carry out certain orders. However, recognising that the safety of the ship and above all the lives of those on board are factors of the greatest importance, the Committee, in the same Conclusions and again in the case of merchant seamen, clarified its concept of non-forced labour and held that "penal measures could, in appropriate circumstances, be justified when they applied in cases where the act giving rise to the charge endangered, or could endanger the safety of the ship or the life or health of those on board. The same was also true, in the Committee's view, of air crew" (Conclusions III, p. 5). The Committee implied that in such cases, restrictions could not go beyond the limitations of Article 31 (protection of national security and public health).

In the same cycle, the Committee held that the particular status of the armed forces could justify penal sanctions for breach of a voluntary engagement, without constituting a breach of the prohibition of forced labour.

Many Contracting Parties were found to be in violation of the Charter in so far as provisions in their legislation imposed penal sanctions on seamen. Some of them consequently amended their legislation and brought it in line with the Charter,[1] whilst others did not and are still found in violation. These Contracting Parties usually argue that their

---

1 The situation was remedied in Germany by the Merchant Shipping Act of 29 October 1974, in Sweden by the Merchant Shipping Act of 18 May 1973, in Norway by an Act of

legislation is no longer applied, but the Committee has constantly held that "the non-application of national legislation containing elements which were in conflict with this principle of the Charter would not be considered sufficient for the purpose of ensuring the application of this provision on this point and that consequently such legislation would have to be amended" (Conclusions V, p. 6) or that "the non-application of national legislation did not suffice to demonstrate a state's compliance with this provision" (see most recently Conclusions XIII-3, p. 66).

Other situations contrary to the prohibition of forced labour

Even though the case law of the Committee concerning the prohibition of forced labour has mainly been established in relation to the merchant navy and the aviation sector, other cases have also been found incompatible with this prohibition, particularly those which go beyond the limitations of Article 31[1] of the Charter such as criminal sanctions against requisitioned civil servants, excessive lengths of compulsory service in the armed forces, and delays in the acceptance of refusals of resignation in certain public services.

Assessment of compliance

The following countries have been found to infringe on the prohibition of forced labour within the meaning of Article 1 para. 2, on the ground that their legislation punishes by penal measures cases where a contract is merely broken or not honoured and where there is no likelihood of persons or property being endangered.

France: Sections 39, para. 4 and 59, para. 1 of the Disciplinary and Penal Code of the Merchant Navy provide a possibility for penal sanctions against seamen in certain cases not involving the safety of the vessel or

---

1975, in Cyprus by Merchant Shipping Act No. 11 of 1976, in Iceland by an Act of 1990, in Spain by an Act of 1992 and in the United Kingdom by an Order of 1994.

1 Under Article 31 of the Charter, the only authorised restrictions or limitations to the rights and principles guaranteed by the Charter are those which "are prescribed by law and are necessary in a democratic society for the protection of the rights and freedoms of others or for the protection of public interest, nationals security, public health, or morals".

the life and health of those on board[1] (see in the last instance, Conclusions XIII-3, p. 62).

Greece: provisions exist for criminal sanctions against seamen in cases where neither the safety nor the lives or health of the persons on board are endangered (Articles 205, 207 para. 1, 208, 210 para. 1 and 222 of the Code of Public Maritime Law of 1973; Section 4 para. 1 of Act No. 3276/1944 on collective bargaining in the Merchant Navy; Section 15 of Act No. 299/1936 on the settlement of collective disputes in the Navy)[1] (*ibidem*, p. 64).

Ireland: under the Merchant Shipping Act of 1894, seamen who fail to rejoin their ship or who do not carry out orders are liable to punishment which may involve their imprisonment (see Sections 222, 224 and 238 for forcible conveyance on board a ship and Sections 221 and 225 1. b. and c. for punishment of disciplinary offences)[1] (*ibidem*, p. 66).

Italy: Sections 1091 and 1094 of the Navigation Code prescribe penal sanctions for seamen and civil aviation staff who desert their posts or refuse to obey orders even if those defaults jeopardise neither the safety of the ship or aeroplane nor the life or health of persons on board[1] (*ibidem*, p. 68).

Spain: the Act of 24 December 1964 relating to airmen includes provisions for criminal sanctions in the event of disciplinary offences, even in cases where neither the safety of the aeroplane nor the life or health of those on board were threatened[1] (*ibidem*, pp. 74 and 75).

---

1 For the twelfth supervision cycle the Committee of Ministers addressed a recommendation to Greece (first part), France, Italy and Spain (second part). Moreover, in the thirteenth supervision cycle (first part), the Committee of Ministers addressed recommendations to France (second recommendation), Greece (second recommendation), Italy (second recommendation), Spain (second recommendation – the first recommendation related to criminal sanctions in the merchant navy and in the aeronautics sector; the second recommendation only concerned those in the aeronautics industry as the law which provided for criminal sanctions for seamen was abolished in 1992) and Ireland (first recommendation). The Committee of Ministers reiterated its recommendations to France, Greece and Italy for the third part of the thirteenth supervision cycle.

Turkey: Article 1467 of the Commercial Code empowers the captain of a ship to use force to bring seamen back on board or with a view to ensuring the proper running of the vessel and the maintenance of discipline. The Committee recalled that any sanction involving compulsory labour should be limited to acts endangering the safety of the ship or the life or health of persons on board, and needed to be strictly defined. As Article 1467 of the Commercial Code did not meet this criteria, the Committee concluded that it was not in conformity with the Charter (*ibidem*, p. 238).

the *United Kingdom:* under Section 30c. of the 1990 Merchant Shipping Act penal sanctions can be imposed in cases where a work contract is merely broken or not honoured because of a strike by the crew or part of the crew and where there is no likelihood of persons or property being endangered.[1] The Committee did not accept the claim of the government that this did not violate the Charter as this section applied only to a strike by the crew or part of the crew of a vessel whilst the vessel was at sea and that no prosecution was ever made under it. The Committee considered that not all strikes on board vessels at sea would endanger the safety of the ship or the life of those on board and that Section 30c. was not in conformity with the Charter (*ibidem*, p. 78).

The following are cases of non-compliance on other grounds:

Cyprus: Defence Regulations 79A and 79B empower the government to requisition employees and to ban strikes in cases non-consistent with the restrictions allowed under Article 31 (*ibidem*, pp. 59 and 60).

Denmark: Sections 198 and 199 of the Criminal Code prescribe criminal penalties for deliberate idleness or lack of means of subsistence for which the person concerned is responsible (*ibidem*, p. 61).

Greece: under Section 64 of Decree No. 1400 of 1973 on compulsory army service, career officers having attended a number of training

---

1 Section 30c. is the last of a series of provisions still in force (see Sections 28-29 and 31) which have been criticised by the Committee since the third cycle The Committee of Ministers addressed a recommendation to the United Kingdom on this point for the third part of the thirteenth supervision cycle.

courses may not leave the army before completing a term of service of up to twenty-five years. The Committee considered that this duration exceeded all reasonable limits and was not justified by the specific nature of a military career and the high cost of training[1] (*ibidem*, p. 64).

The *Netherlands:* under Article 6 of the 1945 Labour Relations (Special Powers) Extraordinary Decree, neither an employee nor an employer may voluntarily terminate a contract of employment without the permission of the director of the Regional Labour Office (*ibidem*, p. 71).

The Committee deferred its conclusion for the following Contracting Parties:

Belgium: a. under certain circumstances the resignation of regular officers or non-commissioned officers may be refused. The Committee asked information on the grounds for refusal and the length of service required; b. the Act of 19 August 1948 on the provision of public services in peacetime provides that joint committees determine measures to be taken, or services to be provided to ensure basic services and criminal penalties can be imposed on workers who refuse to comply with decisions. The Committee recalled that the circumstances in which these measures were taken had to be justified under Article 31 of the Charter and asked a number of questions to enable it to assess the situation (see Conclusions XIII-2, p. 231).

Finland: the Readiness Act No. 1080 of 1991 contained provisions on compulsory manpower placement which could be implemented by the Council of State in emergency conditions, such as in the event of an armed attack directed at Finland, a serious violation of Finland's territorial integrity, when sudden disturbances of international commerce or any other particular event taking place outside Finland, cause a serious threat to the livelihood of the population or to the foundation of the country's economy or in the case of a major disaster. The Committee asked for detailed information as to the meaning of "compulsory place-

---

1 The Committee of Ministers addressed a recommendation to Greece for the first part of the twelfth cycle and for the first part of the thirteenth cycle (second recommendation). The recommendation was renewed for the third part of the thirteenth supervision cycle.

ment" especially in cases of international commerce or any other particular event taking place outside Finland. It also asked whether this act had been applied in practice and if so in what circumstances (Conclusions XIII-3, p. 233)

Greece: Decree No. 17 of 1974 permits the mobilisation of the civilian population in any "unforeseen situation causing disruption of the country's economy and society". This expression appeared to the Committee too wide in its meaning as it could result in some forms of compulsory labour not admissible under Article 1 para. 2 in the light of Article 31 of the Charter. The last report stated that this provision was no longer in force and the Committee asked when and in what way it had been repealed (Conclusions XIII-3, p. 62).

Ireland: the Committee asked for information on cases in which permission for officers to leave the army had been refused or delayed and, having noted that the length of the period of service in the army for which young people could enlist was five years (seven years in the reserve), it asked at what age and under which pecuniary conditions a person enlisted as a minor might obtain discharge from his obligations (Conclusions XIII-3, pp. 66 and 67).

Italy: a. Sections 328, 331 and 333 of the Criminal Code provide prison sentences for civil servants and public service employees guilty of dereliction of duty. The Committee noted that Section 333 on the exercise of the right to strike in essential public services was repealed by Act No. 146 of 12 June 1990 and that according to the Italian report the provisions still in force were applied only where the conduct of the public servant jeopardised the fundamental interests of the community. The Committee asked to be informed of each practical application of them (see Conclusions XIII-3, p. 68); b. Section 2 of Royal Decree No. 773 of 18 June 1931 and Sections 20 and 55 of the Royal Decree of 3 March 1934 empowered prefects to take steps in emergency situations to requisition persons in essential services. The Committee noted that these provisions were still in the statute book although this matter had been revised by the above-mentioned Act No. 146 of 1990 and that a decision of 27 May 1961, handed down by the Constitutional Court, had declared Section 2 of Decree No. 773 to be partially unconstitutional. The Committee wished to know in which services these requisitions could be made and to be informed of any application of these provisions (*ibidem*, pp. 68 and 69).

Portugal: a. Article 436 of the Portuguese Criminal Code provided that any official who abandoned his or her duties or neglected them with the intention of impeding or disrupting a public service would be liable for up to six months' imprisonment or a fine. The Committee asked that the next report state the situations covered by this provision, as well as any practical applications; b. in "particularly serious circumstances", Legislative Order No. 637 of 20 November 1974 (as amended by Legislative Order No. 23-A of 14 February 1979 and Legislative Order No. 123 of 17 May 1980) authorised the government to order civilian requisitioning and take measures to ensure "the proper running of essential public services or vital sectors of the national economy". The Committee took note of the list of public services and enterprises liable to be subjected to civilian requisitioning. In order to determine whether this list was in conformity with the Charter taking into account Article 31, the Committee wished to know the circumstances in which civilian requisitioning could be ordered and particularly, with the exception of strikes, how the Portuguese Government interpreted the concept of "particularly serious circumstances", and whether civilian requisitioning had been applied in practice (Conclusions XIII-3, pp. 234 and 235).

Turkey: the prohibition of forced labour is enshrined in Article 18 of the Constitution. Nevertheless, certain work is not considered to be "forced labour", including *inter alia* work necessitated as a civic obligation (Article 18 para. 2). According to the report, this wording was based on Article 4 para. 3 d) of the European Convention on Human Rights. Act No. 2935 of 25 October 1983 on States of Emergency, one of the laws implemented in application of Article 18 para. 2 of the Constitution, provided that during a state of emergency declared following natural disasters and epidemics, people aged between eighteen and sixty could be assigned to certain tasks. The Committee wished to know whether there were any other laws passed in application of Article 18 para. 2 of the Constitution and if so asked for details of their application in practice (Conclusions XIII-3, p. 238).

B. *Elimination of all forms of discrimination in employment*

According to the Committee, Article 1 para. 2 imposes an obligation upon Contracting Parties to eliminate all forms of discrimination in employment and, in this respect, paragraph 2 must be read in conjunction with the Preamble to the Charter, which provides that "the enjoyment of social rights should be secured without discrimination on grounds of race, colour, sex, religion, political opinion, national extraction or social origin", giving the forms of discrimination that are prohibited.

It is recalled that as the Charter applies *ratione personae* only to nationals of Contracting Parties, it is only such nationals who must be protected from discrimination in employment for reasons of "national extraction".

Furthermore, paragraph 2 is completed by other relevant provisions of the Charter which directly ensure the right to non-discrimination by recognising the entitlement of men and women to equal pay for work of equal value (Article 4 para. 3).[1]

Under Article 1 para. 2, employment is understood in its broadest sense, taken to include all categories of workers, all sectors of activity (public, private, professional and of the self-employed), and all forms of employment (including for the purpose of a private household and in firms not employing more than five persons – Conclusions IX-1, p. 25).

From the earliest supervision cycles the Committee showed a particular interest in the application of the principle of non-discrimination to the admission of women to employment, making it clear that reports on this provision should provide "particulars on the admission of women to certain posts, notably in the civil service; it considered that the rights guaranteed by the Charter, especially in matters of non-discrimination

---

1 The protection of equality between men and women was reinforced by the Additional Protocol to the Charter, adopted in 1988 and brought into force in 1992, Article 1 of which guarantees the right to equal opportunities and equal treatment in matters of employment and occupation without discrimination on the grounds of sex.

against women, required not only that the states remove all legal obstacles to admission to certain types of employment but also that positive, practical steps be taken to create a situation which really ensured complete equality of treatment in this respect" (Conclusions I, p. 15).

Ireland was found to be in violation of Article 1 para. 2 during the first three supervision cycles, because female civil servants were obliged to resign on marriage and because married women were prohibited from entering the civil service.[1]

Furthermore, in its first Conclusions the Committee ruled that, as regards the principle of non-discrimination, this paragraph contained an obligation to "provide appropriate education and training to ensure the full exercise of the right guaranteed therein"[2] (Conclusions I, p. 15).

In the eighth supervision cycle the Committee, welcoming the initiative of Austria to organise a very wide-ranging government campaign to foster public awareness of problems of equality of access to work based on action by numerous international organisations to abolish all discrimination and prejudice against women, observed that this initiative was in keeping with the aims of the Charter and its own concern "to ensure that the principle of non-discrimination between men and women is not only embodied in the positive law of each Contracting Party but is also applied in practice" (Conclusions VIII, p. 29).

In the same cycle, the Committee considered appropriate to clarify that: "the obligation to protect effectively the right of the worker to earn his living in an occupation freely entered upon certainly does not confer upon any worker, whether in the public service or not, the right to employment of his choice regardless of his qualifications. Nevertheless,

---

1 The bar on married women was abolished in 1977 by the Civil Service (Employment of Married Women) Act 1973.

2 David Harris, in his book "*The European Social Charter*" (pp. 33 and 34) regards this ruling as important, because "the absence of discrimination in the employment of qualified or trained candidates is meaningless if there is discrimination in the provision of facilities to obtain the necessary qualifications for training".

certain requirements are not admissible under the Charter such as those based on race, colour, sex, political opinion etc. (see the Preamble). That is to say that the Charter does not prevent an employer from stipulating whatever qualifications he or she may wish, provided that they do not take the form of requirements inadmissible by the Charter (account being taken of Article 31)" (Conclusions VIII, pp. 29 and 30).

Two points may be underlined concerning the elimination of discrimination on grounds of sex: on one hand, the Contracting Parties to the Charter have made considerable efforts to establish the necessary legislation and structures to guarantee the principle of equality, particularly between women and men; on the other, the Committee's supervision does not only extend to the conformity of legislation or regulations with the requirements of the Charter but also to practical applications, and in this respect it must be realised that the *de facto* situation of equality between men and women is nowhere satisfactory, even where the law is sufficient.

Despite the fact that during the early supervision cycles emphasis seems to have been placed on discrimination in access to employment and on discrimination based on sex, it is clear, especially from questions put to the Contracting Parties in the later supervision cycles, (see below) that non-discrimination is also equally important in matters of promotion, training, working conditions and of dismissal on grounds other than sex, such as trade union membership, political opinion, religion, race and national minority.

Concerning discrimination in employment other than that based upon sex, the Committee has examined more closely one particular example of possible discrimination on grounds of political opinion: the duty of fidelity and loyalty to the Constitution, required in the Federal Republic of Germany, for candidates for employment (as well as for those already employed) in the public services. The Committee has never questioned the conformity of this requirement with Article 1 para. 2, but it has expressed doubt as to "whether it was really necessary for the legitimate aim of protecting the state and its constitutional order to extend the requirement of fidelity and loyalty to candidates for fairly routine and even menial jobs such as engine-drivers, postmen and gardeners" (Conclusions VII, p. 6). The Committee defined the limits of this condition with regard to the Charter "The close connection in certain cases between 'loyalty' or 'fidelity to the Constitution' and political behaviour (as the practical expression of political opinion) creates the confusion (in respect, particularly, of "*Berufsverbot*") in this context. The existence of measures based neither on the nature of the service nor on essential elements connected with the qualification of the person concerned or on any overt act putting in doubt his loyalty or fidelity to the Constitution, would constitute a discrimination and would not be considered as being in conformity with Article 1, paragraph 2 of the Charter" (Conclusions-VIII, p. 30). Having considered that "access to the civil service was not the subject of any exemption or reservation in respect of Article 1 para. 2: it was a form of access to work and was therefore covered by this article", the Committee "saw fit, without calling into question the constitutional principle of German law, to draw the government's attention to the fact that one of the main problems arising from the conditions for the application of the duty of loyalty to the Constitution by the federal authorities and the *Länder* authorities – whose practices in this respect differed, moreover – stemmed from the fact that the conditions laid upon applications to and members of the civil service were standard, general ones, irrespective of the jobs in question".[1]

Despite subsequent developments, the Committee once again adjourned its conclusion after its latest study of the situation (Conclusions XIII-2, pp. 230 and 231).

More generally, it may be observed that in the General introduction to Conclusions XI-2, p. 23, under the sub-heading "Equality of Treatment", the Committee remarked that with the exception of one report, all the national reports examined in the eleventh supervision cycle dealt solely with discrimination between men and women. As a result, the Committee drew the attention of the Contracting Parties to the Pre-

[1] In the same way, concerning the provision allowing political, religious or cultural bodies in Norway to enquire as to job applicants'political, religious or cultural opinions when the post to be filled was important to the aims of the organisations or institutions concerned, the Committee "wished to draw the Norwegian Government's attention to the dangers inherent in a wider application of this provision" (Conclusions XI-1, p. 45).

amble of the Charter and urged that "consequently reports relating to the elimination of **all** discrimination in employment (Article 1 para. 2) – which is one of the cornerstones of equality of treatment – ought not to be restricted to discrimination based on sex".

Thus, for example, the Committee asked:

- the United Kingdom to indicate whether the 1990 Employment Act, which *inter alia* makes it unlawful to refuse a person employment on the ground that he is a member of a trade union, provides protection against denial of employment on grounds of past trade union membership or on grounds of trade union activity (Conclusions XII-1 p. 60). It also asked the government to indicate any steps taken or planned to guarantee in practice complete and effective protection against anti-trade union discrimination based on trade union membership or activities (Conclusions XIII-1, p. 57);

- Spain for information on cases of discrimination "in working conditions affecting coloured workers and Muslim workers, as well as difficulties affecting workers belonging to the Gipsy minority" (Conclusions XII-2, p. 52 and Conclusions XIII-1, p. 54);

- Greece to comment on allegations of discrimination in access to employment against persons not belonging to the Greek Orthodox religion, especially in the education sector (Conclusions XIII-1, pp. 48 and 49);

- Turkey for information on discrimination on grounds of political opinion, *inter alia* with respect to: Section 2 of Martial Law Act No. 1402, which imposes an obligation on the competent authorities to comply with any demand by martial law commanders for the transfer or dismissal of public servants whose services are considered dangerous from the standpoint of general security, law and order or public safety, or whose work is not considered necessary; a regulation on security investigation and archive research which affected public servants, magistrates and public prosecutors, university teachers and employees of state enterprises and banks, and which could have repercussions on employment, and on the Fight against Terrorism Act of 12 April 1991 which contains a very broad definition of terrorism and propaganda. The Committee also asked for information on discrimination in practice on the grounds of trade union membership or activities (Conclusions XIII-1, pp. 219 and 220).

– Malta for information on the activities of the Employment Commission set up to ensure that there was no discrimination on grounds of political opinion and on the measures taken in practice to combat forms of discrimination on grounds other than sex or political opinion (Conclusion XIII-2, p. 235).

The repetition of the questions on the elimination of discrimination other than that based on sex has progressively led most of the Contracting Parties to provide all or part of the information requested. In this respect, Conclusions XIII-3 are of particular interest, as they show both the efforts made by states, at least in their legislation, to combat discrimination of all kinds, particularly in the area of employment, and the difficulties encountered.

The importance given by the Committee to the practical application of legislative measures against discrimination is significant, and its purpose is to allow an assessment of their efficiency (see for example, Conclusions XIII-3, p. 74).

Assessment of compliance

There are no cases of non-compliance. The Committee's conclusion is deferred in respect of Finland (first report – Conclusions XIII-3, pp. 231 to 233), Germany (Conclusions XIII-2, pp. 232 and 233), Greece (Conclusions XIII-3, p. 63), Ireland (*ibidem*, p. 66), Italy (*ibidem*, pp. 67 and 68), the Netherlands Antilles (*ibidem*, p. 74), Spain (*ibidem*, p. 74), Turkey (second report – *ibidem*, pp. 236 to 238) and the United Kingdom (*ibidem*, pp. 76 and 78).

Paragraph 3 – Free employment services

Under this paragraph, the Contracting Parties undertake:

"to establish or maintain free employment services for all workers".

In the first cycle of supervision, "The Committee interpreted this provision as placing an obligation on each Contracting State not only to create or maintain such services throughout its national territory but also to ensure that they were properly operated and, where necessary, supervised, in collaboration with both sides of industry" (Conclusions I, p. 16), and it made clear that the "employment services" required are essentially services for the placement of workers in employment (Conclusions I, p. 167).

In the fourth cycle of supervision, the Committee stressed in a general comment that the term "free employment services" implied "the free provision of placement services for both worker and employer. This interpretation is borne out by the text of the paragraph under consideration and is moreover the obvious one if only to prevent an employer passing on any placement costs incurred by him to workers".

Applying this case law in the same supervision cycle, the Committee found that the United Kingdom did not comply with this provision of the Charter because, "employers were charged for the placement of some categories of workers, such as professional, administrative, managerial, executive technical and scientific staff, and this can under no circumstances be compatible with the provisions of the Charter, unless such staff have access to other public placement services which are free of charge for both employee and employer, and receive the same treatment from them as other categories of workers" (Conclusions IV, pp. 10 and 12).

In the fifth, sixth and seventh cycles of supervision, the Committee confirmed its negative conclusion for the United Kingdom, as no comparable services were available to employers free of charge (see also Conclusions XIII-3, p. 241 – Turkey).

In the eighth cycle of supervision, the Committee elaborated further on the "principle that free employment services shall be maintained for all workers". More specifically the Committee explained that this principle: "(being meant in accordance with the very terms of the Charter, to ensure the effective exercise of the right to work) aims above all to match, to the greatest possible extent, supply and demand of manpower with a view to guaranteeing maximum opportunities to workers. Consequently, the principle of free services would be devoid of its meaning if it applied only to the demand of employment by workers and did not include the supply of jobs by employers." Being aware, however, of the fact that: "access to certain occupations of a high level of responsibility or of a highly technical nature entailed, beyond the meeting of supply and demand, additional selection and thorough assessment, calling for appropriate staff and methods", the Committee accepted "that such services, added to the search for and registration of supply and demand by a specialised service for the placement of professional executives, fell outside the scope of application of paragraph 3 of Article 1 of the Charter and could justify payment by the employer for the specific services thus rendered him. Such an interpretation, however, could only be acceptable within very specified limits designed to prevent any failure to comply with the Charter, that is to say:

– that services paid for concern specifically selection or assessment, separate from the registration of supply and demand of manpower, which must remain free;

– that posts justifying recourse to such additional service should be limited in number and correspond to a high level of qualification and responsibility (higher professional executives and managerial staff)" (Conclusions VIII, pp. 36 and 37).

In the ninth supervision cycle, the United Kingdom was found to comply with this provision because since 1983 employers may ask the public employment services, which are free of charge, instead of the special executive recruitment services to recruit professional executives.

During the twelfth supervision cycle, when examining the situation in Denmark where a new Act of 20 December 1989 allowed the free exercise of private placement services and where the Minister of Labour had been authorised to issue rules concerning the payment by employers for certain specified forms of assistance provided by the Public Employment Service, the Committee summarised its case law on this provision, "to the effect, firstly, that the principle of free employment services applied to employers and workers alike, secondly, that the existence of fee-charging placement services was acceptable only if a free placement service were available in all sectors and thirdly, that access to certain occupations of a high level of responsibility could justify payment by the employer for specific services of selection and thorough assessment, but only subject to certain precise limitations".[1] (Conclusions XII-1, p. 62).

Many states are currently changing their placement structures and allow private services to operate. On each occasion, the Committee asks if public – and therefore free – services continue to be available to all workers in all sectors (see, in the last instance, Conclusions XIII-1, pp. 62 to 65, in the cases of Italy, Greece and Sweden and Conclusions XIII-3, pp. 79 (Austria and Denmark), 83 and 84 (Italy), 86 and 87 (Norway and Spain), 88 (Sweden), 239 (Finland) and 240 to 242 (Portugal and Turkey)).

It should also be pointed out that the Committee consistently asks Contracting Parties which have accepted this paragraph to supply it with statistics on the age and sex of applicants and the persons for whom employment is found. It also insists on finding out whether employers' and workers' representatives participate in the operation and control of the employment services. On the latter point see Conclusions XII-1 pp. 66 and 67, the United Kingdom, where the Committee, whilst ruling that the privatisation of the Professional and Executive Recruitment Agency (previously part of the public employment service) was not in itself contrary to the Charter as long as recourse could be made to free employment services for the employment of professional and managerial staff, remarked that workers did not seem to be asked to participate in the operation and control of the employment services and asked for

1 Those indicated in Conclusions VIII; see above.

information on this point (see most recently Conclusions XIII-3, pp. 87 (Spain), p. 89 (the United Kingdom), p. 239 (Finland), p. 242 (Turkey) and Addendum to Conclusions XIII-3, p. 20 (Luxembourg).

The situation of the labour market in the Contracting Parties and the changes having taken place or occurring in the area of recruitment services have led the Committee to strengthen its supervision of the efficiency of free employment services. It has always attached great importance to the correct running of these services and in view of this, has always sought to ascertain that they are located over the whole territory. In Conclusions XII, "the Committee asked all states to outline the geographical distribution of employment services, particularly placement services, over the entire national territory and the action taken to ensure proper conditions of access to such services for all interested persons, which it considered as an indispensable condition for the effective exercise of the rights guaranteed under Article 1 of the Charter" (Conclusions XII-1, p. 19 and XII-2, p. 18; see also most recently Conclusions XIII-3, p. 82 (Greece), p. 86 (the Netherlands Antilles), p. 239 (Finland) and p. 240 (Portugal)).

An essential factor demonstrating the efficiency of recruitment services is their rate of placement; consequently, the Committee asks the Contracting Parties how many job applications are registered, or the numbers of applicants registered and the number of vacancies filled. Where private placement services exist, it asks the same questions for these structures. The Committee also endeavours to find out whether employers are obliged to notify public recruitment services of employment vacancies and if not by what means these services are informed of vacancies, the proportion of placements made by the public services, which other structures exist for recruitment and the proportion of vacancies filled by each (on all these points, see in the last instance Conclusions XIII-1, pp. 58 to 66, pp. 221 and 222, Conclusions XIII-2, pp. 235 to 238, Conclusions XIII-3, pp. 78 to 89 and pp. 238 to 242 and Addendum to Conclusions XIII-3, pp. 19 and 20).

Assessment of compliance

There are no cases of non-compliance with this paragraph. The Committee's conclusion is deferred in respect of Belgium (first report – Conclusions XIII-2, pp. 235 and 236), Greece (Conclusions XIII-3, pp. 81 to 83), Luxembourg (first report – Addendum to Conclusions XIII-3, pp. 13 and 20), the Netherlands Antilles (Conclusions XIII-3, pp. 85 and 86), Portugal (first report – Conclusions XIII-3, pp. 239 to 241), Spain (*ibidem*, pp. 86 and 87) and Turkey (*ibidem*, pp. 241 and 242).

Paragraph 4 – Vocational guidance, training and rehabilitation

Under this paragraph, the Contracting Parties undertake:

> "to provide or promote appropriate vocational guidance, training and rehabilitation".

In the first supervision cycle, the Committee described the obligations deriving from this paragraph as identical to those imposed by Articles 9 (vocational guidance), 10 (vocational training) and 15 (vocational training, rehabilitation and social resettlement for disabled workers) of the Charter and ruled that states which had accepted these three Articles were not required to include in their reports particulars concerning the application of paragraph 4 (Conclusions I, p. 16).

In the second supervision cycle, the Committee recalled its ruling and added that: "Nevertheless the Committee desired to make clear that while this was possible because of the identity, broadly speaking, of the areas covered by those articles and by Article 1, the converse was not implied, viz. that a State which complied with the last-mentioned provision had necessarily fulfilled all the obligations set out in Articles 9, 10 and 15 of the Charter." (Conclusions II, p. 6).

Article 1 para. 4 is a very general provision, whereas Articles 9, 10 and 15 contain precise undertakings in each of the areas covered. The question at issue is therefore whether cases of non-compliance with one or more of the obligations included in Articles 9, 10 and 15 necessarily constitute a violation of Article 1 para. 4. The case law of the Committee has developed around this issue.

Until the seventh cycle of supervision, the Committee's assessment of compliance with Article 1 para. 4 depended on its assessment of compliance with Articles 9, 10 and 15, a fact which it clearly stated: "The Committee had to conclude that this state does not comply entirely with paragraph 4 of Article 1 as it does not comply with paragraph 2 of Article 10", or "...with paragraph 1 of Article 10 and paragraph 1 of Article 15", or "The Committee, having come to the conclusion that this country was not in full compliance with the requirements of paragraphs 1 and 2 of Article 10 and in view of the close connection between paragraph 4 of Article 1 and Articles 9, 10 and 15, concluded that this country was still not entirely fulfilling its obligations under paragraph 4 of Article 1 of the Charter." (Conclusions VII, p. 11).

Since the eighth cycle of supervision, the Committee as a rule does not refer to its assessments given under Article 9, 10 and 15 but to the information on these provisions given in the reports. Concerning the same states as above, it concluded in the following manner: "the Committee noted that vocational training was not being provided equally for all categories of the population and that, in particular, there was discrimination against foreigners. In these circumstances, the Committee had to conclude that Austria was not complying fully with the 'obligation to provide or promote appropriate vocational training'." Also: "the Committee reached the conclusion that vocational training is not adequately provided to certain young foreigners and that this state cannot be considered as fully complying with Article 1 para. 4 of the Charter"; "The Committee took note of the new vocational training programmes in the United Kingdom. It noticed nonetheless that the right to vocational training was not yet fully guaranteed, as certain forms of discrimination against foreign manpower existed in some sectors. The Committee had to conclude that this country does not fully comply with this provision" (Conclusions VIII, pp. 37 and 38).

In the twelfth supervision cycle, the Committee made the following observation of a general character concerning the scope of Article 1 para. 4: "The purpose of Article 1 of the Charter being to ensure the effective exercise of the right to work, the Committee specified that in order to satisfy the requirements of Article 1, para. 4, a state must not only have institutions providing vocational guidance, training and rehabilitation, but must also ensure access to the institutions for all those interested, including foreigners, nationals of the states parties to the Charter, and the disabled" (Conclusions XII-1, p. 67 and Conclusions XII-2, p. 57).

Since then, whenever a negative conclusion is reached under Article 9, 10 or 15 on one of the two grounds mentioned in the above observation (ie. adequacy of services and equality of access) the conclusion is also negative under Article 1 para. 4. On the contrary, when the conclusion under Articles 9, 10 or 15 is negative on another ground, the conclusion under Article 1 para. 4 is not necessarily negative.

Assessment of compliance

Taking into account the scope of Article 1 para. 4 as defined above and information supplied under Articles 9, 10 or 15, as appropriate, the Committee has concluded that the following countries are not complying with the Charter:

Austria: equality of treatment between Austrian nationals and nationals of other Contracting Parties to the Charter is not guaranteed with regard to apprenticeships (Conclusions XIII-3, p. 90);

Greece: in view of the inequality of treatment in the field of vocational training between Greeks and the nationals of other Contracting Parties not members of the European Union (Conclusions XIII-3, p. 91);

Luxembourg: equality of treatment between Luxembourg nationals and those of other Contracting Parties not members of the European Union and not parties to the Agreement on the European Economic Area is not guaranteed in access to institutions providing vocational training (Addendum to Conclusions XIII-3, p. 20).

Malta: priority is given to Maltese nationals in apprenticeship schemes (Conclusions XIII-3, p. 91);

Turkey:[1] due to the inadequacy of existing institutions, which in the Committee's view manifestly do not ensure satisfactory access for all those concerned, particularly disabled persons, to vocational guidance, training and rehabilitation (Conclusions XIII-1, pp. 222 to 224; Conclusions XIII-3, p. 243).

The Committee's conclusion is deferred for:

Finland: pending receipt of replies to the questions asked under Articles 9, 10 and 15 concerning equal treatment for foreign nationals of other Contracting Parties (Conclusions XIII-3, p. 243);

Germany: in the absence of any information on the effect that special conditions such as residence requirements for entitlement to financial training allowances imposed on young foreigners, nationals of Contracting Parties to the Charter not members of the European Union, have on their access to vocational training (Conclusions XII-2, p. 58; Conclusions XIII-2, p. 238);

Italy: because of the ineffectiveness of existing institutions, particularly in the vocational guidance field in the south of Italy (Conclusions XII-2, p. 58 and Conclusions XIII-3, p. 92);

Portugal: pending receipt of the information requested under Articles 9, 10 and 15 (Conclusions XIII-3, p. 243).

---

1 Turkey has accepted Articles 9 and 10 but not Article 15.

Article 2 – The right to just conditions of work

General

"This Article covers matters (hours of work, rest, holidays, etc.) which were among the original concerns of the labour movement and among the early standards established by international labour law" (Conclusions I, p. 17). It consists of five paragraphs which correspond to five types of measure which must be undertaken by Contracting Parties in order to provide the worker with the best conditions in which to carry out his work.

These measures are:

– a reasonable duration of work;

– paid public holidays;

– annual paid holidays;

– specific arrangements for workers engaged in dangerous or unhealthy occupations;

– a weekly rest day.

The whole of Article 2 is subject to the conditions set down by Article 33 of the Charter, which means that the obligations arising from it are fulfilled by a Contracting Party provided that the great majority of the workers concerned (ie. 80%) enjoy the protection stipulated under legislation, collective agreements or otherwise. In view of this it is necessary for the Committee to have sufficient information for each paragraph to determine the proportion of persons covered.

Paragraph 1 – Reasonable working hours

Under this paragraph, the Contracting Parties undertake:

> "to provide for reasonable daily and weekly working hours, the working week to be progressively reduced to the extent that the increase of productivity and other relevant factors permit".

a. The first question which arises is **how to provide for** reasonable working hours. The answer was given by the Committee in its first Conclusions when it stated that: "in view of the wording of this paragraph and of Article 33 of the Charter, a Contracting Party could not be considered as complying with this paragraph unless reasonable daily and weekly working hours were provided either by law or by collective agreement, or by some other process imposing an obligation whose performance is subject to the supervision of an appropriate authority" (Conclusions I, p. 169). This view was reiterated in the Committee's Third report on certain provisions of the Charter which have not been accepted (pp. 11 and 12; see also, in the last instance, Conclusions XIII-1, p. 70).

b. A second question is what constitutes "reasonable working hours" since no precise **number of hours** is mentioned in this paragraph. The approach adopted when drafting it was that it would not be appropriate to prescribe a fixed number of hours because what might have been a meaningful goal when the Charter was drafted might later prove to have been unduly modest. As the Committee pointed out in its Third report on certain provisions of the Charter which have not been accepted: "Clearly the authors of the Charter did not want to specify an exact number of hours in order to allow national situations and economic trends to be taken into account, in the light, of course, of the provision's above-mentioned aim". This was defined earlier in the same report as being "to protect workers' health and safety – hence their lives – without neglecting more general interests, particularly economic ones" (p. 12).

In the first supervision cycle, the Committee "felt that it should first determine the number of hours which might be considered 'reasonable' in the [...] member states of the Council of Europe. It found that what could be thought reasonable under the Charter varied from place to place and from time to time, depending on productivity and other factors. It was therefore out of the question for the Committee to lay down a number of daily or weekly working hours which might be considered reasonable in absolute terms" (Conclusions I, p. 18). As a result, the Committee did not set a particular number of daily or weekly hours that might be considered "reasonable".

Consideration of the Conclusions as a whole shows that the Committee takes actual working hours into account. Thus, for example, "the Committee had [...] considered the situation satisfactory, since, although the statutory limit on weekly working hours was forty-eight, collective agreements had lowered the limit to a reasonable level (thirty-six to forty hours)" (Conclusions XIII-1, p. 71, Italy); or, the Committee observes that "the gap between retail outlets' opening hours could be accounted for either by shift working or by the use of overtime. The Committee wished the next report to provide an explanation as to this situation." (Conclusions XIII-1, p. 67, France and p. 71, Italy). It "also acknowledged that, in order to judge whether a State really fulfilled its obligations under this provision, it was not enough to consider the number of working hours laid down by law in that State. Account had also to be taken of the effect of collective agreements" (*ibidem*).

Each situation is judged on its own merits. In the first supervision cycle, for example, the sixty-hour working week (forty-eight hours and twelve hours overtime) of certain classes of workers in Italy was not considered "reasonable", whereas a forty-five-hour week for the great majority of workers in Norway was considered "reasonable" (Conclusions I, p. 18).

In the most recently published volume of Conclusions XIII-3, a working day of eight hours and a working week of forty hours were considered satisfactory (p. 246, Finland), average hours of forty-seven to fifty hours a week were considered long (pp. 245 and 246, Portugal) and sixty hours including overtime per week were considered very long (p. 204, Ireland).

Among the "relevant factors" taken into account by the Committee in assessing the compliance of a Contracting Party with this paragraph, in addition to the "increase of productivity" mentioned in the text of the provision, is the level of unemployment in a state. In this connection the Committee has underlined that Article 2 para. 1 lays down a special obligation in respect of working hours and their gradual reduction for those Contracting Parties bound by it in which the overall employment situation was marked by the presence of a relatively high number of unemployed persons (Conclusions I, p. 18; Third report on certain provisions of the Charter which have not been accepted, p. 13; Addendum to Conclusions XI-2, p. 11; in the last instance, Conclusions XIII-1, p. 70, Ireland).

In the Third report on certain provisions of the Charter which have not been accepted, the Committee clarified its attitude towards two different factors which affect the length of "reasonable working hours", namely the reference in this provision to "daily and weekly" working hours and the issue of "overtime".

With regard to the former, the Committee took the view that the reference to both **daily and weekly working hours** reflected "a concern to protect workers' health and ensure their safety, as it is well established that accidents occur most frequently at the end of the working day. This fact should be emphasised at a time when in certain countries, a study is being made of the duration of working hours as a whole, ie. not only on a daily and/or weekly basis but also annually and even over the whole of working life, implying that the reduction in working time may be obtained through longer annual holidays and/or the lowering of retirement age. Such a trend would have important repercussions for workers' health and safety and would be incompatible with Article 2 para. 1." (p. 13 of the above-mentioned report).

In the same way, having noted that "extended collective agreements or covenants could provide for an adjustment of working hours, with working weeks exceeding forty-four hours, provided that the average working week over one year does not exceed thirty-nine hours", the Committee noted that "according to the actual wording of Article 2 para. 1 of the Charter, the 'reasonableness' of length of work is required in respect of daily and weekly working hours. In order to assess the situation in this respect, the Committee hoped to find in the next report more detailed and up-to-date information regarding the collective agreements providing for such flexible working time, particularly details as to the maximum length of the working day and week." (Conclusions XIII-1, p. 67, France).

With regard to **overtime**, the Committee stressed in its first Conclusions (p. 18) that "the nature and extent of an employer's right to require overtime to be worked was also, in the Committee's opinion, an important factor" to judge whether a state really fulfilled its obligations under Article 2 para. 1. In its Third report on certain provisions of the Charter which have not been accepted (p. 13), the Committee took the view that since working hours are assessed by taking into account not only normal working hours but also overtime, the latter should also be regulated by limiting its utilisation and/or length, (in order to avoid exposing the workers to the above-mentioned risks), and not be left to the discretion of the employer or the worker. This also ensures reasonable working hours, as otherwise certain employers (or workers) might be tempted to resort to overtime in order to make up for any reduction in normal working hours.

c.   Article 2 para. 1 has been characterized by the Committee as being **dynamic**, since it stipulates a **progressive reduction** in daily and weekly working hours. "Nevertheless, the Committee was aware of the limits to change in this direction, particularly in connection with the fixing of the length of the working week, since the current tendency for the five-day, forty-hour week to become general is already giving rise to new social problems, such as those of the use of leisure time, etc." (Conclusions I, pp. 17 and 18). The concern of the Committee in relation to the question of leisure time was that a worker, instead of enjoying more leisure, might be tempted to hold two or more jobs or work overtime with the result that the protection originally intended by this paragraph would prove futile. The Committee therefore asked to be "informed of the measures taken to alleviate the drawbacks of one worker's holding two or more different employments, as far as total hours are concerned" (Conclusions III, pp. 12 and 13, Germany, Ireland, Italy and Norway).

In its Third report on certain provisions of the Charter which have not been accepted (pp. 13 and 14), the Committee stressed that the expression "to the extent that the increase of productivity and other relevant factors permit" gave "a very relative character to the dynamic nature of this provision. It has already been underlined that, among the 'other factors', the level of unemployment occupied a prominent place. The economic crisis and the resultant unemployment have in recent years fostered reductions in working hours in many European countries as such a measure, which stemmed from the idea of work-sharing, seemed capable of combating growing unemployment." This observation is still topical and the Committee pays great attention to all new arrangements for flexible and reduced working hours (see also below, the general question asked under Article 4 para. 2).

Assessment of compliance

Throughout the supervision cycles the Committee has assessed compliance by obtaining information on working hours (usual and overtime) in the various sectors of the economy, particular attention being paid to the agricultural and forestry sectors where working hours seem to be much longer, and to the proportion of workers in these sectors. On the whole the Contracting Parties have been found to comply with this provision as in most cases the working week is forty hours or less for the majority of workers, a standard considered to be in conformity with the Committee's case law. In some cases no negative conclusion was adopted because the conditions of Article 33 were not fulfilled. However there have been some cases of deferral:

Iceland: the Committee's conclusion has been deferred since the eleventh cycle, as in the tenth cycle the Committee noted that although the standard working week was generally forty hours, the actual average was much higher because there was no limit on overtime (Conclusions XI-1, p. 51; in the last instance, Conclusions XIII-3, p. 197 where the Committee also asks "to be informed of any developments as regards measures adopted to reduce working hours");

Ireland: this is another case of deferral since the eleventh cycle. From a survey it appeared that in Ireland the percentage of workers whose usual hours of work were forty-five or more had continued to increase, the usual average hours in farming were particularly high and overtime was regulated only in industrial undertakings, with sectors where up to sixty hours could be worked in a week (Addendum to Conclusions XI-2, pp. 11 and 12; in the last instance Conclusions XIII-3, pp. 197 and 198).

Malta: the Committee wished to have more information about the number of workers and their working hours in sectors where the working week exceeded forty hours and, in the light of its case law, in what sectors of the economy overtime work is regularly undertaken and the total number of weekly hours (basic and overtime) that are consequently worked regularly (Conclusions XII-2, pp. 60 and 61; in the last instance Conclusions XIII-2, p. 241).

Finland (first report): the Committee asked for information as regards the hours of work for activities not covered by the legislation and the percentage of workers not covered by laws restricting working hours; it also asked for details of the scope and implementation in practice of new collective agreements concerning hours of work, with an estimate of the number of workers concerned (Conclusions XIII-3, pp. 244 and 245);

Portugal (first report): the Committee noted high average working hours for some sectors (including average overtime): forty-seven to fifty hours per week on average over the whole year (for forestry workers the average was fifty-one to fifty-six hours per week depending on levels of qualification); the Committee asked the government to confirm whether these figures were consistent with the statutory limit of fifty hours. It also requested detailed information on the results achieved by the 1990

Economic and Social Agreement which aimed to arrive at a maximum working week of forty hours by 1995 (Conclusions XIII-3, pp. 245 and 246).

Paragraph 2 – Public holidays with pay

Under this paragraph, the Contracting Parties undertake:

"to provide for public holidays with pay".

This provision does not specify the number of public holidays which should be provided, but has been interpreted in a quantitative manner: Contracting Parties with between six and seventeen public holidays a year were found to comply with this paragraph (Conclusions I, p. 19).

Article 33 applies to this paragraph (see above, "General", under Article 2).

Assessment of compliance

There have been no cases of non-compliance with this paragraph, and only two cases of deferral in respect of two Contracting Parties. The Committee, before concluding whether Greece complied or not, asked to be informed if employees who could exceptionally be required to work on public holidays under a decree were entitled to an equivalent number of days off in lieu (see Conclusions XII-1, p. 72; in the last instance, Conclusions XIII-3, p. 205). In respect of Malta it asked for confirmation that part-time employees are also guaranteed public holidays with pay, either by legislation, Wage Regulation Orders or through collective agreements and concluded provisionally that Malta complied with this provision (Conclusions XII-2, p. 61). The reply was that remuneration for public holidays was not guaranteed in the case of part-time workers. However, as these workers only represented 3.83% of paid workers, the Committee was able to reach a positive conclusion (Conclusions XIII-2, pp. 241 and 242).

Paragraph 3 – Annual Holidays with pay

Under this paragraph, the Contracting Parties undertake:

"to provide a minimum of two weeks annual holiday with pay".

From the first cycle of supervision, "the Committee interpreted this paragraph as laying down the principle that workers must not be able to waive their annual holiday even in consideration of an extra payment by the employer. The Committee considered that the need to protect the workers as fully as possible made such a waiver incompatible with the Charter even with the free consent of the workers concerned." (Conclusions I, p. 170).

In the fourth cycle of supervision, "the Committee reiterated that Article 2 para. 3 of the Charter has as its aim the protection of the workers from any abuses which might occur even with his own will or within his own family. It pointed out that legislation permitting renunciation of annual holidays against payment of a lump sum is incompatible with the purpose of the Charter and that family workers in agriculture should as well be protected as much as the other categories of workers" (Conclusions IV, p. 17, Ireland; see also Conclusions VIII, p. 44, the Netherlands). For all the Contracting Parties, the Committee ascertains that renunciation of holidays in the conditions specified is not possible (see most recently Conclusions XIII-1, pp. 74 and 75, Cyprus; p. 76, Italy; Conclusions XIII-2, pp. 243 and 244, Malta and Conclusions XIII-3, p. 250, Portugal).

However, the Committee recognised that "this principle does not prevent the payment of a lump sum to an employee at the end of his employment in compensation for the paid holiday to which he was entitled but which he had not taken" (Conclusions I, p. 170). This point was reconfirmed in a later cycle when the Committee, in examining the situation in Austria where additional wages could only be paid in lieu of leave in cases where following termination of his employment contract the worker in question had been unable to take his leave prior to termination of employment, held that this was not incompatible with the Charter (Conclusions V, p. 14).

Furthermore, according to the case law it is permissible to require a worker to be employed for a qualifying period before he is eligible for annual holidays with pay. Thus in its first Conclusions the Committee ruled that the arrangement under Swedish and Norwegian law, whereby annual holiday may not be taken until the twelve working months for which it is due have fully elapsed, was not incompatible with this provision (Conclusions I, p. 20). The Committee has also accepted more favourable arrangements such as a proportional reduction of holidays when the worker has been employed for eleven months or less (Conclusions VII, p. 14, Ireland), or situations in which the legislation separates the right to leave from the right to payment during such leave: the right to annual leave is therefore independent from the duration of work during the previous year, whereas payment during such leave is proportional to the rights earned during the qualifying year (Conclusions VII, p. 13, Sweden).

Another question to which the Committee was confronted was "whether Article 2 para. 3 requires annual holidays to be taken in one uninterrupted period or allows them to be split up. The French text, which talks of '*un congé payé annuel de deux semaines*', supports the former interpretation; but the English text which uses the phrase 'two weeks' annual holiday' is ambiguous on this point" (Conclusions I, p. 170).

The Committee recognised in the first cycle of supervision that the "exercise of the right to annual holidays might sometimes be affected by the procedure whereby sick leave was taken into consideration when a worker fell ill during his annual holiday" but decided to postpone consideration of the question to a later stage (Conclusions I, p. 20). It did not come back to this point until the twelfth supervision cycle in which, in a general introductory statement under paragraph 3 of Article 2, after recalling its consistent case law according to which the right to leave cannot be waived, it stated that: "As a result, Article 2 para. 3 requires that a worker who is incapacitated for work by reason of illness or injury during all or part of his/her annual holiday must be entitled to take at some other time the days thereby lost, at least in so far as is necessary to guarantee the worker the two-week annual holiday provided for by the Charter".

This requirement applies in all cases, whether the incapacity commences before or during the holiday period, as well as in cases of employment in which there is a fixed holiday period for all workers in an enterprise" (Conclusions XII-2, p. 62).

When examining the Spanish situation in the same cycle, the Committee noted that even though in Spain in the case of illness or accident during annual leave a worker is entitled to make up the days of leave lost, in certain cases Labour Courts had decided that "when a firm had established fixed dates for holidays and these coincided with a period of temporary incapacity for work of one of its employees, the latter was not entitled to take his annual leave at another time". In the light of the aforesaid interpretation, the Committee asked the Government of Spain to inform it "whether these rulings amounted to established case-law confirmed by the higher Courts and, if this were so, what measures the government intended to take to remedy the situation". (Conclusions XII-2, p. 64). Having been informed that these judgements were isolated and that the matter had not been brought before the Supreme Court, the Committee asked for the "percentage (compared to active population) of workers employed in firms where all staff were required to take their annual leave at the same time, who could lose their entitlement to annual leave on account of a period of temporary incapacity for work at that time" (Conclusions XIII-1, p. 77).

Since then, the Committee systematically examines the issue of sick leave during annual holidays in all the Contracting Parties (see Conclusions XIII-1, p. 76, Italy; Conclusions XIII-2, p. 242, Belgium; pp. 242 and 243, Germany; Conclusions XIII-3, p. 248, Finland and p. 250, Portugal; Addendum to Conclusions XIII-3, p. 24, Luxembourg).

Finally, it may be pointed out that paragraph 3 is one of the provisions of the Charter which is now considered outdated, as the two weeks' holiday has been substantially exceeded by all Contracting States. It has therefore been amended by the revised Charter (see below).

Assessment of compliance

On the whole, the Contracting Parties were found to comply with the requirement of this paragraph to provide two weeks' annual holiday, even though some of them did not provide this for all workers. Certain categories such as family workers related to their employer, family workers in agriculture, employees paid on a profit-sharing basis, seafarers and fishermen, were excluded from protection in different Contracting States, but by virtue of the applicability of Article 33 these states were found as being in compliance.

Cases of infringement of this paragraph were mainly on the ground that workers could waive their right to annual holiday. This was the case in respect of Ireland, for example, for certain categories of workers, ie. agricultural wage-earners and family workers in agriculture (Conclusions II, p. 8, III p. 14). However, again as these workers constituted less than 20% of the entire working population of the country, in view of the applicability of Article 33, Ireland was found to comply (Conclusions IV, p. 17). The situation in Ireland continued to be considered satisfactory until the eleventh cycle when the same issue was raised because the 1973 Holidays (Employees) Act of 1973 allowed employees to forgo their leave in return for double pay in cases where board and lodging formed part of the remuneration (Addendum to Conclusions XI-2, p. 12). However, in the thirteenth cycle Ireland was again found in compliance by virtue of Article 33 (Conclusions XIII-1, p. 75).

In the last three supervision cycles the Committee has shown concern over the entitlement to leave of part-time workers or persons employed under atypical contracts and has asked Contracting Parties (for example, Austria, Conclusions XIII-1, p. 74; Finland, Conclusions XIII-3, p. 249; Luxembourg, Addendum to Conclusions XIII-3, p. 23; Malta, Conclusions XIII-2, p. 243; the United Kingdom, Conclusions XIII-1, p. 77) to supply information thereon.

The most recent examination of the situation of the Contracting Parties with respect to Article 2 para. 3 led the Committee to defer its conclusion in three cases (all the other situations having been considered satisfactory): for Finland (first report) the Committee was uncertain as to the possible derogations in lengths of leave, the number of workers not covered by the legislation and the situation of part-time workers (Conclusions XIII-3, pp. 247 to 249); for Malta, the conclusion was deferred because of uncertainty over the possibility of waiving the right to annual holidays (Conclusions XIII-2, pp. 243 and 244); for Portugal (first report), the deferral was due to the lack of information on the situation of part-time workers and to uncertainty as to whether the right to leave was upheld (employers are entitled to deny workers' enjoyment of statutory holidays by paying compensation equivalent to triple pay for the holiday period in question, these holidays being replaced during the first quarter of the following calendar year.) (Conclusions XIII-3, pp. 249 and 250).

The revised Charter provides for a minimum of four weeks' annual holiday with pay.

Paragraph 4 – Reduced working hours or additional holidays for workers in dangerous or unhealthy occupations

Under this paragraph, the Contracting Parties undertake:

> "to provide for additional paid holidays or reduced working hours for workers engaged in dangerous or unhealthy occupations as prescribed".

In applying this provision the Committee ruled that to assess compliance information is needed on:

"*i.* occupations considered dangerous or unhealthy under the country's regulations;

ii. the rules in national legislation, collective agreements or general practice governing reduced working hours;

iii. in view of Article 33 of the Charter, the proportion of workers to whom the standards mentioned in point ii. above did not apply" (Conclusions I, p. 20).

Moreover, according to the Committee, "the term 'as prescribed' did, admittedly, leave the national legislature a certain latitude in the choice of occupations to be classed as dangerous or unhealthy. This choice is however subject to review by the Committee, and were it not to include occupations which were manifestly dangerous or unhealthy, the latter might conclude that the Charter had been violated" (Conclusions II, p. 9).

In the fourth supervision cycle, "the Committee emphasised the close link between the provisions of this paragraph and those of Article 3 of the Charter. Each of these parts should therefore be considered in connection with the other.

It is the issue of safety and health regulations as provided under Article 3 and the supervision of their application and effectiveness which make it possible to identify better the measures taken to protect workers employed in dangerous or unhealthy occupations by providing reduced working hours or additional holidays with pay as stipulated by Article 2, paragraph 4" (Conclusions IV, p. 18; see also the reference made in the conclusion under Article 2 para. 4 to the questions asked under Article 3 para. 1: Conclusions XIII-1, p. 80, the Netherlands).

Dangerous or unhealthy occupations in the different Contracting Parties include, *inter alia*, according to national regulations, quarrying, mining and other underground work, the handling of explosives, asbestos and toxic chemicals, employment in the merchant navy, aerial navigation and such work as steel-making, road transport, ship building, the extraction of peat, the slaughtering of animals, work in high atmospheric pressure and in the nuclear energy sector.

The award of increased pay to employees in the public sector carrying out dangerous or unhealthy tasks without a reduction in working hours seemed to be contrary to this paragraph (Conclusions III, p. 14, Austria). Moreover, the Committee held that a policy to eliminate hazards rather than to restrict working hours or to provide increased holidays was "perfectly valid where the hazards involved are capable of total elimination, for, once an occupation ceases to be dangerous or unhealthy, it ceases by the same token to fall within the ambit of Article 2 para. 4" (Conclusions III, p. 15, Ireland). Where, however, such elimination was not possible, it was important to reduce working hours and provide additional holidays "both because of the need for workers in hazardous situations to be alert, and in order to limit the period of exposure to safety and health risks" (*ibidem*).

The interpretation to be given to this was further clarified in the fifth supervision cycle:

"Whilst the elimination of dangerous or unhealthy occupations was an ideal to strive for, paragraph 4 of Article 2 required that specific measures should be taken as long as these occupations still existed.

It felt in fact that if on the one hand a constant improvement of the technical conditions in which are carried out certain dangerous or unhealthy occupations represents a major factor for the reduction of the risks of accidents or disease, on the other hand, a decrease in working hours and the granting of additional holidays are equally necessary [...] as they allow for a reduced accumulation of physical and mental fatigue and a reduction in the exposure to risk, whilst at the same time granting workers longer periods of rest" (Conclusions V, pp. 15 and 16).

In the eighth supervision cycle, when examining the situation in Ireland, the Committee "reiterated its constant case law on this point to the effect that as long as dangerous or unhealthy occupations were in existence, the need to provide for additional holidays or reduced working hours could not be neglected" (Conclusions VIII, p. 45). The Committee has always maintained and justified this standpoint; thus in the latest instance: "the Committee drew attention to its established case law, namely that while the aim pursued was to eliminate all hazards in the workplace, reduced working hours or increased annual leave as required by this provision of the Charter were, until that aim was achieved, crucial factors in reducing the number of accidents and cases of illness" (Addendum to Conclusions XIII-3, p. 24, Luxembourg).

Assessment of compliance

There have been some cases of non-compliance with this paragraph.

One of the oldest cases for criticism is that of *Ireland*, on the grounds that there are no legislation or collective agreements providing for reduced working hours or additional paid holidays for workers engaged in those occupations which are inherently dangerous or unhealthy, such as mining (this criticism has been constantly made since the first supervision cycle; see in the last instance Conclusions XIII-3, pp. 200 and 201).

Italy and the *Netherlands* are also criticised on similar grounds as Ireland. For Italy this dates back to the fifth cycle (Conclusions V, p. 17); in the case of the Netherlands it was raised in the twelfth cycle (Conclusions XII-I, pp. 74 and 75) and reiterated in the thirteenth cycle (XIII-3, pp. 201 and 202).

The Committee did not accept Italy's argument that efforts were being made to eliminate all risks factors inherent in dangerous and unhealthy occupations. The Committee recalled its case law, according to which "by themselves [these measures] run the risk of being incomplete. They should be coupled with reduced periods of exposure to risk or with increased leave. These are two measures for reducing fatigue, mental and physical, which is a direct or indirect cause of many accidents (Second report on certain provisions of the Charter which have not been accepted pp. 5-7). The Committee also rejected the argumentation of Ireland and the Netherlands who claimed that they emphasised a policy of "prevention" rather than of reduction in working time and reiterated its case law to the effect that: "while the elimination of all risks in the workplace was an appropriate objective, as long as any risk continues, a reduction of working hours [...] is an essential factor in reducing stress/fatigue related accidents and illnesses" (Conclusions XIII-I, pp. 79 and 80).

Austria was also found as not complying on the ground that a reduction in working time was prescribed solely for certain types of dangerous or unhealthy work (Section 13 of the Industrial Code) and that additional annual leave was prescribed only for arduous night work in continuous

shifts (Act of 2 July 1981). The conclusion of the Committee was negative from the fifth (Conclusions V, pp. 16 and 17) to the tenth cycles
(Conclusions X-2, pp. 48 and 49). The Committee did not accept the
argument put forward by the Austrian Government that a Contracting
State which had already reduced the working week to forty hours and
fixed annual holidays to four weeks was exempt from taking any further
action under this paragraph. The Committee held that paragraphs 1 to 3
of Article 2 established a basic level, while paragraph 4 provided for an
improved level of protection and that "it was only just that, if all workers
were entitled to a forty-hour week and four weeks' annual holiday,
those who executed dangerous or unhealthy jobs should receive additional benefits" (Conclusions V, p. 17). In the twelfth and first part of
the thirteenth cycles the Committee adjourned its conclusions, upon
being informed of measures taken to improve the situation by the
Labour Inspectorate and of the revision of the Heavy Nightshift Work
Act (Conclusions XII-2, p. 65 and Conclusions XIII-1, p. 78). The replies
submitted led the Committee to reiterate its negative conclusion as only
dangerous work carried out at night benefits from particular measures
(not necessarily satisfactory with respect to Article 2 para. 4) and not
any dangerous work carried out during the day (Conclusions XIII-3,
pp. 199 and 200).

The revised Charter has amended paragraph 4 to read as follows:

"to eliminate risks in inherently dangerous or unhealthy occupations, and
where it has not yet been possible to eliminate or reduce sufficiently these
risks, to provide for either a reduction of working hours or additional paid
holidays for workers engaged in such occupations."

The amendment places more emphasis on the elimination or reduction of
risks in line with present-day policies. Additional paid holidays or reduced
working hours should only be provided where it has not been possible to
eliminate or reduce sufficiently the risks inherent in dangerous or unhealthy
occupations. Moreover, as pointed out in the explanatory report to the
revised Charter, the amended provision should be seen as a complement to
the revised Article 3, which emphasises the prevention of occupational accidents.

Belgium and *Luxembourg*'s first reports also prompted the Committee to consider that the situation in these two countries was not satisfactory. In Belgium, a very small number of workers benefited from measures in accordance with this provision (Conclusions XIII-2, p. 244); likewise in Luxembourg where persons employed in mines benefited from additional paid holidays, the workers employed in other dangerous or unhealthy occupations being entitled to a rise in salary (Addendum to Conclusions XIII-3, p. 24).

Paragraph 5 – Weekly rest periods

Under this paragraph, the Contracting Parties undertake:

> "to ensure a weekly rest period which shall, as far as possible, coincide with the day recognised by tradition or custom in the country or region concerned as a day of rest."

In the first cycle of supervision, the Committee noted "that this paragraph, read with Article 33, obliged those Contracting Parties who had accepted it to take steps to ensure that the great majority of workers were granted a weekly rest period which should, wherever possible, coincide with the day recognised by tradition or custom in the country or region concerned as a day of rest" (Conclusions I, p. 20). In accordance with tradition or custom in the Contracting Parties, the day of rest normally falls on a Sunday.

"In addition, the Committee interpreted this paragraph in the same way as Article 2 para. 3 on the question of foregoing holidays. In view of the need to protect workers, the Committee decided that here too it would be inconsistent with the Charter to allow a worker to forego his weekly rest period" (Conclusions I, p. 172), even if the worker received a lump sum in compensation (*ibidem*, Ireland; see in the last instance Conclusions XIII-3, p. 253, Finland).

In the eleventh cycle, the Committee recalled that "this provision of the Charter contains two distinct obligations. The first, which is mandatory, provides that workers should be guaranteed the right to a weekly rest period. As Article 33 is applicable, it is sufficient for the great majority of workers, namely 80%, to enjoy this right. The second obligation, less binding in that it must take account of certain special conditions, customs, etc., provides that the rest period should coincide as far as possible with the day recognised by tradition or custom in the country or region concerned as a day of rest." (Conclusions XI-1, p. 55; see in the last instance Conclusions XIII-3, pp. 203 and 204, Ireland).

Further, according to the case law of the Committee, the right to weekly rest must be guaranteed for all workers in all categories of work, including those who, because of their speciality, do not fall within the usual types of industrial workers.

In general, Contracting States have been found to comply with this provision, even though this right is not guaranteed to all categories of workers (for example workers in agriculture and forestry are excluded); this is so by virtue of the applicability of Article 33.

Questions asked by the Committee in assessing compliance with this provision have concerned, *inter alia,* the entitlement of part-time employees to weekly rest (Conclusions XII-2, p. 67, Malta) and the entitlement to compensatory rest of workers obliged to perform overtime work during their day of rest (Conclusions XII-2, p. 67, Cyprus, and Malta, Conclusions XIII-1, p. 81, Austria).

Assessment of compliance

At present, no situations are considered in violation of this provision of the Charter. Conclusions are deferred for four Contracting Parties.

Finland (first report): pending receipt of information on the number of workers not covered by legislation providing for Sunday as a weekly day of rest and on the number of workers covered by collective agreements allowing the renunciation of weekly rest periods in exchange for financial compensation (Conclusions XIII-3, pp. 252 and 253);

Ireland: due to the absence of information on workers who do not benefit from weekly rest periods and those for whom the weekly rest period does not coincide with the traditional day of rest (Conclusions XIII-3, pp. 203 and 204);

Luxembourg (first report): pending the receipt of information on the number of workers excluded from legislation providing for Sunday as a weekly day of rest (Addendum to Conclusions XIII-3, p. 25);

Malta: due to uncertainty as to the legal basis for the right to a weekly rest period for part-time workers and as to the impossibility of waiving the right to weekly rest periods (Conclusions XIII-2, pp. 245 and 246).

In the revised Charter, the following two new paragraphs have been added to Article 2:

"6.   to ensure that workers are informed in written form, as soon as possible, and in any event not later than two months after the date of commencing their employment, of the essential aspects of the contract or employment relationship;

7.   to ensure that workers performing night work benefit from measures which take account of the special nature of the work."

Appendix to Article 2 para. 6:

"Parties may provide that this provision shall not apply:

a.   to workers having a contract or employment relationship with a total duration not exceeding one month and/or with a working week not exceeding eight hours;

b.   where the contract or employment relationship is of a casual and/or specific nature, provided, in these cases, that its non-application is justified by objective considerations."

Paragraph 7 of Article 2, which offers protection for both men and women performing night work, must be read in connection with Article 8 para. 4 of the revised Charter which provides that the employment of women workers for night work must be regulated in the case of maternity (see below).

Article 3 – The right to safe and healthy working conditions

General

"The Committee regarded this Article as establishing a widely recognised principle, stemming directly from the right to personal integrity, one of the fundamental principles of human rights.

...

The second of the three paragraphs comprising Article 3 has, in the opinion of the Committee, a particular importance, since it establishes the need to provide for a system of labour inspection to safeguard the implementation of the rights to safe and healthy working conditions in practice.

The Committee considered that a country which has accepted this Article can only be regarded as fulfilling the undertakings deriving from it if it can prove that safety and health regulations have been issued for all economic sectors, that such regulations are adequately enforced through inspection and civil and criminal sanctions and finally that any necessary consultations on safety and health matters between governments and both sides of industry are arranged and actually take place." (Conclusions I, p. 22).

The guarantees of this Article are supplemented as far as children, young persons and women are concerned by those of Articles 7 and 8 respectively.

In the light of the interpretation it had given in the first supervision cycle to the word "worker"[1] as used in several provisions of the Charter and in the light of its assessment of the extent of the obligations undertaken by a state accepting this Article, the Committee restated in the second cycle "its view that this article, being designed to guarantee the right to safe and healthy working conditions not only for employed persons but also for the self-employed, ought to apply to all sectors of the economy, if only on account of the technical advances and increasing mechanisation manifest in every branch of activity" (Conclusions II, p. 12).

Paragraph 1 – Issue of safety and health regulations

Under this paragraph, the Contracting Parties undertake:

"to issue safety and health regulations".

"The Committee interpreted this provision as requiring the Contracting States to issue safety and health regulations for all economic sectors, ie. a. manufacturing industry, b. mining and quarrying, c. commerce and transport (including shipping), d. agriculture" (Conclusions I, p. 22). As regards road transport, when examining the situation in Ireland, the Committee expressed the view that "the obligation arising under this provision could not be considered as being satisfied unless regulations to ensure the safety and health of professional drivers by, for example, limiting working hours, prescribing safety features on vehicles, etc., were issued" (Conclusions III, p. 18).

---

1 In its first Conclusions, "in the light of the *travaux préparatoires* the Committee arrived at the conclusion that in principle the term "worker" was intended to cover both employed and self-employed persons, but that this interpretation could not be applied in all cases. Where the context so requires, the term "worker" may have to be considered as restricted to employed persons (compare, for example, Article 1 para. 3 with Article 1 paras. 2 and 4, or Article 4 para. 4 with Article 4 para. 3)" (Conclusions I, p. 8).

Moreover, in the eleventh cycle of supervision, the Committee confirmed that this provision applied to seamen (Conclusions XI-2, p. 61, Italy) and in the twelfth that oil rigs were also included (Conclusions XII-1, p. 81, the United Kingdom).

When re-examining the scope of this paragraph in the third cycle "the Committee made it clear that although so far it had not been considered as having a dynamic character, it is up to the governments in the event of technical developments rendering their regulations on health and safety at work seemingly out of tune with the new situation, to prove that the existing regulations were still adequate and, if appropriate, to adapt them continuously to these developments." (Conclusions III, p. 17). Moreover, the Committee pointed out that the obligation to issue safety and health regulations was imposed on the Contracting Parties and it was therefore important for it to know if the regulations issued could be considered as implemented by the government and, consequently, whether their enforcement was supervised by a governmental service or by a private institution (Conclusions III, p. 18).

In assessing compliance with this provision, the Committee requests figures for industrial accidents in the various sectors of the economy, according to the number of occurrences and degree of gravity.

The wide personal scope of this provision has been defined and emphasised throughout the case law of the Committee: as has been stated for Article 3 as a whole, governments must provide for all workers to be covered by safety and health regulations, whether employees or self-employed. The main arguments of the Committee in support of this interpretation may be summarised as follows:

- "the term 'worker' applies not only to employees but also to self-employed persons, except where the context of a provision shows that the term applies only to employees, as where a contract of employment is presupposed. The Committee found nothing in Article 3 to justify the conclusion that its provisions were not intended to protect all workers." (Conclusions II, p. 182);

- the interpretation that both categories are covered "is all the more inescapable because discrimination between employed and self-employed workers as regards safety and health at work would hardly be compatible with current concern to ensure a satisfactory working environment for all workers, especially where employed and self-employed workers were employed on the same work." (Conclusions III, p. 17);

− "there is no impossibility in imposing a duty of self-protection on a self-employed worker, if this is necessary to secure effective regulation and inspection of a dangerous workplace.[...] The activities of the self-employed also affect both the personal health and safety, and the duties in this regard, of other people; these, therefore have an interest in effective regulation and inspection. We [the Committee] can point to:

− the use of the same workplace by other workers (not being employees of the workers in question) − family workers − unpaid helpers − employees of contractors − maintenance men, etc.;

− risks to children (see Article 7, paragraph 10 of the Charter) or third parties generally (Article 11, paragraph 1);

− legal duties owed by landlords, manufacturers, contractors, public utilities, etc... as well as by other workers mentioned above, affecting the health and safety of the workplace.

These considerations lead to the assumption that Article 3, paragraph 1 implies a system of workplace regulation and inspection for non-employed workers as well as the employed, with, of course, derogations for practical reasons, such as to the low risk of certain economic sectors, the difficulty of inspection, lack of co-operation with inspection and so on." (Conclusions IV, pp. 21 and 22).

The Committee, however, "emphasised that the fact that this article applies to all workers, employed or otherwise, does not mean that the same regulations, supervision machinery, etc. should be applied in all cases" (Conclusions III, p. 17). This view was reiterated in the thirteenth supervision cycle when the Committee, noting that the majority of safety decrees in the Netherlands omitted the self-employed, observed that "given the difference in the conditions in which an employee and a self-employed worker carry out their activities, there may, to a certain extent, have to be different rules for applying safety and health requirements. Nevertheless, the objective of providing a safe and healthy working environment, must be the same for both employed and self-employed workers, and the regulations and their enforcement must be adequate and suitable in view of the work being done." (Conclusions XIII-1, p. 89).

Where certain categories of workers other than self-employed workers appear not to be covered, the Committee asks questions in relation to them in order to ascertain that all workers benefit from health and safety regulations. This should also be the case in the Civil Service (see most recently Conclusions XIII-3, p. 207; pp. 255 and 256, Portugal and Addendum to Conclusions XIII-3, p. 26, Luxembourg).

The growing use of home-based workers led the Committee to ask "that all States bound by paragraph 1 and/or 2 of this provision of the Charter indicate, in their next reports, the extent to which home workers are covered by the regulations governing health and safety at work and the measures which exist for the supervision of the enforcement of such regulations" (Conclusions XIII-1, p. 85; see also p. 25). Some replies were submitted in cycle XIII-3 (Conclusions XIII-3, pp. 205 and 206, Italy and the Netherlands) but all the states should give answers to this question in the fourteenth cycle of supervision.

Assessment of compliance

A number of Contracting Parties have been found throughout the various supervision cycles as not complying with this paragraph, mainly as a result of the lack of safety and health regulations in certain economic sectors or their non-application to the self-employed.

These omissions have been remedied in some Contracting States but not in others. Thus, for example, Cyprus was found to be not entirely fulfilling its obligation as there were no safety regulations in the agricultural sector (Conclusions III, p. 17): this situation was remedied by an enactment of legislation for safety and health in agriculture as from October 1982 (Conclusions VIII, p. 49). The same applied to Ireland which extended its legislation to cover self employed-farmers and members of their families. (Addendum to Conclusions XI-2, p. 14).

Countries found in violation of this paragraph during the last supervision cycle are:

Italy: on the ground that legislation and regulations on safety and health at work do not apply to self-employed workers in agriculture, industry and trade or to members of their families working with them. (Conclusions XIII-3, p. 205 and 206);[1]

the *Netherlands:* as self-employed workers are not given the same legal protection as employed workers with regard to safe and healthy working conditions. There are clearly sectors where the self-employed are not ensured the protection envisaged by paragraph 1 (Conclusions XIII-3, p. 206 and 207);

Greece: as there are no general regulations covering self-employed workers (Conclusions XIII-3, p. 205).

Paragraph 2 – Provision for the enforcement of safety and health regulations by measures of supervision

Under this paragraph, the Contracting Parties undertake:

"to provide for the enforcement of such regulations by measures of supervision"

"Proceeding from its interpretation of Article 3 para. 1, the Committee took the view that Article 3 para. 2 likewise relates to all economic

---

1 For the first part of the thirteenth supervision cycle, the Committee of Ministers addressed a recommendation to Italy.

sectors. Moreover it considered that a Contracting State cannot be regarded as meeting the prescribed obligation unless its measures of supervision are enforced by adequate civil and criminal sanctions" (Conclusions I, p. 23). As regards the categories of persons covered, it was also taken to cover the same categories of workers as paragraph 1 (Conclusions II, p. 13).

Throughout all the supervision cycles the Committee has held consistently that a violation of paragraph 1 of Article 3 entails automatically a violation of paragraph 2. In other words, the Committee established a link between paragraphs 1 and 2 in the sense that compliance with paragraph 1 is a necessary condition for compliance with paragraph 2, and defined "the link between the two paragraphs following from the wording of Article 3 para. 2, which refers to such regulations (*ces règlements*). This must refer to those regulations envisaged by Article 3 para. 1, that is those that meet its requirements" (Conclusions XII-1, p. 83)

In order to assess compliance with this paragraph the Committee asks, *inter alia*, for information concerning:

– the number of existing enterprises;

– the number of Labour Inspectors;

– the number of enterprises inspected each year (including agriculture);

– the sanctions imposed for serious breaches of regulations on safety and health;

– the number of infringements committed compared with the number of sanctions and the number of industrial accidents as distinct from the number of occupational diseases for each occupational sector (see, *inter alia*, Conclusions VIII, pp. 54 and 55).

Thus, in fact, statistics on the number of occupational accidents and on work-related illnesses do not suffice (although these are an important indication of the application of health and safety regulations); supervision carried out in the workplace must also be efficient. In the thirteenth cycle of supervision, having noted some shortages in the effective coverage of Labour Inspection services, the Committee addressed a question to all the states having accepted Article 3 para. 2:

"The Committee, in order to be able to evaluate more thoroughly the national situations with regard to Article 3 para. 2 of the Charter, has expressed the wish that the forthcoming national reports submitted by Governments having accepted this provision include, in addition to the information requested in the Form, the following information, concerning:

- the number of visits made by Labour Inspectorate staff, and the number of enterprises subject to inspection, with a breakdown for the different sectors of activity;

- the number and percentage of workers covered by visits in each of these sectors; this information should be broken down if possible by sex and age-groups (adolescents/adults) of the workers;

- the number of staff employed in Labour Inspectorates and details of their assignment to the various sectors of activity;

- the measures taken with a view to maintaining the competence of the inspectors, taking account of technological and legal developments.

This information should be supplied for a period covering the last four years if possible.

The Committee also wished governments would communicate the general reports of the central inspections authorities, *inter alia* those which are periodically communicated to ILO, where these reports existed." (Conclusions XIII-1, pp. 92 and 93; see also p. 25).

As in the case of the general question raised under Article 3 para. 1, all the states having accepted Article 3 para. 2 should submit the information requested during the fourteenth cycle of supervision.

Assessment of compliance

Contracting Parties not complying with this provision during the last supervision cycle are:

Greece: as there is no supervision for the self-employed who are not covered by safety and health regulations (Conclusions XIII-3, pp. 205 and 209); (this situation has been criticised since the tenth cycle (first report);

Italy:[1] for two reasons:

a. the absence of statistical information on the activities of the local health units needed to allow the Committee to assess the situation (the conclusion has been negative since the sixth cycle); and

b. the absence of supervision for the self-employed, who are not covered by safety and health regulations (Conclusions XIII-3, pp. 205-206 and 210-211). On this point, the situation had been criticised since the second cycle;

the *Netherlands:* as there is no supervision for the self-employed, who are only to a limited extent covered by safety and health regulations (Conclusions XIII-3, pp. 206-207 and 211-212) (the situation has been criticised since the ninth cycle – second report).

Paragraph 3 – Consultation with employers' and workers' organisations on questions of safety and health

Under this paragraph, the Contracting Parties undertake:

> "to consult as appropriate employers and workers organisations on measures intended to improve industrial safety and health".

---

1 On point a. the Committee of Ministers addressed a recommendation to Italy for the second part of the twelfth supervision cycle and a second recommendation for the first part of the thirteenth supervision cycle. On point b. the Committee of Ministers addressed a recommendation to Italy for the first part of the thirteenth supervision cycle, which it renewed in the third part of the thirteenth cycle.

"The Committee interpreted this provision and the wording 'as appropriate' as laying upon the Contracting States the obligation not only to make provisions for consultations at either national, regional, local or possibly enterprise level, but also to proceed to such consultations whenever the need arises" (Conclusions I, p. 24).

Moreover, in the fifth cycle, the Committee by reason of the fact that the great majority of the Contracting Parties "confine themselves to confirming that no changes had taken place in the field covered by this paragraph, wished to underline that the rapid development of techniques and its consequences on safety requires a constant updating of health and safety regulations which cannot be achieved without regular consultations with employers' and workers' organisations" and made it clear that in order to assess compliance with this provision information was necessary on "the extent and frequency of consultations which had already taken place with a view to meeting this need" (Conclusions V, p. 23).

This view was reiterated again in the eleventh cycle when the Committee after stating that "the constant adjustment of safety and health regulations in line with technological progress calls for regulars consultations with employers' and workers' organisations" urged Ireland to "provide information on the procedure, extent and frequency of the consultations which had already taken place to that end" (Addendum to Conclusions XI-2, p. 15; see in the last instance for Ireland, Conclusions XIII-1, p. 103; see also Conclusions XIII-3, p. 259, Portugal and Addendum to Conclusions XIII-3, p. 29, Luxembourg).

There are no cases of non-compliance with this provision.

In the revised Charter, Article 3 has been amended as follows:

"With a view to ensuring the effective exercise of the right to safe and healthy working conditions, the Parties undertake, in consultation with employers' and workers' organisations:

1.   to formulate, implement and periodically review a coherent national policy on occupational safety, occupational health and the working environment. The primary aim of this policy shall be to improve occupational safety and health and to prevent accidents and injury to health arising out of, linked with or occurring in the course of work, particularly by minimising the causes of hazards inherent in the working environment;

2.   to issue safety and health regulations;

3.   to provide for the enforcement of such regulations by measures of supervision;

4.   to promote the progressive development of occupational health services for all workers with essentially preventive and advisory functions."

Appendix to Article 3, paragraph 4: "It is understood that for the purposes of this provision the functions, organisation and conditions of operation of these services shall be determined by national laws or regulations, collective agreements or other means appropriate to national conditions."

According to the explanatory report, Article 3 para. 1 "obliges the Parties to formulate, implement and periodically review a coherent national policy on occupational safety, occupational health and the working environment. It emphasises that the aim of this policy shall be to improve occupational safety and health and to prevent accidents and injury to health, *inter alia*, by minimising risks (see above, similarly, the amendment made to Article 2 para. 4 in the revised Charter).

As a result of the inclusion of the requirement for consultation with workers' and employers' organisations in the introductory sentence, this requirement applies to all four paragraphs of Article 3 of the revised Charter. In the Charter, it applies only to the measures intended to improve industrial safety and health (Article 3 para. 3).

Article 4 – The right to a fair remuneration

General

"The Committee considered this right as being the essential corollary of the first three fundamental rights of the Social Charter. Indeed, the right to work, the right to just conditions of work and the right to safe and healthy working conditions would stand in danger of losing much of their meaning without an effective guarantee of the right to fair remuneration, which constitutes one of the basic economic objectives of human activity.

In the Committee's opinion, Contracting Parties who have accepted this article should take the necessary measures to guarantee, in all sectors of the economy, fair remuneration in the full social and economic sense of the term – ie. remuneration which takes account of the basic economic, social and cultural needs of workers and their families, the special efforts made by workers during overtime, and the right to equal pay for work of equal value for men and women workers." (Conclusions I, p. 25).

This Article consists of five numbered paragraphs guaranteeing certain rights aimed at ensuring a fair remuneration and a final unnumbered paragraph which provides that "the exercise of these rights shall be achieved by freely concluded collective agreements, by statutory wage-fixing machinery, or by other means appropriate to national conditions".

Paragraph 1 – Adequate remuneration

Under this paragraph, the Contracting Parties undertake:

> "to recognise the right of workers to a remuneration such as will give them and their families a decent standard of living."

It must be borne in mind that the last, unnumbered, paragraph of Article 4, which defines the method by which the exercise of the rights guaranteed in this Article should be achieved, applies to each of its paragraphs.

As Article 33 does not apply to Article 4 para. 1, its requirement cannot be met by showing that the "great majority" of workers receive remuneration which gives them and their families a decent standard of living. Paragraph 1 applies to the public and private sectors alike.

In the first supervision cycle the Committee interpreted this provision, which obliges Contracting States to take appropriate measures to ensure a decent standard of living for workers and their families, as requiring those states "to make a continuous effort to achieve the objectives set by this provision; this being so, account must be taken of the fact that the socio-economic status of the worker and his family changes and that his basic needs, which at first are centred on the provision of purely material basic necessities such as food and housing, subsequently move towards concerns of a more advanced and complex nature, such as educational facilities and cultural and social benefits" (Conclusions I, p. 26).

Assessment of the implementation of this provision by the Contracting Parties has proved difficult. After four cycles of supervision, the Committee resumed its standpoint on Article 4 para. 1:

"During the first four control cycles the Committee has always had to contend with great difficulties in deciding whether the Contracting States were applying this provision of the Charter.

These difficulties resulted mainly from the paucity of data which could be used directly. It is certainly difficult to collect and produce such data but they are nevertheless necessary for a complete and factual assessment of the position with respect to the provisions of Article 4, paragraph 1, on the basis of the criteria which had been used by the Committee.

To get round these difficulties the Committee felt that it had to work out a more practicable approach to the problem which would require only data which could be collected and produced more easily and without any delay.

For this purpose, recognising that this could only be a first step towards a more sophisticated approach, the Committee, **as a first stage**, took as the basis of its work the considerations which follow:

1.   The concept of a 'decent standard of living' as laid down in Article 4, paragraph 1, must take account of the fundamental social, economic and cultural needs of workers and their families in relation to the stage of development reached by the society in which they live; furthermore this concept must also for the present be judged in the light of the economic and social situation in the country which is being considered.

2.   In a given country and at a given time the wage paid to the largest number of workers can be taken as representative of the wage level in that country.

3.   If the representative wage thus defined were the point of reference, the Committee felt that any lower wage which deviated from this to an excessive extent could no longer be considered as sufficient to permit a 'decent standard of living in the society under consideration.'

However, the statistics needed to assess the situation in each country on this basis are difficult to collect and produce or give rise to problems of interpretation.

At a second stage of its work the Committee observed that recent technical studies[1] which it had read with much interest had arrived at similar results although working on a different basis. These studies concentrated on a 'decency threshold' (in the OECD study a 'poverty threshold') which should be at a level which was either approximately 66% of disposable national income per head (in the OECD study) or around 68% of the national average wage (the Council of Europe study).

These indices seemed to fit in very well with the general considerations which had guided the Committee although the basic reference data differed from those it had previously used.

One of these methods, ie. that which takes a level of 68% seemed to be particularly attractive because it is based on data which are easy to use and few in number. They are also relatively easy for all governments to collect because only the following figures are needed for an assessment:

– the national average wage;

– the lowest wages actually paid in the various sectors of the economy and the various occupations.

This information would enable the Committee to make, on a consistent and comparable basis, a preliminary assessment of the position in the different states and to refine this at a later stage.

Nonetheless the Committee took the view that in the application of this method (which could only be valid for countries with a more or less comparable economic and social structure as is the case within the Council of Europe) a certain number of weighting factors must be taken into account. These indeed result from matters covered in various provisions of the Charter such as: substantial social benefit payments; family and housing subsidies; educational and cultural subsidies; tax conces-

1 Studies on the appropriation of resources (OECD) July 1976; and "Methods of Defining 'Decent' Remuneration", J.-P. Daloz, Council of Europe (1977).

sions; an excessive widening of income distribution; and an effort on the part of the government of a country to ensure sustained progress in the social field for workers." (Conclusions V, pp. 25 and 26).

On the basis of this interpretation, the Committee, in order to be able to assess compliance with this paragraph, asks Contracting Parties to supply, *inter alia*, information on the impact of taxation (ie. tax rebates or exceptions) and social benefits (family allowances, housing allowances etc.) on the disposable income of the lowest paid workers and in particular on the income of three typical categories of worker – a worker supporting a spouse and two children, a single worker supporting two children and a single worker with no dependent children (see for example Conclusions XII-2, p. 79, France; Conclusions XIII-1, pp. 105 and 106, Denmark; p. 106, France; p. 107, Greece; pp. 108 and 109, Italy; p. 110, Spain). Thus if fiscal and social transfers increase the income of the lowest wage-earner so as to satisfy the 68% criterion, the situation is judged as being in conformity with this paragraph.

In response to the argument put forward by one Contracting Party that "comparing the earnings of low-paid workers after tax and social security payments have been taken into account with average earnings before tax is deducted is not making a fair comparison. This could only be made if examples of wages of low-paid workers are compared with net average earnings", the Committee recalled that "its purpose in taking fiscal and social transfer policies into account in assessing the income of the lowest-paid workers, was to allow member states to meet the criteria of this provision of the Charter by using such policies in those cases where wages alone were not sufficient" and observed that in this particular Contracting Party, the family income of low wage-earners was in fact higher after tax and benefits were considered than their gross wages (Conclusions XII-1, p. 93, the United Kingdom).

Furthermore, the Committee, in response to arguments by governments that high unemployment levels, especially among youth, justify the permitting of lower starting wage levels to encourage fuller employment, made it clear that "this cannot be considered as an acceptable reason for allowing wages to fall to such a low level that a worker cannot maintain himself and his family at a 'decent' standard of living"

(Conclusions XI-2, General introduction, p. 29). This view was reiterated in the General introduction to Conclusions XII-1 (p. 28) and in Conclusions XII-2 (p. 26).

Assessment of compliance

In its General introduction to Conclusions XIII-1, the Committee stated that in view of the difficulties encountered by several governments in providing the information required in order for it to reach a conclusion, it had decided to study the modifications which could be made to the method it had used until now to evaluate conformity with this paragraph. Pending implementation of a new method, the Committee used the greatest caution when considering modifying any previous conclusion, while continuing to apply its existing case law (Conclusions XIII-1, p. 25).

With the exception of two cases therefore, (the United Kingdom and the Netherlands) in respect of which the Committee reiterated its negative conclusions given the absence of any change during the reference period, the Committee deferred its conclusions for all the other Contracting Parties which had submitted reports, mainly because of the lack of information on national average wages and/or on the impact of taxation and social benefits on the income of the lowest-paid workers.

The conclusion of the Committee in respect of the **United Kingdom** was negative from the sixth to the ninth cycles, deferred in the tenth and eleventh cycles and negative in the first part of the twelfth cycle and the first part of the thirteenth cycle on the ground that with social benefits and tax deductions taken into account, out of a total of seven hypotheses of family situations presented in the United Kingdom report, only three families would in fact have received an income in 1989 close to or above the threshold considered by the Committee, in application of the 68% rule, as the decency threshold.

In respect of the *Netherlands*, the criticism is based on the ground that workers aged eighteen to twenty-three years with no family responsibilities often receive only a very small percentage of the adult statutory minimum wage, not otherwise compensated for by tax or social benefits, leaving them well below 68% of the national average wage (Conclusions XIII-1, p. 109).

In the thirteenth cycle (part III), having recalled that it had faced particular difficulties in the examination of Article 4 para. 1 and having referred in this respect to Conclusions V (pp. 25 and 26 – see above): "In view of these issues, the Committee asked all states having accepted this provision to provide for each reference period information on:

– the national average wage;

– the statutory minimum wage, if any;

– a sample range of the lowest wages;

– the impact of taxation, social contributions and social transfers on the incomes of three categories of workers on the lowest wages (one worker with a dependent spouse and two dependent children; a single-parent worker with two dependent children; a single worker).

As the governments raised objections and as the Committee was not able to reach a conclusion for certain countries, it requested that additional information be included in the next reports on:

– the minimum wage levels with an indication of the purchasing power they represented;

– the percentage of workers earning the minimum wage;

– the overall trend in the statutory minimum wage and/or the lowest wages compared with the national average wage over the last years;

– the effect of taxation, social contributions and social transfers on the revenue of three categories of workers earning the average national wage (one worker with a dependent spouse and two dependent children; a single-parent worker with two dependent children; a single worker);

– finally, to the extent that these existed, any studies carried out nationally on the amounts of average net wages and minimum net wages.

Pending receipt of this information, the Committee decided not to reach conclusions for this cycle of supervision on the national reports pertaining to this provision. However, all the elements included in the reports would subsequently be taken into consideration by the Committee when it examined the compliance of national situations with Article 4 para. 1 of the Charter." (Conclusions XIII-3, pp. 217 and 218; see also p. 260 and Addendum to Conclusions XIII-3, p. 30: the Committee decided not to assess the compliance of the situations in Finland, Portugal and Luxembourg – first reports).

Paragraph 2 – Increased rate of remuneration for overtime work

Under this paragraph, the Contracting Parties undertake:

> "to recognise the right of workers to an increased rate of remuneration for overtime work, subject to exceptions in particular cases".

Further, it may be recalled that as in the case of paragraph 1, the last, unnumbered, paragraph of this Article also applies here.

In its first Conclusions the Committee stated that "the principle established in this paragraph is based on the assumption that work performed in special circumstances and outside normal working hours requires increased effort on the part of the worker. Not only must the worker receive payment for overtime therefore, but also the rate of such payment must be higher than the normal wage rate" (Conclusions I, p. 28).

Moreover, in the same Conclusions the Committee observed that "the term 'overtime work' is generally taken to mean work performed outside or in addition to normal working hours" (*ibidem*). Nevertheless, it found that in some Contracting Parties normal night work or shift work at night are regarded as overtime and noted that "the precise definition of what is understood by overtime differs slightly from one country to another" (*ibidem*).

Finally, the Committee noted that in some countries overtime may be compensated by the granting of additional leave, in particular for domestic staff (*ibidem*).

As regards the scope of this provision, the Committee has stressed that "since Article 33 was not applicable, all workers (except in special cases, eg. state employees and management executives, etc.) are entitled to higher rates of pay for overtime" (Conclusions IX-2, p. 38). Thus the exceptions allowed in this paragraph are intended for special classes of workers such as personnel in certain jobs with responsibilities who do not normally receive overtime payments, and for special cases such as for example cases of emergency (accident or *force majeure*).

The term "increased rate of remuneration" is a general one. Examples of arrangements considered as acceptable were:

a.   an arrangement by which workers are paid time-and-a-quarter for overtime work on weekdays and time-and-a-half or double time on Sundays and public holidays (Conclusions II, p. 18, Federal Republic of Germany);

b.   a 25% increase in pay for the first eight hours overtime and a 50% increase thereafter (Conclusions VIII, p. 64, France);

c.   a 25% rate of increase for the first 60 hours lawful overtime work in a year and 50% for between 60 and 120 hours overtime and 75% for overtime in excess of 120 hours (Conclusions X-I, p. 58 Greece).

In the tenth supervision cycle the Committee, when examining the situation in a Contracting Party, took the view that the addition of a provision in the relevant legislation to the effect that the increased rates of remuneration to which workers were entitled for overtime work might henceforth be replaced by an equivalent compensatory rest period, was not contrary to Article 4 para. 2 as it did not infringe the workers' right to an increased rate of remuneration and the decision to replace it by an equivalent rest period lay with management and labour (Conclusions X-2, p. 62, France).

Finally, it should be pointed out that in Conclusions XIII-1 the Committee put a general question to Contracting Parties to this provision in view of the observation it had made that, in several states, measures had been taken or were planned regarding flexibility of working time (Conclusions XIII-1, p. 25): "the Committee asked all States bound by this provision to indicate whether such measures provided for the establishment of average, minimum and maximum working hours. It also wished to know what consequences resulted from such measures as concerns the remuneration or compensation of overtime (ie. those hours worked over and above normal legal working hours).

The Committee particularly wished to know whether such a system had to be implemented by provisions established by law or by collective agreements and in the latter case, at what level these agreements were concluded and whether only representative trade unions were authorised to conduct such negotiations" (Conclusions XIII-1, pp. 112 and 113).

The answers to this general question should be given in the fourteenth cycle of supervision.

Assessment of compliance

On the whole, this paragraph has not created any particular problems to Contracting Parties which have been found to satisfy their undertaking by legislation and/or collective agreements and established practice. A common question put to the Contracting Parties applying this provision by collective agreements is whether all workers are covered and if not, what is the position of the workers not covered with respect to the right enshrined in this paragraph (see for example Conclusions VIII, pp. 64 and 65, Denmark, Iceland, Ireland, the Netherlands). An answer considered satisfactory by the Committee was, for example, one to the effect that in the case of workers not covered, "the work contracts take account of conditions applying to the same occupations in the branch of the economy concerned, either explicitly or on the assumption that these conditions are deemed to apply in the event of a dispute" (Conclusions IX-1, p. 40, Denmark). Furthermore, in cases where the overtime was equal to or lower than the normal rate, the Committee asked about the categories of staff and the type of work and circumstances involved in order to ascertain whether these cases fell within the exceptions admitted by the Charter (Conclusions XII-2, p. 86, Malta).

The conclusions are deferred in respect of three Contracting Parties:

the *United Kingdom:* the conclusion was positive until the eleventh cycle of supervision, then deferred from the twelfth cycle. It is interesting to note that in the eleventh cycle, when the Committee discovered that in the United Kingdom as a result of changes in legislation, (the abolition of wages council protection for workers under twenty-one years of age) a significant percentage of workers aged under twenty-one could only enjoy the right provided by this paragraph through custom and practice, it stated that this situation could be considered in conformity with the Charter only if it was proved that in practice all these workers received increased rates of pay for overtime work (Conclusions XI-1, pp. 67 and 68). In the twelfth supervision cycle the Committee, whilst noting the United Kingdom Government's argument that the "very widely held expectation that time worked in excess of normal basic hours will be paid at an enhanced rate" ensured that the custom and practice of paying increased rates for overtime would be observed in all cases, still insisted on having "information evidencing the fact that the 'wisdom and practice' of paying such enhanced rates for overtime work is observed for all these workers" (Conclusions XII-1, pp. 95 and 96). The results of an Earnings Survey to which the government referred were not considered by the Committee as adequate evidence, on the ground that the survey covered only a proportion of the population. As a result of this and of the lack of information about the rights to increased remuneration for overtime work of atypical workers, the Committee deferred its conclusion (Conclusions XIII-1, p. 114). It did the same in cycle XIII-3, recalling "that it was unable to accept a mere assertion and that it was up to the governments of the Contracting Parties to ensure that workers were in fact benefiting from the rights granted to them by the Charter" (Conclusions XIII-3, p. 218).

Finland: the conclusion is deferred pending receipt of information on the sectors not covered by the legal provisions on working hours (Conclusions XIII-3, pp. 260 and 261).

Luxembourg: the conclusion is deferred pending replies to several requests for information, particularly on the rate of remuneration for overtime worked on Saturdays, Sundays and public holidays and those worked by adolescents, on the length of time off in compensation, on increased rates of pay for overtime worked by civil servants on weekdays and during the day and on the applicable collective agreements (Addendum to Conclusions XIII-3, pp. 30 and 31).

Paragraph 3 – Non-discrimination between men and women workers with respect to remuneration

Under this paragraph, the Contracting Parties undertake:

> "to recognise the right of men and women workers to equal pay for work of equal value".

The last unnumbered paragraph of this Article also applies here.

Aware of the importance attached by public opinion to this provision of the Charter, as early as its first Conclusions the Committee felt it necessary to define a certain number of its implications. Moreover, the Committee, emphasising the importance of the right protected by this provision, has stated that this importance "follows directly from one of the fundamental principles of the Charter, namely the enjoyment of social rights without discrimination on grounds of sex, a principle which derives in turn from the Universal Declaration of Human Rights and appears in many of the Constitutions of democratic states" (First report on certain provisions of the Charter which have not been accepted, p. 9).

From the beginning the Committee has held that "this provision obliges the Contracting States who have accepted it to recognise the principle of equal pay for work of equal value, not only in law but also in fact", and has pointed out that "equal pay for men and women for work of equal value (...) presupposes the establishment by the governments of the states concerned of objective criteria for evaluating work, on the basis of appropriate methods (commissions, surveys, etc.). In this connection, the Committee considered that the Charter leaves governments free to choose the methods whereby equality of pay between men and women workers is achieved and that this equality may be ensured either by means of legislation and regulations or by collective agreements, provided only that equality is achieved in practice" (Conclusions I, p. 28).

In the second supervision cycle, the Committee, in a general observation under Article 4 para. 3, elaborated further the issue of the implementation of this provision by making it clear that "if, in a country which had accepted this undertaking, the full exercise of the right to equal remuneration could not be secured for all workers simply through the operation of collective agreements, the state is required to intervene by way of statutory wage-fixing machinery or any other appropriate method. On this point, the Committee had already found that the Charter goes further than ILO Convention No. 100, as is evident from a comparison of the two international instruments, since the Charter included an explicit undertaking to recognise this right, whereas under the ILO Convention the states merely undertake to promote the application of the principle of equal pay for work of equal value and to ensure such application insofar as this is consistent with the methods in operation for determining rates of remuneration. Moreover, the obligation to ensure enjoyment of this right is, in the Charter, absolute" (Conclusions II, pp. 18 and 19). The view that the scope of the Charter is wider than that of ILO Convention No. 100 was repeated by the Committee in its First report on certain provisions of the Charter which have not been accepted (p. 9).

"However, the Committee recognised that while it is possible for a state to require by law, in default of collective agreements, compliance with the rule of equal pay for equal work, implementation of the rule of equal pay for work of equal value involves comparison and assessment of many complicated factors subject to variation in time and space. Accordingly, the undertaking in Article 4 para. 3 could be regarded as being met if, on the one hand, the 'equal pay for equal work' rule was established *de jure* and *de facto* and, on the other hand, the Contracting Party provided evidence that it had taken all steps in its power to achieve equality of remuneration for work of comparable value" (Conclusions II, p. 19).

The latter view was reaffirmed in the third cycle, in which the Committee held that "two criteria should be applied to determine whether the right to equal pay for work of equal value is being respected: firstly to see whether in law and in fact equal pay is guaranteed for equal work, the second whether the state concerned provides evidence that it has taken adequate steps, the nature of which is left to the state's own judgement, to equalise remuneration for work of comparable value" (Conclusions III, p. 26).

The need for state intervention in the form of legislation or any other method where collective agreements failed to secure results which were consistent with the Charter owing to the attitude taken by employers' and workers' organisation, or were proven insufficient, has been recalled by the Committee repeatedly (see for example Conclusions V, p. 31 and Conclusions VII, p. xvi).

Moreover, in its First report on certain provisions of the Charter which have not been accepted (p. 10), the Committee stated that the approach of certain states, which entailed not generally setting out wage regulations in their legislation, "does not in itself seem sufficient to ensure the general implementation of the right enshrined in this Article of the Charter. Thus legislative action is necessary, at least in order to determine the general rules which employers and employees should follow in their negotiations (eg. abolition of differential scales, nullity of discriminatory contracts or clauses etc.)".

By reason of its interpretation that equality of pay must exist in law and in practice, the Committee has been concerned to determine "the reality behind the appearances" and has not been content to consider *de jure* situations only, because "legislation which at first sight may seem very satisfactory is sometimes inadequately or poorly applied. The search for this kind of reality is implicitly required by the terms of the Charter, as in Article 4 (...) which [provides] that certain undertakings may be implemented, otherwise than by law" (Conclusions III, p. xiii).

The examination of these two aspects of national situations – *de jure* and *de facto* – has been observed consistently by the Committee throughout the supervision cycles. In many cases, the Committee found that the situation in law was in conformity with the Charter, but as this was not in itself sufficient it asked Contracting Parties for information on the measures taken to ensure enforcement of the right to equal pay in practice (see for example Conclusions II, p. 19, Conclusions VIII, pp. 67 to 69, Conclusions X-1 p. 60 and 61, Conclusions XI-2 pp. 69 to 71 and Conclusions XII-2, p. 87 and 89) or for "fuller and more accurate statistics on what action has been taken by governments" to ensure application of the principle of equal pay (Conclusions VI, p. xv).

A recent example showing that the Committee also takes into account the situation in practice when assessing whether national situations comply is that of Germany, where the Committee concluded that "although the legal situation was consistent with the Charter, the practical situation posed several problems, and the Committee therefore deferred its conclusion" (Conclusions XIII-2, p. 261; see also p. 260, Belgium and Addendum to Conclusions XIII-3, p. 32, Luxembourg).

In the eighth supervision cycle:

"In the light of the difficulties noticed in the practical application of the principle enshrined in paragraph 3 of Article 4, the Committee agreed to clarify in a more complete manner its scope:

- the legislation of a state which has accepted this provision must prescribe that men and women workers must receive equal pay not only for equal work but also for work of equal value;

- any clauses of collective agreements or individual contracts which contravene this principle must be declared null and void by law;

- the protection of this right must be ensured through adequate remedies;

- workers must enjoy effective protection from measures of retaliation arising from their claim for equal pay (notably protection against dismissal)" (Conclusions VIII, p. 66).

With regard to the first indent, the Committee made it very clear from the outset that the establishment by governments of objective criteria for evaluating work was a necessary prerequisite for the application of the principle of work of "equal value" (see above, Conclusions I, p. 28). Moreover, throughout the supervision cycles the Committee has requested information on steps taken to achieve an objective evaluation of different jobs (see for example Conclusions IV, p. 34 and 35, Federal Republic of Germany, Italy and Sweden; Conclusions V, pp. 32 and 33 for the same Contracting Parties), on systems of objective job evaluation (Conclusions X-2 pp. 63 and 64, Austria and Spain), on methods of assessing the comparative values of different jobs or as to whether "the classification of jobs was made on the basis of an objective appraisal of jobs based on the work to be done (and not on the personal characteristics of the workers)" (Conclusions XII-1, p. 98 and Conclusions XIII-1, p. 126, Greece; see also most recently Addendum to Conclusions XIII-3, p. 32, Luxembourg).

The first procedure on non-accepted provisions of the Charter, which included, *inter alia*, Article 4 para. 3, provided the Committee with an opportunity to recall that the establishment of "objective criteria for assessing equivalence for jobs in all the economic sectors" was one possible approach for the effective protection of the right to equal pay, but it also allowed it to stipulate the limits of the states' obligations: in reply to remarks made by the government of one state in its report, the Committee was unable to accept the suggestion that acceptance of the principle would necessitate compulsory job evaluation throughout the economy: it felt that it would suffice if the right of a woman to equal pay were adequately guaranteed through the judicial system – for example by according her the right to claim job evaluation in her individual case (First report on certain provisions of the Charter which have not been accepted, pp. 10 and 11, the United Kingdom).

The development of objective job evaluation led the Committee to specify that a comparison of wages and corresponding jobs could not be conducted within the same firm and it considered that such a situation represented the application of the principle of equal pay "in a restrictive sense" (Conclusions XII-1, p. 101 and 102, the Netherlands and Norway; in the last instance Conclusions XIII-1, pp. 120 and 121).

The Committee has also noted that certain criteria for determining wages, making objective evaluations or classifying jobs might in practice prove discriminatory (see for example Conclusions XIII-1, p. 121, Norway: "criteria theoretically neutral in terms of gender could be discriminatory in practice (eg. willingness to work overtime, to take on jobs with difficult working hours)"; Conclusions XIII-2, p. 260, Belgium and p. 261, Germany: "emphasis on muscular effort alone to the exclusion of factors that put pressure on workers such as mental strain and stress").

The Committee invariably expresses its concern when a country's legislation on equal pay applies to the "same" work but not to "work of equal value" (see eg. Conclusions VIII, p. 67 and Conclusions IX-1 p. 42, Denmark).[1]

In relation to the second indent, it is pointed out that the nullity of contravening clauses is checked systematically by the Committee. If no provision exists to this effect, the state concerned cannot be considered as satisfying para. 3 of Article 4 (this is the case for Norway; see Conclusions XI-1, p. 72; XII-1, pp. 102 and 103; XIII-1, pp. 120 to 122 and XIII-3 pp. 219 and 220). In the absence of information on this point the Committee puts a specific question (see for example Conclusions-VIII, p. 67, Austria and p. 68, Iceland).

Explaining further its case law on this issue in the tenth supervision cycle, the Committee stated that "compliance with this provision depended either on the existence of an express legislative provision making clauses

---

[1] As a result of legislative reform in 1986 provision was made in Denmark for equal remuneration not only for "the same work" but also for "work of equal value" (Conclusions X -1 p. 59).

contrary to the principle of equal pay null and void (Conclusions VIII, p. 66) or on the existence of a general principle, according to which any provision or clause, which is contrary to a rule of public law must be considered as null and void" (Conclusions X-1, p. 63, Norway).

For the third indent, concerning the protection of the right to equal pay through adequate remedies, the Committee noted that such remedies were included relatively rapidly in the domestic legislation of Contracting Parties, particularly those which were also European Community members. In its First report on certain provisions of the Charter which have not been accepted (p. 10), the Committee observed "a trend towards the granting of judicial guaranties, based on the recognition of an individual right in this matter. Stimulated by certain international standard or directives (...), some states have entitled women workers to take legal action (usually in a labour court) to secure effective protection of this right".

Moreover, the Committee noted the existence "of appropriate legislation in all the states examined, providing both for the individual right to equal pay and for the right of appeal to a judicial authority". (Conclusions IX-I, p. 13). It also noted that "virtually all the countries have commissions responsible for enforcing the principle of equal treatment for men and women. The existence of such bodies does not, however, rule out appeal to the courts as a means of safeguarding the right to equal treatment, in particular the right to equal pay, which is guaranteed in all the states which have accepted the relevant provision of the Charter". (Conclusions IX-2, pp. 10 and 11).

With regard to the fourth indent, the question of effective protection against measures of retaliation was first raised in the seventh cycle of supervision, during the examination of the provisions of an act in a Contracting Party which allowed the dismissal of employees for submitting a claim to equal wages under this act, though in such a case compensation of an amount of not exceeding twenty-six weeks' wages would be payable to them, due regard being given to length of service and to the other circumstances of the case. The Committee considered at that time that "apart from the questions of adequacy of compensation, which would have to be examined further, if a worker is threatened with the possibility of losing his job as a consequence of his exercising a fundamental right, such as the right to equal pay, this could well result in the worker's refraining from submitting his/her claim, so rendering this right devoid of the greatest part of its significance" (Conclusions VII, pp. 26 and 27, Denmark).

In the following cycle, the Committee concluded that "the danger of dismissal was likely to discourage the claims for equal remuneration and that the situation could not therefore be regarded as consistent with Article 4 para. 3 of the Charter" and reached a negative conclusion (Conclusions VIII, p. 67, Denmark). "Considering the fundamental nature of the right to equal pay for men and women for equal work or work of equal value, the Committee stresses that the effective exercise of this right necessarily implies the absence of any retaliatory measures, including dismissal, against persons seeking to avail themselves of it" (Conclusions IX-1, p. 13); the Committee remarked that in Denmark dismissal remained possible in such circumstances and in addition, that the amount of damages that the employer was required to pay did not appear to it to constitute "either a sufficient deterrent for the employer or adequate compensation for the employee concerned" (*ibidem* and p. 41). The same position was taken in the tenth and eleventh cycles, even though in the meantime the amount of compensation was raised to thirty-nine weeks' wages. The Committee also regarded this amount "as too small to represent a sufficient deterrent to the employer or a sufficient compensation for the worker (Conclusions X-1, p. 60 and XI-1, p. 68).

In the twelfth supervision cycle, the Committee maintained the same view and "recalled that the only instance in which it had considered that compensation for such dismissal might be acceptable in lieu of reinstatement was in its Conclusions IX-1, p. 44, where it accepted the following situation: in the country concerned [Sweden] and in respect of the private sector only, where it is not judged possible to order reinstatement because the employer refuses to comply with a court judgement, the contract of employment is deemed to be terminated and the employee is entitled to unlimited damages. In such a case, clearly the employee's rights have been protected as far as it is possible in that unlimited compensation is payable but only when no other solution is possible. The same could not be said of the situation in Denmark where the law merely provides for a maximum compensation of thirty-nine weeks pay for unjustified dismissal on the ground of a claim for equal pay, without even considering reinstatement as a remedy. Such cannot be considered as sufficient protection of the right not to be dismissed for claiming equal pay, as it is sufficient neither to deter the employer nor to compensate the employee" (Conclusions XII-1, pp. 96 and 97).[1]

Finally, it should be mentioned that the Committee is also concerned with reprisals other than dismissal and has examined the issue of the burden of proof. It noted that in one state, "whilst an employer was not entitled to impose a sanction on a worker for the sole reason that he/she had taken court proceedings, he was nevertheless not required to give reasons for dismissal. The dismissed worker thus faced serious difficulties in proving that his/her dismissal was caused by his/her having taken a legal action" (Conclusions IX-2, p. 39, Austria). The Austrian Government itself admitted that this situation was "not entirely satisfactory".

In the twelfth cycle, the Committee considered that where it was left to the worker to substantiate the unlawfulness of the dismissal as being founded on his or her demand that the equal pay principle be applied, "adherence to the principle of equal pay was not fully guaranteed since its practical application was made more difficult" (XII-1, p. 100, Iceland; this has been remedied to a certain extent by reversing the burden of proof in cases of alleged sex discrimination brought before the Complaints Committee; see Conclusions XIII-1, p. 118 and Conclusions XIII-3, p. 219).

Actual examples of retaliatory measures other than dismissal given by the Committee were, *inter alia*, changing jobs, modification of conditions of work (Conclusions XI-1, p. 43, the Netherlands) and transfer,

---

1 The situation was remedied by Act No. 374 of the 10 May 1992 which prohibited the dismissal of employees who had made claims for equal pay or equal working conditions. This act made express provision for reinstatement and in cases where this was deemed unreasonable, the worker concerned would be entitled to compensation of a maximum which had been increased from 39 to 78 weeks (Conclusions XIII-3, pp. 218 and 219).

unilateral alteration in working conditions and down-grading (Conclusions XIII-3, p. 220, Norway).

Assessment of compliance

Up to the sixth supervision cycle, almost all Contracting States were found as not complying with this provision, mainly on the ground of the existence of pay discrepancies[1] between male and female workers doing the same work or work of equal value and the lack of objective criteria or methods of evaluation for comparing and assessing the application of the principle of equal pay for work of equal value in the case of different jobs (Austria, Italy (until the fourth cycle), Norway, Sweden).

As from the seventh cycle on the whole the Contracting States have been found to have made considerable progress towards achieving compliance with this provision, especially through the enactment of legislation establishing the right of equal pay and the intensification of the efforts to ensure *de facto* application of this right, *inter alia* through the establishment of Equality of Treatment or Equal Status Committees or Boards, diffusing information and fostering awareness, reducing the existing wage differentials or raising wages in certain low-paid sectors employing a high proportion of women.

The only Contracting Parties found as not complying in the latest Conclusions are:

Norway: it is still impossible for an individual to have a provision of a collective agreement contravening the principle of equal pay declared null and void. An individual could challenge such a clause before the Courts but if he or she were successful, application of the agreement would be waived in respect only of the individual concerned (see in the last instance Conclusions XIII-3, pp. 219 and 220);

---

1 The Committee however admits that these discrepancies may be due, *inter alia*, to the high proportion of female labour in low-paid sectors, the lack of qualifications and the fact that women are less available for overtime and shift work, which are generally better paid (see for example Conclusions XI-1, p. 73, Sweden).

Turkey: certain sectors of the economy are excluded from any protection with respect to equal pay (Conclusions XIII-3, pp. 265 and 266).

Paragraph 4 – Reasonable notice of termination of employment

Under this paragraph, the Contracting Parties undertake:

> "to recognise the right of all workers to a reasonable period of notice for termination of employment".

Appendix to Article 4 para. 4

> "this provision shall be so understood as not to prohibit immediate dismissal for any serious offence".

This provision was included in Article 4 and not in Article 2 because the purpose of the notice requirement is mainly to ensure that a worker is guaranteed his wages for a reasonable period while he is looking for another job.[1]

Interpreting the notion of a "reasonable" period of notice and its limits in the first supervision cycle, the Committee took the view that no absolute definition of "reasonableness" could be given where a period of notice was concerned and for this reason it confined itself to determining particular cases in which the period of notice could not be considered reasonable (Conclusions I, p. 29). This was reaffirmed in the fourth cycle, when the Committee explained that it "refrained from defining in absolute terms the word 'reasonable' for termination of employment. In fact it follows the reverse procedure and its estimation of what constitutes a clearly 'unreasonable' amount of notice is founded on criteria of fairness, such as a worker's period of service with a firm, as

---

1 Conclusions XII -2, p. 93, Malta; Conclusions XIII-2, p. 264, Belgium; Conclusions XIII-3, p. 267, Portugal.

well as making allowances for the progressive character of the Charter which was envisaged by its authors" (Conclusions IV, p. 35). This view has been maintained throughout all the supervision cycles by the Committee (see in the last instance Conclusions XIII-2, pp. 263 and 264, Belgium and Conclusions XIII-3, p. 267, Portugal).

In the eighth cycle of supervision, when examining the situation in a Contracting Party where legislation laid down, *inter alia*, one week's notice for workers with up to two years' of employment, the Committee took the view that it might possibly be able to regard the situation as complying with the Charter if it were proved that in practice "periods of notice for this category of workers were in fact longer under collective agreements and, more generally, common law" (Conclusions VIII, pp. 73 and 74, the United Kingdom).

The principle of giving the worker compensation in lieu of notice has also been accepted by the Committee (see for example Conclusions XII-1, p. 104, Greece), with the same methods of assessment as for periods of notice. Thus, in the case of Greece, certain workers usually receive financial compensation in lieu of a minimum notice period, such compensation being based on the number and amount of daily wages they should have received during the notice period. "While the Committee considered that providing such compensation in lieu of notice was acceptable, as it had noted in Conclusions XI-1, the minimum notice periods in themselves were not adequate in terms of its case law, and therefore the corresponding compensation could not be considered as satisfactory either" (*ibidem*).

Furthermore, according to the case law of the Committee, the actual period of notice can only be calculated as from the moment when a worker is notified by the employer that the dismissal has been approved. Application to the appropriate office by an employer for authorisation to dismiss or consultations of workers prior to dismissal cannot be regarded as extending the period of notice (Conclusions IX-1, p. 45, the Netherlands). In the same way, the Committee has refused to take into account the Swedish Government's argument that information and consultation for workers prior to dismissal extended the period of notice in practice. "It however was unable to share this opinion, since the period of notice as such cannot commence until after the consultation between the employee – or possibly his local trade union branch – and the employer have taken place" (Conclusions XI-1, p. 75).

Periods of notice considered as reasonable by the Committee were, for example, the following:

- eight days' notice for less than six months' service, one month's notice for less than two years' service and two months' notice for more than two years' service (Conclusions XI-2, p. 71, France);

- two weeks' for two years' service, increasing by one week for every subsequent year of service, subject to a maximum of twelve weeks (Conclusions XII-1, p. 107, the United Kingdom);

- thirty days for two years' service and sixty for over two years (Conclusions XIII-3, p. 267, Portugal).

As regards the personal scope of this paragraph, it is clear from its context that it does not extend to the self-employed.

There is no definition of the term "serious offence" appearing in the appendix to Article 4 para. 4 and which allows immediate dismissal, and the Committee examines situations case by case (see for example Conclusions XIII-2, p. 264, Malta).

Assessment of compliance

Paragraph 4 of Article 4 has been accepted by only thirteen Contracting Parties, of which eight have been found as not complying. Two of these states have had a negative conclusion since the first cycle of supervision and another state since the second cycle.

Contracting Parties not complying are:

Belgium: (first report): because the minimum period of notice for manual workers is insufficient: seven days for less than six months' service; twenty-eight days for less than twenty years' service and fifty-six days for those who have served in the same firm without interruption for more than twenty years (Conclusions XIII-2, pp. 263 and 264);

Greece: because the periods of notice and financial compensation instead of a period of notice for "technicians and workers" (manual or daily wage workers) are insufficient; eight days' notice for service of up to two years; fifteen days for between two and five years' service and thirty days for between five and ten years' service (Conclusions XII-1, p. 104; see in the last instance Conclusions XIII-3, p. 220);

Ireland: the periods of notice criticised are one week for almost two years of service, two weeks for two to five years' service and four weeks for workers with almost ten years of service. The conclusion has been negative since the first supervision cycle (Conclusions I, pp. 177 and 178, Conclusions XIII-3, pp. 220 and 221).[1]

The argument of the Irish Government, that the periods of notice specified in the Minimum Notice and Terms of Employment Act of 1973 were enacted "only after full consultation with the principal organisations representing both employers and workers", was not accepted by the Committee (see Conclusions VI, p. 26);

Italy: on the ground that in the metallurgical industry the periods of notice are still insufficient (six days for a worker with five years' service, nine days for between five and ten years and twelve days for service in excess of ten years). This criticism has been made since the first supervision cycle (Conclusions I, p. 29; Conclusions XIII-3, p. 221).[2] The argument of the Italian Government, that the situation does not pose any problems in practice, because individual cases of dismissal were extremely rare, is not accepted by the Committee;

---

1 The Committee of Ministers addressed a recommendation to Ireland for the first part of the thirteenth cycle.

2 The Committee of Ministers addressed a recommendation to Italy for the second part of the twelfth supervision cycle and a second recommendation for the first part of the thirteenth cycle.

the *Netherlands:* because the existing legislation governing periods of notice is not entirely satisfactory: one week's notice for weekly paid workers below eighteen years of age and for weekly paid adult workers with two years' service or more (see in the last instance Conclusions XIII-3, p. 221);[1]

Portugal: (first report): because periods of notice of dismissal – seven days – for workers employed less than six months is insufficient (Conclusions XIII-3, pp. 266 and 267);

Sweden: because of the periods of notice applicable to young workers in the painting and metal-working trades. According to the collective agreements in force in these fields, workers under thirty years of age are only entitled to one month's notice, which cannot be considered reasonable since some of them may have been in employment for as long as fourteen years. This was a permissible deviation from the Act on Security of Employment, which recommended two months' minimum notice as from the age of twenty-five, increasing by one month every five years up to a maximum of six months' at the age of forty-five. "While considering the Swedish concern to protect older workers as justified and valuable for the purpose of the Charter, the Committee did not find that it did in any way prevent the Swedish Government from also protecting workers on the basis of the length of service. It considered that, in fact, these two approaches to some extent have the same aim and can be combined (which is the case in Sweden except for the workers covered by the two agreements mentioned above)" (Conclusions XII-1, p. 106; see in the last instance Conclusions XIII-3, pp. 221 and 222);

the *United Kingdom:* as the one week period of notice provided by law for workers with between one month and two years' service is considered "unreasonable". The criticism has been made since the second cycle of supervision (Conclusions II, p. 21; Conclusions XIII-3, p. 222).

---

1 Legislation to remedy the situation is under way.

Paragraph 5 – Limitation of deductions from wages

Under this paragraph, the Contracting Parties undertake:

> "to permit deductions from wages only under conditions and to the extent prescribed by national laws or regulations or fixed by collective agreements or arbitration awards".

The last unnumbered paragraph of Article 4 also applies to this provision.

Appendix to Article 4 para. 5

> "It is understood that a Contracting Party may give the undertaking required in this paragraph if the great majority of workers are not permitted to suffer deductions from wages either by law or through collective agreements or arbitration awards, the exception being those persons not so covered".

The nature of the undertaking means that it does not apply to the self-employed. It applies to all employed persons, including part-time workers, employees related to their employer and to those in the public sector (see Conclusions XII-2, pp. 94 and 95 and XIII-2, p. 267, Malta; see also Conclusions XIII-1, pp. 227 and 228 and Conclusions XIII-3, p. 270, Turkey, and Conclusions XIII-3, p. 269, Portugal). With respect to Turkey, the Committee, referring to the appendix to Article 4 para. 5, also wanted to know what proportion of workers did not enjoy the protection provided for in the Charter.

As stated by the Committee in the first supervision cycle, "the worker's right to receive his wages in full has been the subject of long battles in the history of the labour movement. The Social Charter too was bound to establish the principle that deductions from wages can be authorised only 'under conditions and to the extent prescribed by national laws or regulations or fixed by collective agreements or arbitration awards'. The Committee pointed out that a Contracting State cannot be regarded as meeting its obligation under the terms of paragraph 5 unless these conditions and limitations are respected".

In the fifth supervision cycle the examination of the contents of the reports of the Contracting Parties prompted the Committee to clarify its interpretation of the scope of the appendix to this provision. The interpretation given was as follows:

"In fact, if on the one hand this provision obliges Contracting States to permit deductions from wages in respect of all workers only 'under conditions and to the extent prescribed by national laws or regulations or fixed by collective agreements or arbitration awards', thus implying that any other deductions must be considered as contrary to the Charter, on the other hand, the appendix states that 'if the great majority of workers are not permitted to suffer deductions from wages...' the undertaking laid down in the Charter is satisfied.

As the "*travaux préparatoires*" show that the text of the appendix was inserted in order to permit States to satisfy the Charter even if only the great majority of workers were protected as required by Article 4, paragraph 5, the deductions not permitted by the appendix are those which are not authorised either by law or regulations nor fixed by collective agreements or arbitration awards and which are consequently not in conformity with Article 4, paragraph 5, of the Charter. It follows that a State must be regarded as acting in conformity with this provision when deductions from wages are permitted for the large majority of workers only when they are expressly authorised by laws, regulations, collective agreements or arbitration awards" (Conclusions V, pp. 34 and 35).

In the same cycle, the Committee stated in respect of Italy that in order to be able to remove the provisional character of its positive conclusion it was necessary "to know whether or not in Italy, apart from deductions whose nature, conditions and limitations are defined by legal regulation or collective agreement or by arbitration awards, deductions from wages (whether in respect of their nature or amount) can be laid down in individual work contracts or by other methods" (Conclusions V, p. 35).

Deductions from wages for taxation, social insurance, trade union contributions, money paid by the employer for housing or food, money due for damage to an employer's property or for alimony were found to be in line with the Charter when authorised by law, regulations or collective agreements. Even in the case of authorised deductions the Committee has, however, insisted on ensuring that safeguards existed in order that after the deduction the worker retained an amount which enabled him reasonably to support himself and his household (see for example the cases of Greece and Norway for deductions from wages arising from liability for damage or loss caused by an employee through wilful damage or gross negligence (Conclusions XII-1, pp. 108-109 and Conclusions XIII-1, pp. 127 and 128; see also pp. 226-228 and Conclusions XIII-3, p. 270, Turkey, and Addendum to Conclusions XIII-3, pp. 33 and 34, Luxembourg: "the Committee asked that the next report indicate whether there was any overall limitation to such deductions, ensuring that the worker continued to receive a minimum subsistence income").

Assessment of compliance

On the whole, Contracting Parties have been found to be complying with this provision. The only Contracting Party found as not complying is *Italy*. The criticism exists since the eighth supervision cycle when Italy was found as not complying with this provision because "deductions from wages to compensate for debts contracted by workers were neither expressly prohibited nor authorised by law or collective agreements and could be made in application of the principle of contracts of employment, with the consent of the worker. No condition or limitation seems to have been laid down" (Conclusions VIII, p. 75).

The Committee maintained the view that Italy was not complying despite the argument of the Italian Government that "under Article 36 of the Italian Constitution, workers are entitled to remuneration 'proportional to the quantity and quality of the work performed, and at all events sufficing to guarantee a free and decent life for the worker and his family', which constitutes a wage guarantee even in respect of workers' debts towards their employers. The Committee observed, however, that the degree of protection thereby secured was left for the competent judicial authorities to determine" and asked to be informed of the relevant case law. "Nevertheless, having regard to the purpose of this provision of the Charter, the Committee took the view that an effective and more socially acceptable form of protection could only be secured by means of a law clearly establishing precise limits to compensation for workers' debts towards their employers" and reiterated the view that the situation in Italy was not entirely consistent with the Charter (Conclusions X-2, p. 66). This negative conclusion is still maintained (Conclusions XI-2, p. 72; Conclusions XII-2, p. 94; Conclusions XIII-1,[1] p. 127 and Conclusions XIII-3, pp. 222 and 223).

---

1 The Committee of Ministers addressed a recommendation to Italy for the second part of the twelfth supervision cycle and a second recommendation for the first part of the thirteenth supervision cycle, which was renewed for the third part of the thirteenth cycle.

Article 5 – The right to organise

"With a view to ensuring or promoting the freedom of workers and employers to form local, national or international organisations for the protection of their economic and social interests and to join those organisations, the Contracting Parties undertake that national law shall not be such as to impair, nor shall it be so applied as to impair, this freedom. The extent to which the guarantees provided for in this Article shall apply to the police shall be determined by national laws or regulations. The principle governing the application to the members of the armed forces of these guarantees and the extent to which they shall apply to persons in this category shall equally be determined by national laws or regulations."

General

Article 5 together with Article 6 are the two key provisions of the Charter in the field of industrial relations.

The great importance of trade union rights and the difficulties encountered by the Contracting Parties in observing their obligations under Article 5 have given rise to an extensive case law which covers a wide area.

Before presenting this case law, three general points should be underlined:

- even though Article 5 covers the freedom of workers and employers, almost all the case law concerns trade unions, as in practice, the freedom of employers has not caused any problems;

- the restrictions and limitations of the rights guaranteed by the Charter, and therefore by Article 5, should be judged in the light of Article 31 of the Charter;

- the general principle of equality of treatment between nationals and nationals of other Contracting Parties, which according to the Appendix to the Charter applies to all the rights protected by the Charter, is backed up in the case of Article 5 by Article 19 para. 4 which requires Contracting Parties to secure for migrant workers equal treatment with their own nationals in respect of, *inter alia*, "membership of trade unions and enjoyment of the benefits of collective bargaining". Therefore, where the equality of treatment between nationals and nationals of other Contracting Parties is not respected, the Committee's conclusion is negative with respect to Article 5 and Article 19 para. 4, if the state concerned has accepted both of these provisions. This was the case for France.[1] (Fourth report on certain provisions of the Charter which have not been accepted, p. 21).

For the purposes of this presentation the case law has been grouped under four headings. This grouping must not, however, dissimulate the fact that the different aspects of trade union rights are closely linked, and a criticised restriction may consequently constitute an infringement of several of these aspects at the same time.

---

1 According to the Labour Code foreign workers were not eligible for administrative or managerial functions in the trade union to which they belonged until they had worked for a period of five years in France and the proportion of foreign workers among trade union members exercising such functions could not exceed one-third. (Conclusions VI, pp. 30 and 121; see also Conclusions VII, pp. 31 and 102). An Act of 28 October 1982 remedied the sitution (Conclusions VIII, pp. 78, 79 and 207).

1. Freedom to form and join organisations

In a general observation in the first supervision cycle the Committee outlined the obligations of Contracting Parties under Article 5 as follows:

"This article sets out the principle that employers and workers have the right to form national or international associations, for the protection of their economic and social interests. The Committee noted that two obligations were embodied in this provision, having a negative and positive aspect respectively.

The implementation of the first obligation requires the absence, in the municipal law of each Contracting State, of any legislation or regulation or any administrative practice such as to impair the freedom of employers or workers to form or join their respective organisations. By virtue of the second obligation, the Contracting State is obliged to take adequate legislative or other measures to guarantee the exercise of the right to organise and, in particular, to protect workers' organisations from any interference on the part of employers" (Conclusions I, p. 31).

National legislation and practice have revealed different forms of restrictions of the freedom of employers and workers to form and join organisations which is expressly guaranteed by Article 5. These are not necessarily contrary to the requirement of Article 5 when viewed in the light of Article 31. The Committee has assessed them individually, whilst gradually defining certain principles of a more general scope.

The most important issues examined by the Committee in relation to the freedom to form and join workers organisations and the Committee's case law thereon are given below.

a. *Limitations to the freedom of workers to choose the technical and professional framework in which to organise*

When examining the provisions contained in the legislation of Cyprus which limited trade union membership to persons actually engaged in, or working at, the trade or linked to a specific trade union, the Committee, broaching the question from a general standpoint, pointed out that "all workers and all trade union organisations should, in principle under Article 5 of the Charter, be free to decide to which trade union, professional or technical association they wish to belong" (Conclusions II, p. 184).

"The Committee considered, however, that, provided a worker could choose either to join a trade union relating to his trade or profession, or to form another organisation, the situation might be considered as in conformity with the Charter" (Conclusions XII-2, p. 97, Cyprus). On receiving confirmation that the formation of professional or industrial sector trade unions not only were not prohibited but "these organisations represented the general rule and that even if a worker's trade is covered by a trade union, that worker may, along with other workers similarly affected, form another trade union", the Committee concluded that the situation was not in breach of the Charter (Conclusions XIII-1, pp. 129 and 130; see also Conclusions XIII-3, pp. 96 and 97).

Similarly the Committee held in connection with the "excepted bodies" in Ireland (ie. workers groups which could be formed without having to meet the demands imposed on trade unions) that the complete exclusion from the rules of these bodies of the freedom to organise at an inter-professional level was not in compliance with Article 5 (Conclusions IV, pp. 40 and 41).

Responding to arguments from the Government of Ireland that the system of granting of "negotiating licences" aimed at reducing, in the public interest, the number of trade unions so as to improve their bargaining power and organisation, the Committee underlined that "the presence of a high number of trade unions is not a phenomenon exclusive for Ireland and does not necessarily entail a weakening of the labour movement as long as trade unions are in a position to organise 'horizontally' and 'vertically' to defend their interests" (Conclusions VII, p. 31).

b. Compulsory registration or licensing of trade unions

According to the Committee "the principle of the compulsory registration of trade unions is not (...) incompatible with Article 5, so long as the persons concerned have adequate administrative and jurisdictional protection against abuse of the power to refuse to register a trade union" (Conclusions II, p. 184). Moreover "while compulsory registration of a trade union or employers' association is acceptable under Article 5, any pre-condition, including any fee requirement, must be reasonable" (Conclusions XII-2, p. 99).

To assess compliance in cases where registration of trade union is compulsory by law the Committee has inquired into the criteria adopted by the administrative authorities when granting or refusing registration and asked for information on any court decision on the refusal of registration (Conclusions III, p. 31, Cyprus; see also Conclusions XII-2, p. 99 Malta).

c. Minimum membership of an organisation

The Committee touched upon this issue in an indirect manner when examining the condition imposed in Ireland for the granting of a negotiating licence to trade unions, since one of these conditions was for the union to have at least 500 members. The Committee held that the condition of size for a trade union infringed the freedom of forming or joining a trade union (Conclusions III, p. 31; see also below under 3; the requirement of a negotiating licence itself was regarded as impinging on a fundamental trade union prerogative: the right to collective bargaining).

The Committee's view that the requirement of a minimum number of members is incompatible with Article 5, as it can be a restriction of the liberty to constitute workers' and employers' organisations, is clearly shown in the conclusion adopted for Portugal on examination of its first report. The Committee stated here that provisions in legislation:

–   according to which the minimum number of workers required to form a trade union was 10% of the total or 2,000 workers and the formation of an amalgamated union or trade union federation should have a backing of one-third of all trade unions for the region or category concerned;

– and which set the number of employers required to form an employers association at one quarter of those concerned and required that the formation of an amalgamated association or federation of employers should have the backing of at least 30% of the employers concerned,

did not comply with the provisions of the Charter. The Committee's decision, however, in this particular case was deferred pending receipt of additional information, on the ground that these provisions were no longer applied in practice (Conclusions XIII-3, p. 272).

d. Absence of protection for certain trade union members

The omission to protect members of an unlicensed trade union in Ireland (ie. a union not holding a negotiating licence) by the immunities against civil liability provided by the 1906 Trade Unions Act in respect of acts done in furtherance of a trade dispute, as well as the omission to regard the dismissal of a member of an unlicensed trade union for trade union membership or activity as unfair within the meaning of the 1977 Unfair Dismissal Act, were considered to constitute an impairment of the freedom to form and join a trade union of one's choice (Addendum to Conclusions XI-2, p. 19).

e. State intervention in the management of trade unions

The Committee has consistently held that Article 5 is meant to protect freedom of association against any interference on the part of the authorities (Conclusions II, p. 23) and it is for the trade unions to establish their own rules. However, not all forms of state intervention in trade union matters are regarded as being necessarily contrary to the aims of Article 5. Thus, for example, the Committee has considered that Article 5 is not infringed:

- by the development of case law admitting the imposition of liability on trade unions for unlawful strikes. "In this respect, the Committee was able to conclude that such a possibility, whose sole purpose is to allow redress of damage caused by an unlawful act, does not interfere with the right to organise as set out in this provision of the Charter. This is particularly true in view of the fact that should such liability be incurred, there are legislative limits which in any event safeguard such property of a trade union as may be necessary for its activity" (Conclusions X-2, p. 68, France);

- by a law (the Trade Union Act, 1984) which introduced the obligation to vote by secret ballot for the election of union governing bodies, the taking of industrial action and the existence of "political funds" in union budgets (Conclusions X-1, p. 68, the United Kingdom).

On the contrary the Committee has considered as amounting to interference in the constitution and internal regulations of trade unions and thus an impairment of the freedom protected by Article 5 to form an organisation of one's choosing:

- the limitation by legislation of the right of a trade union or confederation to elect or appoint its officers by restricting eligibility for appointment or election to persons actually engaged in the occupation or trade concerned[1] (Conclusions III, p. 31 and Conclusions XI-2, p. 74, Cyprus);

- the prohibition of a trade union from disciplining members who refuse to take part in lawful strikes (Section 3 of the 1988 Employment Act) or from indemnifying a member for a penalty imposed by law for taking part in a strike (Section 8 of the above act) in so far as this limits legitimate activities (Conclusions XII-1, p. 115, the United Kingdom).

---

1 Restrictions abolished by the Trade Unions (Amendment) Law No. 381 of 1991 (Conclusions XII-2, p. 96).

Taking into account the British Government's arguments, the Committee explained its criticisms in more depth in the following cycle:

"Referring to Section 3 of the 1988 Act (Sections 64-67 of the 1992 Act) the Committee noted from the 1993 Observations of the ILO Committee of Experts under Convention No. 87 (Freedom of Association and Protection of the Right to Organise, 1948) that technically these provisions impose no direct or explicit limitation on what may or may not be included in trade union rules. However Section 66 (1) of the 1992 Act allows individual union members to complain to an industrial tribunal on grounds that they have been unjustifiably disciplined. The Committee noted under Section 65 of the Act that disciplinary measures may be regarded as unjustified where an individual fails to participate in or support a strike or other industrial action or indicates opposition to or lack of support for such action (whether by members of the union or by others). Furthermore the Committee noted that recent judicial decisions referred to by both the Government and the TUC demonstrate that, while trade unions are free to adopt any rules they wish in this respect, they may face serious financial penalties if and when they enforce them.

The Committee had to conclude that these provisions removed the right of trade unions to express their dissatisfaction with their members who refuse to comply with or seek to subvert democratic decisions by other union members to take lawful industrial action" and as such, therefore, were not in conformity with Article 5 of the Charter.

"Having regard to Section 8 of the 1988 Act (Section 15 of the 1992 Act), which makes it unlawful for the property of any trade union to be applied so as to indemnify any individual in respect of any penalty which may be imposed in respect of either a criminal offence or for contempt of court, the Committee observed from the report that the provision affords:

- the unions a new statutory right to recover payments made from its fund where such amounts constitute an unlawful indemnity in the above circumstances;

- the individual members of a union with a right of legal redress where, in their opinion, the union, having made such a payment, subsequently fails or refuses to take action to recover such amounts.

The Committee acknowledged that while Section 8 may in some respects be regarded as an interference with the autonomy to be afforded trade unions, in the exercise of legitimate trade union functions, such interference may however be justified, affording individuals, members of a union, both a right and a remedy where, in pursuance of industrial action, the individual believes union funds or property are being used to indemnify individuals against penalties for unlawful acts.

Nevertheless, the Committee emphasised that although according to the information from the Government and the TUC to the ILO Committee of Experts, there had been no judicial proceedings initiated under this provision, the legislation posed a real danger not only for the autonomy of trade unions but also in the exercise of their internal affairs. It therefore asked to be kept informed regarding the practical application of these provisions" (Conclusions XIII-1, pp. 137 and 138; see also Conclusions XIII-3, p. 110: the Committee maintained its negative conclusion under Section 3 of the 1988 Act (Sections 64 to 67 of the 1992 Act) whilst it noted in addition that the information supplied by the TUC confirmed that heavy financial penalties were imposed under these provisions; with respect to Section 8 of the 1988 Act (Section 15 of the 1992 Act), the Committee noted that no judicial proceedings had been initiated under this provision, but "it considered that the existence of this legislation continued to constitute a real risk not only for the autonomy of trade unions but also for the exercise of their internal affairs. It therefore again asked to be kept informed of the practical application of these provisions").

In the third part of the thirteenth cycle, the Committee also noted that other types of interference were introduced by Sections 14, 15 and 18 of the Trade Union Reform and Employment Rights Act 1993:

−   Section 14 introduced changes in the right to membership of a trade union (sections 174 to 177 of the 1992 Act). The Committee noted that Section 14 permitted the exclusion or expulsion of an individual from a trade union in only four restrictively listed cases (Section 174) and that heavy financial penalties were provided for in the event of failure to comply with Section 174 (Section 176). "While noting that Section 14 appeared to strengthen the right of every individual to join the trade union of his choice, the Committee was concerned at the considerable restrictions put to the right of trade unions to establish their own rules and choose their members";

– Section 15 of the Act of 1993 altered the system for the deduction of trade union dues from wages by the employer (Section 68 of the 1992 Act);

– Section 18 of the 1993 Act required trade unions to notify the employer of their intention of holding a ballot on industrial action, "describing (so that he can readily ascertain them) the employees of the employer" who would probably participate in the ballot. According to the information received from the TUC, the courts almost invariably required that the employer be provided with a list of his unionised employees; this was an obstacle to the confidentiality of union membership for those members who desired it and was considered a threat to freedom of association.

Commenting on all of these provisions, the Committee stated that:

"The regular interference that these rules represented and their combined effect greatly concerned the Committee, and it pointed out that, as it had consistently held, Article 5 was meant to protect freedom of association against any interference on the part of the authorities (Conclusions II, p. 23) and that it was for the trade unions to establish their own rules (see for example Conclusions XI-2, p. 74 and XII-2, p. 96). The Committee asked for precise information on the practical application of these provisions, as well as comments from the government on the aim of the 1993 Act and the freedom of trade unions" (Conclusions XIII-3, pp. 109 and 110).

f. *Absence of adequate protection of the freedom to join trade unions*

In the eleventh supervision cycle, the Committee put special emphasis on the requirement for adequate protection of the freedom to join or remain a member of a trade union and made it clear that the absence of this protection is considered in breach of Article 5 (Conclusions XI-1, p. 78; see also below, point 2).

The Committee has criticised various situations in this area.

- In the case of Ireland, "it noted that while the Constitution guarantees the right of citizens to form associations and unions it does not guarantee the right to join such associations and that there is no legislative provision which provides individuals with such rights. While the report states that the courts have established, in principle, that the freedom or right to associate necessarily implies a correlative right not to join any trade union or a particular trade union, the Committee reiterated its statement in Conclusions XI-1 that the absence of adequate protection of such a freedom in national law cannot be considered as consistent with Article 5 of the Charter" (Conclusions XIII-1, p. 133; see also in the last instance Conclusions XIII-3, p. 100; see also above, point d.).

- In respect of the United Kingdom, upon examining the Trade Union Reform and Employment Rights Act 1993 in detail, the Committee noted that its Section 13 had the effect of weakening considerably the protection of the freedom of workers to join or not to join trade unions: court decisions had found illegal the fact that an employer awarded preferential remuneration to employees who accepted individual contracts and relinquished clauses agreed through collective bargaining. Following these decisions, an amendment was introduced to the 1992 Act.

The Committee was of the opinion that the wording of the new legislation (ie. section 148 para. 3 sub-paragraph a.) "was so general that the effect of this provision was that only in exceptional cases would a tribunal be able to rule that the action taken by the employer was unlawful because it violated freedom of association. It considered that this weakening of the protection of freedom of association was not compatible with the requirements of Article 5" (Conclusions XIII-3, p. 108; see also below, under "assessment of compliance").

Protection of the freedom to join trade unions also covers the freedom to join a union "of one's choice". The Committee found that such freedom was infringed by Act No. 408 of 23 June 1988 instituting a Danish International Ship's Register (DIS). This act limited the personal scope of collective agreements concluded by Danish trade unions concerning the wages and working conditions of employees on vessels entered in the register, to persons considered to be residents of Denmark, or put, by virtue of incurred international obligations, on an equal footing with Danish citizens.

The Committee expressed its concern for this restriction, for if a Danish trade union could no longer defend the interests of those of their members who were not "residents of Denmark" or "put on an equal footing with Danish citizens", this might lead those members to join other trade unions or in practice deter them from joining those trade unions (Conclusions XII-1, p. 111; see also Conclusions XIII-1, p. 131 and in the last instance Conclusions XIII-3, p. 97).

2. Negative aspect of the right to organise

An important problem of interpretation which concerned the Committee was whether Article 5, which guarantees expressly the "positive" aspect of the right to organise (ie. the liberty to join a trade union), protects also the "negative" aspect (ie. the right not to belong or to withdraw from a trade union). The main problems which arose in connection with this question concerned trade union security clauses or practices (notably the closed shop) but other cases of non respect of the negative right to organise were also examined.

From the very beginning the Committee held that the "negative" aspect of the right to organise is also protected. Thus in the first supervision cycle it made the following statement as a general interpretation:

"The Committee also noted that, in accordance with the Appendix to the Charter, Article 5 does not rule on the admissibility of union security clauses or practices. The Committee considered, however, that any form of compulsory unionism imposed by law must be considered incompatible with the obligation arising under this article of the Charter" (Conclusions I, p. 31).

The Committee reverted to consideration of the scope of Article 5 as regards the freedom to join workers' organisation in the seventh supervision cycle, after having been made aware of the judgement of the European Court of Human Rights in the case of Young, James and Webster.[1]

The Committee acknowledged this judgment, but felt unable to take a definite stand on the conformity of the United Kingdom 1974 Trade Union and Labour Relations Act, according to which the termination by an employer of the contract of employment of a worker refusing to join any trade union or a particular trade union was regarded as fair because of the existence of a closed shop agreement, until it could receive clarification of the contents of the relevant legislation, the methods of application of this legislation and any relevant cases which it had asked for in the fifth supervision cycle when it first noted the enactment of this act.[2]

Despite postponing its decision on the substance, the Committee reaffirmed in this cycle its earlier case law on Article 5 as follows:

"Without taking a stand on the question whether the Appendix to the Charter concerning Article 1 para. 2 is also applicable to Article 5,[3] the Committee felt that even if this were the case, it would not follow either

---

1 Judgement of 13 August 1981, Series A, No. 44.

2 One of the members of the Committee of Independent Experts, Mr Zanetti, disagreed with the Committee's decision to postpone its stand on the substance and took the view that the provision in English legislation making it lawful for an employer to terminate a contract of employment of a worker who refused to join a trade union was clearly incompatible with Article 5 (Conclusions VII, pp. 113 to 115).

3 Appendix to Article 1 para. 2: "This provision shall not be interpreted as prohibiting or authorising any union security clause or practice".

that the negative aspect of the freedom to organise would fall completely outside the scope of Article 5 or that an obligation to join a trade union would always be in conformity with the spirit of this provision.

In accordance with the statement of the European Court of Human Rights in the above-mentioned case (paragraph 52 of the judgement) concerning Article 11 of the Convention on Human Rights, it should be underlined that also as regards Article 5 of the Charter, to interpret this provision 'as permitting every kind of compulsion in the field of trade union membership would strike at the very substance of the freedom it is designed to guarantee'" (Conclusions VII, p. 32).

In the eighth supervision cycle the Committee further developed its case law, adding the following observation of a general character:

"While conceding that the Appendix to the Charter in respect of Article 1 para. 2 stipulates that this provision 'shall not be interpreted as prohibiting or authorising any union security clause or practice', the Committee considers, in view of the clear wording of Article 5, that no Contracting Party can fail to provide legal remedies or sanctions for practices which unduly obstruct the freedom to form or join trade union organisations, for otherwise the scope of the aforementioned provision of the Appendix would be excessively widened and situations incompatible with the fundamental freedom secured by Article 5 would be considered lawful" (Conclusions VIII, p. 77).

In the light of the above observation of a general nature concerning Article 5 and bearing in mind its previous conclusion, the Committee[1] concluded that the legislation in the United Kingdom was incompatible with Article 5.[2]

---

1 See dissenting opinion of Professor Dr. Fritz Fabricius, shared by Judge Loizou (Conclusions VIII, pp. 223 to 232).

2 The situation in the United Kingdom was subsequently improved by the 1982 Employment Act, which subordinated the possibility of concluding a closed shop agreement to the approval, by secret ballot, of the large majority of the workers concerned and offered workers substantial safeguards against dismissal. The 1988 Employment Act improved the situation further by abolishing the provision whereby the dismissal of a worker refusing to become a member of a trade union could be judged fair because of the existence of a closed shop agreement. The act, by making the dismissal of an employee for not being a

In the same cycle the Committee made a preliminary examination of a new act, namely Act No. 285 of 9 June 1982, which came into force in Denmark outside the reporting period and provided protection against dismissal on grounds of trade union membership. This act provided that membership of a trade union could not be used as a valid reason for dismissing a worker and prohibited dismissal on grounds of non membership of a trade union or of a particular trade union. The Committee noted, however, that pursuant to Section 2 (2) and (3) of the act, this protection against dismissal was not applicable if the worker knew on the date of his engagement that the employer required membership of a trade union or of a particular trade union as a condition of employment, or if a worker belonging to a trade union was informed after his engagement that union membership was a condition of continued employment in the firm. It also observed that, under Section 3 of the said act, workers employed by an employer the express purpose of whose undertaking was to promote certain political, ideological, religious or cultural opinions were not protected against dismissal if membership of a particular trade union had to be considered as important to the undertaking.

Whilst reserving the right to re-examine the Danish legislation on the subject in greater depth during the next supervision cycle, the Committee drew the Danish Government's attention "to the possibility that the above-mentioned provisions of the Act of 9 June 1982 concerning exceptions to the general protection against dismissal on grounds of trade union membership provided by the act, might be contrary to the above conclusion of a general character concerning Article 5" (Conclusions VIII, p. 78).

In the ninth cycle the Committee concluded that Denmark was not fully applying Article 5, as paragraphs 2 and 3 of Section 2 of the above-mentioned act were contrary to the principle of freedom to organise. As regards Section 3, the Committee deferred its conclusion pending receipt of any court rulings (Conclusions IX-1, p. 47).

---

member or for being a member of a trade union unfair, in essence abolished the closed shop in Great Britain (see Conclusions IX-1, pp. 48 and 49; Conclusions X-1, p. 69 and Conclusions XI-1, p. 79). The provisions of this act were extended to Northern Ireland in 1991 (see Conclusions XIII-1, p. 136).

In the next two cycles the Committee explained its position as regards Article 11 of the European Convention on Human Rights and the Young, James and Webster judgment, as the Danish Government claimed, firstly, that since it complied with Article 11 of the Convention it also complied with Article 5 of the Charter and, secondly, that according to the judgment of the European Court of Human Rights, freedom of association did not cover the freedom not to join a trade union.

"With regard to the argument based on a comparison between Article 5 of the Charter and Article 11 of the European Convention on Human Rights, the Committee observed that no decisive weight could be attached to such an argument because of the differences in the content of the relevant provisions of these two instruments as well as its own case law on Article 5 (see Conclusions VIII, p. 77). Moreover, the European Court of Human Rights had taken care to rule solely on the case before it (Young, James and Webster case) and expressly abstained from taking any position as to whether Article 11 of the European Convention on Human Rights also concerns trade union security clauses or 'negative' freedom of association (paragraphs 55 and 52 of the Judgement)" (Conclusions X-1, p. 67, Denmark, see also p. 68, Iceland).

"The tenth Danish report argued that Act No. 285 was not in violation of Article 5 of the Charter because it was enacted to comply with Article 11 of the European Convention on Human Rights as interpreted in the Young, James and Webster case. The Committee observed in particular that although the European Court of Human Rights expressly abstained from ruling on the question of whether Article 11 of the Convention also concerns 'negative' freedom of association, it nevertheless stated that 'a threat of dismissal involving loss of livelihood is a most serious form of compulsion', whereas 'the notion of freedom implies some measures of freedom of choice...'" (paragraphs 52 and 53 of the Judgement)" (Conclusions XI-1, p. 77).[1]

---

1 In its General introduction to Conclusions XIII-1, the Committee, after repeating its consistently held view, that Article 5 guaranteed both the negative aspect and the positive aspect of the right to organise and recalling that, as a result, it had consistently held that a system of closed shop constituted a limitation of the right of association and the right to

In the same supervision cycle (the eleventh), on examination of the situation in Iceland, where the Supreme Court had interpreted Article 73 of the Icelandic Constitution as not protecting the right not to be a member of a trade union and had ruled that international treaties such as the European Convention on Human Rights did not automatically invalidate "ratified" provisions of the Constitution, the Committee, "considering that the freedom to join trade unions, guaranteed by Article 5 of the Charter, necessarily implies the absence of any sort of obligation to become or remain a member of a trade union, [...] held that the absence of adequate protection of such a freedom in national law (either through lack of appropriate statutes or through case law validating practices conflicting with the freedom to organise) cannot be considered as consistent with Article 5 of the Charter" (Conclusions XI-1, p. 78; see also above, under 1 f.). Moreover, after noting that in Iceland collective agreements applicable to industry, shops and offices contained closed shop clauses, the Committee "considered that legislation (or lack thereof) which allows for such practices as stand in contradiction with the very substance of the freedom to organise protected by Article 5 of the Charter cannot be held to ensure the effective application of the principle enshrined in Article 5" (*ibidem*, p. 79).

The statement that the absence of adequate protection in national law of the freedom to join a trade union cannot be considered as consistent with Article 5, was reiterated by the Committee in the first part of the thirteenth supervision cycle in the case of Ireland, where neither the Constitution nor any other law guaranteed the right to join or not to join a trade union (Conclusions XIII-1, p. 133; see also above point 1 f.). It was also recalled in the case of France, when the Committee noted that

organise, "welcomed the decision of the European Court of Human Rights, in the case of Sigurdur A. Sigurjonsson V. Iceland (Case No. 24/1992/369/443), in which the Court had upheld the negative aspect of Article 11 of the European Court of Human rights (right of association, including the right to form and join a trade union. It noted that the case concerned the right of a taxi driver not to join an organisation, a situation which the Committee had criticised for a number of years and noted that the Court had referred to the Committee's conclusions in paragraph 35 of the judgment dated 30 June 1993". (Conclusions XIII-1, pp. 26 and 27).

an agreement concluded in 1900 between the master printers and the "*Fédération française des travailleurs du livre*" gave the members of this trade union the monopoly of recruitment, in response to a statement in the French report that this agreement was not in conformity with the Act of 27 April 1956 prohibiting "closed shop" clauses and that the French Government was not empowered to rule on the legal validity of an "agreement", let alone condemn it. The Committee specified that "the Government of a Contracting Party was responsible for the implementation of the Charter and that it was obliged, using appropriate means, to rectify a situation that was not consistent with the Charter" (*ibidem*, pp. 131 and 132).

In the third part of the thirteenth supervision cycle, the Committee noted that the above-mentioned agreement of 1900 on the "*contrat de label*" had been rendered null and void by the implementation of Section 2 of the Act of 27 April 1956 (now Article L 413 − 2 of the Labour Code); that there were penalties for lack of compliance with the ban on closed shop clauses and that any individual or legal entity suffering discrimination could appeal to the competent administrative or judicial authorities. Nevertheless, it pointed out that closed shop practices were a different problem calling for different measures than those taken to remedy the problem of closed shop clauses or agreements, and that French law as it stood did not provide an effective solution to the situation (Conclusions XIII-3, p. 97).

In addition to the issue of closed shops several other infringements of the freedom not to join a trade union have been examined by the Committee. Thus it found that Iceland did not respect this right:

a.   since non-trade union members were excluded from the payment of unemployment benefit, even though contributions to unemployment funds were financed by public funds and payroll taxes. The Committee held that depriving a worker of his right to economic protection in the event of unemployment represented an inadmissible measure to exert pressure on him/her to become or remain a member of a trade union, which was in conflict with the spirit and the letter of Article 5 of the Charter[1] (Conclusions XI-1, p. 78);

b. as most collective agreements contained a clause granting priority in recruitment to trade union members.

Although this practice did not stem directly from statutes, the Committee noted that the priority clauses had been validated in law by the Labour Court. The Committee considered that "such a legal form of pressure against workers wishing not to become members of trade unions could not be considered as compatible with the freedom to organise as provided for in Article 5 of the Charter" (*ibidem*, pp. 78 and 79).

3.   The exercise of trade union activities and prerogatives

Freedom to organise obviously implies that trade unions and their members, as employers' organisations and their members, have the possibility to act freely in pursuance of the protection of their economic and social interests, this protection being in the wording of Article 5 itself the very reason for constituting workers' and employers' organisations. The case law of the Committee takes into account the difficulties which directly interfere with trade union activities or which restrict and weaken any or all of union prerogatives.

a.   *Dismissal on grounds of trade union activities*

This situation arose in Austria. In the ninth supervision cycle, the Committee learned from the ILO that questions had been raised by the ILO Committee of Experts on the Application of Conventions and Recommendations in connection with the protection of certain workers against

---

1 The situation was remedied by Act No. 54 of 1993 which allowed all unemployed wage-earners or self-employed individuals having ceased their own business operations and who were seeking employment to receive benefit from the Unemployed Benefit Fund (see Conclusions XIII-3, p. 100).

dismissal on grounds of union activity in firms employing less than five persons (Conclusions X-2, p. 67). In the following cycle, the Austrian Government confirmed that workers in firms with five or more employees were adequately protected against dismissal on grounds of the workers' trade union activities, but that such protection did not apply to workers in smaller business concerns. The government explained that its efforts to fill this gap had not succeeded because the social partners had failed to agree. The Committee therefore concluded that the situation, in this respect, could not be considered to be in compliance with the Charter (Conclusions XI-2, p. 73). In the following cycles, the Committee was able to observe improvements in the protection of workers against dismissal, but as there is still no protection in firms with less than five employees, the Committee's conclusion has since remained negative (Conclusions XII-2, p. 96; Conclusions XIII-1, p. 129; see in the last instance Conclusions XIII-3, p. 96).

b. Infringement of trade unions' right to bargain collectively

The Committee's case law on this important issue has evolved progressively in connection with the situation in Ireland.

As early as the first supervision cycle, the Committee observed that "although the right to form trade unions was embodied in principle in Article 40 of the Irish Constitution, there was no information in the report about how this principle was put into practice by legislation or case law. Furthermore, the Irish report shows that, before starting collective negotiations, workers' and employers' organisations must, under an Act of 1941, obtain authorisation for that purpose (negotiating licence). It does not appear from the report, however, whether the grant of that authorisation is subject to the fulfilment of objective conditions which can be reviewed by an independent and impartial authority" (Conclusions I, p. 179).

In the following cycle, the Committee was able to satisfy itself that the granting of such licences was governed by objective conditions and could not, under the terms of the Trade Unions Act 1941, Article 6 (4), and Article 10, be refused if these conditions were met. In the Committee's view, this was perfectly compatible with the Charter. The Committee nevertheless inquired further into the sum required to be deposited by a trade union seeking to obtain the licence and the ratio which apparently existed between the amount of the deposit and the number of members of the unions concerned (Conclusions II, p. 22). The replies given led the Committee to reach a negative conclusion: "It emerged that, in order to obtain a negotiating licence, any trade union had to have at least 500 members and had to deposit a minimum sum of £ 5,000 in the case of trade unions of less than 2,000 members and a maximum one of £ 15,000 for a trade union of more than 39,000 members.

The Committee considered that both the condition in respect of the size of the trade unions and of the deposits required infringed the freedom of forming or joining a trade union and it concluded that Ireland did not fulfil its obligations; it hoped that Irish legislation on this point would be amended" (Conclusions III, p. 31).

It also set out a general rule that "national regulations which make authorisations to create a trade union empowered to exercise the right of collective bargaining conditional upon a minimum number of members, are not consistent with the principle of the freedom to organise; the same holds if this authorisation depends on the deposit of an excessively large sum of money" (Conclusions III, p. 30).

In the following cycle the Committee defined this rule clearly, putting the emphasis on collective bargaining:

"During this cycle of supervision, the Committee felt the need to define the scope and significance of Article 5 of the Charter in greater detail. It pointed out that the right to organise, as defined in article 5, implied that the main object of workers' and employers' right to form organisations was to engage in collective bargaining for the defence of their interests, and that in principle, this could not be qualified by any requirement to deposit money in order to obtain a negotiating licence. At most, the Committee might concede that the Charter has been respected if everyone wishing to organise for purposes that are not prejudicial to "l'ordre public" were automatically entitled to such a licence, or if the payment demanded covered only minimal administrative costs" (Conclusions IV, p. 39).

As a consequence, the conclusion has remained negative for Ireland: "As it is not the case in Ireland however that everyone has a right to organise for purposes not prejudicial to 'ordre public' and since payments required do not cover only minimal administrative costs, as far as the regulations applying to trade unions which possess or apply for negotiating licences were concerned (see Conclusions III), the Committee was forced to conclude that the situation was not satisfactory" (Conclusions IV, p. 40).

As there had been no changes in the situation since then, the Committee's conclusion for Ireland continued to be negative but its justification was defined in more depth in the eleventh cycle by a statement of principle: "while Irish legislation does not affect the right to establish a trade union, the requirement of a negotiation licence, impinging as it did on a fundamental trade union prerogative (the right to bargain collectively) was such as to infringe the very nature of trade union freedom and could not be considered as compatible with this provision of the Charter" (Addendum to Conclusions XI-2, p. 19).

The Committee recalled this statement in the third part of the thirteenth supervision cycle to rebut the argument of the Irish Government that the granting to unlicensed trade unions of the right to negotiate would be counterproductive to the Irish Government's stated objective of facilitating the rationalisation of the number of trade unions in Ireland as provided in the Industrial Relations Act of 1990 (Conclusions XIII-3, p. 100).

It has now been well established by the Committee's case law that "where a fundamental trade union prerogative such as the right to bargain collectively was restricted, this could also amount to an infringement of the very nature of the trade union freedom guaranteed under Article 5". Situations criticised under Article 5 on this basis for violations of the right to bargain collectively include, in addition to that of Ireland, those of Denmark, Malta, Norway and the United Kingdom (see below under "Assessment of compliance").

Other questions examined in connection with collective bargaining concern the withdrawal of negotiating licences because of an absence of secret ballot, which the Committee found to be incompatible with Article 5 (Conclusions XIII-1, p. 133 and Conclusions XIII-3, p. 100, Ireland) and the representation of trade unions: see for example the situation in France, which the Committee has considered satisfactory (Conclusions VI, p. 29) and the situations in Belgium (Conclusions XIII-2, p. 268 and 269) and Luxembourg (Addendum to Conclusions XIII-3, pp. 35 and 36) for which the Committee's conclusion is deferred pending the submission of the explanations or additional information requested.

c. *Interference with trade unions' defence of the interests of their members*

This is one of the Committee's main criticisms of the Act of 1988 applying to the Danish International Ship's Register (DIS) already mentioned. It is recalled that Section 10 sub-section 2 of this act provides that collective agreements concluded by the Danish trade unions in the name of the crew of ships listed on the DIS "may only comprise persons who are considered to be residents of Denmark or who, by virtue of incurred international obligations shall be put on an equal footing with Danish citizens".

"The Committee considered that a restriction of this kind on the personal scope of collective agreements concluded by Danish trade unions, on such fundamental matters as wages and working conditions, constituted a serious violation of the right to organise in so far as it does not enable such trade unions to defend the interests of those of their members to whom the agreements concluded do not apply" (Conclusions XII-1, p. 111; see also Conclusions XIII-1, pp. 130 and 131 and Conclusions XIII-3, p. 97).

The infringements of the right to organise (and of the right to bargain collectively – see below, Article 6 para. 2) resulting from the Danish legislation applying to the DIS have led the Committee to request that all the other states concerned "provide information in their next report as to any similar regulations applicable in their territories" (in a general question under Article 5 appearing in Conclusions XII-1, p. 110 and XII-2, p. 96).

No other state has so far indicated the existence of any such regulations;

d. Infringement of the right of access of trade unions to an enterprise

This issue arose and is still topical in relation to the situation in Germany. In the eleventh cycle, the Committee was informed that in the Federal Republic of Germany, following a judgement by the Federal Constitutional Court in 1981 concerning the protection of the right to organise, trade union officials who did not belong to an enterprise were denied access to the workplace. It asked for information on this subject (Conclusions XI-2, p. 75). In the next cycle, "the Committee noted that trade union representatives not employed by an enterprise had only a limited right of access to that enterprise, restricted to the specific cases provided for in the 1972 Act (*Betriebsverfassungsgesetz*). These cases do not include the trade union activities of information, advice or recruitment. According to the Constitutional Court decision, trade unions have no right of access for such activities where one or more of their members is employed within the enterprise. Where none of their members is employed in the enterprise, the Court decision does not dismiss the possibility that a right of access might be accorded to trade union representatives, but considers that it is up to the legislators to address this issue" (Conclusions XII-2, p. 98).

As the German Government contested the fact that this matter fell within the remit of Article 5, the Committee was obliged to elaborate on its stance: "Unlike the German Government, which maintains that a right of access to workplaces for trade union representatives not belonging to an enterprise cannot be based on Article 5 of the Charter, the Committee considered that the right of access for trade unions to an enterprise is covered by this provision, which protects not only the right of workers to join or not to join a trade union, but also the right of trade unions to organise freely and to perform their activities effectively, which is essential for 'the protection of workers' economic and social interests.'

The Committee therefore considered that states are obliged to ensure, by appropriate means, that trade union representatives can have access to firms for the purpose of their trade union activities. The Committee considered, however, that this right should be exercised taking account of the employer's rights and interests, such as the efficient operation of the firm and the requirements of confidentiality and safety." (*ibidem*, p. 98).

The Committee deferred its conclusion pending receipt of information on the measures taken or planned in order to protect the right of access of trade union representatives to workplaces.

In the thirteenth supervision cycle, the Committee noted "that the Act of 1972 (*Betriebsverfassungsgesetz*) specifically granted the right of access to enterprises for trade union representatives in order to pursue the rights and powers given to trade unions under that law." However, taking into account the decision of the Federal Constitutional Court of 17 January 1981 and noting that there had been no change with regard to the issue of access to workplaces by trade union representatives not employed by the firm concerned, the Committee concluded that this situation was not in conformity with the Charter and asked to be informed of any measures taken to remedy this situation (Conclusions XIII-2, p. 269).

e.   *Intervention in the conduct and organisation of a lawful strike*

The Committee commented on this issue in the twelfth supervision cycle, when it noted that in German public services, civil servants had on several occasions been requisitioned to replace striking employees and manual workers in those services. "On this point, the Committee, regardless of the implications of such measures in terms of respect for the right to strike (see the conclusion under Article 6 para. 4), considered that intervention of this kind by the public authorities in the conduct and organisation of a lawful strike could constitute a restriction on the rights and freedoms guaranteed by Article 5, particularly in cases where unionised civil servants were required to replace employees or manual workers belonging to the same trade union" (Conclusions XII-2, p. 99). The Committee did not, however, reach a conclusion in that cycle because a case was pending before the Constitutional Court on this matter and it wished to see the Court's decision before concluding.

In the next cycle the Committee noted with interest the judgment of the Court that this type of requisition was unconstitutional unless the matter was expressly regulated by law and referred to its observations under Article 6 para. 4 (Conclusions XIII-2, p. 269).

f.   Infringement of the right of assembly

Even though no such infringements have been observed by the Committee, it is clear from questions put to the Government of Austria concerning the dissolution of association or suspension of trade union meetings (Conclusions III, p. 30) and remarks concerning the right of assembly of the police in Cyprus (Conclusions X-2, p. 67, and Conclusions XI-2, p. 74), that it regards the right of assembly as a fundamental trade union prerogative covered by Article 5.

4.   Right to organise of public servants, in particular those of the police and the armed forces

a.   Right to organise of public servants in general

As early as the first supervision cycle, the Committee stated that with the exception of members of the armed forces and of the police, all classes of employers and workers including civil servants "are fully entitled to the right to organise in accordance with the Charter" (Conclusions I, p. 31).

Furthermore, in a general observation in the second supervision cycle the Committee explained that: "Any restrictions prohibiting civil servants from membership of trade unions other than those composed exclusively of officials could not be regarded as compatible with the Charter; this also applied to similar restrictions on the freedom of civil servants' trade union organisations to be members of federations or confederations of their choice" (Conclusions II, p. 184).

Applying this interpretation to the legislation of a Contracting Party, the Committee concluded that although to a great extent this Party applied Article 5 of the Charter by guaranteeing the right to organise both in its legislation and in practice, it did not meet its obligations "since members of the civil service were not permitted to belong to organisations other than those composed exclusively of officials, and these organisations were prohibited from associating with others whose membership was less exclusive" (*ibidem*, Cyprus).[1]

The Committee admitted that public servants' trade union rights could be subject to certain restrictions, but these should fall within the scope of Article 31 of the Charter. This was done in respect of the situation created in the Government Communications Centre (GCHQ) at Cheltenham. The Committee had learned (from a complaint lodged with the ILO supervisory bodies) that trade union rights were infringed at the Centre (Conclusions IX-1, p. 49). Examining whether the provisions by which the United Kingdom Government had deprived 7,000 of the Centre's civil servants of the right to organise were compatible with Article 5 of the Charter, the Committee "recalled first of all that only the two categories whose right to organise could be restricted or abolished under Article 5 were police officers and members of the armed forces. Consequently, the problem concerning the Cheltenham Centre's civil servants had to be considered in the light of Article 31 of the Charter, which permits the placing of 'restrictions or limitations' on the rights guaranteed by the Charter on condition:

- that they are prescribed by law;

- that they are necessary in a democratic society for the protection of

---

[1] This situation was remedied by the Trade Unions (Amendment) Law No. 381 of 1991 which abolished these restrictions (Conclusions VII, p. 31).

the rights and freedoms of others or for the protection of (...) national security (...).

The Committee noted, on the one hand, that the British Government's decision had been taken under the Protection of Employment Acts of 1975 and 1978 and, on the other, that the Cheltenham Centre's activity was essential to national security. However, it wondered whether the Government's decision denoted a 'restriction or limitation' of the right to organise, in accordance with Article 31 or a total abolition of that right, which would be contrary to the Charter.

Having learnt that the civil servants concerned were now able to join a professional association, the Committee hoped that the next report would include some detailed information on the nature of that association, its functioning, the way in which representatives were elected to it and the nature of its relations with the public authority. In the meantime, it postponed its conclusions on this point" (Conclusions X-1, pp. 68 and 69).

The Committee was able to close the matter[1] in the following cycle: "As regards the situation at the Government Communications Headquarters at Cheltenham, the Committee noted with interest that its Staff Federation, officially set up in 1985, has been registered as a trade union and given the right to negotiate on behalf of its members (at present 52% of the staff). It also noted that the membership of the Federation is optional and that its members belong to all the categories of staff employed. In the light of this information, the Committee concluded that the restrictions imposed on this category of civil servants did not exceed the limits prescribed in Article 31 of the Charter" (Conclusions XI-1, p. 80).

---

1 This has not been the case for the ILO. See the observations of the ILO Committee of Experts on the application of Convention No. 87 (Freedom of Association and Protection of the Right to Organise) by the United Kingdom (in the last instance, 1995 and 1996).

b. Right to organise of the police and the armed forces

In the first supervision cycle, after noting that all classes of employers and workers were fully entitled to the right to organise, the Committee stated that "certain restrictions to this right are however permissible under the terms of the two last sentences of Article 5 in respect of members of the police and armed forces. The Charter however lays down different rules in respect of the position of each of these two classes of workers vis-à-vis the right to organise: it is clear in fact from the second sentence of Article 5 (taken in conjunction with the third sentence of the same Article) and from the 'travaux préparatoires' on this clause, that while a State may be permitted to limit the freedom of organisation of the members of the police, it is not justified in depriving them of all the guarantees provided for in the Article" (Conclusions I, p. 31).

The view of the Committee that even though Article 5 authorises in the case of members of the police restrictions on freedom of organisation, the complete suppression of this freedom is not compatible with it, was reaffirmed and further defined in a general observation in the second cycle: "The Charter is not satisfied by statutes or regulations under which such personnel are forbidden to form their organisations or to join organisations of their own choosing, but compelled to become members of an organisation established by or under the statute or regulation itself. The Committee also thinks it right to point out that a distinction exists between the right to establish a union and to join it and the right of negotiation and collective action (provided for in Article 6). The one does not imply the other. Hence, Article 5 is not satisfied merely by the fact that a statutory or other compulsory organisation effectively engages in procedures resembling collective bargaining" (Conclusions II, p. 22).

In the third supervision cycle the Committee summed up its previous views: "Article 5 of the Charter is intended to guarantee the full enjoyment of the freedom to organise to, in principle, every category of employers and workers, including public officials. The terms of Article 5 only permit a few exceptions in the field of its application. For although the text of this Article allows the complete suppression of the right of members of the armed forces to organise, comparison of the second and third sentences of Article 5 and the "*travaux préparatoires*", make it clear that "the Contracting Parties may only limit the freedom of the police to organise on condition that its members are not deprived of all the rights guaranteed by this Article. The Committee is also of the opinion that any form of legally compulsory trade unionism must be considered incompatible with the Charter. The Committee in addition confirmed its view that legislation or regulations which:

i. forbid policemen to set up their own trade union or to join a trade union of their choice,

ii. oblige policemen to join a trade union imposed by statutes,

are contrary to the Charter because they effectively completely suppress the freedom to organise" (Conclusions III, p. 30).

These views have been maintained consistently throughout all the subsequent cycles (see for example Conclusions XII-2, p. 100, Malta; in the last instance Conclusions XIII-2, p. 268, Belgium).

The possibility afforded in some countries to members of the police force to form, instead of trade unions, representative bodies, prompted the Committee to state when these bodies could correspond to "workers organisations" within the meaning of Article 5.

Firstly, these bodies must be actual associations. This was stated clearly in the second supervision cycle in the case of Ireland. This state was found not to comply with Article 5 as "the only bodies permitted could not be considered as workers' organisations within the meaning of Article 5 of the Charter. The bodies in question were not even 'staff associations', since they consisted only of certain representatives elected by the police, who otherwise had no right to form a union nor to affiliate to existing unions" (Conclusions II, p. 23). The Committee concluded negatively for Italy on similar grounds in the sixth supervision cycle. The representative bodies of civilian and military public security personnel, even though they had been constituted democratically and legally, had been joined by almost all staff concerned and were entitled to "express opinions and take initiatives with respect to the legal status and economic situation of their members". It stressed that such a representative body "does not have an 'associative' character, which is the essential feature of the right protected by this provision of the Charter" (Conclusions VI, p. 31).

Secondly, these associations must fulfil certain of the functions of a trade union and benefit from the basic trade union prerogatives. This was stated implicitly in the ninth supervision cycle in the case of the United Kingdom (Conclusions IX-1, p. 49) and directly in respect of the situation in Cyprus, when the Committee learned that a reform of the legislation was planned in order to allow members of the police to form their own professional bodies for the protection of their interests: "The Committee considered it advisable, however, to point out that, in order for the situation to be considered in compliance with the Charter, police organisations should be able to exercise certain trade union type prerogatives, such as the right to negotiate their conditions of service and remuneration and the right of assembly" (Conclusions X-2, p. 67; see also Conclusions XIII-3, p. 273, Portugal).

As part of the restrictions permitted for the police under Article 5, the Committee accepts that their associations be composed exclusively of members of the police force and that they are only allowed to join policemen's trade unions. It also accepts that they are only allowed to join international police trade union organisations (see Conclusions VIII, p. 80, Italy; Conclusions IX-1, p. 49, the United Kingdom and Conclusions XIII-3, p. 106, Spain).

Finally, it is worth mentioning that in the case of the United Kingdom in the ninth supervision cycle the conclusion of the Committee was negative on the ground that membership of the police staff association was compulsory for members of the police force in the lower grades. In the tenth cycle, however, the Committee agreed to no longer revert to this matter, after noting that compulsory affiliation to such associations did not entail the obligation to pay subscriptions (Conclusions X-1, p. 68; see also Addendum to Conclusions XI-2, p. 20, Ireland).

Currently, the only Contracting Party found not to comply with requirements concerning the limitation of the freedom of association of the
police is Malta. Cyprus,[1] Ireland,[2] Italy[3] and the United Kingdom[4] which
in the past were in violation of this aspect of Article 5, subsequently
remedied their situations.

As regards the armed forces, there have of course never been any cases
of non-compliance. The Committee, as a rule, takes note without comment of the information submitted, which is usually included in the first
reports of Contracting Parties.

1 Members of the police force were not allowed to set up one or more professional
protective groups or to join such groups (Conclusions III, p. 31). They were compelled by
law to become members of an organisation established under the law. The situation was
remedied by Police (Amendment) Law No. 27/1989 (Conclusions XI-2, pp. 73 and 74 and
Conclusions XII-2, p. 96).

2 Members of the police were not allowed to form trade unions but only representative
bodies (see above). This situation was remedied by the 1977 Garda Siochana Act which
allowed members of the police to form representative organisations (Conclusions VII,
p. 33). However the Committee's conclusion was deferred in this respect as the 1977 Act
prohibits affiliation to police associations outside the Garda Siochana except in cases
authorised by the Minister of Justice (see in the last instance Conclusions XIII-3, pp. 100
and 101).

3 Armed and civil police personnel were not entitled to form or to join trade unions
(Conclusions I, p. 32). Remedied in 1981 by an act which granted to members of the
police force for the first time the right to form unions empowered to negotiate with the
government directly on such matters as pay, career structure, leave, training and other
additional trade union rights (Conclusions VIII, p. 80).

4 Members of the police force were both obliged by statute to join a special organisation and
forbidden to set up or to join any other trade union (Conclusions II, p. 24). The situation
was considered as remedied when it was established in the ninth supervision cycle that:
  – the members of the police took part in negotiations for their conditions of work at
    various levels;
  – a Police Negotiation Board was created through the 1980 Act whose recommendations
    the Minister was bound to take into consideration;
  – flexibility introduced since 1972 enabled the police to affiliate to international police
    trade union organisations (Conclusions IX-1, p. 49);
  and in the tenth cycle that:
  – compulsory affiliation of police officers below the rank of superintendent to the police
    staff association did not entail the obligation to pay subscriptions to such associations.
    Furthermore, the non-payment of a subscription did not carry any penalty
    (Conclusions X-1, p. 68).

Assessment of compliance

Contracting Parties currently found not to comply with Article 5 are the following:

Austria[1] on two grounds:

a.   legislative protection against dismissal on grounds of trade union activities does not apply to workers dismissed from enterprises with fewer than five employees (Conclusions XI-2, p. 73; in the last instance Conclusions XIII-3, p. 96; see 3 a. above).

b.   as it appears from the 1993 Direct Request of the ILO Committee of Experts on Convention No. 87 (Freedom of Association and Protection of the Right to Organise, 1948), foreign workers are not eligible for election to Works Councils with the exception of workers from states parties to the Agreement on the European Economic Area (Conclusions XIII-3, p. 96).

Denmark[2] on two grounds:

a.   the existence of legislation (Section 2 (2) and (3) of the Act No. 285 of 9 June 1982)[3], which authorises dismissal for failure to respect closed shop clauses. The conclusion has been negative since the ninth supervision cycle (Conclusions IX-1, p. 47; in the last instance Conclusions XIII-3, p. 97; see 2 above);

b.   the existence of provisions (Section 10, sub-section 2 of the Act No. 408 of 23 June 1988 instituting a Danish International Ship's Regis-

---

1 The Committee of Ministers addressed a recommendation to Austria on point a. for the second part of the twelfth supervision cycle and a second one for the first part of the thirteenth supervision cycle.

2 The Committee of Ministers addressed a recommendation to Denmark on point b. for the first part of the thirteenth cycle.

3 Act No. 285 was modified in 1990 by Act No. 347. Whilst the latter act provided for the reinstatement of workers or prescribed compensation for dismissal where employees were dismissed in violation of the rules, the rules as defined were in effect the same as those in the 1982 Act, criticised by the Committee because they authorised dismissal for failure to respect closed shop clauses.

ter) according to which the collective agreements concluded by trade unions concerning the wages and working conditions of employees on vessels entered in the register may only comprise persons who are considered to be residents of Denmark, or who by virtue of incurred international obligations shall be put on an equal footing with Danish citizens (Conclusions XII-1, pp. 110 and 111; Conclusions XIII-1, pp. 130 and 131 and Conclusions XIII-3, p. 97).

The Committee considers that a restriction of this kind of the personal scope of collective agreements concluded by Danish trade unions on such fundamental matters as wages and working conditions constitutes a violation of Article 5 on three counts since:

–   it does not enable such trade unions to defend the interests of those of their members to whom the agreements concluded do not apply (see 3 c. above);

–   it interferes with the right of workers freely to join a trade union of their choice as it might lead the members of Danish trade unions who are not residents of Denmark or put on an equal footing with Danish citizens to join other trade unions or in practice deter them from joining trade union (see 1 f. above);

–   it severely restricts a fundamental trade union prerogative (the right to bargain collectively) under Article 6 para. 2 and thus infringes the very nature of trade union freedom (see 3 b. above).

France: as closed shop practices exist in the book sector (Conclusions XIII-1, pp. 131 and 132 and Conclusions XIII-3, pp. 97 and 99; see 2 above).

Germany: as trade union representatives do not have the right of access to an enterprise if one or more of their members are employed within that enterprise (Conclusions XII-2, p. 98 and Conclusions XIII-2, p. 269; see 3 d. above).

Iceland:[1] as the negative aspect of the right to organise is not ensured. The criticism exists since the ninth supervision cycle (Conclusions IX-1, p. 48; see in the last instance Conclusions XIII-3, p. 99)

Ireland[2] on three grounds:

a.   under the Trade Unions 1941 Act only trade unions holding a negotiating licence, granted subject to compliance with certain conditions, are able to take part in collective bargaining. This criticism dates back to the third supervision cycle (Conclusions III, p. 31; see in the last instance Conclusions XIII-3, p. 100);

b.   negotiating licences can be withdrawn from trade unions failing to comply with the requirement of the Industrial Relations Act to include in their own rules one on secret balloting (Conclusions XIII-1, p. 133 and XIII-3, p. 100);

c.   legal protection of the right of the individual not to join any trade union or a particular trade union is inadequate (Conclusions XIII-1, p. 133 and Conclusions XIII-3, p. 101).

The Committee considers that the absence of adequate protection of such a freedom in national law cannot be considered as consistent with Article 5 of the Charter, despite the statement in the Irish report that the Courts have established, in principle, that the freedom or right to associate necessarily implies a correlative right not to join any trade union or a particular trade union (see 1 f. and 2 above).

---

1 Previous criticisms concerned the non-payment of unemployment benefit to non-union members (remedied by the Unemployment Benefit Act 1993 No. 54; Conclusions XIII-1, p. 100) and the existence of legislation requiring membership of the relevant trade union as a prerequisite for the granting of a taxi driver's operating licence (a bill on taxi cab services brought before the Althing in April 1994 was intended to abolish closed shop practices in taxi services; *ibidem*, p. 99).

2 The issue of the existence of "closed shops" in the merchant shipping industry, which was examined in the ninth supervision cycle (see Conclusions IX-2, p. 44) was not pursued further in subsequent cycles except in relation to the right not to join a union or a particular trade union.

Malta:[1] on two grounds:

a. in the event of failure of statutory machinery for conciliation the Minister may, not only at the request of all the parties but also at the request of one of the parties, refer the matter to an industrial tribunal whose decision is binding on the employers and employees to which it relates and the parties are debarred for at least one year from seeking unilaterally to have the decision altered (Conclusions XIII-2, p. 270 and Conclusions XIII-3, p. 102).

The Committee referred to its conclusion under Article 6 paras. 2 and 3 and considered that the restriction thus imposed on collective bargaining constituted a restraint on a fundamental trade union prerogative such as to infringe the very nature of trade union freedom (see 3 b. above);

b. under the Maltese Constitution the police are excluded from the protection of freedom of association and the 1961 Malta Police Ordinance prohibits the police from becoming members of any trade union, or similar organisation, other than the Malta Police Association, the constitution of which forms part of the Ordinance and which has very limited rights. In addition, membership is compulsory (Conclusions XII-2, p. 100 and in the last instance Conclusions XIII-3, p. 102; see 4 above).

Norway: compulsory arbitration may be imposed in more cases than those provided for under Article 31 of the Charter (Conclusions XIII-3, p. 105).

The Committee has referred in this connection to its conclusions under Article 6 para. 2 and its case law, to the effect that where a fundamental prerogative such as the right to bargain collectively is restricted, this could amount to an infringement of the very nature of trade union freedom.

---

[1] The Committee of Ministers addressed a recommendation to Malta on point b. for the third part of the thirteenth supervision cycle.

Sweden: the negative aspect of the freedom to organise is not ensured because of the existence of closed shops (for hotels and restaurant employees, building workers, electricians and metal workers) (Conclusions XIII-3, pp. 106 and 107).

the *United Kingdom*[1] on two grounds:

a.   the changes introduced by Section 13[2] of the Trade Union Reform and Employment Act of 1993, which amended Section 146 onwards of the Trade Union and Labour Relations (Consolidation) Act of 1992, have had the effect of weakening the protection of freedom of association in that they have limited to exceptional cases the possibility of a tribunal to rule that the action taken by the employer is unlawful because it violates the freedom of association (for instance by awarding preferential remuneration to employees who accept individual contract and relinquish clauses agreed through collective bargaining).

The Committee considers that this weakening is not compatible with the requirement of Article 5. In this connection it points out that under Article 5 "the Contracting Party is obliged to take adequate legislative or other measures to guarantee the exercise of the right to organise and in particular to protect workers' organisations from any interference on the part of the employers" (see most recently Conclusions XII-2, p. 101) (see 1 f. above). It has also referred to its conclusion under Article 6 para. 2 (Section 13 is incompatible with this paragraph which aims at

---

1 The Committee of Ministers addressed a recommendation to the United Kingdom on points a. and b. for the third part of the thirteenth supervision cycle.

2 Section 13 provides that as regards consideration of complaint of action short of dismissal, "in determining what was the purpose for which action was taken by the employer against the complainant in a case where:

a.   there is evidence that the employer's purpose was to further a change in his relationship with all or any class of his employees; and

b.   there is also evidence that his purpose was one falling within Section 146,

the tribunal shall regard the purpose mentioned in paragraph a. (and not the purpose mentioned in paragraph b. as the purpose for which the employer took the action, unless it considers that the action was such as no reasonable employer would take having regard to the purpose mentioned in paragraph a".

Section 146 of the 1992 Act afforded protection to employees against action short of dismissal on grounds of trade union membership or activities.

promoting machinery for voluntary negotiation with a view to the regulation of conditions or employment by means of collective agreements) and to its case law to the effect that where a fundamental trade union right such as the right to bargain collectively is restricted, this could amount to an infringement of the very nature of trade union freedom (see 3 b. above);

b. Sections 64 to 67 of the 1992 Act (Section 3 of the 1988 Act) prohibits trade unions from disciplining members who refuse to take part in lawful strikes (Conclusions XII-1, p. 115; Conclusions XIII-1, p. 137 and Conclusions XIII-3, p. 110; see 1 e. above).

Article 6 – The right to bargain collectively

In the first supervision cycle, the Committee explained in general terms the scope of Article 6.

"This Article seeks to ensure that both employers and workers can exercise the right to bargain collectively. It deals, in four paragraphs, with various aspects of the relations between employers and workers, and between their respective organisations, and with the means which should be used to develop these relations.

The first three paragraphs of this Article set forth the following methods of collaboration which should be established between employers and workers:

a.   consultation on matters of common interest;

b.   negotiation with a view to the conclusion of collective agreements;

c.   conciliation and voluntary arbitration for the settlement of any labour disputes which may arise.

In its fourth paragraph, Article 6 deals with the right of employers and workers to take collective action in cases of conflicts of interest, including the right to strike" (Conclusions I, p. 34).

Paragraph 1 – Joint consultation

Under this paragraph, the Contracting Parties undertake:

> "to promote joint consultation between workers and employers."

In the first cycle of supervision, the Committee interpreted this paragraph "as meaning that any Contracting State which has accepted it is bound to take steps to promote joint consultation between workers and employers, or their organisations, on all matters of common interest and on the following questions among others: productivity, efficiency, industrial health, safety and welfare" (Conclusions I, pp. 34 and 35).

In the fourth cycle of supervision the Committee, having come to the conclusion that the scope of this paragraph of the Charter had not always been correctly understood, felt bound to stress that the text lays down that a Contracting Party should "promote joint (French: *paritaire*) consultation between workers and employers" that is to say that it will assist in bringing together employers and workers or their organisations on terms of equality with a view to consultation on all questions of mutual interest at every level" (Conclusions IV, p. 43).

In the same cycle it also defined the extent of the obligations on Contracting Parties: "According to the Italian report, the development of the situation in industry, especially since the establishment of the trade union works sections, and the attitude of the trade unions hamper any real recourse to joint consultative bodies as provided for in earlier agreements. In the Committee's view such a *de facto* situation cannot relieve the Italian Government of its obligations.[1]

If positive measures to encourage joint consultation (at least that provided for in the agreements in question) are in fact superfluous, the

---

1 In "The European Social Charter", University Press of Virginia, Charlottesville, 1984, David Harris points out that "if adequate consultation occurs as a result of private arrangements made by employers and workers without government assistance, a state need but keep a weather eye on the situation" (p. 70) and cites the example of Norway which was found as complying because of the 1966 Basic Agreement between the Norwegian Employers Association and the National Federation of Trade Unions (Conclusions I, p. 35) as amended in 1969 (Conclusions II, p. 25).

Committee would like to know before it expresses any opinion, by what other means the function expected of joint consultation is fulfilled" (Conclusions IV, p. 44).

In the next cycle, the Committee completed its interpretation of the contents of Article 6 para. 1 and clarified further its scope. It considered that "the expression 'joint consultations' was to be interpreted as being applicable to all kinds of consultation between both sides of industry – with or without any government representatives – on condition that both sides of industry have an equal say in the matter. For the Committee had noted that in some States, consultation takes place within the framework of joint bodies in which the government representative often acted as chairman. This form of joint consultation was deemed to comply with the requirements as set out in Article 6 para. 1" (Conclusions V, p. 41).

It also stated that "This provision did not in fact apply to every organ or body in which representatives of workers and employers or their respective organisations came together for purposes of consultation, and it was not therefore necessary to furnish information on all such bodies. Article 6 para. 1 was solely concerned with collective bargaining in the normal sense of the term, ie. in the sense employed in collective labour law ('*kollektives Arbeitsrecht*'); more specifically, it referred to consultation on the basis of equal representation within joint committees established at national, regional and local level, within firms and various sectors of the economy, as well as the civil service, to enable employers and workers to consult one another on questions of common interest" (Conclusions V, p. 41, Austria).

The areas to which consultation should extend were clearly defined in the seventh supervision cycle. The Committee emphasised the need "for the governments to promote joint consultation, especially in the following areas:

– occupational problems (working conditions, vocational training-retraining, industrial health and safety, etc.);

– economic problems (the organisation and management of the business enterprise, working hours, production rates, structure and number of staff etc.)

— social matters (social insurance, social welfare, etc.)" (Conclusions-VII, pp. 35 and 36). The view that, in order to comply with Article 6 para. 1, a state is obliged to promote joint consultation in all these areas, has been reiterated throughout all the supervision cycles (see for example Conclusions XII-2, p. 104, Malta).

The personal scope of this provision covers all employed persons, since Article 33 is not applicable. As its wording indicates, it does not apply to the self-employed. The Committee also held "the provisions of Article 6 as a whole to be applicable not only to employees in the private sector, but to public officials subject to regulations, though with the modifications obviously necessary in respect of persons bound not by contractual conditions but by regulations laid down by the public authorities. Article 6 para. 1 can only be regarded as respected where such officials are concerned if consultation machinery is arranged for the drafting and implementation of regulations, which should not give rise to any special difficulty" (Conclusions III, p. 33, Federal Republic of Germany). Public employees whose employment is governed by a contract of employment are governed by this paragraph in the same way as private employees.

Moreover, the Committee has taken the view that joint consultations must be promoted at all levels,[1] national, regional and local, and in all economic sectors including agriculture (Conclusions II, p. 25, Ireland). The Committee has on several occasions stressed the importance it attaches to joint consultation at all levels, particularly that of the undertaking, and in all sectors of the economy, dealing with all the areas listed above (see, *inter alia*, Conclusions V, p. 43 and Addendum to

---

1 In "The European Social Charter" (p. 70), David Harris points out that this interpretation is too strict, as the Social Committee at its fifth session during the *travaux préparatoires* omitted for this reason the wording "both on the level of the undertaking and on the industrial and national level". The level should be determined by the Contracting Parties themselves.

Conclusions XI-2, pp. 22 and 23, Ireland; Conclusions XII-2, p. 104, Malta).

The latest supervision cycles show that the Committee now devotes great attention to two other questions:

- the manner in which consultation procedures operate in practice (see for example Conclusions XIII-1, p. 141, the United Kingdom; Conclusions XIII-2, p. 275, Malta; Conclusions XIII-3, p. 113, Ireland; p. 114, Malta; p. 274, Portugal);

- the participation of non-unionised workers in joint consultation procedures (see Conclusions XIII-1, p. 141, the United Kingdom; Conclusions XIII-2, p. 273, Belgium; Conclusions XIII-3, p. 274, Finland).

The inclusion of the undertaking to promote joint consultations in an Article designed to safeguard the right to collective bargaining indicates that the consultations concerned form part of the more general concept of collective bargaining. In fact, consultations between workers and employers, especially if they take place regularly, facilitate collective bargaining and can avoid disputes between the social partners.

Assessment of compliance

The only Contracting Party currently found as not complying is *Ireland*, on the ground that even though satisfactory arrangements exist for joint consultations at national level, at regional and local level joint consultations are confined to certain undertakings and certain sectors of the economy and concern only a limited number of issues. These restrictions were particularly noticeable in the agricultural sector. The criticism was raised in the second cycle (Conclusions II, p. 25) and still stands (see in the last instance Conclusions XIII-3, p. 113). In the eleventh cycle, the Committee recalled that the Joint Labour Committees, which established minimum wages and conditions of employment in various sectors of the economy, particularly in agriculture, did not offer true joint consultation, especially at company level, with regard, *inter alia*, to occupational, economic and social issues (see Addendum to Conclusions XI-2, p. 23).

The Committee did not accept the argument of the Irish Government that it had done everything that could be expected of it under this paragraph but that its efforts had not been well received by employers and unions. The Committee recalled that it had interpreted this provision "as meaning that any Contracting State which has accepted it is bound to take steps to promote joint consultation" (Addendum to Conclusions XI-2, pp. 22 and 23).

The Committee's conclusion is deferred for three Contracting Parties: Finland, (first report – Conclusions XIII-3, p. 274), Luxembourg (first report – Addendum to Conclusions XIII-3, p. 37) and the United Kingdom (Conclusions XIII-3, pp. 116 and 117).

Paragraph 2 – Promotion of machinery for voluntary negotiations

Under this paragraph, the Contracting Parties undertake:

> "to promote, where necessary and appropriate, machinery for voluntary negotiations between employers or employers' organisations and workers organisations, with a view to the regulation of terms and conditions of employment by means of collective agreements".

According to the Committee's interpretation, "in accepting the terms of this provision Contracting Parties undertake not only to recognise, in their legislation, that employers and workers may settle their mutual relations by means of collective agreements, but also actively to promote the conclusion of such agreements if their spontaneous development is not satisfactory and, in particular, to ensure that each side is prepared to bargain collectively with the other. Where adequate machinery for voluntary negotiation is set up spontaneously, however, the government in question is not, in the Committee's opinion, bound to intervene in the manner prescribed in this paragraph" (Conclusions I, p. 35).

The Committee's case law covers mainly three issues: the link between Article 5 and paragraph 2 of Article 6, the rights of public employees and the intervention of the state in collective bargaining.

To assess compliance with this paragraph, the Committee expects the Contracting Parties to provide it with detailed information on the existing system of collective bargaining and the extent of its application in the different economic sectors, by furnishing statistics concerning particularly the number and categories of enterprises and workers concerned and the number and categories of organisations on both sides (Conclusions I, p. 35).

1. The link between Article 5 and Article 6 para. 2

According to the case law of the Committee, paragraph 2 of Article 6 "presupposes the guarantee of a complete freedom to organise" (Conclusions IV, p. 46, Ireland). This rule was laid down when the Committee dealt with the question of negotiating licences in Ireland (see under Article 5 above). In the light of its conclusions regarding Ireland's application of Article 5 of the Charter, from which it had emerged that the conditions under which negotiating licences were granted were not compatible with the freedom to form or join trade unions, "the Committee decided that this incompatibility extended also to the right to bargain collectively provided for under Article 6 para. 2" (Conclusions III, p. 35).

The Committee confirmed the rule in the sixth supervision cycle, again in the context of the Irish situation: the Committee felt bound to recall that "a precondition of satisfactory compliance with the obligations arising out of Article 6 para. 2 was full observance of Article 5" (Conclusions VI, p. 36). Thus the interdependence of trade union rights and collective bargaining is fully established (for the effect of non-compliance with Article 6 para. 2 on Article 5, see under Article 5, point 3 b. above). This is clearly illustrated by the Committee's conclusions in the cases of Denmark, France, Malta and the United Kingdom mentioned under the heading "assessment of compliance" below.

2. *The rights of public employees*

As regards public employees, the Committee pointed out that even though in the case of those whose employment was subject in some degree to regulation by law (and not by a contract of employment) it was not possible for the ordinary collective bargaining procedures to apply, these employees must participate in the drafting of the regulations which were to apply to them (Conclusions III, p. 34, Federal Republic of Germany and Conclusions IV, p. 45, Austria). This interpretation was confirmed once again in the tenth supervision cycle in connection with the situation in Spain, when the Committee concluded that even though there was no genuine right to collective bargaining in the civil service, paragraph 2 of Article 6 was not infringed, as the law authorised the most representative trade unions to participate in the determination of working conditions, including remuneration, in the civil service (Conclusions X-2, p. 73).

It must, however, be ascertained whether the persons concerned have the status of civil servants or of employees in the private sector. This question arose for the United Kingdom in relation to primary and secondary school teachers in England and Wales. Until 1987, their terms and conditions of employment were determined by collective bargaining. In 1987, a temporary mechanism for pay awards was introduced, which gave a discretionary power to the Secretary of State for Education to determine pay awards without being obliged to consider the view of the teaching unions. The Committee, recalling its case law according to which the right of civil servants to collective bargaining may be limited to a certain extent, asked whether teachers were to be considered as civil servants or private sector employees. The reply was that teachers are not civil servants but, as employees of local authorities, they are "public servants". "The Committee noted that although they are public servants, until the 1987 Act, their terms and conditions of employment were determined by collective bargaining, the outcome of which had to be followed by the Secretary of State under the legislation previously in force (1965 Remuneration of Teachers Act). Thus, the 1987 Act, in contradiction to the obligation contained in Article 6 para. 2 to promote collective bargaining, in fact placed limitations on an existing right to bargain collectively. The Committee considered that this situation could not be considered as compatible with Article 6 para. 2 of the Charter" (Conclusions XII-1, pp. 125 and 126).

The 1991 School Teachers Pay and Conditions Act introduced a new system which represented an improvement on the system put in place in 1987 (Conclusions XIII-1, pp. 149 and 150) but the Committee felt that it did not give teachers the same negotiating rights they had prior to 1987, in that the new system offered consultation rather than negotiation, "which was a backward step". "In order to make a full assessment of the situation, the Committee requested that the next report explain precisely if the teachers concerned were covered by a statute or by contracts" (Conclusions XIII-3, pp. 128 and 129).

3.   Intervention of the state in collective bargaining

The power of the state to intervene in free collective bargaining is an issue which has concerned the Committee on repeated occasions, mostly since the ninth cycle of supervision.

The Committee first turned its attention to this issue in the eighth supervision cycle following comments made by a Dutch trade union federation on the first Dutch report, criticising the interference of government in wages and conditions of work in the private sector (by fixing limits to wage increases). In its General introduction to the conclusions of this particular cycle, the Committee stated that "though the state should not normally interfere in negotiations between workers' organisations and employers, public interest may require that in order to overcome serious economic and social problems, the state should intervene in a more concrete manner in the economic life of the nation and take steps in matters which normally fall within the scope of collective bargaining" (Conclusions VIII, p. 11).

In the ninth supervision cycle, the Committee re-examined the issue of government's statutory powers to intervene in free collective bargaining, not only in the private sector but also in the so-called "trend follower" sector by reason of the comments of the Dutch unions (CNV (National Federation of Christian Trade Unions), FNV (Confederation of the Netherlands Trade Union Movement) and MHP (Federation of Middle and Senior Staff personnel)).

As regards the private sector, the Committee confirmed its opinion that "in order to remedy a particularly serious economic situation, a government should be able to set certain limits to collective bargaining, particularly where wages increases are concerned. However, the Committee emphasised that such restrictions should be imposed only after extensive consultation of all the parties concerned, notably trade unions and employers' associations, and that they should be of an exceptional kind and of limited duration. Furthermore, they should not be imposed unless it has been proved that no other measures can produce the same effects without recourse to such government intervention." (Conclusions IX-1, p. 53).

With regard to state intervention in collective bargaining in certain "trend-follower" sectors, the Committee, after recognising that "the situation in these sectors had a number of special features: on the one hand the sectors are dependent on public funds, namely the state budget or social insurance contributions while, on the other, employees in these sectors are clearly in a different position compared with state officials, since the state is not their employer and moreover they have always had the right to bargain collectively and to strike. Furthermore, their wages have traditionally followed trends in the private sector", expressed the belief that the problem of collective bargaining in this sector "should be solved through consultation and negotiation between government and all the parties concerned" (Conclusions IX-1, p. 54). In the following supervision cycle, the Committee was informed that under an Act of 1985 the responsible Minister retained the power to establish ceilings to increases in wages costs, but had first to hold very wide-ranging consultations with the trade union concerned. In view of this, the Committee found that the situation in the Netherlands did not conflict with the Charter (Conclusions X-1, p. 73).

Equally in this cycle (the tenth), the Committee, commenting on an act passed by the Danish Parliament in 1985 calling a halt to industrial action, extending the validity of collective agreements for two years and limiting pay rises to a certain percentage in the first year and a lower one in the next year when widespread industrial action threatened to cause serious disruption of the economy, recalled that "such a temporary restriction to the exercise of the right to collective bargaining is a very serious measure which could only be justified according to the relevant conditions laid down in Article 31, paragraph 1 of the Charter. Moreover, such a measure should be taken only for the time needed to return to a normal situation in which the exercise of the right to collective bargaining would again be fully ensured". (Conclusions X-1, p. 72).

In the twelfth cycle of supervision the Committee, applying the above-mentioned case law on state intervention in collective bargaining:

- found an act passed in Iceland in May 1988 (Act No. 14) which, *inter alia*, prohibited all collective bargaining and strike action and which was implemented without prior consultations with the unions as not in conformity with Article 6 para. 2. "The Committee considered that a total suspension of all collective bargaining rights on the basis of the economic well-being of the state cannot be justified under the terms of Article 31 of the Charter" (Conclusions XII-1, pp. 120 and 121; this case also came before the ILO Committee on Freedom of Association, case No. 1458);[1]

- found to be incompatible with Article 6 para. 2 Sections 10 and 11 of the WAAGS Act, enacted in the Netherlands in 1985 and allowing the Minister of Social Affairs and Employment to limit wage increases in national insurance funded and subsidised sectors (the "trend-follower" sectors)[2] (Conclusions XII-1, pp. 122 and 123);

- found as incompatible with Article 6 para. 2 the Danish Government's intervention in 1987 to end industrial action in certain sectors and prolong existing agreements. These agreements were prolonged for four years, but certain pay-related matters could be

---

1 Act No. 14 of 1988 remained in force for only nine months and so by the end of the reference period, the right guaranteed by Article 6 para. 2 had been fully restored.

2 The infringing sections of the act were repealed by Act No. 557 of 27 October 1993 (Conclusions XIII-3, p. 123); in the first part of the thirteenth cycle, as this repeal had only reached the draft stage, the conclusion was still negative (Conclusions XIII-1, p. 146).

negotiated as early as spring 1989. In addition, the Public Conciliator had used the linking provision of the Act on Conciliation in Industrial Disputes to extend a general draft agreement concluded on 11 February 1987 to one part of the private sector, where negotiations were taking place with a view to the renewal of an agreement. "While considering that these interventions, which made collective bargaining in the above-mentioned sectors impossible for the first part of the period under review, interfered with the rights guaranteed under this provision of the Charter, the Committee noted that in spring 1989 there were negotiations covering practically all agreements – although on limited items – in the private and public sectors and that the parties agreed on average wage increases of 2,5%. The Committee expressed the hope that in the future the social partners would be able to negotiate all conditions of their agreements free from any interference by the authorities" (Conclusions XII-1, p. 118).

Another type of intervention which interferes with collective bargaining is the use of compulsory arbitration: "insofar as any compulsory binding arbitration went beyond the limitations permitted by Article 31 of the Charter, this would constitute a limitation on the effective exercise of the right to voluntary negotiation protected by this provision of the Charter [Article 6 para. 2]" (Conclusions XII-2, pp. 107 and 108). The issue of compulsory arbitration is covered by Article 6 para. 3 (see below), but has an obvious effect on collective bargaining which may be hindered if the compulsory arbitration applies to situations of voluntary negotiation of collective agreements, which are also covered by Article 6 para. 2.

Thus in Malta, the faculty to refer a dispute to compulsory binding arbitration at the request of only one of the parties to the dispute is criticised from the viewpoint of Article 6 para. 3 (see below). Under Article 6 para. 2, the Committee asked "to what extent, having regard to Article 31, the provisions regarding binding arbitration at the request of one only of the parties were applied to situations of voluntary negotiation of collective agreements" (Conclusions XII-2, pp. 107 and 108; see also Conclusions XIII-2, p. 277 and XIII-3, p. 122 where the question is repeated because the government has not yet given an answer).

Similarly with regard to Ireland, the Committee has asked questions under Article 6 para. 3 on the subject of the possible use of compulsory arbitration without the consent of the parties to a dispute (Conclusions XIII-3, p. 131) and under Article 6 para. 2, referring to its case law, it asked what the situation was with respect to the effective exercise of the right to voluntary negotiation (Conclusions XIII-3, p. 121).

Assessment of compliance

Six Contracting Parties currently do not meet the requirements of Article 6 para. 2: Denmark, France, Ireland, Malta, Norway and the United Kingdom.

Denmark: Section 10 of the 1988 Act on a Danish International Ship's Register violates Article 6 para. 2 (it is also in contradiction with Article 5 on several counts; see above). This section provides, *inter alia:*

- that collective agreements on wages and working conditions for employees on vessels in the Ship's Register, concluded by a Danish trade union organisation, may only comprise persons who are considered to be residents of Denmark or who, by virtue of incurred international obligations, shall be put on an equal footing with Danish citizens; and

- that such collective agreements, concluded by a foreign trade union organisation, may only comprise persons who are members of the organisation concerned or persons who are citizens in the country where the trade union organisation is domiciled.

On the basis of information submitted to the ILO, the Committee examined whether the reasons given by the Danish Government could justify these restrictions in the light of Article 31 of the Charter and concluded negatively. The Committee's reasoning was as follows: "Before the ILO Committee on Freedom of Association the Danish Government contended *inter alia* that compelling reasons of national economic interest justified this intervention in private sector collective bargaining;

a crisis had arisen because of flagging out and the competitiveness of Danish ship-owners needed to be improved. It also argued that the standard of living of Danish seamen was guaranteed by the legislative package, since any reduction in wages they might have to accept was balanced by tax relief; that the act by its nature was a general regulation allowing negotiation on more detailed conditions of employment and that other countries already had similar legislation allowing ship-owners to free themselves of collective agreements.

Taking these arguments into consideration, the Committee found that Denmark was in breach of Article 6 para. 2, also in this respect, as the 1988 Act, which not only interfered with existing collective agreements, but also limited the scope of future agreements, constituted such a restriction of the exercise of the right to free collective bargaining as could not be justified under Article 31 of the Charter. It noted in addition that this restriction had not been imposed only for the time needed to return to a normal situation in which the exercise of the right to collective bargaining would again be fully ensured (Conclusions X-1, p. 72), but was a permanent measure.

The Committee underlined that it considered equality of treatment for all 'nationals of other Contracting Parties lawfully resident or working regularly within the territory' (see appendix to the Charter) in the enjoyment of the benefits of collective bargaining to be one of the fundamental principles of the Charter" (Conclusions XII-1, pp. 119 and 120).

On this basis, the conclusion has remained negative: "The restrictions on the freedom to bargain collectively and the inequality of treatment between nationals of the Contracting Parties in this field led the Committee to reiterate its negative conclusion. In this regard it also referred to its conclusion under Article 5" (Conclusions XIII-1[1], pp. 142 and 143; see in the last instance Conclusions XIII-3, p. 118).[2]

---

1 The Committee of Ministers addressed a recommendation to Denmark for the first part of the thirteenth cycle; see also under Article 5.

2 By reason of its conclusions under Articles 5 and 6 para. 2 in the twelfth cycle (first part) on the Danish International Ships's Register, the Committee also asked, in a general question

France: having concluded under Article 5 (see above) that the closed shop practices in the book sector did not comply with the requirements of this provision, the Committee "referred to its established case law (Conclusions VI, p. 36; see most recently Conclusions XIII-1, p. 145 and Conclusions XIII-2, pp. 276 and 277) according to which 'a precondition of satisfactory compliance with the obligations arising out of Article 6 para. 2 was full observance of Article 5'. Under these circumstances, the Committee had to conclude that the situation in the book sector did not comply with the requirements of Article 6 para. 2" (Conclusions XIII-3, pp. 119 and 120).

Ireland: referring to the obligation for trade unions to apply for a negotiating licence, which is in violation of Article 5 (see above), the Committee has concluded negatively with respect to Article 6 para. 2 (in the last instance, Conclusions XIII-3, p. 121).

Malta:[1] the Committee referred to its conclusion under Article 5 as to the rights of the police force to organise and to bargain collectively (see above). It stressed that "as long as the situation was not in conformity with Article 5 on this point, the restrictions on the right to bargain collectively resulting therefrom could only be considered as being in breach of Article 6 para. 2" (Conclusions XIII-3, p. 122).

Norway: The Committee's conclusion has been negative since the first part of the thirteenth cycle, when the Committee found out from the report of Norway under paragraph 4 of Article 6 and from a recommendation of the ILO Committee on Freedom of Association (Case No. 1576) that after the breakdown of negotiations over a new collective agreement between the Norwegian Trade Union Federation of Oil Workers and the Confederation of Norwegian Business and Industry, the workers had gone on strike and the government had resorted to compulsory arbitration. The Committee, recalling its case law according

under these two provisions, all other states (other than Denmark) to report on any similar regulation applicable in their territories (Conclusions XII-1, p. 118 and XII-2, p. 105). No state has as yet reported any such legislation (see above, under Article 5).

1 The Committee of Ministers addressed a recommendation to Malta for the third part of the thirteenth supervision cycle.

to which state intervention "which made collective bargaining... impossible,... interfered with the rights guaranteed under this provision of the Charter (Conclusions XII-1, pp. 118 to 120)" found the situation in Norway unsatisfactory (Conclusions XIII-1, p. 147). In the third part of the thirteenth cycle, the Committee noted under Article 6 para. 3 that there was still no law specifying the circumstances in which the authorities could impose arbitration to settle a labour dispute and that as a result compulsory arbitration could be imposed in more cases than those provided for under Article 31 of the Charter. Under Article 6 para. 2, referring to its conclusion under Article 6 para. 3 and to its case law, it maintained its negative conclusion (Conclusions XIII-3, p. 125).

The *United Kingdom:*[1] on the one hand, "having considered that the United Kingdom's Government did not satisfy the requirements of Article 5, the Committee felt it important to reiterate that according to its established case law, "a precondition of satisfactory compliance with the obligations arising out of Article 6 para. 2 was full observance of Article 5." (Conclusions VI, p. 36, see also Conclusions XIII-1, p. 145 and Conclusions XIII-2, pp. 277 and 278)"; and on the other, the Committee considered that Section 13 of the Trade Union Reform and Employment Rights Act 1993, which is not in compliance with Article 5 of the Charter (see above), is not in compliance with Article 6 para. 2 either: "the Committee referred to its conclusion under Article 5 which contained a detailed presentation and analysis of this provision. With regard more specifically to the right to collective bargaining, the Committee recalled that in application of Article 13, cases such as that of Wilson or Palmer in which the employers had the clear intention of persuading their staff to relinquish union representation and collective bargaining, could no longer be deemed to be illegal except in exceptional circumstances. This was not compatible with Article 6 para. 2 which was aimed at promoting machinery for voluntary negotiations with a view to the regulation of conditions of employment by means of collective agreements" (Conclusions XIII-3, pp. 127 to 129). The Committee also asked questions on other points.

---

1 The Committee of Ministers addressed a recommendation to the United Kingdom for the third part of the thirteenth supervision cycle.

The conclusion is deferred in the case of Belgium (first report – Conclusions XIII-2, pp. 275 and 276), Finland (first report – Conclusions XIII-3, pp. 275 and 276), Luxembourg (first report – Addendum to Conclusions XIII-3, pp. 37 and 38), the Netherlands (Conclusions XIII-3, pp. 123 and 124) and the Netherlands Antilles (pp. 124 and 125), Portugal (first report – Conclusions XIII-3, pp. 276 and 277).

Paragraph 3 – Conciliation and arbitration

Under this paragraph, the Contracting Parties undertake:

> "to promote the establishment and use of appropriate machinery for conciliation and voluntary arbitration for the settlement of labour disputes".

The Committee established from the very beginning that "the machinery for the settlement of labour disputes may be established by legislation, collective agreements or industrial practice and its object may be the settlement of any labour dispute".

It took the view that "where conciliation machinery, established for example on the basis of collective agreements, is sufficiently efficacious, then there is no need for the government concerned to establish arbitration procedures or to promote their use" (Conclusions I, p. 37).

As regards the disputes covered, the Committee, in a general observation, stated that "this provision concerned disputes which would arise when collective agreements were being negotiated or concluded and included the obligation for states to promote the establishment and use of machinery for conciliation and voluntary arbitration for the settlement of these disputes" (Conclusions V, p. 45). The Committee's restrictive interpretation was based on the introductory sentence to Article 6.

The Committee also stressed that "it was evident that if the machinery was operating satisfactory, the State did not need to intervene" (*ibidem*).

In the twelfth cycle when examining the Maltese situation, the Committee developed its case law further, by stating that "binding arbitration procedures cannot be considered as in conformity with the Charter unless they represent restrictions which fall within Article 31 of the Charter (ie. restrictions or limitations which are prescribed by law and are necessary in a democratic society for the protection of the rights and freedoms of others or for the protection of public interest, national security, public health or morals)" (Conclusions XII-2, p. 110).

Assessment of compliance

This provision is widely complied with by the Contracting Parties to the Charter, which appear to have well-developed machinery for conciliation and arbitration. Malta and Norway are the only countries found as not complying.

Malta, on two grounds:

– in the event of failure of statutory machinery for conciliation the Minister, not only at the joint request of all the parties but also at the request of one of the parties, may refer the matter to an industrial tribunal whose decision is binding on the employers and employees to whom it relates, and the parties are debarred for at least one year from seeking unilaterally to have the decision altered;

– in the public service neither conciliation nor arbitration exist. (Conclusions XII-2, pp. 110 and 111; see also Conclusions XIII-2, pp. 279 and 280 and in the last instance Conclusions XIII-3, p. 132).

Norway: on the ground that the government had used compulsory procedures on several occasions, notably in June 1991 in order to end a lawful strike by oil workers in the North Sea. The Committee considered that these restrictions did not fall within the scope of Article 31. Also there was no law specifying the circumstances in which the authorities could resort to compulsory arbitration to settle a labour dispute (Conclusions XIII-I, p. 152); see in the last instance, on the latter point, Conclusions XIII-3, p. 133).

The conclusion is deferred for Finland (first report – Conclusions XIII-3, pp. 277 and 278), Ireland (Conclusions XIII-3, pp. 130 and 131), Portugal (first report – Conclusions XIII-3, pp. 278 and 279).

Paragraph 4 – The right to collective action

Under this paragraph, the Contracting Parties recognise:

> "the right of workers and employers to collective action in cases of conflicts of interest, including the right to strike, subject to obligations that might arise out of collective agreements previously entered into."

Appendix[1] to Article 6 para. 4

> "It is understood that each Contracting Party may, in so far as it is concerned, regulate the exercise of the right to strike by law, provided that any further restrictions that this might place on the right can be justified under the terms of Article 31".

General

This provision concerns the right of workers and employers to take collective action in cases of conflicts of interest. In its first Conclusions the Committee noted that "by this provision, the right to strike is for the first time explicitly recognised in an international convention. Hence, the Committee had to elaborate to a great extent its own principle of interpretation" (Conclusions I, p. 34).[2]

---

1 The provision of the Appendix of the Charter relating to paragraph 4 of Article 6 only intends to make clear that the restrictions mentioned in Article 31 are applicable to that paragraph, in addition to those which the latter contains, namely the obligations arising out of collective agreements.

2 As David Harris points out in his book "The European Social Charter", "from the standpoint of the worker Article 6 para. 4 is a landmark in international labour law. It represents the first occasion on which the right to strike has been expressly recognised by a treaty in

In the first cycle of supervision, the Committee adopted the following general interpretation of this paragraph:

"*a.*   It is clear from the text that this provision relates to both strikes and lock-outs – even though the latter are not explicitly mentioned in the text of Article 6 para. 4 of the Charter, or in the gloss to this provision in the Appendix. The Committee came to this conclusion because the lock-out is the principal, if not the only, form of collective action which employers can take in defence of their interests.

b.   This provision recognises the right to collective action only in cases of conflicts of interest. It follows that it cannot be invoked in cases of conflicts of right, in particular in cases of disputes concerning the existence, validity or interpretation of a collective agreement, or its violation, eg. through action taken during its currency with a view to the revision of its contents. This interpretation should be adopted even where a collective agreement contains provisions purporting to permit such industrial action.

c.   It follows from the wording of the Charter that restrictions on recourse to collective action even in cases of conflicts of interest are compatible with the Charter, if they are imposed by a collective agreement.

d.   The same applied to a 'cooling-off' period prescribed by legislation, for periods of negotiation or conciliation or arbitration proceedings between employers and workers; the Committee is of the opinion that such a provision does not impose a real restriction of the right to collective action, since it merely regulates the exercise thereof.

e.   Where the limits within which the right to strike may be exercised have been determined, in a State, not by legislation but by the courts, it is for the Committee to examine whether the case law thus established is in accordance with the requirements of the Charter.

---

force". This right is expressly recognised in Article 8 d. of the International Covenant on Economic, Social and Cultural Rights, but this Covenant came into force in 1976. It is also recognised by implication in ILO Convention No. 87 and mentioned indirectly in ILO Convention No. 105.

f.	Legislation denying the right to strike to persons employed in essential public services may, by virtue of Article 31, be compatible with the Charter whether such restriction be total or partial. Whether or not, in a given case, it is so compatible depends on the extent to which the life of the community depends on the services involved. The same applies to legislation for the compulsory settlement of conflicts of interest which are likely to expose the national economy to serious danger.

g.	As regards the right of public servants to strike, the Committee recognises that, by virtue of Article 31, the right to strike of certain categories of public servants may be restricted, including members of the police and armed forces, judges and senior civil servants. On the other hand, the Committee takes the view that a denial of the right of strike to public servants as a whole cannot be regarded as compatible with the Charter.

h.	The Committee is of the opinion that no violation of the Charter is involved in the application of legal provisions or principles making individual members of trade unions or employers' associations criminally or civilly liable in the event of their organisation resorting to illegal collective action, on the understanding that legislation enacted in this field be in keeping with the Charter.

i.	Lastly, the Committee examined the compatibility with the Charter of a rule according to which a strike terminates the contracts of employment. In principle, the Committee takes the view that this is not compatible with the respect of the right to strike as envisaged by the Charter. Whether, in a given case, a rule of this kind constitutes a violation of the Charter is, however, a question which should not be answered in the abstract, but in the light of the consequences which the legislation and industrial practice of a given country attaches to the termination and resumption of the employment relationship. If, in practice, those participating in a strike are, after its termination, fully reinstated and if their previously acquired rights, e.g. as regards pension, holidays and seniority, in general, are not impaired, the formal termination of the contracts of employment by the strike does not, in the opinion of the Committee, constitute a violation of the Charter" (Conclusions I, pp. 38 and 39).

All these points have been confirmed, defined and developed over the successive cycles of supervision. As a result, the Committee's case law covers a wide area: therefore it was considered appropriate to group it under four headings for the purpose of this presentation.

1. Strikes covered by Article 6 para. 4

As early as the first cycle, the Committee interpreted Article 6 para. 4 as recognising the right to collective action, including the right to strike, only in cases of conflicts of interest: see b. of the general interpretation under the heading "General" above. In the same cycle, the Committee completed this interpretation by clarifying that "any limitation to this right to strike connected with the conclusion of new collective agreements could not be considered compatible with the provision of the Charter" (Conclusions I, p. 183).

In the following cycle, the Committee confirmed and explained further its interpretation:

- "Political strikes are not covered by Article 6, which is designed to protect 'the right to bargain collectively', such strikes being obviously quite outside the purview of collective bargaining;

- Restrictions on the right to strike as, for example, a ban on strikes that are contrary to the public interest or morals are permitted, provided that they are within the terms of Article 31;

- On the other hand, provisions are not consonant with the Charter when they are designed to restrict the right to strike solely to strikes to secure the conclusion of collective agreements and to make its exercise dependent on trade union action" (Conclusions II, pp. 27 and 28); Putting this interpretation into practice, the Committee adopted the following conclusions with regard to Germany:

"To the extent that German law prohibits strikes in breach of a currently valid collective agreement or during a cooling-off period, and regards as illegal any strike action taken for political ends or for immoral reasons and any strike contrary to the public interest, the Committee considered that the German regulations were not in conflict with the Charter. This conclusion is founded on the interpretation given above, on the Committee's own practice or on Article 31 of the Charter, as the case may be.

As to the prohibition, under German law, of all strikes which are not aimed at obtaining a collective agreement or led by a trade union, the Committee, basing itself on the interpretation set out above, found German law on this point to be inconsistent with the Charter. For example, the Committee considered that a strike aimed at compelling an employer to comply with safety regulations imposed by law could not be regarded as outside the terms of Article 6 para. 4 of the Charter. Similarly, the Committee was of the opinion that a group of workers ought to be able to take strike action even outside the trade union framework" (ibidem).

In the fourth cycle of supervision, replying to the arguments of the German Government to support its attitude with respect to the prohibition of strikes not aimed at the conclusion of a collective agreement and of all strikes not called or recognised by a trade union, the Committee explained its position in even greater detail:

"As regards prohibition of strikes not aimed at the conclusion of a collective agreement, the attitude of the Government of the Federal Republic of Germany is based on Article 6 of the Social Charter, whereby the right of workers to collective action in cases of conflicts of interest, including the right to strike, is recognised 'with a view to ensuring the effective exercise of the right to bargain collectively'. It does not, however, seem possible to accept that there should be no other type of collective bargaining in labour relations than that aimed at concluding a collective agreement. There are many circumstances which, apart from any collective agreement, call for 'collective bargaining', such as when dismissals have been announced or are contemplated by a firm and a group of employees seeks to prevent them or to serve the re-engagement of those dismissed. Any bargaining between one or more employers and a body of employees (whether "de jure" or "de facto") aimed at solving a problem of common interest, whatever its nature may be, should be regarded as 'collective bargaining' within the meaning of Article 6. To the extent that the legislation of the Federal Republic of Germany does not allow strike action in all instances where such bargaining may occur, it is contrary to the provisions of Article 6, paragraph 4.

There is no provision in Article 6 or indeed any other article of the Charter that allows the exercise of the right to strike to be restricted to trade unions. Paragraph 6 of Part I of the Charter lays down the principle that 'all workers and employers have the right to bargain collectively'. Since therefore an ordinary group of workers without any legal status may engage in such bargaining, it can and should be given the right to strike under Article 6 para. 4, so that it may effectively exercise its right to bargain collectively. In this respect, too, the legislation of the Federal Republic of Germany cannot be considered to conform to the requirements of the Charter" (Conclusions IV, p. 50).

This case law on both points, which remained unaltered in all supervision cycles, was not only applied in the case of Germany (see in the last instance Conclusions XIII-2, p. 282) but also of Iceland: "The Committee also noted that it is still the case that Section 14 of Act No. 94/1986 limits the right to strike of civil servants to situations where the strike is called with the aim of reaching a collective agreement, which is contrary to Article 6 paragraph 4, as interpreted by the Committee's case law (see for example Conclusions VIII, p. 96 '... the persistence of provisions prohibiting all strikes not aimed at the conclusion of a collective agreement and all strikes not called or recognised by a trade union are contrary to the Charter')" (Conclusions XII-1, pp. 128 and 129; in the last instance, Conclusions XIII-3, p. 135).

The Committee has observed that "trade unions alone seem to enjoy the right to call a strike in connection with negotiations for the conclusion or the total or partial renewal of collective agreements. Workers not members of a trade union signatory of a collective agreement may, apparently, stop work, depending on the terms of their contract of employment, but stoppages are not regarded as a strike within the meaning of Act No. 80/1938. The Committee was obliged to conclude that this state of affairs is not compatible with Article 6 para. 4 of the

Charter" (Conclusions IX-1, p. 56; see in the last instance Conclusions XIII-3, p. 135).

As regards strikes in breach of a currently valid collective agreement, the Committee was led to clarify one issue in relation to Malta: it had observed that collective agreements provided that during their period of application, the parties concerned would not make any new demands concerning the contents of the agreements or those matters which had been subject to bargaining before signature. "Admittedly, the Committee had always accepted the fact that collective action could not be taken with regard to matters governed by collective agreements if legal disputes, rather than conflicts of interest, were at stake (see Conclusions I, p. 38), however this did not apply to matters subject to bargaining during the negotiations but not covered by the agreement, which could not be considered an obstacle to such action" (Conclusions XIII-2, p. 283).

2. Right to strike of public servants

The right of public servants to strike was one of the issues covered by the general interpretation given to Article 6 para. 4 by the Committee in the first supervision cycle (see paras. f. and g. of this interpretation under "General" above, or Conclusions I, p. 38). The Committee's case law on this point was further developed between the first and the seventh cycles of supervision in relation to the position of German public servants who did not have the right to strike.

In the first supervision cycle, the Committee pointed out that a comparison of Articles 5 and 6 and an examination of the provisions of the Appendix showed that the complete suppression of the right to strike for public servants was not permissible. In this connection, the Committee also took note of the letter, dated 28 September 1961,[1] "in which the Permanent Representative of the Federal Republic of Germany to the Council of Europe sent a declaration to the Secretary General according to which civil servants (*Beamte*), judges and members of the armed

---

[1] Before ratification of the Charter by the Federal Republic of Germany.

forces entitled to a pension do not enjoy the right to strike for reasons of public order and State security. Nevertheless, in the Committee's opinion, that declaration is not sufficient to exclude a whole category of persons covered by the Charter from the benefit of such fundamental provisions as Article 5 and 6. On that point, the Committee also took note of the text of the letter sent to the governments interested by the Deputy Secretary General of the Council of Europe on 11 October 1961, informing them of the content of the said declaration" (Conclusions I, pp. 184 and 185).

In the third cycle of supervision, the Committee rejected the position of the German Government that public officials were not considered as "workers" under Federal law: it "confirmed its previous position on the coverage of the term 'worker' which in the sense of the Charter embraces public officials. Although the provisions of Article 31 of the Charter and of its Appendix make it possible, in the case of public officials:

a. to restrict the right to strike or in some instances, exclude it altogether, for certain officials who, if they were to use it would endanger public order, national security public health or morality;

b. to lay down legislative rules for the exercise of this right which may differ according to whether public officials or employees in the private sector are concerned,

the Committee reaffirmed that a global prohibition of the right to strike directed at public officials or at any other category of workers is incompatible with the prescriptions of Article 6 para. 4 of the Charter" (Conclusions III, p. 36).

In the fourth cycle of supervision, the Committee gave details of the criteria for and scope of the permissible restrictions to the right to strike of public servants:

"As regards the denial of the right to strike to all established civil servants ('*Beamte*'), the Appendix to the Charter, amplifying Article 6, para. 4 thereof, lays down that 'it is understood that each Contracting

Party may, insofar as it is concerned, regulate the exercise of the right to strike by law, provided that any further restriction that this might place on the right can be justified under the terms of Article 31'. The latter Article does not permit any restrictions to the rights and principles set forth in the Charter except 'such as are prescribed by law and are necessary in a democratic society for the protection of the rights and freedoms of others or for the protection of public interest, national security, public health or morals'. The study undertaken showed however that it was manifestly impossible for a total denial of the right to strike, as embodied in Article 6 para. 4, to all established civil servants to be considered justifiable in the light of Article 31.

In the first place, although some established civil servants undoubtedly carry out tasks whose nature justifies strikes being prohibited under Article 31, this is not the case with a large proportion of them whose work may equally well be performed by non-established public employees (*Angestellte*), whereas only the latter are entitled to strike. The distinction between *'Beamte'* and *'Angestellte'* is thus based not on the nature of the duties performed but on a difference in legal status totally unconnected with the grounds on which the right to strike may be restricted under Article 31.

Secondly, it appears equally inadmissible that denying the right to strike to all *'Beamte'* should be regarded as 'necessary in a democratic society' for the protection of the rights and freedoms of others or for the protection of public interest, national security, public health or morals when no such denial is to be found in many democratic States that are Contracting Parties to the Charter.

While therefore the legislation of the Federal Republic of Germany could, without violating the European Social Charter, prohibit a strike by any *'Beamte'* – and even *'Angestellte'* – who perform functions affecting the public interest, national security, public health or morals, such a prohibition must be deemed contrary to the provisions of Article 6 para. 4 as amplified by the Appendix to the Charter, if it applies to all civil servants without distinction" (Conclusions IV, p. 48 and 49). In addition, the Committee held that the declaration of the Federal Republic of Germany could not have the force of a "reservation" restricting the scope of the Federal Republic's acceptance of the Charter's requirements (*ibidem*).

However, in the seventh cycle of supervision, in the light of the new situation brought about by the then recent ratification of the Charter by the Netherlands with a reservation concerning Article 6 para. 4 which had been accepted by all the member states and which did not affect the minimum requirements of Article 20, the Committee once more examined whether Germany's declaration could be regarded as a reservation of a similar nature. Even though the Committee considered that this was not the case, it decided not to revert to the German situation again since "it appeared that the Government of the Federal Republic of Germany had intended its declaration to have a similar effect to a reservation, and since if it had been made in due form such a reservation would have been acceptable, given that it would not have affected the minimum requirements of Article 20" (Conclusions VII, p. 39).

Since then, the Committee has ceased to refer to this issue concerning Germany, but the principles set out in that context have remained valid. Their application has led the Committee to adopt a negative conclusion for Denmark on the ground that civil servants are denied the right to strike by the Civil Servants Act. The ban on strikes applicable to the civil service takes the form of a general prohibition and as such could not be warranted by the restrictions authorised under the terms of Article 31 of the Charter (situation criticised since the fifth cycle; see in the last instance Conclusions XIII-1, p. 154 and XIII-3, p. 135).

For Cyprus, the question of the right to strike of public servants has remained pending: Article 27 para. 2 of the Constitution provides, *inter alia*, that a law may extend the prohibition on the right to strike for the armed forces and the police to the members of the public services. The Committee stressed that the adoption of such a law would not be in conformity with the Charter (Conclusions II, p. 187). However, this provision has never been applied and the Committee was informed that members of the public service had gone on strike on many occasions and that Section 63 of the 1990 Public Service Law provided that "the freedom of association and the unhampered exercise of the rights related to it are secured to the public officials". The Committee asked whether according to this provision, the right to strike was "one of the rights attached to freedom of association" and deferred its conclusion (Conclusions XIII-3, p. 134).

If all civil servants have the right to strike, "with the exception of certain categories, such as judges and officials in key administrative positions or responsible for essential services (health and security)", the Committee asks for a list of civil servants who do not have the right to strike (Conclusions XI-1, pp. 87 and 88, Iceland) and it considers the list in the light of Article 31: "From this list the Committee noted that not only personnel whose presence is indispensable were prohibited from striking, but also other categories such as janitors, cooks and telephone operators. In some cases, the limitation is restricted to one or two members of staff, such as the requirement that there should be at least one long-distance operator per shift in the Reykjavik telephone station. The Committee asked for an explanation as to why workers in apparently non-essential positions were denied the right to strike" (Conclusions XII-1, p. 128; see also Conclusions XIII-1, p. 155 and XIII-3, p. 135).[1]

The Committee has not as yet admitted any restriction of the right to strike for other categories than public servants. Thus, for example, it considered as not compatible with Article 6 para. 4:

a.   the restriction whereby workers belonging to a union which does not hold a negotiating licence under the Trade Unions Act 1941 do not enjoy the right to strike (Conclusions I, p. 185, Ireland; see in the last instance Conclusions XIII-3, p. 136).

b.   the restriction whereby salaried workers employed in non-profit making activities (restriction established by case law) do not enjoy the right to strike (Conclusions I, p. 185, Ireland).[2]

---

1 Iceland supplied a list of posts for which a minimum service must be maintained and the situation seems to be satisfactory.

2 This situation appears to have been remedied by the Trade Disputes (Amendment) Act which extended the personal scope of the 1906 Act to all employees (Conclusions VIII, p. 96).

3. Restrictions and limitations of the right to strike other than those covered under 1 and 2 above

a. Restrictions imposed by collective agreements

It must be recalled that restrictions on recourse to collective action are compatible with the Charter, if they are imposed by a collective agreement (see above, under "General", paragraph c. of the general interpretation given to Article 6 para. 4). Thus, the Committee considered as in conformity with Article 6 para. 4 restrictions on collective action imposed by mutual consent of the parties concerned for the purpose of limiting recourse to such action in the interests of the community or for users of essential services (Conclusions VIII, p. 98). This view was expressed by the Committee in relation to the Swedish Codetermination Act of 1976 which made it possible to impose, by collective agreement, severer restrictions than those laid down by the act itself.

b. Intervention of public authorities in strikes

It should be recalled that, according to the case law of the Committee, "an intervention of the public authorities to limit the exercise of the right to collective action is a very serious measure which could only be justified according to the relevant conditions laid down in Article 31 para. 1 of the Charter. Moreover the time during which this limitation takes place should be as short as possible and in any case should not exceed that which is needed to return to a normal situation" (Conclusions X-1, p. 74 and 75).

The Committee took this stand in the tenth cycle of supervision when examining the Danish Collective and Other Agreements (Renewal and Extension) Act of 31 March 1985, one of the main effects of which was to put a stop to current strikes and prevent further action in both the private and public sectors throughout the two-year period for which collective agreements had been extended (a complaint had been brought to the ILO Committee on Freedom of Association in respect of this act).

In the next (eleventh) supervision cycle the Committee criticised:

- Denmark, *inter alia*, for intervention in certain areas of the public sector to stop action and prolong existing agreements, thereby prohibiting strikes for the duration of these agreements through Act No. 246 of 8 May 1987 (Junior hospital doctors), Act No. 542 of August 1987 (computer workers) and Act No. 657 of May 1987 (seamen of the state-owned company). The Committee found that the legislative action taken went beyond the limits fixed in Article 31 (Conclusions XI-1, p. 87);

- Norway, on the ground that on several occasions it had imposed compulsory arbitration to end strikes in the public and private sector and specifically the oil and chemical industry under circumstances not justified within the meaning of Article 31 (Conclusions XI-1, pp. 89 and 90).

In the twelfth cycle of supervision, the Committee criticised:

- Denmark, in so far as the agreements prolonged by the acts adopted in 1987 were still in force during the reference period (Conclusions XII-1, p. 127);

- Iceland, as for a period of eleven months during the reference period Act No. 14 of 1988 prohibited all strikes and other industrial action. The Committee stressed that "a complete denial of the right to strike can hardly be considered as a "restriction" which might be justified under Article 31 of the Charter" (Conclusions XII-1, p. 128);[1]

- Norway, as the state intervened to bring to an end a strike by nurses by passing a law obliging the nurses to enter into compulsory arbitration under circumstances not justifiable within the terms of Article 31: it appeared that, while the strike in question clearly represented an inconvenience for a number of patients who were awaiting planned surgery (which might have been postponed had the strike continued), there was no question of cancelling or post-

---

1 This act was no longer in force at the end of the reference period; the situation was thus considered to be in conformity with the Charter on this point.

poning any emergency operation, so that it could not be contended that the government's intervention was justified under Article 31. Furthermore, the government intervened at the very beginning of the strike, before its effect could be validly assessed.

In addition, the Committee pointed out that its previous criticism, namely that the Norwegian Government effectively had the power to impose compulsory arbitration and thus to prohibit strikes in an unlimited manner, could only lead it to reach a negative conclusion in each supervision cycle where such power is exercised in an abusive manner, that is, beyond the limitations of Article 31. "The Committee considered that the apparent absence of any limitation on the government's power to intervene in strike action and the consequent absence of any protection of workers in itself constitute a breach of Article 6 para. 4, since without any such protection there is no real recognition of the right to strike as required by this provision of the Charter" (Conclusions XII-1,[1] p. 130; on the latter point, see in the last instance Conclusions XIII-3, pp. 141 and 142).

In the thirteenth supervision cycle, the Committee criticised:

Norway, as it had again resorted to compulsory arbitration to end a lawful strike by oil workers in the North Sea, only thirty-six hours after the beginning of the work stoppage. The ILO Committee on Freedom of Association had expressed doubts as to the compelling need for recourse to such arbitration (Conclusions XIII-1, pp. 158 and 159).

The Committee applied the principles defined in the context of public authority intervention to all the other limitations or restrictions put to the right to strike brought to its attention.

c.   Replacement of strikers

The Committee had to examine the issue of the replacement of strikers in the twelfth supervision cycle in connection with Germany where civil

---

1 The Committee of Ministers addressed a recommendation to Norway for the first part of the twelfth cycle.

servants (*Beamte*) were requisitioned in certain cases to replace striking state employees and manual workers (*Angestellte*) in the public services. Even though the Committee did not take a stand on the issue pending the result of an appeal to the Federal Constitutional Court against the judgement of the Federal Labour Tribunal which had accepted the principle of replacement, nevertheless it emphasised that "the requisitioning of civil servants was such as to seriously restrict the right of workers to strike as a means of defending their professional and economic interests and that requisitioning of any kind could be justified only in the light of Article 31 of the Charter" (Conclusions XII-2, pp. 113 and 114). In the next cycle the Committee noted that the Constitutional Court had ruled (2 March 1993) that such requisitions were incompatible with the German Constitution unless the matter was expressly regulated by law and drew attention to the fact that "if a law should be made in this field, requisitioning could be justified only with respect to Article 31 of the Charter as confirmed by its case law" (Conclusions XIII-2, p. 282).

d.   Restrictions on collective action imposed by the Courts

In the first supervision cycle the Committee had held that "where the limits within which the right to strike may be exercised have been determined, in a state, not by legislation but by the courts, it is for the Committee to examine whether the case law thus established is in accordance with the requirements of the Charter" (see above, under "General", para. e. of the general interpretation given by the Committee to Article 6 para. 4, or Conclusions I, p. 38).

The Committee applied this interpretation in the eleventh cycle of supervision when, for the first time, it had to examine judgments by the national courts of a Contracting Party in which Article 6 para. 4 and Article 31 of the Charter had been directly applied.

More specifically, in that cycle, the Netherlands' report provided the Committee with information on recent judgments relating to collective action. The Committee noted in particular the terms of the judgment of 30 May 1986, in which the Netherlands Supreme Court ruled that Article 6 para. 4 and Article 31 of the Charter were directly applicable in internal law by virtue of both Article 93 of the Netherlands Constitution and the wording of these two provision of the Charter.

After examining the criteria on which the Supreme Court had based its decision that the collective action launched in that particular case was a lawful measure[1] coming within the scope of Article 6 para. 4 and on examination of the comments submitted by workers' and employers' organisations under Article 23 of the Charter regarding the application of this provision, the Committee made the following comments:

–   "the Committee noted that the aforementioned judgment of the Supreme Court confirming the direct applicability in domestic law of Article 6 para. 4 and of Article 31 of the Charter thereby bestowed force of law on these two provision and afforded workers and employers the right to take legal action in the national courts to have the relevant provisions applied;

–   the different courts called upon to enforce Article 31 of the Charter will determine, by way of interpretation, and in relation to the circumstances of each case, whether the condition imposed by this provision to the application of any restrictions on the exercise of the right have been complied with. The Committee nevertheless reserves the right to verify in future whether the direct application of Article 31 by the Netherlands' courts conforms to its own case law" (Conclusions XI-1, pp. 88 and 89). It also asked the government to furnish in its reports information on cases restricting the right to strike brought before the courts.

In the first part of the thirteenth cycle the Committee examined the judgments reported by the government (Supreme Court Judgments of 22 August 1988, 19 April 1991 and 22 November 1992) and concluded that the Netherlands complied with the Charter. However, examining the Supreme Court judgment of 22 November 1992 concerning a con-

---

1 The Supreme Court considered that the collective action in question could be regarded as a means of defending the workers' right to negotiate their working conditions. Accordingly, the circumstances entailed a conflict of interests and thus, as borne out by the Committee of Independent Experts' case law, came within the scope of Article 6 para. 4.

flict between public health sector trade unions and the association set up to defend patients' and consumers' interests, the Committee noted that the court had based its judgement on Article 1401 (now Article 162) of the Civil Code (civil responsibility of a person acting unlawfully) to limit a collective action in time. The Supreme Court appeared to consider that damages caused to third parties could render the strike unlawful. Moreover, the Committee learned that, on the basis of Article 1401 of the Civil Code, first instance courts had limited the means or duration of collective action on the grounds of financial losses sustained by an employer. The Committee recalled its case law and "held that, on the basis of Article 31 of the Charter, damages caused to third parties and financial losses sustained by the employer could only be taken into consideration in exceptional cases, when justified by a pressing social need". It therefore asked for detailed information on cases brought before the Netherlands courts in which account had been taken of such considerations, on the persons who could request that a court limit the means or duration of collective action and on whether it was possible to appeal against the judgements of First Instance Courts in this field (Conclusions XIII-1, p. 158 and in the last instance Conclusions XIII-3, p. 139; see also p. 140, the same issue raised with respect to the Netherlands Antilles).

4.   The consequences of strikes

The Committee's case law reflects two types of consequence of strike action, which according to their circumstances may not be in compliance with the requirements of the Charter: one concerns the termination of an employment contract, the other civil and criminal responsibility and other sanctions.

a.   The effect of a strike on contracts of employment

In the first supervision cycle, the Committee analysed in depth the compatibility with the Charter of a rule according to which a strike terminates the contract of employment, as it had noted that in their legislation Norway, the United Kingdom and Denmark regarded strikes as constituting a termination of contracts of employment (see above under "General", paragraph i. of the general interpretation). In short the Committee took the view that such a rule is "in principle" contrary to Article 6 para. 4 as it constitutes a restriction of the right to strike, but if in practice those participating in a strike are, after its termination, fully reinstated and if their previously acquired rights are not impaired, the formal termination of their contract of employment by the strike does not constitute a violation of the Charter.

In the second supervision cycle the Committee concluded that Norway complied with the Charter, since it ascertained that despite the termination of the contract of employment, workers were granted the same rights after the strike (Conclusions II, p. 29).

This was not the case for the United Kingdom, however. The Committee concluded that this country was not complying with the Charter (*ibidem*). The conclusion has remained negative up to the last (thirteenth) supervision cycle. Criticism of the United Kingdom is based on the fact that legislation allows an employer to dismiss collectively all employees carrying out strike action, and to reinstate them on a selective basis three months after dismissal. The ILO Committee of Experts on the Application of Conventions and Recommendations also recommended that the United Kingdom amend its legislation to bring it in line with ILO Convention No. 87 (Conclusions XIII-1, p. 160).

The Committee does not accept the arguments of the United Kingdom Government that the situation is not contrary to the Charter on the ground that employees are fully aware, when deciding, on a secret ballot, to take collective action, that their action entails the breach of their contract, that it would be impracticable to require employers to keep jobs open indefinitely and that the power of the employer to dismiss employees on strike ensures a "proper balance" between management and labour. Collective dismissal is seen as the counterpart of strike action.

The Committee considered that "the possibility for all strikers to be dismissed, although rarely resorted to by employers, represents a threat of such an importance that it unduly restricts the exercise of the right to collective action as protected by Article 6 para. 4 of the Charter"

(Conclusions XI-1, p. 90; see most recently Conclusions XIII-1,[1] pp. 159 and 160 and XIII-3, pp. 144 and 145).

Another Contracting Party found as not complying is Ireland, as under the 1977 Unfair Dismissals Act the possibility exists for an employer to dismiss collectively all employees for taking strike action (Addendum to Conclusions XI-2, p. 25; in the last instance Conclusions XIII-3, p. 136).

b.   Other sanctions

The other consequences of strike action which have been found in violation of the Charter are cases of civil or criminal responsibility of trade unions or their members in Ireland, as well as another type of sanction in France.

In Ireland, the right to strike is not specifically guaranteed by law but is rather protected by granting striking workers immunity from the criminal and civil consequences of their strike action (Addendum to Conclusions XI-2, p. 26).

It must be recalled that the Committee is of the opinion that criminal or civil liability of individual members of trade unions or employers' associations in the event of illegal collective action is in keeping with the Charter (see above, under "General", paragraph h. of the general interpretation given to Article 6 para. 4).

With respect to Ireland, the situations criticised concern legal strikes. They are as follows:

–   state employees could be prosecuted under Section 9 sub-section 2 of the 1939 Offences against the State Act for taking industrial action (ie. striking is an offence).[2] Even though this provision appears

---

1 The Committee of Ministers addressed a recommendation to the United Kingdom for the first part of the thirteenth supervision cycle and a second recommendation for the third part of the thirteenth cycle.

2 The last Irish report explained that following the entry into force of the 1982 Trade Disputes (Amendment) Act, the right to strike was guaranteed in all branches of the public

not to have been enforced in practice the Committee felt that the potential for prosecution rendered the situation not in conformity with the Charter (Addendum to Conclusions XI-2, pp. 24 and 25);

– there is no protection for a trade union not holding a negotiating licence and for its members against civil action by the employer for damages in the event of peaceful incitement to collective action or against an action seeking an injunction to put an end to a strike.[1] The Committee did not accept the arguments of the Irish Government that the great majority of workers were members of a trade union holding a negotiating licence. In its view, this lack of protection for members of trade unions not holding a negotiating licence and workers who are not members of trade unions, was not compatible with Article 6 para. 4 (Conclusions XIII-1, p. 156; in the last instance, Conclusions XIII-3, p. 136);

– under Section 16 of the 1875 Conspiracy and Protection of Property Act merchant seamen in Ireland were not protected from criminal prosecution for conspiracy in respect of acts in contemplation or furtherance of trade disputes (these provisions no longer had a practical application) and by Section 225.1e of the 1894 Merchant Shipping Act, it is a criminal offence, punishable by imprisonment, for seamen to combine to disobey lawful demands or to neglect duty. The Committee held that "these provisions act effectively as a prohibition to strike action on the part of merchant seamen". After recalling its case law according to which "while in accordance with the Appendix to Article 6 para. 4 a Contracting Party may regulate the right to strike, it must do so by law (Conclusions X-1, p. 76) and may only impose such restrictions as may be justified under Article 31 of the Charter (Conclusions II, p. 27, Conclusions X-1, pp. 74-75, Conclusions X-1, p. 76, Conclusions X-2, p. 75)", the Committee concluded that a review of the above two acts showed that "the lack of immunity from prosecution is not limited in any

---

sector except the *Garda Siochana* and the armed forces. The Committee asked which restrictions were put in practice on the right to strike (Conclusions XIII-3, p. 136).

1 The 1990 Industrial Relations Act continued to protect only trade unions holding a negotiating licence and its members.

way, so that it cannot be contended that the consequent limitation of the right to strike of merchant seamen was justified under Article 31 of the Charter" (Addendum to Conclusions XI-2, p. 26; see most recently Conclusions XIII-1,[1] p. 156 and Conclusions XIII-3, p. 136 in which the Committee considered that even if these provisions were no longer applied, the fact that they existed was contrary to the Charter).

In France, salary deductions in the case of state civil servants (not civil servants in local government and the hospital service) exercising their right to strike are not proportional to the length of the strike because of the application of the rule of the indivisible thirtieth, which was abolished in 1982 but reintroduced in 1987. This rule, according to which salary deductions are assessed in daily thirtieths whether the civil servant works for a day or an hour, and which makes possible deductions in salary larger than the length of the strike, was considered by the Committee as being a form of sanction which did not appear to be compatible with the free exercise of the right to strike (situation criticised for the first time in the thirteenth cycle: Conclusions XIII-1, pp. 154 and 155; see in the last instance Conclusions XIII-3, p. 135).

In a general question (Conclusions XIII-1, p. 153), the Committee asked that all states having accepted Article 6 para. 4 indicate "the extent to which deductions from salaries of striking workers are in proportion to the actual duration of the strike, in the private and public sector". Until now, no reference has been made to situations similar to that of France.

5.   Lockout

As already stated, the Charter does not mention explicitly the right to lock out but it should be considered as protected, as otherwise the words "the right of employers to collective action" would be devoid of any meaning as the lockout is the principal, if not the only, form of such action at the disposal of employers.

---

[1] The Committee of Ministers addressed a recommendation to Ireland for the first part of the thirteenth cycle.

In 1971, on the basis of this interpretation, the Committee found Italy, where locking out was considered as a "civil delict" as not complying with the Charter (Conclusions II, p. 29). The conclusion remained negative until the ninth cycle of supervision as the compensation which employers had to pay in cases of lockout showed that this right could not be freely exercised (Conclusions III, p. 38) whereas case law recognised the employer's right to close his firm only when illegal action made such closure inevitable (Conclusions IV, p. 51 and V, p. 51).

In the eighth supervision cycle, the Committee made the following more precise statement concerning lockouts in a general observation:

"The Committee pointed out in the first place that if, by virtue of Article 6 para. 4, the Charter recognises the right of workers and employers to collective action where conflicts of interest arise, it does certainly not raise any obstacle to the existence of legislation regulating the exercise of the right to call a lock-out, as well as of the right to strike, provided that neither legislation nor judicial decisions affect the very existence of the right thus recognised.

However, subject to the aforesaid, the Charter does not necessarily imply that legislation and case law should establish full legal equality between the right to strike – which the Charter indeed mentions explicitly and which is recognised as a fundamental right by the Constitution of several member States – and the right to call a lock-out. Consequently, the Committee thought, in the first place, that a State party to the Charter cannot be found at fault for not having passed legislation regulating the exercise of lock-out and, in the second place, that the competent tribunals were entitled to place certain restrictions of the exercise of lock-out in specific cases where it would in particular constitute an abuse of right or where it would be devoid of justification on the ground of 'force majeure' or of the disorganisation of the enterprise caused by the workers' collective action" (Conclusions VIII, p. 95).

Putting this stand into application in the next supervision cycle, the Committee found France, where the tendency of case law was to move "away from the conception of lockout as a breach of contract by the employer and towards justification of lockout by reference to circumstances such as *force majeure*, abuse of the right to strike by the employees, compelling circumstances or disorganisation of the company by the workers' collective action" to be in compliance with the Charter. It also mentioned, as a further possibility of justifying the lockout, the authority of the head of the company to manage, when order and the safety of property and persons are endangered on company premises (Conclusions IX-2, pp. 47 and 48).

In the same cycle, as regards Italy, the Committee noted the information on lock-out showing that "an employer can lawfully decide to close the firm down during a collective dispute if the action of the striking workers takes violent or extreme forms (sabotage, interference with the right to work of non-striking employees and violence). In such cases, the employer's action is designed to preserve the means of production and prevent disruption of the work process. The courts are able to verify whether this is in fact the case, and the Committee thought that these circumstances conformed to the principles which it had itself considered admissible (see Conclusions VIII) as justification for 'regulating recourses to lock-out'. That being so, the Committee was able to conclude that Italy complied with this provision of the Charter" (Conclusions IX-2, pp. 48 and 49).

Summary of assessment of compliance

The Committee's conclusion is currently negative in respect of:

Denmark: civil servants are denied the right to strike (Conclusions XIII-3, p. 135; see 2 above).

France: salary deductions in the case of state civil servants exercising their right to strike are not entirely proportional to the length of the strike (Conclusions XIII-3, p. 135; see 4 b. above).

Germany: the only lawful strikes are those aimed at the conclusion of a collective agreement and called or endorsed by a trade union (Conclusions XIII-2, p. 282; see 1 above).

Iceland: the right to strike of civil servants is limited by law to situations where the strike is called with the aim of reaching a collective agreement. Also, the right to call a strike in connection with negotiations for the conclusion or the total or partial renewal of collective agreements is exclusively in the hands of trade unions (Conclusions XIII-3, p. 135; see 1 above).

Ireland:

a. legislation allows an employer to dismiss collectively all employees for taking strike action (Conclusions XIII-3, p. 136; see 4 a. above);

b. protection against civil action taken by the employer in the event of a strike is not extended to trade unions not holding a negotiating licence and their members (Conclusions XIII-3, p. 136; see 4 b. above);

c. merchant seamen are not protected by law from criminal prosecution for conspiracy in respect of acts relating to trade disputes (Conclusions XIII-3, p. 136; see 4 b. above).

Norway: the government may intervene during a strike and impose arbitration in circumstances which go beyond those provided for in Article 31 of the Charter (Conclusions XIII-3, pp. 141 and 142; see 3 above).

The *United Kingdom:* legislation permits an employer to dismiss collectively employees taking part in a strike and to reemploy them selectively three months after dismissal (Conclusions XIII-3, pp. 144 and 145; see 4 a. above).

The Committee's conclusion is currently deferred in respect of Belgium (first report – Conclusions XIII-2, pp. 280 to 282), Cyprus (Conclusions XIII-3, p. 134), Finland (first report – Conclusions XIII-3, pp. 279 and 280), Italy (Conclusions XIII-3, pp. 137 and 138), Malta (Conclusions XIII-3, p. 138) and Portugal (first report – Conclusions XIII-3, pp. 280 and 281).

Article 7 – The right of children and young persons to protection

General

This Article provides for the protection of children and adolescents, a category of the population considered as being comparatively vulnerable and therefore in need of special protection. This protection extends to the areas of health, education and employment and working conditions.

It consists of ten paragraphs, covering various aspects of the safeguards of the right to protection of children and young persons which the Committee in Conclusions I (p. 41) defined as follows:

–   minimum age of admission to employment (paragraphs 1 and 2);

–   working hours (paragraphs 4 and 6);

–   exclusion from employment in certain types of activity (paragraphs 3 and 8);

–   right to fair remuneration (paragraph 5);

–   length of paid annual holidays (paragraph 7);

- the right to regular medical control in certain cases (paragraph 9);

- protection against physical and moral dangers (paragraph 10).

In its first Conclusions the Committee made a comparison between the scope of the first nine paragraphs of Article 7 and its paragraph 10 and examined the possibility that Article 7 could coincide in its scope with other provisions of the Charter, especially Article 17.

With respect to the former issue, the Committee noted that "paragraph 10 is far broader in scope than the first nine paragraphs. In fact, paragraphs 1 to 9 cover the protection of children and young persons against the dangers of working life, whereas paragraph 10 places an obligation upon the states which accept it to protect young people against any dangers which threaten them, even if these dangers are not connected with their work".

With respect to the second issue the Committee, whilst accepting that "in fact both these Articles of the Charter are particularly concerned with providing 'protection' for children" and admitting that "two or more provisions in the Charter might well have the same content in part, since the Contracting Parties were free to accept the Charter only in part" took the view that "when the Charter was drawn up, it had not been intended that these two Articles should overlap and that the two provisions in question were different in scope. According to the Committee, the provisions of Article 17 applied to children of pre-school age, while children and young people were covered by Article 7 once they had reached school age". (Conclusions I, pp. 40 and 41).

In its General introduction to Conclusions XII-1, the Committee expressed concern at the fact that these provisions of the Charter, which should constitute a common minimum standard of protection, were still not accepted by all the Contracting Parties or fully complied with by those which had accepted the undertakings therein. The Committee counts among the chief causes of non-compliance unduly long working hours, particularly for children below school-leaving age, and gaps in legislation which exclude from protection certain categories of young workers.

In Conclusions XIII-2 (p. 77), the Committee asked all Contracting Parties to indicate the following in their next report on Article 7:

"1.   Exactly which regulations governed the work of children employed in family businesses;

2.   What was the supervision machinery;

3.   An estimate of the numbers of children employed in family businesses."

Paragraph 1 – Minimum age of admission to employment

Under this paragraph, the Contracting Parties undertake:

> "to provide that the minimum age of admission to employment shall be fifteen years, subject to exceptions for children employed in prescribed light work without harm to their health, morals or education".

The main purpose of this provision was defined by the Committee as being "to ensure that young people below the age of fifteen are effectively protected against the dangers of admission to employment which is likely to have a harmful effect on their health, morals, development or education". However, since it would be impossible or undesirable "to impose an absolute ban on the employment of children" (because for example of the educational value of work) "the Charter provides for an exception to the general rule prohibiting the employment of children". It specifies that children can be employed "in prescribed light work" which does not expose them to the risks mentioned. (First report on certain provisions of the Charter which have not been accepted, p. 12).

The case law of the Committee regarding this paragraph can be summed up as follows:

a.   paragraph 1 applies to all categories of work including agricultural, domestic work and work in the services sector and to all types of enterprises, including family businesses.

The Committee took the view that agricultural and domestic work cannot *a priori* be regarded as "light" work within the meaning of this paragraph and on this basis found, throughout all the cycles of supervision, Contracting Parties which allowed in general the admission of children below fifteen to such work as not complying with the Charter (Conclusions I, p. 42; Conclusions II, p. 30; Conclusions III, p. 39; Conclusions IV, p. 53; Conclusions V, p. 56; Conclusions VI, p. 44; Conclusions VII, p. 41; Conclusions VIII, p. 101; Conclusions X-2, p. 80; Conclusions XI-2, p. 82; Conclusions XII-2, p. 119; Conclusions XIII-2, p. 78, Italy).

Moreover, the Committee considered the general exclusion of children who work in family businesses from the prohibition of work to be incompatible with the Charter. (Conclusions VI, p. 44, France). In the seventh cycle of supervision, when examining the situation in France, the Committee recalled its established case law to the effect that the regulations prohibiting the employment of children below fifteen must be applied to all economic sectors and to all types of business, including family enterprises, exceptions being allowed only for light work and laid down in limitative lists. It considered that the situation in France, where children worked in family enterprises, could not be considered as complying with paragraph 1 in the absence of complete information on the manner in which the competent authorities ensure adequate protection of children against the risks of exploitation, even within family enterprises (Conclusions VII, p. 41, France).

In addition, when examining the reports on non-accepted provisions of the Charter, the Committee stressed that "the protection guaranteed by Article 7 of the Charter must be afforded, without distinction, to all young people below the age of fifteen, whether or not they were bound to their employers by employment or apprenticeship contracts" (First report on certain provisions of the Charter which have not been accepted, p. 17);

b. to comply with paragraph 1, a state not only has to fix the minimum age of admission to employment at fifteen years but also has to take the necessary steps to ensure that this rule is adequately enforced (Conclusions XI-2, p. 82, Spain);

c. in general, admission to any type of work is contrary to the Charter. The types of work to which children may be admitted by derogation must:

– be laid down clearly in a limitative list;

– be genuinely light;

– in no way prejudice the moral, welfare, health or education of the children concerned (Conclusions V, p. 55).

To assess whether the work involved is in fact light, the Committee has regard in particular to the nature of the work permitted, the maximum working hours authorised, the time at which the work may be performed (before or after school, on public holidays, throughout the school holiday period, etc.) and the existence of a statutory rest period (First report on certain provisions of the Charter which have not been accepted and Conclusions VIII, pp. 101 and 102, France and the Netherlands).

Exceptions to the general prohibition of work considered acceptable under paragraph 1 include:

i. children authorised to work in the performing arts;

ii. children following preparatory courses for apprenticeship during the last two years of their schooling; and

iii. children authorised to work during part of their school holidays (Conclusions VI, p. 43, France). Time worked during school holidays by children subject to compulsory school attendance is also relevant to this provision, as exceptions for prescribed light work are admissible only if they are unlikely to harm the child's health or education (Conclusions VIII, p. 103). Allowing children to work throughout the holidays and without a statutory rest period (apart from the thirty-six hour per week of rest which is clearly inadequate), was considered as inconsistent with paragraph 1 (Conclusions VIII, p. 103, Sweden).

In the tenth cycle of supervision the Committee, when examining the situation in Spain, summed up its case law on this provision as follows: "Contracting Parties had to ensure that work carried out by young people who were under fifteen or were required to attend school was indeed 'light', that it was not performed in the morning before school, that it was of reasonable length and that the child was free from any work for at least one day of the week and for half the school holidays" (Conclusions X-2, p. 81).

The term "prescribed" qualifying light work implies that in each Contracting Party where children are allowed to carry out light work, there must be a list of light occupations to which children under fifteen could be admitted. There could also be a negative list, indicating the occupations in which these children could not be permitted to be employed. The lists may be established by legislation, regulations, case law or administrative practice. It is with the help of lists or other appropriate means that the competent bodies can objectively judge the genuinely light character of the work which children under fifteen may be permitted to do and the dangers to which their physical health, morals and education may be exposed in consequence (see for example the First report on certain provisions of the Charter which have not been accepted, p. 12).

In the thirteenth cycle of supervision, the Committee, finding the description of light work given by a Contracting Party in its report to be very general recalled that "the prescription of work authorised on an exceptional basis could not be left to the entire discretion of the supervisory bodies and that in the absence of a list of types of work, each state must indicate in its legislation or regulations, for all sectors of activity, the criteria for assessing the light nature of such work, and those for assessing the risks of adverse effects on children's health, morals or education. It asked whether such criteria were established and requested that the next report include examples of light work permitted before the legal age of admission to employment" (Conclusions XIII-3, p. 285, Portugal).

d.   the fulfilment of the obligation deriving from this provision entails implementation of a series of general measures (enforcement of compulsory school attendance, supervision by the health authorities, raising of school-leaving age to sixteen, etc.) as well as specific measures to be taken by the Labour Inspectorate (Conclusions VIII, p. 101).

Assessment of compliance

The Contracting Parties found as not complying are:

France: because of the absence of specific regulations protecting children related to their employer and working in family business (Conclusions XIII-2, p. 77 and 78);

Greece:[1] the 1989 Act on the protection of minors, providing *inter alia*, for an age limit for admission to employment in conformity with the Charter's requirements, does not include agricultural, forestry or livestock work of a family nature (Conclusions XIII-2, p. 78);

Italy:[2] Act No. 977 of 1967 authorises the employment of persons under fifteen in agriculture and domestic work. There are no regulations governing the situation of young workers related to their employer and no effective system of supervision (Conclusions XIII-2, pp. 78 and 79);

Spain: there is no minimum age of admission to employment for children working in family businesses without an employment contract, since the Workers' Statute, which prohibits work by persons under sixteen does not, in principle, apply to work in a family business (Conclusions XIII-2, p. 79);

Sweden: on two grounds; the continuing absence of legislation on the minimum age of admission to employment in the employer's household, and the absence of protection of children under fifteen years against

1 The Committee of Ministers addressed a recommendation to Greece for the first part of the thirteenth supervision cycle.

2 The Committee of Ministers addressed a recommendation to Italy for the second part of the twelfth supervision cycle, which was renewed for the second part of the thirteenth cycle.

excessive working hours during school holidays, as they may work throughout the holidays without a compulsory period of rest and the working hours during the school holidays – eight per day or forty weekly – are considered excessive (Conclusions XIII-2, pp. 79 and 80).

Paragraph 2 – Higher minimum age in certain occupations

Under this paragraph, the Contracting Parties undertake:

> "to provide that a higher minimum age of admission to employment shall be fixed with respect to prescribed occupations regarded as dangerous or unhealthy."

The Committee interpreted the expression "minimum age" as covering the same minimum age as indicated in Article 7 para. 1, which is fifteen years, regardless of whether the Contracting State concerned by paragraph 2 has accepted paragraph 1 (Conclusions I, p. 186).

The obligation of Contracting Parties is to set a higher minimum age for occupations regarded as dangerous or unhealthy. The precise age to be attained is not indicated in the Charter. In the second part of the thirteenth cycle of supervision, however, the Committee set the minimum age for admission to work involving exposure to benzene at eighteen.

In this respect, in the tenth cycle of supervision, the Committee noted that in Italy by virtue of the Men and Women (Equality at Work) Act (No. 903 of 1977) the minimum age of employment for work involving exposure to benzene, (which was previously fixed at sixteen for men and eighteen for women) was lowered to sixteen for both sexes. It asked for detailed explanations of the technical or medical considerations on which this change was made and on the situation concerning benzene-related occupational diseases (Conclusions X-2, p. 82, Italy). In the twelfth cycle of supervision, the Committee asked additionally how the above-mentioned change was reconciled with the government's obligations under ILO Convention No. 136 (Benzene, 1971) which Italy had ratified.

In the thirteenth cycle of supervision (second part), the Committee noted:

a.   the recognition in the Italian report that there were no medical or technical reasons inherently justifying a reduction to sixteen years of age for both sexes of the minimum age for access to employment involving exposure to benzene and that the amendment was intended solely to ensure equality between the sexes;

b.   the statement of the Italian Government that it was unable to provide statistics on benzene-related occupational diseases affecting young people. The Committee reiterated its case law, according to which the minimum age referred to in this paragraph should in any event be higher than fifteen and underlined that compliance with it meant that, in drawing up the list of occupations regarded as dangerous or unhealthy, the Contracting Parties were required to take into account the nature of each of the occupations concerned and the extent to which it was dangerous or unhealthy, and fix the appropriate minimum age at which adolescents could be employed in that occupation without disproportionate health risks.

"Regarding the specific case of occupations involving exposure to benzene, the Committee noted that:

–   scientific research demonstrated both that benzene is particularly dangerous (because of the risks to health and of fire and explosion) and also that adolescents were particularly vulnerable to this danger;

–   that ILO Convention No. 136, ratified by Italy in 1981, set the minimum age for admission to occupations involving exposure to benzene at eighteen for both sexes, with the sole exception of training or educational activities, where adequate technical and medical supervision was required;

–   in the European Union, the Directive of 22 June 1994 on the Protection of Young Persons at Work provided for a ban on the employment of young people under the age of eighteen in 'work involving harmful exposure to substances which are toxic, carcinogenic, cause heritable genetic damage, or harm the unborn child or which in any other way chronically affect human health' (such work included, *inter alia*, 'work involving harmful exposure to the physical, biological and chemical agents' indicated in an appendix which referred to a list of agents including benzene).

The Committee therefore considered that a country could not be regarded as complying with Article 7 para. 2 if it established at lower than eighteen the age for which employment in occupations involving exposure to benzene was normally prohibited and was therefore obliged to adopt a negative conclusion in respect of Italy" (Conclusions XIII-2, pp. 81 and 82).

This was the first time the Committee specified that the "minimum age" in this paragraph should be eighteen in respect of a specific occupation.

The term "prescribed occupations" suggests that a Contracting Party has some discretion to determine which occupations are to be treated as dangerous or unhealthy, although this is subject to the restriction that Article 7 para. 2 cannot be limited to exclude manifestly dangerous or unhealthy activities from its scope.

Acting on this basis, the Committee rejected the view of a Contracting Party that jobs in the commerce, transport, hotel or catering sectors did not qualify as "dangerous or unhealthy", as in fact "certain activities carried out in these sectors were beyond all doubt dangerous or unhealthy". (Conclusions III, p. 39, Germany). Moreover, in the twelfth cycle of supervision, the Committee asked the Maltese Government to indicate whether the prohibition of the employment of young people under eighteen in specified work processes regarded as dangerous applied only to factory work or whether it also covered other economic sectors, in particular agriculture and work in family businesses or jobs involving the shifting of loads, as some of these jobs might also be dangerous or unhealthy (Conclusions XII-2, p. 120, Malta). In the thirteenth cycle of supervision it asked for additional information on any other measures to protect children and young persons from other risks, such as those incurred through chemical products in general (and benzene and asbestos in particular) carcinogenic products and agents, certain types of machinery, air pollution, noise and vibration and so on (Conclusions XIII-2, p. 287, Malta).

Assessment of compliance

On the whole, the Contracting Parties have been found to comply with this provision, as the minimum age for admission to such occupations was fixed at sixteen, seventeen or eighteen. Some of them have even improved the protection afforded by extending further the list of dangerous occupations in which the employment of children and adolescents is forbidden (see for example Conclusions XI-1, p. 92, Sweden).

The only Contracting Party found as not complying is:

Italy: the situation was found not to be in conformity because of the minimum age for admission to work involving exposure to benzene (Conclusions XIII-2, p. 80 to 82).

In the revised Charter, Article 7 para. 2 reads as follows:

"With a view to ensuring the effective exercise of the right of children and young persons to protection, the Parties undertake:

...

2. to provide that the minimum age of admission to employment shall be 18 years with respect to prescribed occupations regarded as dangerous or unhealthy;"

The appendix to this provision specifies that:

"This provision does not prevent Parties from providing in their legislation that young persons not having reached the minimum age laid down may perform work in so far as it is absolutely necessary for their vocational training where such work is carried out in accordance with conditions prescribed by the competent authority and measures are taken to protect the health and safety of these young persons."

Paragraph 3 – Safeguarding the full benefit of compulsory education

Under this paragraph, the Contracting Parties undertake:

> "to provide that persons who are still subject to compulsory education shall not be employed in such work as would deprive them of the full benefit of their education."

In the first supervision cycle, the Committee interpreted this provision as requiring a state which had accepted it to ensure that children still subject to compulsory education were not employed in work likely to deprive them of the full benefit of education. The measures taken should at the very least limit the employment of children still attending school to work after school hours or at weekends (Conclusions I p. 43). This interpretation was confirmed in the third cycle of supervision when the Committee reiterated that this provision required governments to take specific measures which, *inter alia*, set a maximum limit on the duration of work done by children before or after school hours and restricted the permissible types of work to prescribed light occupations. (Conclusions III, p. 40).

In the fifth supervision cycle, the Committee stressed that "the aim of this provision is primarily that of permitting children and young persons to draw the full beneficial effects from compulsory school attendance and of ensuring that any occupational activity exercised outside school hours does not have an adverse effect on such compulsory education. It therefore follows that mere school attendance would not suffice, if the necessary measures are not taken by Contracting States to avoid any interference, through occupational activities, with such education" (Conclusions V, p. 57).

The view that school attendance alone, even if satisfactory, is insufficient evidence that work performed outside school hours does not detract from the full benefit of education was again stated in the eleventh cycle (Conclusions XI-2, p. 85, Italy).

Whilst accepting that work during holidays can give children valuable experience, the Committee pointed out that the main purpose of holidays is to let young people rest after a year of study in order to derive greater benefit from the following year's course (Conclusions XII-1, p. 136 referring to Conclusions XI-1, p. 92).

According to the case law of the Committee:

– children under school-leaving age related to their employer are also covered by this provision, (Conclusions V, pp. 57 and 58, Conclusions VI, p. 46, Ireland). This applies even to children related to their employer when they are not employees (Conclusions XI-2, p. 85, Spain);

– in all sectors of the economy, only light work should be permitted and the conditions governing the performance of such work should be laid down to ensure that its nature and duration are suited to the age and development of those concerned, (Conclusions VI, p. 47, Italy and Norway). Work over a certain number of hours per week could stop children benefiting fully from education, as rest periods would not be sufficient. A total of twenty-five hours per week was held not to be in conformity (Conclusions II, p. 32). Three hours maximum working time on school days and six to eight hours on weekdays when there is no school were also considered excessive. (Conclusions IV, p. 54, Austria);

– the ratification of ILO Convention No. 10 on the Age for Admission of Children to Employment in Agriculture does not necessarily mean that Article 7 para. 3 is being complied with, since the scope of the protection of the two instruments is not the same. Although Convention No. 10 ensured regular school attendance, in the sense of children being physically present at school, the Social Charter went further as it imposed an obligation on Contracting Parties to prohibit employment outside school in such work as would deprive children of the full benefit of education (Conclusions VIII, p. 106, Austria);

– important factors in assessing compliance are: minimum age of exemption, maximum permissible working time, rest periods and authorised (or prohibited) work (Conclusions XIII-2, p. 83, Austria). Authorised work should not take place at night, before school, on the weekly rest day, on public holidays or throughout the entire school holiday period (Conclusions VIII, p. 108);

- as regards the question of the hours which children can be required to work during their school holidays and the possibility of working throughout their holidays, the Committee emphasised that "the existence of a compulsory weekly rest period would not be sufficient if the child worked for up to eight hours a day and forty hours a week for the entire duration of holidays, since in such a case the aim of this provision would not be attained. It would indeed seem that in such circumstances, uninterrupted employment during the school holidays could have adverse effects on compulsory school attendance, inasmuch as it might impair the receptive capacity of a child who had not had a sufficient period of rest" (Conclusions VIII, p. 109, Sweden).

Work during school holidays can give children valuable experience. As, however, the main purpose of holidays is to let young people rest in order to derive greater benefit from the next year's course, if the possibility of working during holidays does exist for young persons, this work must be undertaken under certain conditions, namely the daily and weekly work should not be excessive and at least half of their school holidays should be devoted to an obligatory rest period (Conclusions XI-1, p. 94, Sweden; Conclusions XII-1, p. 136 and Conclusions XIII-2, p. 85, the Netherlands).

Assessment of compliance

The Contracting Parties found as not complying are:

Austria: on two grounds; with regard to the agricultural sector, the provisions at the national level governing the employment of young persons still subject to compulsory education (the Agricultural Labour Act No. 287 of 1984) were too general and there remained an absence of adequate and precise regulation in the Länder, although the act itself stipulated that the necessary steps for its application were to be taken by the Länder (Conclusions XIII-2, pp. 83 and 84). The criticism was first made in the tenth cycle;

France: for the same reasons as in paragraph 1 – due to the absence of specific regulations protecting children related to their employer and working in a family business (Conclusions XIII-2, p. 84);

Greece:[1] on the same grounds as for paragraph 1 – employment in agriculture, forestry and livestock work of a family nature was not covered by Act No. 1837 of 1989 (Conclusions XIII-2, pp. 84 and 85);

Ireland:[2] a. children related to their employer enjoyed none of the protection required by this provision of the Charter and b. for other children over fourteen, the length of work permitted during school holidays was excessive (Conclusions XIII-2, p. 85). The criticism was first made in the second supervision cycle for point a. and in the seventh cycle for point b.;

Italy: because of the absence of an effective supervision system. The legislation prohibiting the employment of children subject to compulsory education was still widely and frequently infringed (Conclusions XIII-2, p. 85). The criticism was first expressed in the eighth cycle of supervision;

the *Netherlands:* adolescents of compulsory school age and over fifteen could work throughout the school holidays for up to eight hours a day and forty hours a week. They could also deliver newspapers from 6 am onwards on school days (Conclusions XIII-2, p. 85). The conclusion has been negative as regards the delivery of newspapers since the eighth cycle (first report) and as regards holiday work since the ninth cycle;

Norway:[3] It was possible for children over thirteen still subject to compulsory education to work during school terms for a total of forty-nine

---

1 The Committee of Ministers addressed a recommendation to Greece for the first part of the thirteenth supervision cycle.

2 The Committee of Ministers addressed a recommendation to Ireland for the first part of the thirteenth supervision cycle.

3 The Committee of Ministers addressed a recommendation to Norway for the first part of the twelfth supervision cycle, which was renewed for the second part of the thirteenth cycle.

hours at school and out of school which was excessive for children of that age (even though the total number of working hours and school hours cannot exceed eight hours a day, taking into account the duration of classes, it is possible for children to work for nineteen hours per week) (Conclusions XII-1, p. 136 and Conclusions XIII-2, p. 86). The conclusion has been negative since the eleventh cycle (eleventh report);

Sweden: on the ground that the working hours during school holidays of children subject to compulsory education are excessive (Conclusions XIII-2, p. 87). The Committee omitted from the latest Conclusions its previous criticism for lack of legislation stipulating a minimum working age for work performed in the home of the employer, which had been made from the sixth to the thirteenth cycles (Conclusions XIII-1, p. 164);

Spain: for the same reason as for paragraph 1, which was that children related to their employer and not remunerated were not protected by the employment legislation which set the minimum age of employment at sixteen years (Conclusions XIII-2, p. 86);

Turkey:[1] the Labour Act of 25 August 1971, which fixed the minimum age for employment and regulated the working hours of children attending school, excluded from its scope many sectors of the economy, in particular the agricultural sector, craft and construction activities, domestic work, etc. (Conclusions XIII-1, pp. 229 and 230 and Conclusions XIII-3, p. 293);

the *United Kingdom:* children under school-leaving age were allowed to work as from 7 am (in light non-industrial work) and for up to twenty-five hours a week in Great Britain and twenty-seven in Northern Ireland if under fifteen (Conclusions XIII-2, p. 87). The criticism for excessive working hours of children still subject to compulsory schooling was first made in the sixth cycle (Conclusions VI, p. 49).

---

1 The Committee of Ministers addressed a recommendation to Turkey for the third part of the thirteenth supervision cycle.

Paragraph 4 – Working hours for young persons under sixteen years of age

Under this paragraph, the Contracting Parties undertake:

> "to provide that the working hours of persons under sixteen years of age shall be limited in accordance with the needs of their development, and particularly with their need for vocational training".

Article 33 of the Charter applies to this paragraph, which means that it is complied with by showing that "the great majority of the workers concerned", in this case persons under sixteen, benefit from its terms. The application of Article 33 also means that the undertaking in this paragraph can be satisfied by legislation, collective agreements or other means.

Paragraph 4 is concerned with the employment of persons under sixteen who have left school. The question as to the work which can be carried out by young persons still in compulsory schooling is examined under Article 7 para. 3 (Addendum to Conclusions XI-2, p. 28, Ireland).

If the school-leaving age is sixteen, there should be no problems in the implementation of this paragraph. A problem might, however, arise in connection with the protection of young workers who have completed compulsory schooling a few months before reaching sixteen, if in respect of this short period of time there is no provision limiting their hours of work. Such a situation was identified by the Committee in two Contracting Parties (see Second report on certain provisions of the Charter which have not been accepted, pp. 10, 12 and 13).

As stated by the Committee in its Second report on certain provisions of the Charter which have not been accepted (p. 10) "This provision of the Charter [....] forms part of a number of provisions contained in Article 7, whose principal aim is the protection of children and young persons against the occupational hazards arising from their immaturity; these concern their health, their physical, intellectual and moral development and their vocational training".

Moreover, "the daily and weekly working hours for young persons of less than sixteen years of age have particular significance, not only because of the need for their development, but also in view of their specific needs in regard to vocational training, which is so important in today's world of work" *(ibidem)*.

No uniform and precise rule has been fixed with regard to the limitations on working hours required by this paragraph which, as all other paragraphs of Article 7, applies to all economic sectors and all types of work including work in the employer's home and family enterprises.

In order, however, to judge compliance with this paragraph the Committee asks for quantitative data on working hours. The limitation of working hours to eight per day and forty per week was regarded as not meeting the requirements of the Charter. Such working hours were considered as not allowing young persons to enjoy the benefit of vocational training. (Conclusions I, p. 44). Moreover, in view of the application of Article 33 in the absence of legislation restricting the hours of work in all sectors of the economy or for all persons under sixteen, statistical data is required in order to establish whether the limitation of working hours applies to the "great majority" of workers under sixteen.

Assessment of compliance

The Contracting Parties found as not complying are:

Ireland: Despite the restriction of working hours to eight hours per day and forty per week for workers under sixteen by the 1977 Protection of Young Persons (Employment) Act, more than two-thirds of fifteen-year-olds work for forty hours a week or more and eight daily, which the Committee regarded as excessive and likely to impair their development (Conclusions XIII-2, p. 87). Moreover, no information was given on the number of young people not subject to the above legislation and therefore not subject to any limit on working hours or on the proportion of all workers under sixteen represented by this figure. The criticism has been made since the seventh cycle (seventh report).

Italy:[1] Young people between fifteen and sixteen are subject to a working week of forty hours and eight hours daily which is regarded as excessive, having regard to their developmental and vocational training needs. (Conclusions XIII-2, p. 88). The criticism has existed since the second cycle of supervision (second Italian report).

Turkey: No provision is made for any limitation of working hours in the case of children under the age of sixteen who no longer attend school. Moreover, the majority of children in employment have no legal protection as regards working hours as the Labour Act does not cover some important sectors of the economy. Moreover the average working hours are forty to forty-nine per week for young people aged between twelve and fourteen and forty-seven to forty-eight per week for those aged between fifteen and nineteen (Conclusions XIII-1, p. 230, and Conclusions XIII-3, p. 296).

In the revised Charter, Article 7 para. 4 reads as follows:

"With a view to ensuring the effective exercise of the right of children and young persons to protection, the Parties undertake:

…

4. to provide that the working hours of persons under 18 years of age shall be limited in accordance with the needs of their development, and particularly with their need for vocational training".

Paragraph 5 – Fair remuneration for young workers and apprentices

Under this paragraph, the Contracting Parties undertake:

"to recognise the right of young workers and apprentices to a fair wage or other appropriate allowances".

---

1 The Committee of Ministers addressed a recommendation to Italy for the second part of the thirteenth supervision cycle.

This paragraph is intended to guarantee an appropriate remuneration to apprentices and young workers and prevent them from being exploited or employed as cheap labour. (Third report on certain provisions of the Charter which have not been accepted, pp. 18 to 20). As Article 33 does not apply here, the required level of wages or allowances must be paid to all persons covered.

The Committee has applied this paragraph by relating the wage paid to young workers and apprentices to that paid to adults doing the same job at the beginning of their career.

Regarding the type of information needed for assessing compliance, the Committee made it clear that Contracting Parties should supply full information on the wages and allowances actually paid, including minimum rates, to young workers and apprentices for all branches of industry and in all parts of the national territory and the minimum wages paid to adults in the corresponding trades (Conclusions I, p. 44 in combination with Conclusions VI, p. 52, France). This view has been maintained throughout all cycles of supervision. However, aware that general surveys of wages are not always possible, the Committee later stated that "significant examples and estimates would equally be acceptable, provided that they are not limited to a few sectors and do take into account the entire range of wages according to recognized qualifications" (Conclusions VII, p. 48, Italy; Third report on certain provisions of the Charter which have not been accepted, p. 18).

The Committee accepted from the beginning that paragraph 5 does not require the same wages for young people as for adults. Thus in Conclusions II the Committee stated, with regard to young workers, that certain reductions might be justified but made it clear that these should not be too substantial and ought to be for a limited period. Moreover, in the case of apprentices the Committee expressed the view that the value of training ought to be taken into account, but at the same time account should also be taken of the fact that after two or three years apprenticeship an apprentice was fitted to render such services that he could hardly still be considered as an apprentice (Conclusions II, p. 33).

On examination of reports on non-accepted provisions, the Committee also clarified the following two points:

"*a.* that the enactment of legislation is not necessary in order to comply with paragraph 5 of Article 7 as long as a network of collective agreements or some other arrangement guarantees that all young workers and apprentices receive a fair wage or appropriate allowances;

b. although this is not explicitly stated in paragraph 5, the age of eighteen sets a limit to the personal scope of Article 7. This indication is given in other paragraphs of the same Article; in addition all international instruments concerning 'adolescents' and 'young persons' refer to persons under the age of eighteen. With particular reference to paragraph 5 of Article 7, it should be noted that after this age the guarantee of a fair wage is provided by paragraph 1 of Article 4."

Regarding the question of what should be understood as a "fair wage" or "appropriate allowances" the Committee admitted in its Third report on certain provisions of the Charter which have not been accepted that this raised a major difficulty. In this respect, the Committee pointed out that it had always made a distinction between apprentices and young workers as their situations were different and justified a separate assessment of their remuneration and summed up its case law on the matter and the practice followed regarding each category.

Apprentices

By definition, apprentices are provided as they work with vocational training, the value of which should be taken into account. At least temporarily, therefore, their remuneration may justifiably be lower than that of young workers.

However, the apprenticeship system should not be deflected from its objective and used to underpay a worker. That is why the Committee has always combated a tendency to prolong apprenticeships unduly. It has underlined that if they last too long (for example, five years), the difference between apprentices and young workers tends to disappear and a worker would not then receive an adult remuneration until he was twenty-one (rather than eighteen) (Conclusions I, p. 188).

As regards the amount of the remuneration or the allowance, it is felt that, as in the case of young workers, this should be assessed in relation to that of an adult worker at the beginning of his career and that it may be reduced fairly considerably to take account of the cost of the vocational training provided and possibly of the apprentice's lower productivity. However, on account of the skill acquired during such training, the reduction should progressively diminish and, as already underlined, should be limited in time.

On an indicative basis (as no precise rule has ever been laid down, and as a certain degree of flexibility as well as some margin of discretion seem desirable), it transpires from the assessments made during the various cycles of supervision that the remuneration/allowance of an apprentice could vary from one-third of the wage of an adult worker at the beginning of his career (minimum at the beginning of the apprenticeship) to two-thirds of the same wage (minimum at the end of the apprenticeship).

Young workers

In providing that young workers are entitled to a "fair remuneration", the Charter entertains the possibility of their receiving a lower wage than adult workers at the beginning of their career because of such factors as a generally lower output. However, the differential should be reasonable and limited in time. On an indicative basis (for the same reasons as those mentioned in respect of apprentices), differentials of about 30% in comparison with the wages of an adult worker at the beginning of his career which are generally applied to young workers have been considered excessive. Differences of about 20%, have been considered admissible and a 25% differential was accepted since it concerned young workers of less than sixteen years of age (Conclusions V, p. 63).

The importance the Committee attaches to keeping young workers' wages reasonably proportionate to those of adult workers at the beginning of their career should be stressed here, since in certain countries there has been a tendency in recent years to reduce young workers' wages in order to foster their employment. The Committee does not accept this trend, as it exceeds the limits set by its case law; it has underlined the risk of disproportionately imposing "the sacrifices necessary to the country's economic recovery on one section of the work force" (Conclusions X-1, p. 84).

Finally, it should be noted that in accordance with the case law of the Committee, if paragraph 1 of Article 4 is not satisfied because the starting wages for adults are themselves not sufficient, as a general rule paragraph 5 of Article 7 cannot be considered to be satisfied either. Arguments of Contracting Parties to the effect that the low starting salaries for young workers are justified in the interests of providing more job opportunities for such persons are not accepted by the Committee on the grounds that there are "dangers inherent in such a policy, which may impose on this category of people the sacrifices necessary for the improvement of the economic and employment situation" (Conclusions XI-1, p. 28, General introduction and Conclusions XII-1, pp. 140 and 141, the United Kingdom)

Assessment of compliance

The Contracting Parties found as not complying are:

Luxembourg: because young workers aged fifteen and sixteen are paid 40% less than the minimum wage of those over the age of eighteen (Addendum to Conclusions XIII-3, p. 42);

the *Netherlands:* the wages of young workers under eighteen are considerably lower by comparison with the starting wages of adults paid at full rate (those aged twenty-three); 34,5% for sixteen-year-olds, 39,5% for seventeen-year-olds, 45,5% for eighteen-year-olds (in 1992). These minimums are not regarded as fair. Moreover the Committee referred to its conclusion under Article 4 para. 1, namely that it was unclear whether adult minimum wages themselves could be considered as sufficient (Conclusions XIII-1, p. 167). In Conclusions XIII-2 the Committee referred to its case law and the examples given on this issue in its Third report on certain provisions of the Charter which have not been accepted and reiterated its negative conclusion, since the number of workers affected amounted to 11% of all young workers and Article 33 was not applicable to this paragraph. (Conclusions XIII-2, p. 91);

Spain: workers under the age of eighteen earned 34% less than those over the age of eighteen. (Conclusions XIII-2, p. 92);

the *United Kingdom:* whilst the wages of young workers represent an adequate percentage of adult wages, the fact that adult wages themselves (ie. for workers aged eighteen and over) could not be considered as meeting the requirements of Article 4 para. 1, necessarily led to the result that the wages of young persons were insufficient (Conclusions XIII-2, pp. 92 and 93).

Although there are only four cases of non-compliance, there are nine deferrals (Belgium, Finland, Germany, Ireland, Italy, Malta, Norway, Portugal and Turkey), mainly because of a lack of information in respect of wages and allowances in all branches of activity and the wage situation of young workers not covered by collective agreements or owing to the connection with the assessment of the fairness of remuneration made under Article 4 para. 1.

Paragraph 6 – Treatment of time spent in vocational training as forming part of the working day

Under this paragraph, the Contracting Parties undertake:

> "to provide that the time spent by young persons in vocational training during the normal working hours with the consent of the employer shall be treated as forming part of the working day".

As in the case of paragraph 4 of Article 7, Article 33 is applicable. This means that the Contracting Parties must ensure that for the great majority of young persons (ie. 80%) the time spent in vocational training during normal working hours is treated as part of the working day and is remunerated as such.

As stated by the Committee in its Third report on certain provisions of the Charter which have not been accepted, pp. 24 and 25, this provision is intended "to facilitate the vocational training of young persons, afford them fair conditions of work and protect their health. They might, in fact, be discouraged from taking up vocational training – which has become increasingly necessary of late – if it involved lower remuneration or additional working hours".

The Committee made it clear on several occasions that the personal scope of this provision is not restricted to apprentices, but also includes young workers receiving vocational training (see for example Conclusions VIII, p. 116 and Conclusions IX-1, p. 63, Norway).

In order to remove any ambiguity which might influence the interpretation of this provision in view of the expression "with the employer's consent", the Committee made it clear in the fifth cycle of supervision that "these words should not be interpreted in such a way as to constitute a 'condition *sine qua non*' for recognising that young workers should be granted the right under this provision although the employer's consent might have some bearing in defining the way in which this is to be exercised. For on the one hand, any other interpretation would result in this provision being deprived of any scope at all, on the other, it would seem that this type of situation is being regulated by law more and more, and that this consent is more often the outcome of a legal obligation, as has been borne out by several laws relating to apprentices, than of the employer's own consent, which continues to be required when the law remains silent" (Conclusions V, p. 67).

Stated more simply, the words "with the consent of the employer" must not be read as meaning that the employer can be allowed to refuse permission but rather as an indication that he may within reason be permitted to set the time and the conditions for the exercise of the right to release studies.

In the same cycle the Committee also clarified that "the fact that the time spent by young persons on their vocational training during working hours shall be treated as forming part of the working day implies, in particular:

- that such time be remunerated (by either the employer or from public funds, as the case may be); and

- that it does not give rise to any form of recuperation which would result in the total number of hours of work of the person concerned being extended accordingly" (Conclusions V, p. 67).

The aforesaid interpretation of the expression "forming part of the working day" was reconfirmed by the Committee in its Third report on certain provisions of the Charter which have not been accepted, p. 24.

When examining the reports of Contracting Parties which did not accept this paragraph, the Committee availed itself of the opportunity to underline that as in the case of paragraph 5 legislation is not necessary for compliance with this provision, "though if there is no legislation 'the authorities should produce evidence' of the following:

- that the time spent by young persons in vocational training during normal working hours with the consent of the employer is effectively included in the working day (in the sense mentioned above, ie. remunerated and not recuperated);

- that these measures are applicable to the great majority of the young workers concerned, ie. of all young persons (up to eighteen years of age) who work and receive vocational training during working hours".

The Committee also underlined on this occasion that:

"1. Article 7 para. 6 is not intended to regulate vocational training in general – which is governed by Article 10 of the Charter – but to ensure basic training ('initial training', according to the *travaux préparatoires*) for young persons having entered working life at an early stage,

2.   moreover without any exhaustiveness being claimed on this point, it may be supposed that an employer cannot be expected to provide everything that a young worker requests. The latter should, of course, be encouraged and indeed helped to acquire an occupational qualification, but this should not preclude a personal effort on his part. If he has different ambitions, he can use his own free time to acquire qualifications unconnected with his work" (*ibidem* p. 25).

In order to assess compliance the Committee needs precise data on the percentage of young workers receiving training in accordance with paragraph 6.

Assessment of compliance

The only country found as not complying is:

the *Netherlands:* for lack of information which would enable the Committee to determine if the great majority of young workers, whether covered by collective agreements or not, benefit from the measures provided for by this paragraph, which require that training time during normal working hours with the consent of the employer is not to be made up by the trainee but remunerated as time worked (Conclusions XIII-2, pp. 93 and 94).

It should be mentioned, however, that throughout the various cycles of supervision the Committee has repeatedly been unable to reach a conclusion in respect of some Contracting Parties. In most cases this was due – but not solely – to the absence of precise data on the percentage of young persons (other than apprentices) receiving training in accordance with this paragraph in view of the applicability of Article 33. This was the case for example in France up to the eighth cycle of supervision (Conclusions VIII, p. 115) and the United Kingdom up to the seventh cycle (Conclusions VII, p. 50). From the Committee's latest Conclusions it appears that the conclusion is currently deferred for six Contracting Parties (Belgium, Luxembourg, Norway, Portugal, Spain and Turkey; Conclusions XIII-2, p. 296; Addendum to Conclusions XIII-3, pp. 42 and 43; Conclusions XIII-2, p. 94; XIII-3, p. 300; XIII-2, pp. 94 and 95 and XIII-3, pp. 300 and 301 respectively).

Paragraph 7 – Annual holidays of young persons under eighteen

Under this paragraph, the Contracting Parties undertake:

> "to provide that employed persons of under eighteen years of age shall be entitled to not less than three weeks' annual holiday with pay".

Article 33 applies here, which means that Contracting Parties are complying with it if they can show that the "great majority" (80%) of employed persons under eighteen are treated in accordance with this paragraph by virtue of legislation, collective agreements or otherwise.

This provision is intended to "ensure that young workers' annual holidays are longer than the two weeks provided for in respect of adult workers (Article 2 para. 3 of the Charter), in order to protect both their physical and their mental health, at a time when they are still growing and may be experiencing psychological difficulties that are an acknowledged feature of adolescence" (Third report on certain provisions of the Charter which have not been accepted, pp. 29 and 30).

The Committee interpreted this provision as imposing on Contracting States an obligation to guarantee three weeks' leave, the number of working days granted depending on the length of the working week (Conclusions I, p. 45). Thus a person employed on a five-day-week basis is entitled to fifteen days' holiday, whereas a person employed on a six-day-week basis to eighteen days' holiday.

On the occasion of the examination of the reports of Contracting Parties which had not accepted this provision, the Committee felt it necessary to point out that its decision in relation to Article 2 para. 3, namely that "not permitting annual holiday to be taken until the twelve working months for which it is due have fully elapsed" (Conclusions I, p. 20), is not incompatible with the Charter also applies to this paragraph.

It also stressed that the principle which it had laid down in connection with Article 2 para. 3, that "workers must not be able to waive their annual holidays, even in consideration of an extra payment since the need to protect the workers as fully as possible made such a waive incompatible with the Charter, even with the free consent of the workers concerned" (Conclusions I, p. 170) was applicable, even with greater force, to Article 7 para. 7 (Third report on certain provisions of the Charter which have not been accepted, pp. 29 and 30).

Assessment of compliance

There are no cases of non-compliance with this paragraph. There are three cases of deferral: for Belgium, whose first report the Committee examined in Conclusions XIII-2 (pp. 296 and 297) and for Finland and Portugal, whose first reports were examined in Conclusions XIII-3 (pp. 301 and 302).

In the revised Charter, Article 7 para. 7 reads as follows:

"With a view to ensuring the effective exercise of the right of children and young persons to protection, the Parties undertake:

...

7. to provide that employed persons of under 18 years of age shall be entitled to a minimum of four weeks' annual holiday with pay;"

Paragraph 8 – Prohibition of night work for young persons under eighteen

Under this paragraph, the Contracting Parties undertake:

"to provide that persons under eighteen years of age shall not be employed in night work with the exception of certain occupations provided for by national laws or regulations."

Appendix to Article 7 para. 8

"It is understood that a Contracting Party may give the undertaking required in this paragraph if it fulfils the spirit of the undertaking by providing by law that the great majority of persons under eighteen years of age shall not be employed in night work."

Having regard to the Appendix to the Charter, this paragraph requires that the prohibition on night work should apply by law to the great majority of young workers.

To assess compliance with this provision Contracting Parties must supply information on:

"*a.* the period defined in national regulations as "night" for the purpose of the prohibition of night work;

b. the occupations in which night work by minors under eighteen is permitted, either in general or by special decision;

c. the extent of such derogation (maximum hours allowed, minimum age, etc.);

d. hours during which night work is altogether prohibited;

e. the numbers:

– of all people under eighteen years at work;

– of young people who in fact are normally required to work at night." (Conclusions I, p. 46).

Legislation which prohibited night work of persons under sixteen between 7 pm and 6 am and young persons under eighteen between 10 pm and 5 am is considered satisfactory.

Assessment of compliance

The Contracting Parties found as not complying are:

Cyprus: in respect of young workers aged sixteen to eighteen, the prohibition of night work is limited to industrial work and is subject to the possibility of exemption (Conclusions XIII-2, pp. 96 and 97).

Malta: there are no legislative or statutory provisions prohibiting night work by young people between sixteen and eighteen years of age and the ban on the employment of workers under eighteen on night work is not valid for the great majority of persons concerned. (Conclusions XIII-2, pp. 298 and 299).

Turkey: although night work is prohibited in industry for young workers by Labour Act No. 1475, these provisions do not apply to other categories of work, including in particular agricultural work and services, sectors in which according to labour statistics furnished by the Turkish authorities, many young workers are employed. (Conclusions XIII-3, p. 305).

There are six cases of deferral (Belgium, Finland, Greece, Norway, Portugal and Spain). For Belgium, Greece, Portugal and Spain the deferral is due to the absence of information to enable the Committee to assess whether the prohibition of night work applied to the great majority of workers concerned, as required under the Appendix (Conclusions XIII-2, p. 298; XIII-2, p. 97; XIII-3, p. 304; XIII-2 p. 98, respectively). For Finland and Norway the Committee has asked for further information concerning the possible exceptions to the prohibition of night work by young persons, the conditions in which exceptions are made, the prescribed working hours and an estimate of the number of young people involved (Conclusions XIII-3 pp. 302 and 303 and Conclusions XIII-2, p. 98). For Spain, the Committee asked to know the number of young people under eighteen years of age related to their employer who are not covered by national legislation (Conclusions XIII-2, p. 98).

Paragraph 9 – Provision of regular medical control for young workers under eighteen

Under this paragraph, the Contracting Parties undertake:

> "to provide that persons under eighteen years of age employed in occupations prescribed by national laws or regulations shall be subject to regular medical control".

States accepting this paragraph must provide comprehensive information on the nature of the occupations of persons covered by this provision for whom regular medical control is prescribed, on the organisation and operation of the medical services and on the frequency of medical examinations (Conclusions I, p. 47).

It is up to national legislation to prescribe the occupations concerned but the Committee insists on "examining" them. Replying to a question by a Contracting Party, the Committee explained that it needed to have a list of "occupations in which regular medical examinations were prescribed (either for workers under eighteen or for all workers) in order to be able to establish what the competent services of the various member states consider, on the basis of the technical and medical knowledge and experience of each country, to be occupations or processes or industries covering such occupations which require regular medical control of some or all of the persons who worked in them" and "expressed the view that the adequacy of such prescribed lists, particularly in relation to persons under eighteen, must be judged in the light of the available medical advice and attention outside the place of work, eg. at school." (Conclusions VI, p. 58, the United Kingdom). There have been cases where the Committee has held that a greater number of occupations should be covered. (see for instance Conclusions III, p. 46 and Conclusions VI, p. 57, Germany, and Conclusions XI-1, p. 66, the United Kingdom).

"Regular medical control" means periodic medical examination on a continuing basis. (Conclusions II, p. 37). Thus a law which makes compulsory only the pre-recruitment examination and an examination which takes place after one year of employment, but which fails to require further medical examinations at reasonable intervals up to the age of eighteen, is not in keeping with the Charter (Conclusions VI, p. 57, Germany).

Moreover, medical examinations must be compulsory. "A regulation providing merely for the possibility of a young worker undergoing a regular medical check" is not adequate. Medical examination is "an important aspect of social protection that should not be left to the discretion of the parties concerned, not even to the protected persons themselves". (Conclusions IV, p. 61).

In addition, the Committee held in a general observation that "considering the development of regular medical examination for the benefit of all workers and the extension of medical services in a certain number of countries, the protection of young workers' health does not necessarily require widespread legislative provisions, calling for a specific organisation of medical services for young workers. However, this can only be envisaged in a state whose medical services and examinations for the benefit of workers have reached the necessary level of development, and should be wholly compatible with the development of a policy of prevention and protection of young workers which constitute the very scope of Article 7, paragraph 9. The Committee considered it essential, in this case, that precise guidelines and instructions are expressly given to the bodies responsible for carrying out medical examinations of workers, so that, when such examinations concern young workers, prevention and protection of their health be taken into account" (General observation under Article 7 para. 9 in Conclusions VIII, p. 119).

In order to be able to assess the situation in a Contracting Party in which there was no specific organisation of medical supervision for young workers, the Committee, referring to the above-mentioned general observation, stated that it needed to know:

"*a.* the frequency of medical examinations of workers under eighteen years of age;

b. is medical supervision a specific obligation in the case of workers under eighteen who are authorized to engage in activities listed in the 1980 Ordinance;

c. are specific instructions issued to the industrial medical services in order to adopt medical examinations to the specific situation of young workers and to the particular risks to which they are exposed" (Conclusions VIII, pp. 120 and 121, Sweden).

As regards the personal scope of protection, according to the Committee this provision applies also to young workers employed in family businesses who did not have the status of paid employees and young self-employed workers. (Conclusions XIII-2, p. 100, Spain).

Assessment of compliance

Sweden was found as not complying with this paragraph from the ninth cycle of supervision up to the eleventh cycle, as the new AFS 1987 Ordinance concerning the work of young people under eighteen had not introduced a mandatory regular medical examination for all young people in unhealthy occupations.

Now the conclusion is deferred, pending receipt of information regarding the medical examination of young persons at school and of young persons outside school. The question in respect of young persons at school is whether the medical control, which they must undergo to be authorised to perform work which is considered dangerous or unhealthy, concerns the capacity to exercise a particular occupation and if the results are indeed taken into account when deciding whether or not to grant authorisation. The question in respect of young persons outside school, who according to the Swedish report are required to complete a vocational training course on covering the risks of the work and safe working methods before being authorised to carry out a dangerous or unhealthy activity, is whether medical examinations are provided at all and whether these are indeed carried out not just on recruitment, but also at regular intervals (Conclusions XIII-1, p. 170 and XIII-2, p. 100).

The Contracting states found as not complying are Spain and Turkey.

Spain: on the ground that no legal provision guarantees the specific protection afforded by Article 7 para. 9 to young workers employed in family businesses who do not have the status of paid employees and young self-employed workers still not covered by labour legislation (Conclusions XIII-2, pp. 99 and 100).

Turkey: because as a result of the limited scope of the Labour Act No. 1475, young people under eighteen years of age employed in agriculture as well as craftsmen and shopkeepers do not undergo any medical examinations. The same is true for apprentices under eighteen, who do not undergo periodical medical examinations (Conclusions XIII-1, pp. 232 and 233 and Conclusions XIII-3, pp. 306 and 307).

Paragraph 10 – Special protection for children and young people from physical and moral dangers to which they are exposed

Under this paragraph, the Contracting Parties undertake:

> "to ensure special protection against physical and moral dangers to which children and young persons are exposed, and particularly against those resulting directly or indirectly from their work".

As already stated under "General" above, the Committee in its first Conclusions noted that "paragraph 10 of this Article is far broader in scope than the first nine paragraphs. In fact, paragraphs 1 to 9 cover the protection of children and young people against the dangers of a working life, whereas paragraph 10 places an obligation upon the states to protect young people against any dangers which threaten them, even if these dangers are not connected with their work". (Conclusions I, p. 41).

The view that the scope of paragraph 10 is appreciably broader than that of the other provisions of Article 7, which cover the protection of children and young persons mainly from the point of view of employment and working conditions, was reiterated in the fifth cycle of supervision in a general observation. In this cycle the Committee, after underlining that "although paragraph 10 states that the world of work is one of the fields to which it principally applies, it extends its protection well beyond this content to include all dangers of a physical and moral kind to which children and young persons are exposed", observed that the Contracting Parties should bear in mind the special character of paragraph 10 of Article 7 and give in their reports the fullest possible information on measures specifically designed to protect children and young persons against physical and moral dangers, children and young persons in the family, at school and in society as a whole as well as in the world of work, from the age at which they are required to attend school until the age at which they become adults (Conclusions V, p. 73).

The legal importance of the Charter as regards the protection of child and youth welfare, by reason of the commitment of Contracting Parties under paragraph 10 of Article 7 to provide comprehensive protection for children and adolescents not only where working life is concerned but also more generally against all physical and moral dangers to which they are exposed, was once more underlined General introduction in the twelfth cycle of supervision. In this connection the Committee, prompted by the information supplied in the United Kingdom report for the protection of children against sexual abuse – the incidents of which had increased – expressed its concern that the reports of Contracting Parties did not contain updated information regarding the aspect of comprehensive protection of children and young persons including information as to the ill-treatment of children. (Conclusions XII-1, p. 31, General introduction).

The Committee explained that the special character of the dangers to which young persons may be exposed because of the changing moral and technological environment made it necessary for Contracting Parties to update regularly the information furnished in this area, even if the situation had been considered satisfactory in previous cycles (Conclusions V, pp. 73 and 74).

In later cycles of supervision the Committee also emphasised the need for Contracting Parties to supply information on preventive measures taken in the fields of drug addiction, alcoholism and juvenile delinquency as well as on measures taken with a view to safeguarding children employed in the performing arts or other occupations against moral dangers (Conclusions VIII, p. 122 and Conclusions X-1, p. 90).

Other information requested by the Committee concerns the bodies responsible for supervising the application of relevant provisions, the way in which they function and the methods employed to carry out such supervision.

With a view to examining more closely the problem of ill-treatment of children (including sexual abuse and ill-treatment within the family) the Committee, in its General introduction to Conclusions XIII-2, asked all Contracting Parties to supply in their next reports "all relevant information about the extent of this problem and the measures they have taken or planned to take to guarantee children and adolescents the protection to which they are entitled, including not only preventive but also other measures, together with information about the setting up and role of the various services responsible for these matters (in particular the social and legal services) and about the regulations governing these services" (Conclusions XIII-2, p. 100).

Assessment of compliance

There are no cases of non-compliance with this provision. There are four cases of deferral (Belgium, Luxembourg, the Netherlands and Portugal). For Belgium, this was pending receipt of information from the government concerning measures to combat family violence, juvenile delinquency, the spread of alcoholism, smoking, drug addiction and sexually transmitted diseases (particularly Aids) (Conclusions XIII-2, pp. 300 to 302). The Committee asked Luxembourg for information in reply to Questions B, C and D of the Form for Reports concerning the existing measures to protect young persons who are exposed to physical of moral danger at their work or outside work and to the general question put in Conclusions XIII-2, p. 100 (Addendum to Conclusions XIII-3, p. 45). In the case of the Netherlands, the deferral concerned preventive measures in the area of drug addiction, alcoholism and juvenile delinquency (Conclusions XIII-2, p. 104). The Committee asked Portugal for information on measures to protect young persons from undertaking physical work in the transport sector, to prevent accidents of children and young persons at work, for the social protection of children of groups at risk and on the supervisory system to ensure that children did not endure corporal punishment or abuse (Conclusions XIII-3, p. 311).

Article 8 – The right of employed women to protection

General

In the first supervision cycle, the Committee stated that "the aim of this article is to ensure the effective exercise of the right of employed women to protection, and it accordingly established specific provisions concerning:

- maternity protection;

- general protection of women at work.

As regards maternity protection, Article 8 is concerned with:

- maternity leave (paragraph 1);

- prohibition of dismissal during absence on maternity leave (paragraph 2);

- time off for nursing mothers (paragraph 3).

The provisions of article 8 concerning the general protection of women at work deal with night work in industry, and work of a dangerous, unhealthy or arduous nature (paragraph 4)." (Conclusions I, p. 49).

As far as the personal scope of the protection provided by this Article is concerned, the Committee again in the first cycle, interpreted it "as applying solely to women in paid employment, and not to self-employed women. This interpretation is based on the following:

- regarding all four paragraphs making up the Article, on the expression 'employed women' used in the English text of the first sentence of the Article;

- regarding more especially paragraphs 2 and 4, on the use in their text of the word 'employer' or 'employment' which is fairly conclusive" (*ibidem*, pp. 49 and 50).

The Committee seeks to ensure that all female paid workers without exception should benefit from the protection guaranteed under Article 8, including civil servants and public service employees, as well as in accordance with the Appendix to the Charter paid foreign workers, nationals of other Contracting Parties lawfully residing or working regularly within the territory of a Contracting Party.

The Committee's standpoint, clarified from the first supervision cycle, is constantly confirmed (see most recently Conclusions XIII-3, pp. 313 and 314, Portugal). This poses a problem for several Contracting Parties, whose legislation does not cover all categories of workers. Those most frequently excluded are domestic employees (see most recently Conclusions XIII-2, p. 213, Austria and pp. 213, 215 and 216, Italy), although other categories may be affected, as for example part-time workers or workers related to their employer (Conclusions XIII-1, pp. 174 and 175, Ireland[1] and Conclusions XIII-2, pp. 305 and 308, Malta) or women employed at sea (Conclusions XIII-1, p. 178, Greece).

---

1 Certain employees were still excluded, despite the subsequent extension of the scope of the 1981 Act by the Worker Protection (Regular Part-time Employees) Act 1991 to all regular part-time female employees who have worked at least eight hours per week (previously eighteen hours) over a period of not less that thirteen weeks with the same employer. This exclusion was abolished under the Maternity Protection Act No. 34 of 1994 (outside the reference period).

Negative conclusions have been reached for Austria[1] and Italy[2] by reason of the exclusion of domestic employees.

A negative conclusion has also been reached for Greece and Malta as equality of treatment is not ensured between nationals and nationals of other Contracting Parties (see Conclusions XI-1, p. 103 and Conclusions XII-1, p. 148, Greece;[3] and Conclusions XII-2, p. 137 and Conclusions XIII-2, pp. 306 and 307, Malta).

Paragraph 1 – Maternity leave and maternity benefits

Under this paragraph, the Contracting Parties undertake:

> "to provide either by paid leave, by adequate social security benefits or by benefits from public funds for women to take leave before and after childbirth up to a total of at least twelve weeks".

The purpose of this paragraph is to allow women workers to reconcile the requirements of maternity with the constraints of working life.

From the very first supervision cycle, the Committee interpreted this provision "as meaning that all Contracting Parties having accepted it are bound to ensure a twelve weeks' maternity leave, not merely allowances over a period of twelve weeks, to expectant mothers in paid employment; it agreed, however, that the terms used in the first paragraph of Article 8 were such that it was nonetheless possible for such women to elect not to avail themselves of this right over a part of the twelve weeks' period in question" (Conclusions I, p. 50).

The view that this provision of the Charter involves two obligations, that is:

---

1 The Committee of Ministers addressed a recommendation to Austria on this issue, concerning Article 8 para. 2, for the second part of the twelfth supervision cycle.

2 The Committee of Ministers addressed a recommendation to Italy on this issue, concerning Article 8 paras. 1, 2, and 3, for the second part of the twelfth supervision cycle.

3 The situation was remedied by Act No. 1902 of 1990 which repealed Section 4 1. of the Emergency Law No. 1846 of 1951, which excluded foreigners temporarily working in Greece from access to the Social Insurance Institute (IKA) (Conclusions XIII-1, p. 173).

"*a.*   to provide for women to take at least 12 weeks' maternity leave, and

b.   to ensure that women are adequately compensated for their loss of earnings during the period of leave"

was reaffirmed by the Committee in the third supervision cycle (Conclusions III, p. 48).

1.   *Maternity leave*

With regard to the first obligation, the Committee's case law, in addition to the issue of personal scope (see under "General") covers three other issues: the establishment of a right to maternity leave, the length of the leave and its nature. Each of these issues is dealt with separately for reasons of clarity.

a.   *Establishment of the right to maternity leave*

The Committee established that the right to maternity leave must be guaranteed by legislation.

Thus in the second supervision cycle, the Committee urged a Contracting Party to include the right of working women to maternity leave in its legislation (Conclusions II, p. 39, the United Kingdom). In the third cycle, whilst noting that in certain countries women workers benefited from maternity leave in practice rather than by virtue of legislation, the Committee held that "a right of such capital importance ought to be guaranteed by law" and made it clear that it was "unable to accept the assertion that legislation is unnecessary when the customary rights in question are solidly based" (Conclusions III, p. 49, the United Kingdom).

The Committee rejected the argument of the Irish Government that the obligation under this paragraph was simply to make provision for one of the three forms of payment mentioned therein and not for a right to maternity leave. The Committee maintained its interpretation for the following reasons:

"*i.* the wording of paragraph 1 of Article 8 clearly imposed the obligation '... to provide... for women to take leave... of at least twelve weeks' and not merely to provide for allowances over that period of twelve weeks;

ii. to ensure that women were compensated for loss of earnings during the period concerned. It was true that this paragraph allowed a choice of three means for this latter purpose; the 'choice' referred to by the Irish Government did not, however, affect the fundamental obligation to establish entitlement to twelve weeks' maternity leave but concerned only the means of compensation for loss of earnings, namely i. paid leave, ii. social security benefits or iii. benefits from public funds";

and concluded that as Ireland had not met the aforesaid fundamental obligation under this paragraph, which was that an employee was entitled to resume her employment after her twelve weeks' absence on maternity leave, it was still not complying with the Charter. (Conclusions V, p. 76, Ireland).

b. *Length of the leave*

The importance attached by the Committee to the fact that the length of leave provided under the Charter (twelve weeks) is a minimum, is illustrated by the last quotation. It is also stressed in the Committee's First report on certain provisions of the Charter which have not been accepted (p. 19): "As the Charter makes clear, the twelve-week period of leave, partly before and partly after the birth, is to be regarded as a minimum, since it is important both to allow the mother sufficient time to prepare properly for the confinement and for her subsequent return to work, and to enable the special needs of the child to be met." As a result no inferior length of leave is admissible.

c. *Nature of leave (compulsory/optional)*

The third issue examined by the Committee with regard to the first obligation was whether maternity leave should be compulsory or not or, in other words, whether women should be prohibited from working during the period of maternity leave.

As already pointed out, the Committee agreed "that the terms used in the first paragraph of Article 8 were such that it was nonetheless possible for [expectant mothers] to elect not to avail themselves of the right over a part of the twelve week's" maternity leave (see Conclusions I, p. 50 above).

In the fourth supervision cycle, the Committee drew attention to the fact that in a Contracting Party "employed women were free to give up a substantial part of their maternity leave and return to work or go on working. In the Committee's view this option, coupled with the relatively low rate of maternity allowance (...) seemed to make substantial inroads in the protection provided for by this clause." (Conclusions IV, p. 66, the United Kingdom). Moreover, in the fifth supervision cycle, when examining the situation in another Contracting Party, the Committee considered that "maternity leave should be compulsory for a part, at least, of the twelve week period" (Conclusions V, p. 76, Sweden). The Committee did not, however, state how long the compulsory leave should be. In the sixth supervision cycle, the Committee asked this Contracting Party to inform it whether under the new legislation on parental leave "it would be possible for a female worker after childbirth, to forego wholly parental leave in favour of the child's father (...), or whether in any event the mother is entitled to *maternity leave* up to the 29th day after childbirth even if she does not have the child in her care" (Conclusions VI, p. 62 Sweden).

In the eighth supervision cycle the Committee stated that women should not be allowed to work for six weeks after childbirth. The full reasoning of the Committee behind this conclusion was as follows:

"The provision of Article 8, para. 1 of the Charter should be examined in the light, in particular, of developments in national legislation and international conventions. They were designed both to grant working women increased personal protection in the case of maternity and to reflect a more general interest in public health – ie. the health of the mother and child.

In connection with the first point, the Charter prescribes a minimum of twelve weeks' leave entitlement, matched by adequate financial safeguards. With regard to the second point, the aim is to prevent any work which might be harmful to the health of the mother or the child.

It should be pointed out, however, that the justifiable trend in most countries towards extending women's entitlement to maternity leave does not imply that the period for which they are prohibited from actually working must necessarily be the same as the period of leave to which they are entitled.

Having carefully studied the relevant national legislation and international conventions in force, the Committee considered that the two requirements mentioned above were reconcilable in so far as national legislation on the one hand allowed women the right to use all or part of their recognised entitlement to stop work for a period of at least twelve weeks, allowing them freedom of choice by means of a scheme of benefits set at an adequate level, and, on the other hand, obliged the woman concerned and the employer to observe within this total period, a minimum period of cessation of work, which had to be taken after the birth and which it was reasonable to fix at six weeks" (Conclusions VIII, p. 123).[1]

The view that the woman and the employer must both observe a minimum period of cessassion of work after childbirth, which is fixed at six weeks, has been maintained by the Committee consistently from the eighth cycle up to the last supervision cycle (thirteenth) (Conclusions XIII-I, pp. 172 to 177).

Assessment of compliance

The Contracting Parties found as not complying are:

---

1 See the dissenting opinions of Professor Fabricius (Conclusions VIII, pp. 233 to 238) and of Ms Billum (Conclusions XII-1, pp. 253 and 254).

Denmark: employees are not obliged to stop working because of childbirth (Conclusions VIII, p. 124; in the last instance Conclusions XIII-1, p. 172);

Ireland: legislation provides for work to be interrupted for only four weeks after confinement (Conclusions VIII, p. 125; in the last instance XIII-1, p. 174);

Malta: the duration of post-natal leave is five weeks instead of six. In addition, the rules governing the breakdown of leave before and after childbirth makes no provision in the event of premature childbirth for the unused period of pre-natal leave to be deferred until after the birth. Moreover, women who fail to give their employer three weeks' notice of maternity leave before its beginning are, according to the relevant legislation, only entitled to leave comprising the day of childbirth and the following five weeks. Though this legislative provision had never been applied in practice, the Committee recalled that "the fact that a rule contrary to the Charter was not applied was not sufficient to render the situation satisfactory" (Conclusions XIII-2, p. 304);

Portugal: in some cases (the physical or psychological incapacity of the mother, the mother's participation in theoretical or practical training courses, stillbirth, miscarriage or death of the child during post-natal leave) the ninety days' total maternity leave before and after confinement can be reduced to between thirty and sixty days and post-natal leave amounts to less than six weeks (Conclusions XIII-3, pp. 312 to 314);

Sweden: the relevant legislation allows a female worker to forego her right to maternity leave and return to work (Conclusions VIII, p. 126; in the last instance Conclusions XIII-1, p. 176);

the *United Kingdom:* there is no obligation on the worker to stop work for a minimum of six weeks after confinement (Conclusions VIII, p. 127; in the last instance Conclusions XIII-1, p. 177).

Past cases of non-compliance which have been remedied included the following:

Greece:[1] civil servants who gave birth to a still-born child were only entitled to a month of sick leave which would be regarded as maternity leave (Conclusions XII-1, p. 148);

Ireland:[2] there were no statutory provisions for paid maternity leave (Conclusions III, p. 48);

the Netherlands:[3] in the event of premature childbirth, the period of maternity leave was less than the twelve week minimum (Conclusions XII-1, p. 149);

the United Kingdom:[4] there were no statutory provisions for paid maternity leave (Conclusions III, p. 49; Conclusions IV, p. 66).

In the revised Charter the length of maternity leave has been increased to fourteen weeks (Article 8 para. 1)

---

2.   Maternity benefits

Article 8 para. 1 of the Charter lays down that maternity leave shall be provided, "either by paid leave, by adequate social benefits or by benefits from public funds", which implies a choice of means of payment.

---

1 The situation was remedied by Act No. 2085 of 1992 which prescribes the same leave for such civil servants as for those having given birth to a living child (two months before and two months after confinement) (Conclusions XIII-1, p. 173). However, as this act came into force outside the reference period, the conclusion remained negative for this reason in Conclusions XIII-1.

2 The absence of legal guarantee of maternity leave was remedied by the Maternity Protection of Employees Act 1981, which entitled the employees to whom the act applied to at least fourteen weeks' maternity leave if they satisfied the contribution conditions to the general maternity scheme (Conclusions VIII, p. 125).

3 The situation was remedied by the Act of 22 February 1990 amending the 1913 Sickness Insurance Act which increased from twelve to sixteen the number of weeks' payment of maternity benefits and thus ensured maternity leave, whether or not the birth was on the expected date (Conclusions XIII-1, p. 175).

4 The situation was remedied by new legislation in 1975 and 1976 on employment protection which, *inter alia*, entitled female workers to resume their occupation any time within twenty-nine weeks from childbirth (Conclusions V, p. 76).

The Committee has specified that it left the choice "to governments to select, from a number of alternatives, the methods best suited to national circumstances" (First report on certain provisions of the Charter which have not been accepted, p. 19). A combination of several methods may be accepted, as, for example, a combination of a fixed social security allowance and a supplementary payment by the employer (Conclusions VIII, p. 124, Germany).

As regards the level of payments or benefits during the period of maternity leave, the terms used in Article 8 para. 1 are very general. Reference is made to "paid leave" and "adequate social security benefits or benefits from public funds". The qualifying word "adequate" does not refer to paid leave.

In the first supervision cycle, the Committee felt obliged to give an interpretation of the term "adequate benefit": "As in the similar instance of the first paragraph of Article 2, it was felt inadvisable to make any absolute definition" (Conclusions I, p. 50). The practice followed, therefore, is to decide on a case-by-case basis whether benefits are adequate or not.

Moreover, in its First report on certain provisions of the Charter which have not been accepted (p. 19), the Committee, commenting on the developing drive for equality between the sexes, stressed that "the protection of maternity provided for in Article 8 para. 1 should not be regarded as discriminatory *vis-à-vis* the interests of the woman worker, but as a social right on a par with paid holidays, benefiting both the mother and the child"; it explained that "to ensure that this is really the case, the Committee has always insisted on the importance of income maintenance during the mother's absence on maternity leave as it is essential that the mother should not suffer prejudice in the form of a substantial reduction in her income, implying a kind of sanction on maternity, for this would constitute a socially harmful instance of discrimination".

Up to the sixth cycle of supervision, the level of benefits in Contracting Parties was found to be adequate in most cases. More details on "adequate benefit" may be found from Conclusions VI onwards.

Thus in Conclusions VI concerning Ireland "pay-related maternity benefits representing 40% of weekly earnings between 14 and 50 Irish punts were thought to be "not sufficiently high to constitute an adequate income maintenance guarantee". In Conclusions IX-2, 80% of the pregnant woman's average earnings in Ireland was considered sufficient. The 70% to which it was reduced was not seen as sufficient in Conclusions X-2. In Conclusions XIII-1, the Committee noted that the 70% allowance was related to gross earnings and that in view of taxation procedures the income of female workers on maternity leave was close to 100% of their net wage, which was satisfactory. Whether and how this allowance, which was subject to a ceiling of 154 Irish punts per week, was supplemented for female workers whose wages were higher that the ceiling, remained a question to be clarified.

According to Conclusions X-1 concerning Greece, "70-85% of salary" was adequate, the balance being paid by the employer.

In Conclusions XI-2 the reduction in France of maternity benefit from 90% to 84% was not considered as inconsistent with the Charter, as it was intended to ensure that the amount of actual earnings would not be exceeded, something which could happen when the 90% rate was applied, as the benefit was calculated on the basis of gross salary. In Conclusions XII-1, 90% of monthly income was mentioned as sufficient for Denmark, but in Conclusions XIII-1 the Committee adjourned its conclusion for this country, because the legal maximum amount of benefits represented only 69% of the average wage. The Committee asked to be informed whether and in what way collective agreements provided for supplements (paid by employers or public funds) to offset the difference between maternity benefits and previous wages and whether all female wage-earners received such supplements.

It may be said that the Committee generally finds compensation during maternity leave adequate only when its amount approaches that of a woman's previous earnings.

Since the twelfth cycle of supervision, the Committee has examined in greater detail another aspect of the concept of "adequate benefits". It observed that the amount of maternity pay was often subject to a ceiling which directly modified this amount or resulted in a limit being set to the amount of wages taken into account for calculation. It thus began to ask the states concerned whether and how compensation was given between the maximum benefit and the amount of wages for women workers earning more than the ceiling, as in this case benefit may represent a rather small percentage of the worker's wages (see Conclusions XII-2, p. 134, France: the maximum maternity allowance only equalled 58% of the average monthly salary of women executives; Conclusions XIII-1, p. 174, Ireland: the maternity allowance was subject to a ceiling of 154 punts per week; p. 175, the Netherlands: an upper limit of 286.4 florins applied to maternity benefit, Conclusions XIII-2, p. 303, Belgium: the capped gross wage was fixed at 3,416 Belgian francs per day in 1992).

Finally, with the above-mentioned concern of ensuring that all paid women workers without exception benefit from the protection provided under Article 8 and taking into account the fact that the payments made in relation to maternity leave are often social security benefits, the Committee asked the following general question:

"The Committee asked all states which have accepted Article 8 para. 1 to indicate in their next report under this provision if the payment of maternity benefit is subject to conditions as to the length of affiliation to a social security insurance scheme, a specified period of occupational activity or of employment with one or more employers (indicating whether periods of unemployment are counted as working time for this purpose) and/or a specified salary level" (Conclusions XIII-1, p. 172).

Assessment of compliance

Three Contracting Parties are currently found infringing Article 8 para. 1 on grounds of insufficient level or duration of maternity benefits provided: Ireland, Malta and the United Kingdom.

Ireland: some women (those who do not satisfy the required contribution conditions) receive a maternity allowance of only 50 Irish punts per week (at July 1991), considered by the Committee as too low, in relation to the wages of female employees, to be acceptable (according to the Irish report, the average female industrial wage was 132 Irish punts per week – Conclusions XIII-1, p. 174).[1]

Malta: maternity benefits payable under the Social Security Act to employees not covered by the 1952 Employment Conditions (Regulation) Act are considered very insufficient. (Conclusions XII-2, p. 137: 16% of the minimum wage and Conclusions XIII-2, p. 306: 17.2% of the minimum wage). Moreover this benefit was reserved solely for Maltese citizens and the wives of Maltese citizens "ordinarily resident in Malta" (see above under "General")

the *United Kingdom:* the situation is considered unsatisfactory, as statutory maternity pay (SMP), which amounts to 90% of the usual wage and is thus considered by the Committee as "adequate", is only paid to certain employed women (those with two or more years' service with the same employer) and only for six weeks instead of the twelve required by the Charter. Moreover, the Committee considered inadequate the weekly statutory maternity allowance (SMP) of 36 pounds paid for a further twelve weeks to the aforesaid women and for a further eighteen weeks to employed women with between six months' and two years' service with the same employer, as well as the maternity allowance (MA) of 33 pounds paid for eighteen weeks to women not entitled to SMP but who had paid sufficient national insurance contributions (Conclusions XII-1, pp. 150 to 152, the United Kingdom).[2] The negative conclusion was maintained in Conclusions XIII-1 (pp. 176 and 177), despite the increase of SMP to 44.50 pounds and MA to 40.60 pounds, as the Committee considered the increase still not sufficient to ensure to women an income close to their previous income (minimum adult wage was fixed at 129.43 pounds per week in 1991). Employed women with

---

1 However, the Committee noted with satisfaction in the same Conclusions the extension of the scope of the 1981 Maternity Protection of Employees Act and the Social Welfare (Employment of Inconsiderable Extent) (No. 2) Regulations 1991 which guarantee the full range of benefits, including maternity allowance, for employees whose weekly earnings are 25 punts or more, but it observed that a number of female workers continued to be denied access to maternity benefits.

2 See Professor Fabricius' separate opinion (Conclusions XII-1, pp. 246 to 252).

less than six months' service with the same employer could, subject to certain conditions concerning the length of national social insurance contributions, claim sickness benefit (£39.60) for eight weeks.

A fourth Contracting Party which does not satisfy the requirements for payments is *Italy*,[1] for whom the conclusion is negative since domestic employees dismissed during pregnancy are still not entitled to maternity benefits in cash, which is contrary to the Charter (Conclusions XIII-2, p. 213; see also above, under "General").

Paragraph 2 – Illegality of dismissal during maternity leave

Under this paragraph, the Contracting Parties undertake:

> "to consider it as unlawful for an employer to give a woman notice of dismissal during her absence on maternity leave or to give her notice of dismissal at such a time that the notice would expire during such absence".

The protected period is therefore limited to the time granted to women as maternity leave. The Committee considered in this connection that "it would obviously have been better if the prohibition had covered the entire period of pregnancy" (First report on certain provisions of the Charter which have not been accepted, p. 23).

As regards the personal scope of this provision (see also above, "General" under Article 8) the Committee, throughout all the supervision cycles, has consistently held that all women workers without exception should be entitled to protection under paragraph 2. In the fourth cycle of supervision, when reiterating its negative conclusion in respect of a

---

1 The Committee of Ministers addressed a recommendation to Italy on this subject; see above, under "General".

Contracting Party which did not protect all women, the Committee stated that "the text of Article 8 clearly demonstrates that no limitation of the personal scope of its provisions is admissible and that its paragraph 2 is not among the provisions in the Charter in respect of which Article 33 authorises some of the beneficiaries to be excluded." (Conclusions IV, p. 67, Austria).

The Committee, from the very first supervision cycle, interpreted this provision "as not laying down an absolute prohibition which could be removed, for instance, in the following cases:

1. if an employed woman has been guilty of misconduct which justifies breaking off the employment relationship,

2. if the undertaking concerned ceases to operate,

3. if the period prescribed in the employment contract has expired." (Conclusions I, p. 51).

This view has been retained by the Committee throughout all the supervision cycles (see for example Conclusions XIII-2, p. 215, Spain; in the last instance, Conclusions XIII-3, p. 315, Portugal).

When national laws permit dismissal during maternity leave in some cases, the Committee is careful to ensure that these correspond to the authorised reasons under its case law, especially when only very general terms are used in the reports, such as "urgent reasons" (Conclusions XIII-1, p. 179, the Netherlands), "objective reasons" (Conclusions XIII-2, pp. 215 and 216, Spain) or "serious grounds" (Addendum to Conclusions XIII-3, p. 49, Luxembourg).

The Committee also shows concern over the wrongful employment of women on the basis of fixed-term contracts, aimed to avoid the prohibition of dismissal during maternity leave (Conclusions XII-2, p. 139 and Conclusions XIII-2, pp. 213 and 214, Austria; Addendum to Conclusions XIII-3, p. 49, Luxembourg).

Commenting in general on this provision in its First report on certain provisions of the Charter which have not been accepted (p. 21), the Committee stated that this paragraph "is complementary to paragraph 1 of Article 8 since it is designed to protect maternity as such against certain possible negative effects on a woman's working life. By prohibiting dismissal of a woman worker during her absence on maternity leave, the Charter seeks to protect her not only against the economic effects of such action, but also against the psychological effects which normally accompany it". The Committee went on to point out that Article 8 para. 2 "is intended to protect not only the financial security of female workers, but also their security of employment" (Conclusions VII, p. 54). This statement has been made repeatedly in the Committee's conclusions (see most recently Conclusions XIII-2, p. 307).

Thus defined, the purpose of Article 8 para. 2 means that in cases of dismissal in breach of the prohibition contained in this provision, the worker should be reinstated in her employment, as this is the only solution which effectively guarantees job security: "The Committee pointed out that the purpose of Article 8 para. 2 was to safeguard the jobs of women workers during maternity leave and drew the [...] authorities' attention to its case law on Article 4 para. 3 on dismissal, which could be applied to this provision. In this regard, it is stated that reinstatement should be the rule that only in exceptional circumstances should compensation be the sole remedy and that the compensation should be sufficient to deter the employer and compensate the employee. It asked that the next report specify whether [...] legislation provided for reinstatement of women workers and, if not, whether this reinstatement was envisaged." (Conclusions XIII-2, pp. 307 and 308, Belgium and pp. 308 and 309, Malta; see also Conclusions XII-2, p. 140, Cyprus and Conclusions XIII-3, p. 314, Finland).

Assessment of compliance

Contracting Parties found as not complying with this provision are Austria, Italy, Greece, Portugal and Spain.

The conclusions for Austria and Italy have been negative since their first report: for *Austria*[1] because the relevant Maternity Protection Law, which prohibits the dismissal of a pregnant woman, does not apply to domestic employees between the end of the fifth month of pregnancy and childbirth (Conclusions III, p. 49, IV pp. 66 and 67, V p. 77, VI p. 63, VII p. 54, VIII p. 127, IX-2 p. 61, X-2 p. 95, XI-2 p. 94, XII-2 p. 139 and XIII-2 pp. 213 and 214), and for *Italy*[1] because the Act on the protection of working mothers does not provide any protection from dismissal for this category of workers during the protected period. (Conclusions I, p. 51, II p. 39, III p. 49, IV p. 67, V p. 77, VI p. 63, VII p. 55, VIII p. 127, IX-2 p. 61, X-2 pp. 95-96, XI-2 pp. 94-95, XII-2 p. 140 and XIII-2, p. 215).

As regards Austria, the Committee did not accept the government's argument that it had ratified and complied with ILO Convention No. 103 (Protection of Maternity), to which reference was made in the Form for Reports for this paragraph. The Committee held that the Convention was "referred to with the sole aim of helping governments to prepare their reports without any suggestion that the personal and material scope of Convention No. 103 is the same as the Charter's" (Conclusions IV, p. 67). Nor did the Committee consider the special financial assistance granted in case of dismissal as relieving Austria of its obligation, as this paragraph was designed to safeguard not only the financial security of female employees but also their jobs. (Conclusions-VIII, p. 127).

The other negative conclusions were reached for the following reasons:

Greece: there is no legislative provision prohibiting the dismissal of women seafarers (Conclusions XIII-1, p. 178);

Portugal: none of the specified objective grounds of dismissal provided for in the labour law falls within the exceptions to the prohibition

---

1 For the second part of the twelfth cycle, the Committee of Ministers addressed recommendations both to Austria and to Italy in order that they amend their legislation to protect this category of workers; see above under "general".

contained in Article 8 para. 2 allowed by the Committee's case law (Conclusions XIII-3, p. 315);

Spain: the grounds of dismissal provided for in the Workers' Statute are wider than those for which the Committee allows an employed woman to be dismissed during maternity leave or at such a time that the notice of dismissal expires during maternity leave (Conclusions XIII-2, pp. 215 and 216).

Article 8 para. 2 of the revised Charter has been amended to extend the protected period. It reads as follows:

"With a view to ensuring the effective exercise of the right of employed women to the protection of maternity, the Parties undertake:

...

to consider it as unlawful for an employer to give a woman notice of dismissal during the period from the time she notifies her employer that she is pregnant until the end of her maternity leave, or to give her notice of dismissal at such time that the notice would expire during such a period."

Moreover, an appendix to Article 8 para. 2 was added which reads as follows:

"This provision shall not be interpreted as laying down an absolute prohibition. Exceptions could be made, for instance, in the following cases:

a.   if an employed woman has been guilty of misconduct which justifies breaking off the employment relationship;

b.   if the undertaking concerned ceases to operate;

c.   if the period prescribed in the employment contract has expired."

Paragraph 3 – Time off for nursing mothers

Under this paragraph, the Contracting Parties undertake:

> "to provide that mothers who are nursing their infants shall be entitled to sufficient time off for this purpose".

1.	As regards the personal scope of the protection provided under this paragraph, the Committee has consistently held the view that all female workers, without exception, are covered, as Article 33 does not apply (see also above, "General", under Article 8).

For this reason Italy,[1] where female domestic workers and women working at home are not covered by the Act on the protection of working mothers, has been found as not complying with this paragraph (Conclusions IV, p. 67, V p. 78, Conclusions VI, p. 64, VII p. 55, VIII p. 128, IX-2 p. 61, X-2 p. 97, XI-2 p. 96, XII-2 p. 143 and in the last instance Conclusions XIII-2, p. 215).

Sweden[2] was also found as not complying with this provision in the seventh cycle, on the ground that domestic employees did not benefit under legislation from the right to time off for nursing their children as opposed to other employees who were protected by the Work Environment Act of 1978. (Conclusions VII, p. 55).

2.	According to the Committee, time off for nursing mothers must be provided as part of working hours and be paid as such (see, in the first instance, Conclusions I, p. 51, Italy, and most recently Addendum to Conclusions XIII-3, p. 49, Luxembourg).

In this respect, the Netherlands has been found as not fulfilling its undertaking under this paragraph as there are certain gaps in the legislation relating to the right of employed women to remunerated time off

---

1 The Committee of Ministers addressed a recommendation to Italy for the second part of the twelfth supervision cycle concerning, *inter alia*, Article 8 para. 3 (see above under "general").

2 The situation of domestic employees was remedied by the transfer of the provision of Chapter IV, Section 4 of the 1978 Work Environment Act which stipulates that "a mother may not be denied time off for the purpose of nursing her child" to the Act concerning the right to leave of absence or the care of a child which came into force on 1 January 1983 and also covers household employees. (Conclusions VIII, p. 128 and Conclusions IX-1, p. 72).

for breast-feeding which have not been filled by collective agreements (Conclusions X-1, p. 97, XI-1 p. 107). In Conclusions XII-1 (p. 155), the Committee noted that these gaps concerned the remuneration and the taking into consideration of time off for breast-feeding as working time. The Committee did not find convincing the explanations of the Netherlands' Government that general legislation guarantees women's right to time off for breast-feeding and that the obligation to act as "good employer(s)" contained in the Civil Code ensures that employers paid women for such time off, on the ground that the legislation providing for time off for breast-feeding (the Labour Act of 1919) does not state that such time should be regarded as working time nor that it should be paid. Moreover, according to information provided to the ILO by the Netherlands Trade Union Confederation and which was brought to the attention of the Committee, in practice many employers require women to make up for any time taken off for breast-feeding or refuse to pay them for this time. (Conclusions XIII-1, p. 180).

The Committee has also been prompted to point out that the breaks for breast-feeding are necessarily to be given during working hours. For this reason it has reached a negative conclusion for Belgium, where employers are not required by law to grant time off with pay for nursing mothers during working hours. The Committee considers that the possibility of part-time work or leave which may be taken after childbirth, although interesting in itself, does not correspond to the commitment entered into under Article 8 para. 3 (Conclusions XIII-2, p. 309).

This situation may be compared to that of Sweden: under the Child Care Leave Act women have the right to time off for breast-feeding, but employers are not legally bound to grant this time off during working hours; following confinement there are also possibilities for part-time work, the hours not worked being financially compensated by the parental allowance. The Committee has deferred its conclusion (Conclusions XIII-1, pp. 180 and 181); it will be interesting to note the replies given and the Committee's future assessment of them.

3. As regards arrangements for time off for breast-feeding, the Committee has given no general definition of "sufficient time off" and

assesses each situation individually. For example, it has considered the following situations to be satisfactory:

–   two periods of rest per day for a year for the purposes of feeding, of one half-hour each, in cases where the employer provides creche or nursing room facilities for mothers, and of one hour each where these are not provided, in which case the mother is entitled to leave the premises (Conclusions I, p. 51, Italy, see also p. 191, Federal Republic of Germany);

–   one hour per day for the purpose of nursing infants up to the age of one year (Conclusions V, p. 78, France);

–   one hour per day for mothers of children up to nine months of age, which may be divided into two half-hour periods or replaced by a reduction of one half-hour in daily working hours (Addendum to Conclusions IX-2, p. 22, Spain);

–   two daily rest periods of not more than one hour, to be taken at different times, for as long as breast-feeding continues or until the child's first birthday (Conclusions XIII-3, p. 315, Portugal);

–   two periods of forty-five minutes each, granted to nursing mothers who so request, for breast-feeding at the beginning and at the end of the working day, which two periods may be combined in a single period of at least ninety minutes where there is only one break of less than one hour in the course of the working day or where the employee is unable to breast-feed her baby near the workplace (Addendum to Conclusions XIII-3, p. 49, Luxembourg).

Assessment of compliance

The Committee's conclusion is negative for three Contracting Parties: *Italy*, for the reasons set out in point 1; *Belgium* and the *Netherlands* for those set out in point 2.

Paragraph 4 – Regulation of night work and prohibition of dangerous, unhealthy and arduous work for women workers

Under this paragraph, the Contracting Parties undertake:

"a. to regulate the employment of women workers on night work in industrial employment;

b. to prohibit the employment of women workers in underground mining, and, as appropriate, on all other work which is unsuitable for them by reason of its dangerous, unhealthy or arduous nature".

Unlike the first three paragraphs of Article 8, which are concerned exclusively with maternity, this paragraph is concerned with the general protection of women at work. Consequently, this provision could imply a contradiction between the principle of equality between women and men and the special protection afforded to women which is often considered as being discriminatory except in the case of maternity. The case law of the Committee has endeavoured to reconcile these two conflicting aspects of the protection of women, both set out in the Charter.

The Committee's comments on its own case law, made in the General introduction to Conclusions XII-1, may summarise paragraph 4 of Article 8: "conflicts between the principle of equality between sexes and the specific protection of women posed certain problems with regard to Article 8 of the Charter. On the one hand, although measures relating to pregnancy and maternity are not traditionally considered to be discriminatory, a contradictory tendency is beginning to emerge. On the other hand [...], it has been remarked that there might be some difficulty in reconciling the rules of Article 8 paragraph 4 with equality". The Committee stated clearly that in the interpretation of this provision which it had adopted in the course of the tenth supervision cycle it had taken "note of sociological, scientific and technological developments in an attempt to reconcile these contradictory trends". Commenting on its entire case law, which the Committee reconfirmed, it stated that it "reflects the consideration which the Committee has always given to real equality between women and men in employment, while bearing in mind such specific forms of protection as are necessary. It has thus arrived at, on the one hand, affirming the egalitarian requirements of Article 1 para. 2, while continuing, on the other, to stress the necessity for the specific protection of women provided for in Article 8 para. 4" (Conclusions XII-1, pp. 22 to 24).

Paragraph 4a requires states to *regulate* the employment of women on night work, whilst paragraph 4b requires states to *prohibit* the employment of women in underground mining, etc.

1.   Regulation of night work for women in industrial employment (Article 8 para. 4a)

In the first supervision cycle, the Committee decided that the expression "industrial employment" could not be interpreted as referring to non-industrial employment in industrial enterprises. The Committee reached this conclusion by comparing the text of this sub-paragraph with the corresponding text of ILO Convention No. 89, which in this respect employs a different term (Conclusions I, p. 192).

As far as the requirement of paragraph 4 to "regulate the employment of women workers on night work" is concerned, the Committee considered it appropriate "to indicate what degree and nature of regulation is here called for, and whether, if such regulation applies to men equally with women workers, the requirements of this provision are met. The Committee concluded that in the context of this whole Article (the right of employed women to protection), the regulations should be such as to afford women workers protection against the harmful physical (and sociological) effects of night work; if this protection is afforded to women by measures of general application, it is not necessary to take further measures to afford them additional 'special' protection over and above that given to men. The adequacy of the regulations applicable to night work must be judged by their effectiveness in securing to women the protection to which they have a right" (Second report on certain provisions of the Charter which have not been accepted, p. 15).

The Committee first gave some details of what the regulations should contain in the ninth supervision cycle. It accepted that a Contracting

Party whose legislation allowed exceptions to the prohibition of night work by women in factories and craft workshops provided that there was compulsory notification of such exceptions to the Labour Inspectorate and that these were permitted only if the particular requirements of production made them necessary, and if due account was taken of conditions in the work environment and the organisation of the enterprises concerned, was complying with the Charter. In the opinion of the Committee, night work was duly "regulated", within the meaning of Article 8 para. 4a (Conclusions IX-2, pp. 62 and 63, Italy).

In the tenth cycle (second part), "the efforts of governments to establish *de facto* and *de jure* equality between women and men in all fields, and expressly that of work, involving the gradual and constant elimination of all forms of discrimination based on sex, prompted the Committee to define the scope of Article 8, paragraph 4 of the Charter more precisely.

With regard to the undertaking 'to regulate the employment of women workers on night work in industrial employment' (sub-paragraph a.), the Committee confirmed its case law to the effect that, to comply with this provision, a state is not obliged to enact specific regulations for women if it can demonstrate the existence of regulations applying without distinction to workers of both sexes. Such regulations must specify the conditions governing night work, such as the need to secure permission from the Labour Inspectorate (if necessary), the laying down of working hours, breaks, days of rest following periods of night work, etc. These regulations are designed in particular to limit the adverse effects of night work on the worker's health and family life and to prevent abuses" (Conclusions X-2, p. 97; see also Conclusions XII-1, General introduction, pp. 22 and 23).

Since then the Committee has always requested that the Contracting Parties include in their reports information on the content of the applicable regulations "with respect to the conditions laid down in its jurisprudence" (Conclusions XII-2, pp. 144 and 145, France; Conclusions XII-2, p. 145 and 146 and XIII-2, p. 218, Italy; Conclusions XII-2, p. 146 and XIII-2, p. 311, Malta; Conclusions XIII-1, p. 181, Greece; Conclusions XIII-2, p. 310, Belgium).

In the light of its case law and given the information received, the Committee concluded that a Contracting Party in which legislation lifted for a period of three years the ban on night work by women in factories and workshops but under another act night work was still authorised and its duration as well as the duration of rest periods was regulated, complied with the Charter (Conclusions XI-1, pp. 108 and 109, the Netherlands). This view was reiterated even when by a new Act of 1989 the prohibition of night work was removed completely, so long as the other legislation made it necessary to obtain authorisation for night work and controlled the length of work and rest hours (Conclusions XII-1, p. 157);

A negative conclusion was reached for Ireland: the Committee had found that the provisions of the 1936 Conditions of Employment Act, which were cited by the Irish Government as the regulations applicable to night work in industry, did not specifically apply to night work, but to various forms of shift work. Moreover it had found (Conclusions X-2, p. 98) that these provisions were not really designed to "limit the damaging effects of night work and to prevent abuse". In the absence of any reply to its question as to what regulations, if any, applied to night work in industry and "given that the regulations already submitted neither were consistent with the aims of this provision of the Charter nor afforded sufficient protection and that no regulations in industry had been indicated", the Committee concluded that Ireland was not complying with the Charter (Conclusions XIII-1, pp. 182 and 183).

There have been recent developments concerning night work for women: following the judgement delivered by the Court of Justice of the European Communities on 25 July 1991 in the Stoeckel case (Case C 345/89), Contracting Parties which had ratified ILO Convention No. 89 (Night Work – Women)[1] and are member states of the European Union have denounced this ILO Convention; consequently, changes were to

---

1 This Convention prohibits the employment of women workers on night work in industry, with some exemptions. In 1990, a protocol to this Convention, introducing further exemptions from the ban, and a new Convention (No. 171) regulating night work performed by both men and women, with special provisions to protect maternity, were adopted.

be expected in the national laws of these states, under which night work for women was formerly prohibited. "In this context, the Committee drew attention, and particularly that of the Community member states when they come to amend their legislation, to its case law according to which 'regulations must specify the conditions governing night work, such as the need to secure permission from the Labour Inspectorate (if necessary), the laying down of working hours, breaks, days of rest following periods of night work, etc.' (Conclusions X-2, p. 97). It would like the particular situations of pregnant women, women who have recently given birth or nursing mothers to be taken into account under this provision of the Charter" (Conclusions XII-2, pp. 23 and 24).

Since then, when needed, the Committee asks these states for information on "any new provisions that might be implemented with regard to night work" and "whether the particular situation of pregnant women, women who have just given birth or were nursing is taken into account for the purpose of this provision of the Charter" (see, for Belgium, Conclusions XIII-2, p. 310; for France, Conclusions XII-2, p. 145; for Greece, Conclusions XIII-1, p. 181; for Italy, Conclusions XII-2, p. 146 and Conclusions XIII-2, p. 218; for Malta, Conclusions XIII-2, p. 312).

Assessment of compliance

Only one Contracting Party does not meet the requirements of Article 8 para. 4a: Ireland (see above).

2. Prohibition of the employment of women in certain dangerous, unhealthy or arduous work (Article 8 para. 4b)

This sub-paragraph provides for the prohibition of certain tasks for women; the risk of potential discrimination is therefore greater than in the case of night work, which requires only to be regulated. For this reason the Committee decided to restrict the scope of this sub-paragraph, which contains two distinct prohibitions.

a. Prohibition of employment in underground mining

As regards this prohibition, the Committee examined in the sixth cycle the compatibility with this provision of a change in the legislation of a Contracting Party "to allow employment of women below ground in mines worked for minerals (eg. female doctors, nurses, etc. going underground in a working mine in the course of their work), provided they do not spend a significant proportion of their time below ground and also to allow women to work underground in mines no longer worked for minerals eg. to cultivate mushrooms, guiding tourists, etc." The Committee noted that "there appeared to exist a difference between the wording of the French and the English texts of paragraph 4b of Article 8. The French text prohibited 'the employment of women workers on underground work in mines', whereas the English text prohibited such employment '[...] in underground mining'. The French text thus seemed to be wider in its purview in that it excluded underground work in mines even if such work was unconnected with mining proper as opposed to the English text which covered a less wide ground, ie. cases concerned with mining proper underground." (Conclusions VI, p. 65, the United Kingdom).

The Committee, solving this problem of interpretation by referring to ILO Convention No. 45 (Underground Work – Women) which, despite the fact that its wording in French was in agreement with the French text of Article 4b, allowed exemptions from the prohibition of employment on underground work in the case of "females employed in health and welfare services or females occasionally entering the underground parts of a mine for non-manual occupations", decided to adopt the more limited meaning of the English text: "The Committee therefore took the view that this provision of the Charter prohibited employment of women in 'underground mining' in the sense indicated above and not *any* work carried out underground in a mine, unless, of course, such work was 'unsuitable by reason of its dangerous, unhealthy or arduous nature' as provided for in paragraph 4b of Article 8" (*ibidem*); it concluded that the Contracting Party concerned was complying with the Charter since the amendment introduced in its legislation corresponded to the derogations of the ILO convention and since in all other cases the employment of women underground remained prohibited (*ibidem*).

As in the case of sub-paragraph a. of Article 8 para. 4, the growing importance of the principle of equality between men and women led the Committee to further define its standpoint in a general observation: "The efforts to establish de facto and de jure equality between women and men in all fields, and especially that of work, involving the gradual and constant elimination of all forms of discrimination based on sex, have prompted the Committee to define the scope of Article 8, paragraph 4 of the Charter more precisely.

...

With regard to the undertaking to "prohibit the employment of women workers in underground mining" (first part of sub-paragraph b) the Committee clarified its case law by specifying that the above-mentioned prohibition is concerned only with the employment of women on underground extraction work in mines, to the exclusion of all other occupations, and in particular those of a social or medical nature, management, inspection, etc." (Conclusions X-2, p. 97).

The Committee accepted that where there is no mining industry, this provision has no relevance (see Conclusions XII-2, p. 147, Malta).

Assessment of compliance

The prohibition of employment in underground mining work should exist in the legislation of Contracting Parties which have accepted this provision, otherwise the conclusion is negative.

Thus the conclusion for Italy is negative on this point, as by a change in legislation the employment of women workers in underground extraction is no longer prohibited, except in the case of pregnant women. It has been maintained despite the fact that according to the report of Italy, of the very few women working in mines none actually carried out extraction work. (Conclusions XI-2, p. 97, Conclusions XII-2, p. 145 and Conclusions XIII-2, p. 217).

With respect to Ireland, "the Committee had noted that Ireland had denounced ILO Convention No. 45 (Underground Work – Women) with effect from May 1989 (ie. during the present supervision cycle). It had asked to be kept informed of any developments in the situation, in particular, whether the ban on the employment of women on manual work in mines had been repealed. The Committee strongly regretted that the report contained no information on the matter and insisted that the next report should answer these questions. In the absence of information on the new situation created by the denunciation of ILO Convention No. 45, the Committee deferred its conclusion" (Conclusions XIII-1, p. 183).

b. Prohibition, as appropriate, of all work of a dangerous, unhealthy or arduous nature

In the general observation referred to under point a. and for the same reasons, the Committee has defined the scope of this prohibition:

"As regards the second part of sub-paragraph *b.*, prohibiting employment of women 'as appropriate' on all other work which is unsuitable for them by reason of its "dangerous, unhealthy or arduous nature" the Committee clarified that the "expression 'as appropriate' permits states bound by this provision of the Charter to limit the prohibition of employment of women in the above-mentioned occupations to the sole cases where this is necessary, in particular to protect motherhood, notably pregnancy, confinement and the post-natal period, as well as future children." (Conclusions X-2, pp. 97 and 98).

Within these limits, the Committee pays particular attention to activities entailing exposure to lead (Conclusions XIII-1, p. 182, Greece; Conclusions XII-2, p. 145 and XIII-2, p. 217, Italy; Conclusions XII-2, p. 147, Malta; Conclusions XI-2, p. 98, Spain), to benzene (Conclusions XII-1, p. 156 and XIII-1, p. 182, Greece; Conclusions XII-2, p. 145 and XIII-2, pp. 217 and 218, Italy) or to ionising radiation (Conclusions XIII-1, p. 182, Greece; Conclusions XI-2, p. 97, Italy; Conclusions XII-2, p. 147, Malta; Conclusions XI-2, p. 98, Spain).

The example of Italy is particularly significant: in the eleventh cycle, having noted that legislation prohibited dangerous unhealthy and arduous work for pregnant women and excluded women of child-bearing age from activities involving the risk of exposure to ionising radiation, the Committee concluded that the situation complied with this part of Article 8 para. 4b. (Conclusions XI-2, pp. 97 and 98).

In the twelfth supervision cycle however, the Committee, having learnt from ILO sources that there was some difficulty with regard to the employment of women exposed to lead and to benzene, asked for information on the measures taken to protect women of child-bearing age from the risks of exposure to lead at work, as well as steps taken to protect nursing mothers from the risks of exposure to benzene, regardless of the duration of nursing. (Conclusions XII-2, p. 145). In the thirteenth cycle the Committee noted that a legislative decree had been adopted to bring Italian legislation into line in particular with Community Directive 82/605. This decree provided, *inter alia*, for measures to protect workers against the risks relating to exposure to lead, with specific exposure limits for women of child-bearing age. Moreover, legislation was in preparation for protection against risks relating to exposure to benzene with a view to implementing Community Directive 90/394. The Committee asked what medical checks such women received under the legislative decree, whether the Italian authorities would not consider banning the employment of such women in work involving exposure to lead and whether the new legislation would provide for an extension of the prohibition of employment of nursing mothers beyond seven months after birth so as to cover the entire nursing period (Conclusions XIII-2, pp. 217 and 218).

Assessment of compliance

The Committee adopted a negative conclusion in respect of *Greece* as it noted that as regards dangerous, unhealthy or arduous occupations for women workers, other than underground mining which is forbidden to women, "almost all other provisions relating to protection against dangerous activities applied to workers of both sexes and that, according to the Greek authorities, these standards did not afford adequate protection to women of child-bearing age. The Committee expressed concern at this situation which appeared to imply that, even in occupations as dangerous to motherhood and future children as those which involved exposure to ionisation radiation, benzene or lead, for example, the standards are inadequate." (Conclusions XIII-1, p. 182).

In order to take into account the principle of equality, this Article has been modified in the revised Charter so as to protect women exclusively in the case of maternity.

In addition to the amendments to paragraphs 1 and 2 mentioned above, Article 8 para. 4 makes it compulsory to regulate the employment in night work of pregnant women, women who have recently given birth and women nursing their infants. Protection for workers of both sexes performing night work is now provided for exclusively under Article 2 para. 7. Article 8 para. 5 limits the prohibition of employment of women in underground mining and in all other work which is unsuitable by reason of its dangerous, unhealthy or arduous nature to the case of maternity as defined above.

Article 8 reads as follows:

"Article 8 – The right of employed women to protection of maternity

With a view to ensuring the effective exercise of the right of employed women to the protection of maternity, the Parties undertake:

1.   to provide either by paid leave, by adequate social security benefits or by benefits from public funds for employed women to take leave before and after childbirth up to a total of at least fourteen weeks;

2.   to consider it as unlawful for an employer to give a woman notice of dismissal during the period from the time she notifies her employer that she is pregnant until the end of her maternity leave, or to give her notice of dismissal at such a time that the notice would expire during such a period;

3.   to provide that mothers who are nursing their infants shall be entitled to sufficient time off for this purpose;

4. to regulate the employment in night work of pregnant women, women who have recently given birth and women nursing their infants;

5. to prohibit the employment of pregnant women, women who have recently given birth or who are nursing their infants in underground mining and all other work which is unsuitable by reason of its dangerous, unhealthy or arduous nature and to take appropriate measures to protect the employment rights of these women.

Article 9 – The right to vocational guidance

This Article, which consists of a single paragraph, reads as follows:

> "With a view to ensuring the effective exercise of the right to vocational guidance, the Contracting Parties undertake to provide or promote, as necessary, a service which will assist all persons, including the handicapped, to solve problems related to occupational choice and progress, with due regard to the individual's characteristics and their relation to occupational opportunity; this assistance should be available free of charge, both to young persons, including school children, and to adults".

In the first supervision cycle, the Committee made the following general statement:

"The purpose of this Article is to make it compulsory for those states having accepted it to operate a service that helps all persons, free of charge, to solve their problems relating to vocational guidance. Article 9 is a considerable innovation in the history of international labour law, this being the first time that there has been any international undertaking concerning vocational guidance; until now, the principle appeared in international law only through various recommendations" (Conclusions I, p. 53).

It also made a number of points in connection with the interpretation of Article 9. It emphasised first that the expression "as necessary" used in Article 9 "bound those states which still had a fairly high level of unemployment to make a special effort as regards vocational guidance", and pointed out that "vocational guidance facilities should be placed at the disposal not only of unemployed persons but of all categories of students and particularly young people leaving school" (*ibidem*).

Secondly it made it clear that adequate information on the following was needed for assessing compliance:

"1. the functions, organisation and operation of public and private vocational guidance services;

2. measures to improve and co-ordinate these services, including measures to assist handicapped persons;

3. measures taken to promote social advancement through vocational guidance (including measures to inform the public);

4. the financing of vocational guidance services, the size of their professional staff and the number of people assisted by them" (*ibidem*).

Three cycles later, having noted that the period under review (1972-1973) had been characterised by an economic crisis – one of its consequences being rising unemployment – the Committee stressed that "this overall situation emphasises particularly the importance of the social and economic commitments arising out of the Charter". In this context, the Committee expressed the view, *inter alia*, that "in accordance with Articles 9 and 10 of the Charter, governments should take steps to facilitate young people's entry and adjustment to working life. The problem is particularly acute in the case of migrant workers and their families" (Conclusions IV, p. XIV). The Committee "stressed the importance of vocational guidance in a modern economy especially at times of economic recession and defined it as the service which assists all persons to solve problems related to occupational choice and with due regard to the individual's characteristics and their relation to occupational opportunity" (Conclusions IV, p. 69).

Since then, vocational guidance has taken on a growing importance in national policies and consequently in the Committee's case law, which lends particular attention to the more vulnerable categories which constitute the labour market (young persons, the disabled – these two categories being expressly targeted by Article 9 – women, the unemployed and foreigners – for whom the Appendix to the Charter provides equal treatment if they are nationals of the other Contracting Parties legally residing or working regularly within the territory of the Contracting Party in question). The Committee has also greatly stressed the steps to be taken to increase awareness of vocational guidance services and emphasised "the importance of information on the effective exercise of the right to vocational guidance" (see in the last instance Conclusions XIII-2, p. 314, Belgium and Conclusions XIII-3, p. 318, Finland).

The Committee devoted the thematic part of the General introduction of Conclusions XIII-3 to the topic of vocational guidance and training, stressing that "action in this field had become essential in the current European context, not only in the combat against unemployment, but also in responding to technical advances and the conversion of industries, as well as to all the changes linked to the transitional periods in the countries of central and eastern Europe" (General introduction to Conclusions XIII-3, p. 30).

It retraced the changes which had occurred and resumed the principal aspects of its case law in the area of vocational guidance (*ibidem*, pp. 30 to 32):

"In the first stages of the economic crisis in Western Europe, vocational guidance and training were seen as remedies for increasing unemployment, used to orient workers towards developing sectors and to give them the necessary training or retraining. Since then, the economy has undergone profound transformations, whether these be technological developments which have totally shaken the labour market by eliminating some traditional jobs and creating others requiring different skills, or the transition of central and eastern Europe to a market economy which has entirely transformed every aspect of the labour market.

In this context, vocational guidance and even more so vocational training are elements needed to ensure that the labour available meets demands.

The states under consideration therefore continued their efforts over the reference period in order to adapt vocational guidance and training schemes to these economic transformations.

The Committee thus observed the greater importance taken on by careers advice and vocational guidance activities, demonstrated in many states by a concern to extend and improve guidance services, inter alia through computerisation (Norway) or the setting up of specific departments in schools (Spain), as well as increases in the relevant expenditure. The Committee stressed that Article 9 requires these services to be free of charge.

A comparative study of data submitted in relation to Article 9 revealed that there was no systematic provision of information on the amount of public expenditure set aside for vocational guidance, the number of people benefiting from such guidance, levels of staff assigned to guidance or on the geographical distribution of services. This information is necessary in order to allow the Committee to adopt the most objective possible approach to national situations and thereby constitutes a vital element in the assessment of the conformity of these situations. The Committee therefore emphasised that such information should be provided in the next supervision cycle.

The study also revealed that in most Contracting Parties there were two levels of vocational guidance, one carried out within the education system and the other in the labour market. Since these complemented each other, the Committee wished national reports to give relevant information for each reference period, including figures, making a distinction between careers guidance in schools and vocational guidance within the labour market.

A number of the countries examined had encouraged measures to promote careers guidance for young people within the education system by increasing the numbers of staff assigned to this task (Denmark and

Ireland) or through special programmes designed to give young people a better idea of their occupational abilities and in this way to help them choose a career, an example being the 'Active Vocational Guidance' programme in Greece.

Where adult guidance was concerned, some countries had given particular attention, as the text of the Charter suggests, to the disabled. Thus in Malta a Special Needs Unit for people with disabilities had been set up within the employment office, while experimental activities for the benefit of disabled people launched within the framework of the Horizon programme had had positive effects in Portugal and Spain. A lack of information on measures to help people with disabilities has in several cases led the Committee to request that the next report be more comprehensive.

Various initiatives taken for women were also observed: measures had been adopted in Cyprus to improve the quality and quantity of vocational guidance for women, with a view to encouraging them to enter the labour market; the setting up of guidance services for women in Austria had enabled a larger number of women to find employment.

As the Committee has emphasised since the first supervision cycle, a particular effort must be made in the field of guidance for the unemployed.[1] Guidance services have indeed proved to be increasingly important and efficient contributors to the reintegration of unemployed people, particularly those out of work for long periods. Thus in Ireland priority was given to vocational guidance for the long-term unemployed, while in the United Kingdom thought was being given to methods of improving and adapting the guidance services available to them. An OECD study on employment revealed that the French Government had launched a scheme in 1992 to combat long-term unemployment through individual interviews to ascertain the employment prospects and training needs of people who had been unemployed for more than a year.

1 Conclusions I, p. 53.

Lastly, because of the often more vulnerable position in society of foreigners and, *inter alia*, the greater difficulty they have in obtaining information, the Committee considered it necessary systematically to ask the states which had not yet dealt with this problem whether and how they ensured equal treatment for foreign nationals of Contracting Parties in the area of vocational guidance."

Assessment of compliance

Throughout the various supervision cycles, the Committee has on the whole found that Contracting Parties are satisfying their obligations under this Article by providing adequate vocational guidance services, noting with satisfaction the constant and substantial efforts made to expand and improve these services from the point of view of the number of persons benefiting from them, the staff they employ, the funds allocated to them and their organisation.

There is one case of non-compliance with this Article: Turkey, and two cases of deferral – Belgium and Italy (Conclusions XIII-2, pp. 313 to 315 and Conclusions XIII-3, pp. 148 and 149 respectively).

In respect of *Turkey*, the conclusion is negative because "in spite of these recent efforts to improve vocational guidance and counselling services, the Committee had to note that the number and geographical distribution of such services, the number of staff at their disposal and the level of state expenditure on vocational guidance (150 million Turkish lira) could not guarantee access to these services for all the people concerned (8.193 persons benefited from these services before the reform of May 1991)" (Conclusions XIII-1, pp. 234 and 235). The Committee reiterated its negative conclusion in the next supervision cycle as the report did not contain information concerning developments in the situation and repeated its request for information (Conclusions XIII-3, pp. 321 and 322).

Article 10 – The right to vocational training

General

This Article was the first international provision to guarantee the right to vocational training as such; until the Charter, this matter had not been dealt with internationally, except in two recommendations of the ILO and in directives adopted within the framework of the European Communities (see Conclusions I, p. 55). It consists of four paragraphs, to all of which Article 33 applies. This means that Contracting Parties accepting these paragraphs must give concrete evidence to show that "the great majority", ie. 80%, of the workers concerned enjoy the protection afforded by them either by legislation, by collective agreements or otherwise.

Article 10 applies to the self-employed where relevant.

As already mentioned, the Committee devoted the thematic part of the General introduction of Conclusions XIII-3 to the topic of vocational guidance and training and in particular retraced the developments which had occurred in these areas (see under Article 9 above). It also underlined the specific difficulties faced by foreigners and the disabled: "The Committee noted that in some countries specific action had been taken for migrant workers (Spain, Portugal, Sweden). Economic reconstruction does in fact affect immigrants particularly, in so far as they are often in especially insecure employment and do not have sufficient capacities to easily adapt themselves and retrain. The Committee has attached particular importance to this issue, and has considered obvious the fact that 'economic difficulties can obviously have much more serious consequences for this group [migrant workers and their families] than for other sections of the population; that is why a special effort should be made on their behalf, so that unemployed migrant workers may benefit from the same help in the matter of vocational training and retraining as nationals'.[1] The Committee has therefore always urged states to provide information about how they ensure equal treatment for the nationals of other Contracting Parties, including people with disabilities, in the field of vocational training (access and means of access to vocational training), and considers national situations not guaranteeing such equal treatment as failing to comply with the requirements of the Charter (Austria, Greece, Malta).

The Committee further emphasised that the obligation stemming from Article 19 para. 4 to grant migrant workers equal treatment in respect of employment and working conditions, including vocational training,[2] 'goes beyond merely guaranteeing equality of treatment as between foreign and national workers in the sense that, recognising that migrants are in fact handicapped, it provides for the institution by the Contracting States of measures which are more favourable and more positive in regard to this category of persons than in regard to the states' own nationals'.[3]

Aware of the fact that training and rehabilitation play a major role in efforts to arrange employment opportunities for them, the states had,

---

1 Conclusions IV, p. xv. The Committee also specified, in a general observation relating to Article 1 para. 4, that access to vocational guidance, training and retraining institutions should be available to foreign nationals of States Parties to the Charter (Conclusions XII-1, p. 67 and XII-2, p. 57).

2 In the introduction to the Fourth report on certain provisions of the Charter which have not been accepted, the Committee gave the Maltese Government a clear reminder of the importance it gave under Article 19 para. 4 to the absence of *de jure* and *de facto* discrimination in employment, including training, recruitment and promotion and working conditions.

3 Conclusions I, p. 81.

during the reference period, continued their policy of helping people with disabilities. They were given priority access to training in Spain under the FIP plan (National Vocational and Employment Promotion Plan), and also in Sweden; specific programmes had also been implemented, for example in the United Kingdom. Special efforts had also been made in certain countries to make the special training provided for people with disabilities more suited to the labour market (France and Finland). The Committee nevertheless regretted the general absence of information on the total number of people with disabilities able to carry out a professional activity, the proportion of those having requested to benefit from training and/or retraining measures and the number that had effectively received them during the reference period. It therefore insisted that information should be provided in the next supervision cycle" (Conclusions XIII-3, pp. 36 and 37).

In conclusion, the Committee underlined that:

"In a transformed economy, whatever the reasons for and characteristics of this transformation, vocational training is thus an essential component of the labour market. In the current context of expansion for the Council of Europe, training for young people and adults should be adapted to new ways of working and in-depth consideration should be given to this issue by all the participants in the labour market, on the basis of the most accurate forecast possible. The frequently noted imbalance between the demand and supply of jobs and especially the lack skilled labour are proof of the efforts necessary in this area. The Committee was anxious to underline the fact that these issues should not only be approached from the standpoint of unemployment, but much more widely in terms of the general framework of vocational training in the light of the present demands of employment. For this reason, the Committee insisted that in their subsequent reports the Contracting Parties give the actual structure of vocational training as a whole as well as describing all its aspects, whilst indicating modifications planned or considered" (ibidem, p. 37).

Paragraph 1 – Promotion of technical and vocational training and the granting of facilities for access to higher technical and university education

Under this paragraph, the Contracting Parties undertake:

> "to provide or promote, as necessary, the technical and vocational training of all persons, including the handicapped, in consultation with employers' and workers' organisations, and to grant facilities for access to higher technical and university education, based solely on individual aptitude".

In the first supervision cycle, the Committee stated that "the obligations implicit in this provision are twofold:

- the obligation to promote technical and vocational training for all persons, and

- the obligation to provide facilities for access to higher technical and university education, subject to no other criterion than individual fitness" (Conclusions I, p. 55).

Therefore, Contracting States which have accepted this provision must provide information on both of these aspects in order to enable the Committee to assess compliance (*ibidem*, pp. 55 and 56).

Moreover, the Committee held that this paragraph lays emphasis upon making access to higher technical and university education more democratic, by providing that individual fitness is the only criterion to be observed in granting facilities for access to education. A Contracting Party must have enough establishments, a reasonable level of educational fees and offer scholarships and other grants or benefits. (*ibidem*).

Even though reference to handicapped persons is only made in the first part of the undertaking, it appears from comments of the Committee on the application of this paragraph by some Contracting Parties that it regards the second part of the undertaking as also covering this category (see Conclusions II, p. 43 and Conclusions III, p. 54, Norway).

Information requested for assessing compliance includes, *inter alia*, the following;

– "the measures taken to make vocational training available to all persons;

– the financial and other facilities for access to higher technical and university education based on the criterion of individual aptitude" (Conclusions II, p. 42, Denmark);

– "the total number of handicapped persons who, bearing in mind their age, would be capable of taking up employment;

...

– the number of persons who had the benefit within a specified period of vocational training in the agricultural sector" (*ibidem*, Ireland);

– "the facilities granted to immigrant workers in the field of vocational training and their proportion to the total number of persons receiving vocational training with particular reference to adult migrant workers" (Conclusions IV, p. 71, Federal Republic of Germany);

– "the powers, organisation, operation and financing of the vocational training services;

...

– action taken to prevent discrimination (in law and in practice) against nationals of other Contracting Parties in respect of admission to vocational training;

– the consultation of employers' and workers' organisations in establishing vocational training programmes" (Conclusions V, p. 81, France);

– as well as the number of technical and higher educational establishments, the number of pupils and students attending them, the number of teachers employed in them and the number of students and pupils assisted out of public funds (summary of the questions put to all of the Contracting Parties).

In connection with the consultation of employers' and workers' organisations the Committee, when examining the United Kingdom's report in the twelfth supervision cycle, observed that "while Article 10 of the Charter does not require that the field of vocational training be the responsibility of a tripartite body, paragraphs 1 and 4 of this provision expressly provide for consultation with employers' and workers' organisations" and asked for detailed information as to the manner in which new structures for training in the United Kingdom (replacement of the Training Commission, a tripartite organisation, by the Training Agency, a non-tripartite organisation) ensure the consultation of workers' organisations in decision-making in relation to vocational training. The employers' participation was not in doubt, as United Kingdom policy aims at involving them more and more in formulating and implementing training programmes (Conclusions XII-1, p. 165).

The German situation led the Committee to clarify the scope of Article 10 paragraph 1 in relation to financial assistance, that is the link between paragraphs 1 and 4 of Article 10 on this point.

In the seventh cycle of supervision, Germany was found as not complying with this paragraph, on the ground that there were restrictions put to the issue of work permits to young foreigners, nationals of Contracting Parties, for the purpose of signing a training contract (young persons had to have been admitted into Germany before the age of eighteen through family reunion procedures) and also for the granting of allowances to young foreign trainees (one of their parents had to have lived in Germany for at least three years (Conclusions VII, p. 59).

In the eighth cycle, the Committee held that "notwithstanding the non-acceptance of paragraph 4,[1] the scope of paragraph 1 is so general

1 Germany has not accepted Article 10 para. 4.

('to provide or promote as necessary the technical and vocational training of all persons') that it also covers the granting of allowances to young trainees.

Moreover, by virtue of the Appendix to the Charter, such financial assistance must be guaranteed to the nationals of the other states bound by the Charter.

Finally, the application of Article 33 should not lead to the exclusion of a given category of beneficiaries composed solely of foreigners, including nationals of other states bound by the Charter.

The importance of financial assistance in the framework of vocational training is, in fact, so great that the very existence of the right to vocational training may depend on it" (Conclusions VIII, p. 136).

In the ninth supervision cycle, the Committee, whilst rejecting the arguments of the German Government that these restrictions were justified by reason of the application of Article 33, that Article 10 para. 4 had the force of a "*lex specialis*" in relation to Article 10 para. 1 and that only a small number of persons was concerned, decided to postpone its conclusion pending receipt of statistical information concerning the number of persons who failed to meet the requirements for the award of a work permit which was necessary to be admitted to in-plant training as well as on the number of such persons who did not qualify for financial aid under the Act of 3 June 1982[1] (Conclusions IX-2, pp. 66 and 67).

In the tenth cycle of supervision, the Committee determined that "while the granting of economic aid is not outside the scope of Article 10 para. 1, because it is concerned with the provision of grants and other forms of assistance to make access to technical and university education easier, the financial assistance granted to young persons during voca-

---

1 Three members of the Committee (Mr Ohilinger, Mr Fabricius and Mr de Gaay Fortman) expressed a dissenting opinion on the conclusion that the Federal Republic of Germany did not comply with Article 10 para. 1. They held the view that Germany was provisionally complying and based their opinion on a different interpretation of Article 10, especially para. 1 and a different evaluation of the actual situation (Conclusions IX-2, p. 103).

tional training within firms is more closely connected with Article 10 para. 4, which the Federal Republic of Germany has not accepted" (Conclusions X-2, p. 103).

In the twelfth cycle, "the Committee reiterated its case law regarding the applicability of Article 10 para. 1 to vocational assistance allowances for young trainees in general (Conclusions VII, p. 59) and the incompatibility of residence and employment conditions for vocational assistance allowances with these provisions of the Charter in particular (Conclusions VII, p. 62). The Committee expressed its concern at this unequal treatment between German nationals and nationals of non-European Community Member States bound by the Charter and wished to be informed on a. the number of young foreigners, nationals of non-European Community Member States bound by the Charter, eligible for vocational assistance allowance and b. the number of those foreigners who failed to fulfil the requirements for vocational assistance allowance" (Conclusions XII-2, p. 154; see in the last instance Conclusions XIII-2, pp. 320 and 321).

In the General introduction to Conclusions XIII-3, the Committee noted that:

"As in the past, the main element of active measures in the labour market related to vocational training. Training activities, usually for the benefit of specific groups, had frequently been combined with advisory activities, with a view to guiding job-seekers towards training which would improve their employment prospects. The Committee noted a greater variety of activities and training programmes in this context, and a clear increase in expenditure on vocational training in such countries as Austria, France and Italy.

The Committee was also aware of endeavours to adapt the training system to meet the needs of the working world. Emphasis now seemed increasingly to be placed upon the complementary roles of school and enterprise in training processes" (Conclusions XIII-3, p. 32).

...

"The Committee nevertheless regretted that states did not give regular updates on the way in which this training was organised, particularly its legal framework, the respective roles of technical and professional schools and industry, staff and pupil levels, the distribution of training facilities within the different sectors of the economy, the participation of the social partners in the elaboration and supervision of vocational training policies and finally on the functioning of this training (questions which appear on the Form for Reports)" (*ibidem*, p. 33).

...

"Finally, it wished to recall that Article 10 para. 1 of the Charter also covered access to university studies and underlined the importance of the means which Contracting Parties should provide (particularly by awarding grants) in order that the sole condition for access should be individual aptitude" (*ibidem*, p. 37).

Assessment of compliance

The only country currently found as not complying is *Greece*, on the ground that foreigners not born and living there are not usually accepted on the OAED (Manpower Employment Organisation) apprenticeship schemes, which is in breach of the Appendix to the Charter as it guarantees to foreigners from other states bound by the Charter the same treatment as nationals in respect of access to vocational training and apprenticeship systems. This criticism has been made since the eleventh supervision cycle (Conclusions XI-1, p. 112; Conclusions XII-1, pp. 161 and 162; Conclusions XIII-1, p. 185 and Conclusions XIII-3, p. 155[1]).

The Committee has deferred its conclusion for six Contracting Parties, essentially (although not solely) for matters relating to equal treatment

---

1 In Conclusions XIII-3, "the Committee took note of the adoption, outside the reference period, of Act No. 2224 of 1994 which provided for equal treatment between Greek nationals and nationals of other Contracting Parties to the Charter in respect of access to vocational training. However, as the situation had remained unchanged during the reference period, it was obliged to reiterate its negative conclusion on this point."

between nationals and nationals of the other Contracting Parties: Belgium (first report – Conclusions XIII-2, pp. 317 and 319); Finland (first report – Conclusions XIII-3, pp. 323 and 324); Germany (Conclusions XIII-2, pp. 320 and 321; see also above); Luxembourg (first report – Addendum to Conclusions XIII-3, pp. 54 to 56); Malta (Conclusions XIII-3, p. 157) and Turkey (Conclusions XIII-3, pp. 326 to 328).

Paragraph 2 – Promotion of apprenticeship

Under this paragraph, the Contracting Parties undertake:

> "to provide or promote a system of apprenticeship and other systematic arrangements for training young boys and girls in their various employments."

In the first supervision cycle, the Committee defined as follows the meaning of the expression "system of apprenticeship" as used in this paragraph:

"the apprenticeship facilities referred to in the Charter should not be purely empirical or aim solely at manual training duty but should be conceived in broad terms and comprise full, coordinated and systematic training" (Conclusions I, p. 57).

It also held that "the provision of Article 10 para. 2 should not be understood as preventing a State which had accepted it from making arrangements aimed at gradually replacing apprenticeship by more institutionalised vocational training" (ibidem).

Furthermore, in the third supervision cycle, the Committee explained that "it considers the compulsory periods of partial experience forming part of the training of, for example, students in medicine, dentistry, law and education, whether in the course of their university studies or after, are within the scope of paragraph 2 of Article 10" (Conclusions III, p. 55).

With a view to the assessment of compliance with this paragraph, the Committee pointed out as early as its first Conclusions that adequate information must be supplied in respect of:

"1. steps taken to promote "the systematic arrangements" referred to in this paragraph;

2. approximate number of young persons trained;

3. how vocational training arrangements are divided among the various kinds of occupational activity;

4. public financial support for private apprenticeship schemes" (Conclusions I, pp. 56 and 57).

Commenting on Article 10 para. 2 in the General introduction to Conclusions XIII-3, the Committee observed that:

"National reports refer mainly to the existence of occasional or temporary 'schemes' or 'campaigns' set up to integrate young people into the working world and concentrating on sandwich courses.

The Committee thus noted in France the different types of sandwich integration contracts available to young people (fixed-term contracts) such as qualification, retraining and guidance contracts (see General introduction to Conclusions XII-2, p. 19).

In Italy, programmes for training and work contracts (part-time contracts) were made more readily available to young people in application of Act No. 863 of 1984.

The number of temporary jobs for young people had also seen a significant increase in Spain, mainly in the form of trainee-ship contracts and training contracts, fundamental instruments of the FIP Plan (the National Vocational Training and Employment Promotion Plan), although these were losing their impetus, and apprenticeship contracts and work experience contracts had recently been developed.

These provided young people with a professional activity accompanied by a varying proportion of training. Employers received recruitment assistance and usually benefited from exemption from charges.

Although these programmes represent a means of entry into the labour market for a number of young people in countries with high rates of youth unemployment, they do not ensure permanent access to working life. On this occasion the Committee emphasised the risk of insecurity in employment, as firms are tempted by the advantages they are offered to give preference to and repeatedly use replaceable labour instead of offering long-term contracts, and not to continue the training that workers had received. It therefore raised a question as to the impact of these various types of contracts on the beneficiaries' effective and lasting integration into the labour market.

Through these various arrangements, vocational training is increasingly seen as a half-way house between employment and unemployment: as a result, the Committee decided no longer to deal with this subject under Article 10, but to consider it under Article 1 para. 1" (Conclusions XIII-3, pp. 33 and 34).

Assessment of compliance

The Committee's conclusion is currently negative for four Contracting Parties: Austria, Greece, Luxembourg and Malta, owing to the inequality of treatment between nationals and nationals of the other Contracting Parties.

Austria: because of the exclusion from apprenticeship of young foreigners, nationals of the states bound by the Charter.

The Committee, made aware of this problem in the seventh supervision cycle, found in the eighth supervision cycle the argument of the Austrian Government, that the number of foreigners who were denied the work permit required for entry into apprenticeship contracts represented only 5% of the total number of apprentices, whereas Article 33 allowed even 20% to be excluded from Article 10 para. 2, as irrelevant since those excluded all appeared to be foreigners, a situation which the Committee considered to be incompatible with the Charter (see Conclusions VIII, pp. 138 and 139).

The Committee postponed its conclusions in the following cycles, in view of information given by the Austrian Government that the competent authorities had been given directions to grant work permits to foreigners who found employment as apprentices and pending receipt of information on intended changes to the legislation. However, in the twelfth cycle, the Committee repeated its criticism as the Aliens Employment Act, as amended in 1988 and 1990, still imposed restrictions related to the length of residence in Austria either of young foreigners' parents or of themselves and moreover according to the 1975 Aliens Employment Act, which was not amended by the aforesaid Act of 1988 or 1990, apprentices were granted a work permit only if the situation in the "apprentices market" so permitted and if there were not serious grounds for refusal in the rest of the labour market. Nevertheless, the Committee deferred its conclusion pending receipt of information on how many young foreigners, nationals of Contracting Parties, were a. granted exemption certificates (and how many were refused) and b. precluded from gaining access to apprenticeship training (Conclusions XII-2, pp. 156 and 157). A negative conclusion was again reached in the thirteenth cycle (Conclusions XIII-3, p. 162);

Greece: on the ground that young nationals of other states bound by the Charter are only admitted to apprenticeship schools if they were born and are resident in Greece. Such an exclusion contravenes the Appendix to the Charter (Conclusions XI-1, p. 114; see in the last instance Conclusions XIII-3, pp. 163 and 164);[1]

Luxembourg (first report): because nationals of the other Contracting Parties not members of the European Union and not parties to the Agreement on the European Economic Area wishing to attend a course or undergo an apprenticeship first have to apply for a work permit valid

---

1 The situation was remedied by Act No. 2224 of 1994 – outside the reference period – providing for equal treatment between Greeks and the nationals of other Contracting Parties.

for the period of the course or apprenticeship. "The Committee pointed out that, according to its case law, a prior requirement for a work permit to enable the nationals of other Contracting Parties to start an apprenticeship constituted discriminatory treatment contrary to Article 10 para. 2 (Conclusions XII-2, pp. 156-7, XIII-2, p. 220 and XIII-3, p. 165)" (Addendum to Conclusions XIII-3, pp. 56 to 58);

Malta: because priority is given to Maltese nationals wishing to participate in apprenticeship schemes, "a situation which was contrary to the requirements of Article 10 para. 2, when read in conjunction with the Appendix to the Charter" (Conclusions XIII-2, p. 323 and Conclusions XIII-3, pp. 165 and 167).

There are also four cases of deferral (Belgium, Finland, Malta and Germany). In respect of Germany the conclusion is deferred pending receipt of the information requested under paragraph 1 on the conditions for the award of vocational training allowances to nationals of Contracting Parties not members of the European Union as, according to the Committee, "the requirements of Article 10 para. 2, were the same in this respect as those of paragraph 1". (Conclusions XIII-2, p. 323).

Paragraph 3 – Vocational training and retraining of adult workers

With a view to ensuring the effective exercise of the right to vocational training, the Contracting Parties undertake:

> "to provide or promote, as necessary: a. adequate and readily available training facilities for adult workers; b. special facilities for the re-training of adult workers needed as a result of technological development or new trends in employment."

Whereas the previous paragraph contains an undertaking in respect of young boys and girls, this paragraph contains an undertaking in respect of adult workers.

The words "as necessary" after the words "promote or provide" permit some discretion. As the Committee held in its first Conclusions (p. 58), "this provision lays a particular obligation on any Contracting State that still has a considerable number of unemployed". This was found to be the case in Italy and the United Kingdom, for example, in the first cycle. In respect of Italy the Committee considered the situation unsatisfactory as the number of unemployed who received training was very small compared to the general employment situation and in the United Kingdom on the ground that the facilities offered were modest in relation to the size of the working population (Conclusions I, p. 58). These conclusions were changed to positive ones in the third cycle, both for Italy and the United Kingdom, in the light of new information furnished by the governments.

Information asked by the Committee in order to assess compliance with this paragraph includes:

- "the structure, operation, number and geographical distribution of public training centres for the unemployed and of private or public centres for agricultural workers;

- permanent training facilities for self-employed workers (craftsmen, tradesmen, etc.) and for the professions (doctors, lawyers, dentists, etc.);

- measures to ensure equality of treatment for indigenous workers and migrant workers from other Contracting States in the matter of access to training programmes;

- the means used to bring the importance of permanent training home to the public" (Conclusions V, p. 84, France).

An interesting question was raised by the Committee in the fifth cycle in relation to the application of this provision by Germany. The Committee feared that the conditions laid down in new legislation in Germany for eligibility to vocational training assistance and retraining (ie. three years' employment in the case of trained workers and six years in the case of untrained workers) might create difficulties in respect of foreign workers and asked to be informed whether in the case of nationals of other Contracting States, periods of employment in such states were taken into account in this respect. Upon being informed that they were taken into account, the Committee concluded that there was equality of treatment between nationals and non nationals and, therefore, conformity with this paragraph (Conclusions V, p. 84 and Conclusions VI, p. 73).

In the General introduction to Conclusions XIII-3, the Committee observed that: "Training was also used on the labour market in order to improve the mobility of the workforce. Denmark had adopted legislative provisions to encourage training leave, public assistance for such leave being subject to the worker concerned being replaced by an unemployed person. Also in France the Committee noted that employees holding fixed-term contracts could now take individual training leave.

The Committee noted that several countries had adopted measures with a view to setting up an independent training and further training framework within enterprises, particularly with a view to boosting productivity by increasing employees' skills and versatility within their firms (Iceland and Ireland)" (Conclusions XIII-3, pp. 34 and 35).

More generally, the Committee noted that: "In addition, states had continued their efforts to develop adult training and retraining facilities, particularly for the benefit of those groups most severely disadvantaged on the labour market" (*ibidem*, p. 35). These groups are long-term unemployed women, migrant workers and people with disabilities (for the two latter, see above, in "General" under Article 10):

"The Committee noted with interest that taking into account the increase in long-term unemployment, special training measures had been taken in several countries to assist this category of the unemployed (Ireland, Portugal, Spain, Sweden and the United Kingdom). The importance of the link between training and long-term unemployment was further emphasised by the inclusion in the draft revised Charter of an additional provision to Article 10, aimed at the provision or promotion of "special" measures for the retraining and reintegration of the long-term unemployed. The Committee nevertheless emphasised the necessity to ensure a true balance between the needs of the labour market and to give everyone suitable training on the one hand and on the other, the legitimate and reasonable aspirations of the individual facing the choice of a career, when examining the situation in the United Kingdom, where unemployment benefit may be denied to anyone not accepting training offered to them.[1]

The Committee noted that there were specific training programmes designed for women in several countries, to which they had priority access (Ireland, Portugal, Spain and Sweden). In Turkey it noted the efforts made to give women training which would allow them to have access to traditionally male-dominated professions and encourage them to enter employment requiring higher levels of skills, as well as the launching of a project entitled 'Support for the creation of businesses by women'.

Even before considering these specific steps for the benefit of women, emphasis ought to be laid on the need to promote equal opportunities and treatment, *inter alia* in the field of vocational guidance and training enshrined in Article 1 of the Additional Protocol to the Charter. In this respect, different measures had been taken in the Netherlands and in Sweden to counter the division of the labour market according to gender" (*ibidem*).

Assessment of compliance

One Contracting Party is currently found as not complying with Article 10 para. 3: *Austria*. When examining the Austrian situation in the eighth supervision cycle, the Committee reiterated the view that the exclusion of nationals of other Contracting States from access to training opportunities on the sole ground of the nationality of the persons concerned was incompatible with the Charter. (Conclusions VIII, p. 142). As the Austrian Government stated that there was no differentiation between Austrians and foreigners as far as vocational training and retraining for adults were concerned, the Committee deferred its

---

1 Question already raised in respect of the United Kingdom in Conclusions XII-1, p. 172.

conclusion and asked to learn the legal basis for this statement (Conclusions IX-2, p. 69); the conclusion was again deferred in the tenth supervision cycle, when the Committee noted that specific training programmes were directed at foreigners having resided for several years in Austria and members of their families, including young second generation members. The Committee asked whether all the other training and retraining programmes for adult workers, ie. those not specifically designed for foreigners, were also available to foreigners on equal terms with nationals (Conclusions X-2, pp. 106 and 107); in the eleventh cycle the Committee was unable to examine the Austrian report in respect of this provision (see Conclusions XI-2, pp. 13 and 105); the conclusion was also deferred in the twelfth cycle since the Committee wished to receive further clarification as to whether access to further training and retraining was granted on an equal basis (Conclusions XII-2, p. 160);

As from the thirteenth supervision cycle, the conclusion has been negative, as it appears that financial assistance for training and retraining is only granted to foreigners, nationals of Contracting Parties, if it is believed they will remain in Austria in the future, which is assumed if they have already been in the country for one year. "The Committee, recalling its Conclusions VI, (p. 72), decided that such a condition of residence could not be considered as being in conformity with the Charter as it was discriminatory. For this reason the Committee found that Austria was not complying with this provision of the Charter." In the same conclusion, the Committee noted that "access for adult workers to vocational training and retraining was open under the same conditions to Austrian nationals and to foreigners, nationals of Contracting Parties to the Charter who were in possession of a work permit or an exemption certificate. In order to assess whether all discrimination in this field was excluded, it wished to know if vocational training and retraining was also open, and subject to what conditions, to unemployed foreign workers", and deferred its conclusion on this point (Conclusions XIII-2, pp. 220 and 221; Conclusions XIII-3, pp. 168 and 169).

The conclusion is deferred for Belgium (first report – Conclusions XIII-2, pp. 324 and 325), Finland (first report – Conclusions XIII-3, pp. 323 and

324), Greece (Conclusions XIII-3, pp. 170 and 171), Italy (*ibidem*, p. 171) and Turkey (*ibidem*, pp. 326 to 328).

Paragraph 4 – Encouragement for the full utilisation of available facilities

Under this paragraph, the Contracting Parties undertake:

> "to encourage the full utilisation of the facilities provided by appropriate measures such as:
>
> a.   reducing or abolishing any fees or charges;
>
> b.   granting financial assistance in appropriate cases;
>
> c.   including in the normal working hours time spent on supplementary training taken by the worker, at the request of his employer, during employment;
>
> d.   ensuring, through adequate supervision, in consultation with the employers' and workers' organisations, the efficiency of apprenticeship and other training arrangements for young workers, and the adequate protection of young workers generally."

In order to assess whether a Contracting State that has accepted this provision is in fact satisfying the obligations implicit therein, adequate information must be provided as to the measures taken for giving effect to each one of the points comprised in this paragraph. It is pointed out, however, that the list of measures enumerated in a to d is not an exhaustive but an indicative one.

Until now, the Committee has not gone beyond the measures listed.

When the Contracting Parties submit their first reports, the Committee examines whether the requirements of each sub-paragraph are met. Insufficient information on any of them justifies a deferred conclusion (for recent first reports, see Conclusions XIII-1, pp. 241 and 242, Turkey; Conclusions XIII-2, pp. 327 and 328, Belgium; Conclusions XIII-3, pp. 337 to 339, Finland and Portugal; Addendum to Conclusions XIII-3, pp. 60 to 62, Luxembourg).

Turkey's first report led the Committee to be more explicit as to the meaning of sub-paragraph *b.* in relation to sub-paragraph *a.:* "with regard to the granting of financial assistance in appropriate cases, the Committee reminded the Turkish authorities that this meant providing financial assistance to persons who would not otherwise be in a position to undergo apprenticeship or training. It entailed, in addition to free or low-cost training, the provision of assistance in the form of grants, allowances or other arrangements where necessary (Conclusions XIII-1, p. 242; see also Conclusions XIII-3, p. 339).

Another interesting question was raised in relation to the situation in the United Kingdom: "having been informed that new legislation would stop unemployment benefit for anyone not accepting the training offered, the Committee wanted to know how a proper balance was maintained between labour market needs and the wish to give everyone a valid training on the one hand, and on the other hand the legitimate and reasonable aspirations of the individual faced with choosing a career" (Conclusions XII-1, p. 172; see also Conclusions XIII-3, pp. 177 and 178).

Assessment of compliance

The only Contracting Party found as not complying with Article 10 para. 4 is *Greece*, because equality of treatment between Greeks and the nationals of other Contracting Parties is not secured in the matters covered by this provision. The conclusion has been negative since the twelfth cycle (Conclusions XII-1, p. 171; in the last instance Conclusions XIII-3, p. 175).[1]

---

1 This situation was remedied by Act No. 2224 of 1994, outside the reference period.

In the last cycle, the Committee deferred its conclusion in respect of Belgium, Finland, Luxembourg and Turkey:

– Belgium (first report): given the very incomplete nature of the information supplied, which does not cover "either all the sub-paragraphs of Article 10 para. 4" or all the territory of Belgium (Conclusions XIII-2, pp. 327 and 328);

– Finland (first report): information has been requested on "how the efficiency of apprenticeship and other training arrangements for young workers was ensured through adequate supervision, in consultation with employers' and workers' organisations, as well as the adequate protection of young workers generally (Article 10 para. 4 d.)" and on whether foreigners, nationals of Contracting Parties to the Charter legally resident or regularly working in Finland, are treated on an equal footing with Finnish nationals in respect of this provision (Conclusions XIII-3, pp. 337 and 338);

– Luxembourg (first report): further information and clarification have been requested concerning the four sub-paragraphs of the provision and the Committee has also raised a question on the equal treatment of the nationals of other Contracting Parties with respect to financial assistance (Addendum to Conclusions XIII-3, pp. 60 to 62);

– Turkey (second report): the Committee has not been able to determine whether financial assistance is granted in appropriate cases; it has also asked for further information on sub-paragraph *c.* (inclusion in working hours of time spent on supplementary training taken by the worker, at the request of his employer, during employment) and from which financial advantages nationals of the other Contracting Parties may benefit and in what conditions (Conclusions XIII-3, pp. 339 and 340).

On the whole, implementation of this paragraph has not presented difficulties to Contracting Parties, all of which were found in compliance until the twelfth supervision cycle.

In the revised Charter one paragraph has been added to Article 10 (paragraph 4); the others remain unchanged, therefore paragraph 4 of the Charter has become paragraph 5 of the revised Charter.

This new paragraph reads as follows:

"to provide or promote, as necessary, special measures for the retraining and reintegration of the long-term unemployed;"

The idea behind this paragraph is that it is necessary to adopt "special" measures for the cases mentioned, as opportunities for the long-term unemployed to re-enter the labour market are particularly few.

Article 11 – The right to protection of health

General

Commenting on Article 11 as a whole in its first Conclusions, the Committee stated that it contained undertakings of a very general nature and expressed the opinion that in the wording of the text as it stood, a country bound by it "should be considered as fulfilling its obligations on this point if it provides evidence of the existence of a medical and health system comprising the following elements:

1. Public health arrangements making generally available medical and para-medical practitioners and adequate equipment consistent with meeting its main health problems.

Such arrangements must ensure:

   a. proper medical care for the whole population;

   b. the prevention and diagnosis of disease.

2. Special measures to protect the health of mothers, children and old people.

3. General measures aimed in particular at the prevention of air and

water pollution, protection from radio-active substances, noise abatement, food control, environmental hygiene, and the control of alcoholism and drugs.

4.   A system of health education.

5.   Measures such as vaccination, disinfection, and the control of epidemics, providing the means of combating epidemic and endemic diseases.

6.   The bearing by collective bodies of all, or at least a substantial part, of the cost of the health services" (Conclusions I, p. 59).

After examining the Contracting Parties' first reports, the Committee observed that as the field covered by this Article was so large, it would be difficult to arrive at a definite opinion on what might lack in the work accomplished by various countries.

The impression obtained was that these gaps did not give grounds for concluding that a country had failed to satisfy its obligations; the Committee therefore "confined itself to suggesting that the attention of the governments concerned should be drawn to the points on which the information available was felt to be inadequate so that more complete data might be obtained in later reports" (ibidem). This policy seems to have been followed consistently throughout all the supervision cycles.

The observations made by the Committee in its first Conclusions were as follows:

"On a more general level, and subject to the remarks made about particular countries, the Committee felt bound to point out that greater all-round efforts seemed desirable on a number of points:

1.   While all the countries appear to have medical and para-medical staff and health equipment in accordance with their needs, it is not possible to judge whether or not the geographical distribution of such staff and equipment satisfactorily meets the needs of the population as a whole. In order to cover this point, with a view to subsequent reports,

the Committee reserves the possibility of suggesting an amplification of the present form.

2.   The organisation of preventive care does not always appear to be as advanced as that of curative treatment. This is especially true:

   a. in the field of mental illness, though this appears to be a problem of increasing importance in European countries;

   b. in respect of vaccination and the control of epidemics which, perhaps because of the decrease in epidemic diseases, no longer appear to occupy a sufficient place in the thinking of the governments.

3.   The special effort needed for the care of old people, bearing in mind that the proportion of old people in the population is on the increase, is still generally insufficient.

4.   With a few exceptions, health education remains fragmentary and is not sufficiently systematically organised, bearing in mind the part it can play in the prevention and treatment of disease" (Conclusions I, pp. 59 and 60).

In the first supervision cycle, the Committee analysed all the paragraphs of Article 11 together, but in subsequent cycles it took the option of treating them separately.

In the fourth cycle, the Committee "regretted that the States which had accepted this Article frequently failed, in their biennial reports, to amplify the measures taken for control of environmental pollution which has become a serious problem. In this connection, the Committee hoped that the questions contained in the Form would be answered regularly and accurately.

The Committee also considered the recrudescence of certain epidemic and venereal diseases, as well as the appearance of hitherto unknown or unrecognised diseases, such as viral hepatitis, and it emphasized how important it was not to neglect prophylactic measures in order to prevent the spread of such diseases.

Among the health problems to which governments should pay particular attention and which should be covered by special regulations, the Committee emphasised the importance, at the present time, of iatrogenic diseases often caused by the common misuse of medicines and of new risks to consumers resulting from the composition and processing of certain foods, household products and other everyday articles" (Conclusions IV, p. 75).

Development in health policy

The idea of the protection of health itself – and, of course, its reality – has changed over the years. In this respect, the Committee's observations on health and on the environment made in the General introductions to its Conclusions are significant:

– in the fourth and fifth supervision cycles, the Committee only took the environment into consideration (Conclusions IV, p. xvi and V, p. xviii);

– in the sixth cycle, after having stressed the existing relation between safety and health at work *stricto sensu* and living conditions in general, the Committee underlined that though it is "bound in any event to examine Articles 3 and 11 of the Charter separately in view of their different content, the matters contemplated under these provisions could only be considered in relation to the common aim pursued, namely, the protection of the quality of life" (Conclusions VI, p. xiii);

– in the eighth supervision cycle, the Committee stated that "the obligation laid on states by the three paragraphs of Article 11 of the Charter implies the implementation in various fields of a very considerable number of measures, constituting a health policy in the fullest sense and geared to prevention as well as treatment". In respect of the quality of the environment, it stressed the importance of the effective enforcement of the existing standards and of rigorous supervision of certain kinds of plants "which discharge large quantities of polluting substances, including sulphur dioxide, the cause of 'acid rain'" (see also under Article 11 para. 1) (Conclusions VIII, pp. 12 and 13);

- in the ninth supervision cycle, it examined "the trends in the health policies" and noted that "owing to the constant increase in health costs, states were focusing their efforts in particular on improving and developing prevention policies" (Conclusions IX-1, pp. 16 and 17); for the first time, dealing with the existence of new diseases, it mentioned Aids and, in respect of the environment, pollution from motorised vehicles (Conclusions IX-2, pp. 12 and 13);

- in the tenth supervision cycle, it noted *inter alia:* a series of preventive measures geared, in particular, to groups at risk, such as pregnant women, newborn babies, children and the elderly; it also mentioned recent incidents in certain nuclear power stations and measures taken by governments to improve security and provide the public with information. Later, developing its considerations on Aids, it "stressed that the protection of health cannot be treated in isolation from other social rights, and emphasised the wide-ranging social effects of certain diseases such as Aids" (Conclusions X-2, pp. 25 and 26); as regards the environment, it noted that the accident in the Tchernobyl nuclear reactor had prompted governments to take new measures (*ibidem*, pp. 27 and 28);

- in the eleventh cycle, the Committee observed that particular efforts had been made to increase public awareness and responsibility through improved health education (Conclusions XI-1, p. 31); as regards the protection of the environment, noting the necessity of concerted action co-ordinated at international level, the Committee stated that: "as an international legal instrument imposing on sixteen European states the obligation to ensure a healthy environment (Article 11), the Social Charter may constitute an appropriate common basis around which Contracting Parties can co-ordinate their efforts. A common effort is, in fact, necessary at European level in order to stimulate scientific research on these matters and the adoption of the necessary counter-measures." (Conclusions XI-1, p. 34; see also Conclusions XI-2, pp. 40 to 42);

– in the twelfth cycle, the Committee observed that prevention and health education were now foremost in health policies, in particular in the campaigns against the spread of Aids, alcoholism, smoking and drug addiction; as regards Aids, "while it fully appreciated the scale of the difficulties posed by the efforts to prevent the spread of Aids, and the need for stringent measures to cope with the epidemic, the Committee stressed that it is essential to guarantee respect for patients' private life and dignity. It also considered this an area where international co-operation might be helpful in laying down common principles and co-ordinating plans of action on medical research and epidemiologic survey". It drew attention to Recommendation No. R (89) 14 of the Committee of Ministers of the Council of Europe on the ethical issues involved in HIV infection as regards social and health matters, as well as Recommendation 1116 (1989) of the Parliamentary Assembly on Aids and human rights (Conclusions XII-1, pp. 34 to 36 and Conclusions XII-2, pp. 31 and 32); it recalled its "constant concern as to the need for greater international consultation" in the field of protection of the environment, especially in association "with the possible health implication of radioactive pollution" (Conclusions XII-1, pp. 36 and 37 and Conclusions XII-2, pp. 32 and 33; see also under Article 11 para. 1 the general question on the latter point).

Paragraph 1 – Removal of the causes of ill-health

Under this paragraph, the Contracting Parties undertake:

"to remove as far as possible the causes of ill-health."

The views of the Committee in relation to the undertakings of Contracting Parties under this paragraph are shown in the introductory comments it has made on Article 11 as a whole. In the Committee's opinion, a Contracting Party is fulfilling its undertaking under this paragraph if it can prove that it possesses a medical and health system comprising the elements mentioned in 1, 2, 3 and 6 as cited under "General" above.

In the third cycle of supervision, the Committee felt obliged to point out, in response to information in the Cypriot report which stated that industrial medicine was concerned only with occupational diseases, that "it does not see industrial medicine as limited to this aspect, but that in its view it should also cover problems concerning the adjustment of individuals to their occupational surroundings, accident prevention, etc." (Conclusions III, p. 58, Cyprus).

The Committee consistently asks Contracting Parties for information on measures taken to protect the elderly and the mentally ill and to protect the health of mothers and infants, to combat drug addiction and alcoholism and to prevent smoking. It also asks questions on the steps taken in the fight against Aids. In respect of protection of the environment and of its effects on health, the Committee asks for information on measures taken to control environmental pollution, to reduce water and air pollution, to combat various types of pollution and to regulate waste disposal and noise. The Committee notes the measures taken and asks to be kept informed of developments.

With the apparition of new diseases endangering public health (such as Aids) or new environmental hazards which seem to represent a particular threat to health, the Committee endeavours to find out the extent of the problems, either by asking for information from states which have submitted none in this field, or by drafting a "general question".

An example of the first procedure, in addition to the questions automatically put to all the states on the measures taken to combat Aids, is the request for information on "the measures taken to reduce the release of sulphur dioxide and other acid pollutants in the atmosphere" addressed to Austria, Cyprus, Denmark, the Federal Republic of Germany, France, Italy, the Netherlands, Norway and Spain in Conclusions VIII (pp. 147 to 149), when the phenomenon of "acid rain" reached an alarming level. (see *ibidem*, p. 13: having stressed that sulphur dioxide was the cause of acid rain, the Committee stated that "increased atmospheric acidity is in fact a danger to health and seems to be one of the main causes of the serious damage done to forests and of the disappearance of lacustrian fauna in certain parts of Europe").

Later, the Committee "was in particular concerned with the possible health implications of radioactive pollution" (Conclusions XII-1, p. 36) and decided to put a general question under Article 11 para. 1:

"The Committee asked that the next report of each state which has accepted the first paragraph of Article 11 indicate the measures taken by that state to protect the health of the population living in the vicinity of nuclear power plants or working therein, as well as the particular measures for the protection of the population in the event of an incident at such a plant" (Conclusions XII-1, p. 174 and Conclusions XII-2, p. 166). The replies to this general question should be included in the coming supervision cycles.

The Committee also systematically takes into account the main causes of death in each Contracting Party, as well as the measures taken to combat them, or asks questions on the subject when the necessary information has not been given (see in the last instance Conclusions XIII-1, p. 245 and XIII-3, pp. 345 and 346, Turkey; Conclusions XIII-3, p. 341, Finland and p. 343, Portugal).

Assessment of compliance

The only negative conclusion under Article 11 para. 1 concerns *Turkey*. The Committee concluded negatively, particularly because of insufficient measures taken to lower the rate of perinatal and infant mortality in the country:

"The report showed that in 1993, only 33% of mothers and children had access to the Maternity and Child Health Care Centres and that 24% of all deliveries had occurred without the help of health personnel. It also stated that the maternal mortality rate was about 100 in 100,000 during the reference period. The Committee, having previously considered that a maternal mortality rate of 10 per 100,000 was high, found that 100 for 100,000 was a cause for concern. In addition, infant mortality was a significant problem in Turkey: 49.3 per 1,000 live births in 1993 according to the OECD, which is very high in comparison with other Contracting Parties which vary from 4.8 to 9.3 for 1,000 live births. The Committee expressed its concern regarding these high rates and hoped to find information in the next report to confirm that measures were being taken to remedy the situation. It also wished to be kept informed of any initiatives taken to make health services more readily available to women and children.

In the light of these elements and particularly of the insufficient number of measures taken to lower the rate of perinatal and infant mortality, the Committee had to conclude that Turkey did not satisfy this provision of the Charter" (Conclusions XIII-3, pp. 345 and 346).

On the whole, other Contracting Parties have been found to comply with this paragraph.

A positive conclusion was provisionally adopted in respect of the first Finnish report in the thirteenth cycle, where additional information was requested on various acts that had entered into force (Conclusions XIII-3, p. 341 and 342, Finland).

The Committee deferred its conclusion after examining the first reports of Belgium and Portugal during the thirteenth cycle. It considered that further information was required in order for it to reach a positive conclusion on a large section of the population and on subjects including general health and environmental measures (Conclusions XIII-2, p. 330, Belgium), and on measures taken or planned to lower the number of road accidents and to reduce the number of perinatal and infant deaths (Conclusions XIII-3, p. 343, Portugal).

Paragraph 2 – Advisory and educational facilities

Under this paragraph, Contracting Parties undertake:

> "to provide advisory and educational facilities for the promotion of health and the encouragement of individual responsibility in matters of health".

In the first supervision cycle, the Committee was generally critical of the provision made by Contracting Parties for health education. It considered that "with a few exceptions, health education remains fragmentary and is not sufficiently systematically organised, bearing in mind the part it can play in the prevention and treatment of diseases" (see above, "General" or Conclusions I, p. 60); in later cycles the Committee acknowledged the progress made (see above, "General" or Conclusions XI-1, p. 31).

To assess compliance with this paragraph, the Committee asks Contracting Parties to update the information requested in the Form for Reports and to indicate the sums devoted to health education. Information sought concerns, *inter alia*, health education in school curricula, advisory and diagnostic services for schools and other age groups, and the measures taken to inform the public of the effects of drugs and alcohol; the Committee's questions have also gradually been oriented towards health education for the prevention of Aids.

In the tenth cycle, for example, Spain was asked to provide information about medical examinations in schools, age groups, the nature and frequency of the screening carried out and the financial resources provided by the Autonomous Communities as well as details of the steps taken to reduce smoking, alcoholism and drug addiction (Conclusions X-2, p. 111, Spain).

Some indication of what the Committee considers satisfactory for compliance with this undertaking can be found in the twelfth cycle of supervision, in which it concluded that the Netherlands continued to comply since health education was part of primary and secondary school curricula, public information campaigns on drugs, Aids, alcohol, tobacco and sporting accidents had been carried out, and pilot projects to promote health education at work had been launched (Conclusions XII-1, pp. 176 and 177, the Netherlands); see also in the same Conclusions: Iceland, for the fight against cancer which included public information campaigns, screening programmes and research projects (p. 176); Norway, for the organisation of health education committees (p. 177); and in Conclusions XII-2, see: France, for local health education policy (p. 169); Italy, for the prevention of Aids by information campaigns and compulsory notification of cases in order to monitor the spread of the disease (p. 169); the latest examples of a positive conclusion in the light of a first report were that of Belgium in Conclusions XIII-2, pp. 331 and 332, and Luxembourg in the Addendum to Conclusions XIII-3, (pp. 65 and 66).

Assessment of compliance

There are no cases of non-compliance with this paragraph.

The Committee has adopted a provisionally positive conclusion in the third part of the thirteenth cycle for the first Finnish and Portuguese reports: in respect of Finland, it wishes to know whether health education in schools includes programmes of awareness aimed particularly to combat Aids and drug and alcohol abuse and to receive further information on measures taken to improve national strategy on health promotion, in particular with regard to the prevention of suicide and coronary diseases whose rates are reported to be exceptionally high (Conclusions XIII-3, pp. 346 and 347); in respect of Portugal, it wishes to receive more information on issues such as alcohol abuse and its prevention and measures to discourage smoking (Conclusions XIII-3, p. 347, Portugal).

It has deferred its conclusion in respect of Turkey pending receipt of information on a number of important outstanding questions (see Conclusions XIII-1, pp. 245 and 246 and XIII-3, p. 348).

Paragraph 3 – Prevention of diseases

Under this paragraph, the Contracting Parties undertake:

"to prevent as far as possible epidemic, endemic and other diseases."

The undertaking in this paragraph seems to partially overlap with those in paragraphs 1 and 2 of this Article. Questions A, B and C of the Form for Reports under Article 11 para. 3 relate to "the main forms of ill-health", "the way in which public health services are organised" and "the measures taken to further health education" respectively, and are identical to questions A, B and E under paragraph 1. For this reason, Contracting Parties which have answered the questions contained in paragraph 1 are not required to reply to the duplicated questions under paragraph 3 (question C, concerning "measures taken to further health education" also appears in paragraph 2). Indeed, the only new question in this paragraph concerns "the measures taken to prevent epidemic, endemic and other diseases (compulsory or optional vaccination, disinfection, epidemics policy)".

In applying paragraph 3, the Committee has sought to ensure that a Contracting Party has an adequate vaccination programme. In this connection, it asks, for example, for information on the number of vaccinations carried out in the course of a year or on the proportion of the population actually vaccinated.

Another issue for which the Committee has shown specific concern under this paragraph is that of adequate school health services, even though this issue seems to be covered more directly under paragraphs 1 and 2. In the case of Ireland, which has not ratified paragraphs 1 and 2, the Committee stated in the third cycle of supervision that it would only maintain its positive conclusion if the next report indicated the progress made in covering all schools by health services (Conclusions III, pp. 60 and 61, Ireland).

The Committee has consistently requested information concerning the measures taken by Contracting Parties to control the spread of serious epidemic diseases (see, for example, Conclusions IV, p. 78, Denmark and Germany, Conclusions VIII, p. 152, Spain, Conclusions XI-1, p. 121, Norway). In one instance, the United Kingdom explained that an increase of epidemic diseases was due to seasonal conditions particularly favourable to their appearance and that the situation had since become normal. This led the Committee to conclude that this Party continued to fulfil its obligations under that provision (Conclusions VI, p. 80, the United Kingdom). Moreover, the Committee noted with interest the development in Italy of an epidemiological monitoring system which allowed information on twenty-one infectious diseases to be updated weekly and transmitted to all concerned. This therefore clearly improved the system of prevention of epidemic, endemic and other diseases in the country (Conclusions IX-2, p. 73).

In the tenth supervision cycle, the Committee asked all Contracting Parties to provide information on measures taken to prevent Aids when this information had not yet been submitted (Conclusions X-1, p. 109 and Conclusions X-2, p. 111).

Assessment of compliance

Contracting Parties have generally been found to comply with their undertaking, despite the fact that they have often been asked to update previously provided information, particularly on measures taken to prevent the spread of infectious diseases.

In the thirteenth cycle of supervision, the Committee deferred its conclusion in respect of Belgium (first report), for lack of information on the Flemish Community (see Conclusions XIII-2, p. 333) and for Ireland, whose report still did not contain the information requested in reply to each of the questions in the Form for Reports (Conclusions XIII-1, p. 187). The Committee decided that the first Portuguese report lacked sufficient information on vaccinations, procedures for isolating contagious people and funding for Aids programmes: it adopted a provisionally positive conclusion (Conclusions XIII-3, pp. 349 and 350).

In the revised Charter, this paragraph reads as follows:

"to prevent as far as possible epidemic, endemic and other diseases, as well as accidents".

According to the explanatory report, what is required from the Parties, by the addition of "accidents", is that they implement accident prevention policies, but each state will be able to decide on its own measures to that end.

The conclusions in respect of Turkey's first and second reports were both deferred during the thirteenth cycle of supervision as a result of the existence of a number of important health issues such as the fall in the number of vaccinated children and the increase in the number of cases of malaria (Conclusions XIII-1, pp. 247 and 248 and XIII-3, pp. 350 and 351).

Article 12 – The right to social security

General

"This Article, necessarily of a very general character because of the complexity of the matters dealt with, guarantees the effective exercise of the right to social security firstly by establishing the principle of the institution or the maintenance of a social security system (paragraph 1), then by defining a minimum level for this system (paragraph 2) and providing that it should be progressively brought up to a higher level (paragraph 3) and, finally, by encouraging measures to ensure equality of treatment between the nationals of one Contracting Party with the nationals of the other Contracting Parties, as well as the granting, maintenance and resumption of social security rights (paragraph 4)" (Conclusions I, p. 62).

In the General introduction to Conclusions XII-1, commenting in general on Article 12, the Committee observed that the period under examination like the period covered by the eleventh cycle "was marked by attempts on the part of almost all the Contracting Parties concerned to control and limit the increasing costs of social security, particularly in the light of the ageing of the population, which affected nearly all the countries concerned. To this effect the various governments introduced a number of measures focusing on the improvement of the management of resources, more effective control on rising expenditure and more accurate channelling of resources to those in need, particularly the long-term unemployed.

...

Generally, all social security schemes introduced more flexibility in their benefits, giving individuals a wider choice and, at the same time, more responsibility. This development could be seen as beneficial, as individuals now had more options, for example in the United Kingdom where there was increasing privatisation of the retirement pension schemes, to choose what proportion of their salary they wish to allocate to a pension plan. At the same time, it should be noted that increased flexibility and individual choice in social security schemes could also lead to the marginalisation of the more vulnerable members of the community. The Committee will therefore monitor carefully all developments of this nature in future cycles of supervision.

The Committee was also concerned to note that, while overall the average level of benefits increased, there were a number of changes to the social security systems in nearly all the Contracting Parties concerned which could be seen as restrictions in benefit provision. These changes were dictated in particular by the wish to limit the ever increasing costs of social security and to link social security more closely to the wage structure".

After citing examples of such restrictions in Contracting Parties the Committee concluded "given the increasing concern over the cost of social security and the consequent attempts to curb costs, often involving individuals and employers in a share of those costs, as well as the (in general) welcome initiatives in making social security systems more flexible and adaptable to individual needs, it is of paramount importance that social security systems are adequate to protect the population, particularly as regards families, the disabled, the elderly and migrant workers". (Conclusions XII-1, pp. 32 to 34, General introduction).

In its General introduction to Conclusions XII-2 (p. 29) the Committee, "noting the preoccupation of all the Contracting Parties with the increasing costs of social security, called their attention to the fact that social security has a major role to play in protecting the more vulnerable members of the community". The Committee put a general question to all Contracting Parties, asking whether and how social security was provided to refugees and to stateless persons within their territory (Conclusions XII-1, p. 185 and XII-2, p. 177).

As to the meaning of "social security", a term which is not defined by the Charter itself, the Committee considered that social security benefits covered by Article 12 could be non-contributory as well as contributory. It held that "social security, as a socially more advanced means of social protection, had thus taken over a certain area which traditionally belonged to social assistance" and that this was considered as a positive development on many grounds (Conclusions VII, p. 74, France).

Paragraph 1 – Establishment or maintenance of a social security system

Under this paragraph, the Contracting Parties undertake:

> "to establish or maintain a system of social security".

Paragraph 1 was characterised by the Committee in its first Conclusions as a very general provision. It is difficult to be specific about what is required of Contracting Parties.

From the case law of the Committee it can be seen that it hesitated during the second and third supervision cycles to recognise the provisions made in a Contracting Party as amounting to a social security system within the meaning of this paragraph. The Committee felt that, despite the existence of social insurance legislation which provided benefits covering certain risks, "there were substantial gaps in it and many benefits were so low as to warrant serious doubt as to whether the measures in force could be termed a social security system" (Conclusions III, p. 62, Cyprus).

When this Contracting Party later amended its legislation and improved substantially the protection afforded, the Committee held that there was compliance with the provisions of this paragraph because, even though some risks (such as benefits in the form of sickness, maternity and family benefits) were still not covered, the new regulations could be regarded as a genuine system of social security (Conclusions IV, p. 81, Cyprus).

Therefore, it may be said that a "system" may be regarded as coming within the meaning of this paragraph even if there is no provision at all for care or benefits of one or more of the kinds listed in the nine Parts of ILO Convention No. 102. In general the approach adopted by the Committee is that a system exists when care or benefits are provided in respect to most, but not necessarily all, of the areas covered by Convention No. 102 or the European Code of Social Security.

Assessment of compliance

There are no cases of non-compliance with this provision.

Paragraph 2 – Maintenance of a social security system at a satisfactory level at least equal to that required for ratification of International Labour Convention No. 102

Under this paragraph, the Contracting Parties undertake:

> "to maintain the social security system at a satisfactory level at least equal to that required for ratification of the International Labour Convention (No. 102) Concerning Minimum Standards of Social Security".

The original intention of those who drafted the Charter was to specify that the "level" required for compliance with this paragraph should be that required for ratification of the European Code of Social Security which was in preparation at the same time as the Charter. As, however, the final text of the Code had not yet been adopted in 1961 when the Charter was signed, it was decided to make the required level that necessary for ratification of the ILO Convention, which had a lower standard. It is worth noting that the Committee of Ministers, which was apparently not happy with the replacement of the reference to the Code with the reference to the ILO Convention, agreed that when the Code was eventually adopted, it would be desirable to consider amending the Charter to implement the original intention (CM (61) 95 rev. 2).

It should be pointed out that the Code and the ILO Convention contain the same undertakings but a state has to accept three of the nine parts of the Convention,[1] whereas for the Code it must accept at least six of the same nine Parts. Furthermore the Code covers all workers without exception, whereas under the Convention seamen and seafishermen may be exempted.

According to the case law of the Committee a Contracting Party which has a social security system at least equal in level to that required for ratification of ILO Convention No. 102 and which is found by the ILO Committee of Experts on the Application of Conventions and Recommendations as complying with Convention No. 102, fulfils the undertakings of Article 12 paragraph 2 of the Charter (see Conclusions I, p. 62 and Conclusions VIII, p. 153).

In the same way a Contracting Party which does not satisfy Convention No. 102 (either because the level of benefits does not reach the prescribed minimum or because certain risks are not covered) will, as a rule, be found as contravening Article 12 para. 2 of the Charter. This was for example the case in the fourth cycle for Austria, found to fulfil only two of the four parts of Convention No. 102 which it had accepted. As the standard laid down by this Convention is only reached if the requirements of at least three of its parts are met, Austria was considered as not fulfilling Article 12 para. 2 of the Charter (Conclusions IV, p. 81).

However, there are cases in which Contracting Parties may be considered as complying with paragraph 2 of Article 12 even though the ILO Committee of Experts on the Application of Conventions and Recommendations may have found them as not complying with a particular branch of the Convention. This can happen when the Contracting Party

---

1 These parts are: Medical care (II), sickness benefit (III), unemployment benefit (IV), old-age benefit (V), employment injury benefit (VI), family benefit (VII), maternity benefit (VIII), invalidity benefit (IX) and survivors' benefit (X).

has accepted a greater number of parts than the minimum required for ratification of the Convention (Conclusions I, p. 62).

Moreover, if a Contracting Party to the Charter has not ratified the ILO Convention and therefore its law and practice are not subject to examination by the ILO when assessing the conformity of this state to the Charter, the Committee itself examines whether the requirements of the ILO Convention are respected (see Conclusions XII-2, p. 176, Malta).

Assessment of compliance

There are no cases of non-compliance with this provision by the Contracting Parties.

One of the newest Contracting Parties, Finland, was considered as meeting the requirements of this paragraph even though it had not ratified ILO Convention No. 102, since it had ratified several other ILO Conventions under which it undertook commitments concerning a larger number of fields than necessary for ratification of Convention No. 102 (Conclusions XIII-3, p. 354).

In the revised Charter, Article 12 para. 2 reads as follows:

"to maintain the social security system at a satisfactory level at least equal to that necessary for the ratification of the European Code of Social Security;"

Paragraph 3 – Progressive improvement of the social security system

Under this paragraph, the Contracting Parties undertake:

"to endeavour to raise progressively the system of social security to a higher level".

The Committee stressed in the first supervision cycle the dynamic character of this provision "which requires States which have accepted it to make a continuous effort to bring their social security systems progressively to a higher level and to inform the Council of Europe regularly of any steps taken" (Conclusions I, p. 62 and more recently Conclusions XIII-3, p. 357, Turkey).

In the second supervision cycle the Committee specified that "in order to satisfy Article 12 para. 3, a Contracting Party whether or not it accepted Article 12 para. 2, is expected progressively to raise its system of Social Security to a level higher than that of Convention 102" and indicated that a State which does not comply with paragraph 2 of this Article because its social security system fails to attain the minimum level laid down by Convention No. 102 cannot be found as complying with paragraph 3. This was the case in respect of Cyprus during several cycles (Conclusions II, p. 191 and Conclusions III, p. 63) and of Austria (Conclusions IV, p. 82).

From the case law it appears that the Committee on the whole has been able in most cases to find sufficient evidence of actual improvements on the previous situation and therefore to confirm compliance. Even an improvement in just one kind of benefit or care was regarded by the Committee as sufficient improvement (eg. improvements in Italy in the field of maternity protection, Conclusions III, p. 64). However, according to the Committee an improvement can only be regarded as satisfying paragraph 3 if the social security system already complies with the minimum level laid down by Convention No. 102. Thus in the third cycle the Committee stated in connection with Austria that despite the improvements it had made during the reporting period with regard to the sphere of application of sickness and old age insurance and to the level of certain benefits, it would consider that Austria complied with paragraph 3 only if its system complied with the minimum level laid down by Convention No. 102. As the Committee at the time was not able to ascertain the compliance of Austria with paragraph 2, it deferred its conclusion (Conclusions III, p. 63). Furthermore, ratification of the European Code of Social Security has been considered as evidence of a state's constant determination to raise the standard of its social security scheme. (Conclusions IV, p. 83, Denmark).

In trying to decide whether there has been an improvement or not and therefore compliance with this paragraph, the Committee has asked for information on increases in the cost of living because, in its view, an increase in benefits which only keeps pace with increases in the cost of living does not constitute an improvement: it considered that a rise in all benefits ranging from 27 to 69% while the cost of living index rose by no more than 21.9% was an improvement (Conclusions IV, p. 83). Other information considered as relevant by the Committee concerns the effects of the taxation of benefits as in its view there might be cases in which they result in cut-backs in the level of coverage provided. (Conclusions IV, p. 84).

A question raised in connection with this provision is whether its dynamic character has a limit and if so at what level. In its earlier Conclusions the Committee showed no signs that it regarded this paragraph as finite in its aim. In the tenth cycle, however, when examining the Netherlands report, the Committee noted that "the Committee of Ministers of the Council of Europe recently held that the Netherlands complied with at least the minimum number of provisions necessary for the ratification of the Protocol to the European Code of Social Security. On account of the Committee of Ministers' position in this respect (the maximum effort which could be required from Contracting Parties by virtue of Article 12 para. 3 of the Charter, is to attain the minimum level necessary for the ratification of the Protocol to the European Code of Social Security) the Committee was able to conclude that the Netherlands comply with this provision of the Charter" (Conclusions X-1, p. 113). In the eleventh supervision cycle the Committee "observing that the Netherlands continue to fulfil the minimum requirements for ratification of the Protocol to the European Code of Social Security" upheld its previous positive conclusion (Conclusions XI-1, p. 125). In the twelfth cycle the Committee noted from the *travaux préparatoires* of the Charter that, had the European Code on Social Security and its Protocol been in force at the time the Charter was signed, satisfaction of the requirements of the Protocol would have constituted the basic requirement for fulfilment of this provision of the Charter. As the Netherlands satisfied the requirements of this Protocol the Committee was able to renew its positive conclusions (Conclusions XII-1, pp. 183 and 184).

Finally it is worth pointing out that this paragraph is the only one in the Charter in which the obligation for a Contracting Party is to "endeavour", ie. to make an effort, to achieve something. This distinction proved important in the case of Denmark in the third cycle. Despite the fact that during the reporting period under examination (1970-1971) no improvements were made in the Danish social security system, the Committee found Denmark as having complied with this paragraph because the preparatory work for the major improvements which came into effect in 1972 had been carried out during the reporting period. Denmark had provided evidence that it had been endeavouring to improve its system (Conclusions III, p. 63).

Assessment of compliance

There are no cases of non-compliance. Nevertheless, in the thirteenth cycle the Committee, expressing its concern for the regression in the social security systems of some member states, requested the Contracting Parties concerned to indicate the reasons for this and its impact on the overall system of social security.

There are two cases of deferral, Portugal (first report) and Turkey.

Portugal: pending receipt of information on the development of social security schemes in the past and the efforts made to progressively bring these schemes to a higher level (Conclusions XIII-3, p. 356).

Turkey: the Committee noted that the gaps in insurance cover of the active population recorded in its previous Conclusions still existed (family allowances paid to a limited number of recipients, non-existence of unemployment insurance) and stated that it expected more significant developments (Conclusions XIII-3, p. 357).

Paragraph 4 – Equal treatment for the nationals of the other Contracting Parties with respect to social security

Under this paragraph, the Contracting Parties undertake:

"to take steps, by the conclusion of appropriate bilateral and multilateral agreements, or by other means, and subject to the conditions laid down in such agreements, in order to ensure:

a. equal treatment with their own nationals of the nationals of other Contracting Parties in respect of social security rights, including the retention of benefits arising out of social security legislation, whatever movements the persons protected may undertake between the territories of the Contracting Parties;

b. the granting, maintenance and resumption of social security rights by such means as the accumulation of insurance or employment periods completed under the legislation of each of the Contracting Parties."

Appendix to Article 12 para. 4

"The words 'and subject to the conditions laid down in such agreements' in the introduction to this paragraph are taken to imply *inter alia* that with regard to benefits which are available independently of any insurance contribution a Contracting Party may require the completion of a prescribe period of residence before granting such benefits to nationals of other Contracting Parties".

According to the wording of Article 12 para. 4 and to paragraph 1 of the Appendix, which defines the scope of the Charter in terms of the persons protected, paragraph 4 of Article 12 applies to the nationals of **all** the Contracting Parties to the Charter and not only to nationals of Contracting Parties which have accepted this paragraph. It applies to all such nationals irrespective of whether they lawfully reside or work regularly within the territory of the Contracting Party concerned.

In the third supervision cycle, the Committee explained the differences between sub-paragraphs a. and b. of Article 12 para. 4, stating that the provisions of Article 12 para. 4 comprise:

- "an undertaking by each Contracting Party *to ensure equal treatment* with its own nationals of the nationals of other Contracting Parties.

These undertakings cannot be regarded as having been honoured unless *equality is effectively safeguarded under national legislation;*

- an undertaking to endeavour to enable migrants to maintain or restore their rights which can only be achieved by means of bilateral or multilateral agreements.

These undertakings cannot be regarded as having been honoured unless *adequate efforts are made to conclude and implement international agreements whereby migrants' rights are retained*" (Conclusions III, p. 64 and 65).

In the sixth supervision cycle, the Committee recalled that equality of treatment must be accorded to the nationals of other Contracting Parties either by bilateral or multilateral agreements or by other means and specified that "other means" was to be interpreted as including unilateral measures (Conclusions VI, p. 84). This was reiterated in subsequent cycles, together with the view "that equal treatment should be effectively safeguarded under national legislation" (Conclusions XII-2, p. 178 and Conclusions XIII-2, p. 118, France).

In the thirteenth supervision cycle, the Committee recalled further that Article 12 para. 4 "did not require that bilateral agreements exist, nor was it based on principles of reciprocity. Any state having accepted it could comply either through bilateral agreement or through unilateral action" (Conclusions XIII-2, p. 122, Norway). Furthermore, the Committee accepts the absence of bilateral agreements when the countries concerned have no migration exchange. (Conclusions VII, p. 73, Austria). The latter point was confirmed several times (see for example Conclusions XIII-2, p. 117, Cyprus and p. 121, the Netherlands).

Finally the Committee stressed that equality should be ensured in two respects:

- a Contracting Party cannot restrict a social security benefit to its nationals or lay down conditions only for non-nationals, except for a period of residence, in principle allowed under the provisions of the Appendix to the Charter relating to Article 12 para. 4 (see below "assessment of compliance");

- requirements which applied equally to nationals and non-nationals but affected exclusively or mainly non-nationals were an example of indirect discrimination (see the Committee's requests for clarification under "assessment of compliance" below).

Nevertheless, the Committee retained some margin of appreciation in assessing the respect of the principle of equal treatment. Whilst regretting the situation, it considered that as long as indirect discrimination had not been seen in practice, there would be no violation of Article 12 para. 4 in this respect (Conclusions XIII-2, p. 122, the Netherlands). Moreover, it reserved its position concerning the payment of reduced family allowance rates for children resident in another Contracting Party because of the considerably lower cost of living in the Contracting Party concerned, pending receipt of information on the basis on which these rates were fixed (Conclusions XIII-2, p. 341, Germany).

As mentioned above, the Appendix to Article 12 para. 4 specifies that the granting of non-contributory benefits may be conditional on the completion of a prescribed period of residence. However, the Committee reserves the right to examine the proportionality of any residence requirements (Conclusions XIII-3, p. 358, Finland).

Assessment of compliance

The following situations have in the past been considered by the Committee as not complying with the undertaking of Contracting Parties to ensure equality between their nationals and nationals of other Contracting Parties:

France:

a.   the restriction of the award of allowances for disabled adults (AAH) to nationals of Community member states resident in France and to nationals of other states with which a reciprocal agreement had been concluded resulted in depriving nationals of the other Contracting Parties of this allowance. The Contracting Parties affected in the thirteenth supervision cycle were Austria, Cyprus, Finland, Iceland, Malta, and Norway (negative conclusion since the sixth cycle);

In the tenth cycle, in response to the French Government's point of view that this allowance was a specific social benefit to which, by reason in particular of its non-contributory character, the Appendix to paragraph 4 of Article 12 applied (which did not oblige states to grant such a benefit unilaterally) and that France was prepared to enter into bilateral agreements, the Committee, whilst not disagreeing with this view and admitting that formal or informal arrangements should be sought for determining the period of residence referred to in the Appendix, observed that in the absence of agreements or arrangements covering such matters, the French Government was compelled under the Charter to determine unilaterally one or more periods of residence upon which the provision of such benefit to nationals of the other Contracting Parties would be made conditional. In view of this it asked the French Government to indicate the measures it intended to take to ensure the payment of this allowance to nationals of other Contracting Parties with which it had no agreement and were not European Community countries (Conclusions X-2, p. 116; the criticism was repeated in Conclusions XII-2, p. 177 to 178 and Conclusions XIII-2, p. 117);

b.   the restriction of the supplementary allowance from the National Solidarity Fund (FNS) only to nationals, to nationals of European Community member states and to nationals of other states with which a reciprocal agreement had been concluded resulted in depriving nationals of the other Contracting Parties of the allowance. The Contracting

Parties affected in the thirteenth cycle were Cyprus, Finland, Iceland, Malta, Norway and Turkey[1] (Conclusions XII-2 p. 178 and Conclusions XIII-2, p. 118).

Italy:[2] the "Social Pension", a non-contributory pension granted to persons over sixty-five without an income or income below a ceiling, was restricted to Italians and nationals of member states of the European Communities resident in Italy (Conclusions III, p. 65), with the result that the pension was denied to nationals of Contracting Parties to the Charter not members of the European Economic Community (Conclusions III, p. 65 and Conclusions VII, p. 74);

In the fourth cycle the Committee explained that this discriminatory treatment could not be compatible with paragraph 4 of Article 12 and that the only permissible restriction to equality between nationals and non-nationals under this paragraph and the Interim Agreements was to make the payment of non-contributory benefits conditional on a certain period of residence (Conclusions IV, p. 84 and 85);

Norway:[3] benefits for disablement and for survivors to persons living abroad were not granted unless they were of Norwegian nationality. Such discrimination could not be accepted as being in conformity with Article 12 (Conclusions III, p. 66). The subsequent authorisation of the payment of these benefits to nationals of Contracting Parties, parties to the Council of Europe Interim Agreements, did not change the negative conclusion since the parties to these agreements were not the same

---

1 In Conclusions XIII-2 (p. 118) the Committee took note that bilateral reciprocal agreements with Austria and Sweden were the only bilateral agreements which provided for the supplementary allowance from the FNS to those entitled to old age or invalidity contributions. The Committee wished to know if this allowance was identical to that accorded to French nationals.

2 Italy made a reservation in respect of the European Interim Agreements on Social Security in relation to old-age, invalidity and survivors' benefit, which excluded the Italian social pension from the scope of the agreement. As a result, Italy was not required to grant this benefit to nationals of other states bound by the Charter and the Committee concluded that Italy complied with the Charter (Conclusions IX-2, p. 77).

3 The situation was remedied by the National Insurance Act of 14 June 1974 which came into force on 1 July 1974.

countries as those of the Charter and one state had not ratified the Interim Agreements (Conclusions IV, p. 85);

In addition, it should be pointed out that the Committee asks for clarifications in respect of family benefits. It has noted that the legislation of several Contracting Parties submits grants to residence requirements for the beneficiary and/or his or her children and that these requirements also apply in principle to nationals of the Contracting Parties concerned. In each case, whilst stressing that from a strictly legal point of view the rule is the same for nationals and non-nationals, the Committee has expressed concern over this matter as it could constitute a form of indirect discrimination, in so far as in practice there would be proportionally more non-nationals than nationals affected.

Cases in which the Committee has observed that restrictions are imposed and has asked for clarifications include the following:

Belgium: the Committee noted that family allowances were only paid for children brought up in Belgium or in a European Union country, or else in a country with which a reciprocity agreement had been signed (Conclusions XIII-2, p. 340);

Finland: the Committee noted that family allowances were granted to both non-nationals and nationals on the condition that the children were resident in Finland (Conclusions XIII-3, p. 358);

France: the Committee noted that French legislation submitted family allowances to residence requirements in France or, apart from exceptions, in a country which is party to the Agreement on the European Economic Area for the beneficiary and his or her children (Conclusions XII-2, p. 179 and Conclusions XIII-2, pp. 118 and 119);

Germany: family allowances are paid in respect of children who are resident in Germany or in a European country with which Germany has a bilateral agreement, with the result that nationals of other Contracting Parties (ie. in the thirteenth cycle Cyprus and Malta) have no entitlement to family allowances if their children are not resident in Germany

(Conclusions XI-2, pp. 115 and 116, Conclusions XII-2, p. 179 and Conclusions XIII-2, pp. 340 and 341);

the Netherlands: the payment of family allowances in respect of unemployed children aged between sixteen and twenty-one is granted only if the children are registered with an employment office in the Netherlands or in other European Community member states, or in a country with which a treaty covering social security has been concluded. This restriction means that nationals of other Contracting Parties not members of the European Union or of states with which a social security agreement has been signed (ie. in the thirteenth cycle Cyprus and Malta) who work in the Netherlands are denied the right to family allowances in respect of their children registered with an employment office in their own country (Conclusions XII-1, p. 187 and Conclusions XIII-2, p. 122).

The clarifications sought by the Committee concern in particular the types of family benefits in question, their amounts and the number of people affected, nationals of the Contracting Party and nationals of other Contracting Parties.

Article 13 – The right to social and medical assistance

General

This Article, which consists of four paragraphs, ensures for persons without adequate resources the right to social and medical assistance.

As the Committee pointed out in the first supervision cycle an attempt was made when the Charter was drafted to break away from the old idea of assistance which was bound up with the dispensation of charity. This is reflected in the wording used in this Article, where the term "persons without adequate resources" was chosen instead of "poor", and "want" was used instead of the word "poverty". The attempt to eradicate the stigma attached to public assistance is also evident from the undertaking in paragraph 2 which makes it compulsory for the states accepting it to eradicate from their legislation any remnants of social and political discrimination against persons receiving assistance (Conclusions I, p. 64).

Paragraph 1 – Social and medical assistance for those in need

Under this paragraph, the Contracting Parties undertake:

> "to ensure that any person who is without adequate resources and who is unable to secure such resources either by his own efforts or from other sources, in particular under a social security scheme be granted adequate assistance, and, in case of sickness, the care necessitated by his condition".

From the very first supervision cycle, the Committee established that this paragraph bound Contracting Parties to recognise that persons in need were entitled to public assistance as of right. It has insisted that social assistance should be granted as a "subjective right (*droit subjectif*)", in other words it should not depend solely on a decision at the administration's discretion. It found that such a right should furthermore be supported by a right of appeal to an independent body (Conclusions I, p. 64; Conclusions X-1, p. 116, Iceland; Conclusions X-2, p. 121 and XI-2, pp. 119 and 120, Spain; Conclusions XII-1, pp. 188 and 189 and XIII-1 pp. 188 and 189, Greece).

In order to enable it to exercise its supervisory role on the first point, the Committee asks whether uniform national criteria are laid down (see Conclusions XIII-1, p. 188, Greece; Conclusions XIII-3, p. 361, Finland).

In order to ascertain the independence of the body before which appeals may be brought, the Committee asks by whom and how its members are appointed, the length of their term of office, their qualifications, the procedures applied and what statutory factors ensure their independence (Conclusions XIII-1, p. 189, Iceland). It also asks whether the body concerned is empowered to take enforceable decisions (Addendum to Conclusions XIII-3, p. 71, Luxembourg). A prefect or a minister cannot be considered as independent bodies (Conclusions XIII-2, p. 127, Greece) Assuming that independence has been established, the Committee asks for examples of their case law (Conclusions XIII-3, pp. 362 and 364, Finland and Turkey).

The phrase without "adequate resources" has not been defined expressly by the Committee, but its assessment of national situations suggests that a person comes within this paragraph when he or she lacks sufficient resources to provide for the necessities of life as determined by reference to the prevailing cost and standard of living within the Contracting Party concerned.

On this point, the Committee asks the Contracting Parties to supply information on the procedure for determining whether a person is without adequate resources (Conclusions I, p. 66) and in particular, the methods used to investigate needs and resources; they should also report on the criteria according to which "want" is assessed (Conclusions I, p. 66; Addendum to Conclusions IX-2, p. 33, Spain), including at what level (national, regional, municipal).

As regards the word "in particular", it is clear from the *travaux préparatoires* that it does not mean that "benefits made under a social security scheme" are the only "other sources" to which an indigent person may be expected to resort before a Contracting Party must provide him or her with social assistance. Although the Committee has never used this information in order to reach a conclusion, it nevertheless asks whether an indigent person's family is obliged to support him, if so whether the family support is required before or after the social assistance and who are deemed "family" (Conclusions XIII-1, p. 188 and Conclusions XIII-2, p. 128, Greece).

Subject to the rule concerning the scope of the Charter *ratione personae*, "any person" eligible for it is entitled to assistance. The system of assistance should cover, at least notionally, the entire population (see, on this point, Conclusions IV, p. 88, Italy; Conclusions X-2, p. 121, Spain; Conclusions XIII-3, pp. 362 and 363, Portugal and Turkey; Addendum to Conclusions XIII-3, p. 73, Luxembourg). This does not prevent particular benefits being limited to certain categories of recipient (such as elderly or disabled persons), on condition that other categories who might be in need also qualify for assistance (Conclusions X-2, p. 121, Spain; Conclusions XIII-3, pp. 362 and 363). According to the case law, the imposition of age, health, length of residence or nationality[1] requirements may potentially exclude particular groups of the population from assistance, thus failing to comply with the Charter (see below, "assessment of compliance"). The imposition of residence or place of birth requirements is also incompatible with the Charter (Conclusions II, p. 49, Italy; Conclusions XIII-2, p. 131, Spain; see also "assessment of compliance" below).

The assistance to which a person is entitled may be in cash or in kind and must be adequate. The term "adequate" is not defined in the Charter but it appears that the Committee regards assistance as adequate if it is sufficient to allow the person concerned to provide for the necessaries of life in accordance with the prevailing cost and standard of living in the Contracting Party concerned. In this regard, adequate information must be supplied on the amount of benefits under the social assistance system (basic and maximum amounts, percentage of minimum legal wage and so on); the Committee retaining the right to determine whether this is appropriate (Conclusions III, p. 67, Austria; Conclusions XIII-2, pp. 124, 126 and 182, Austria, France and Malta; Conclusions XIII-3, pp. 363 and 364, Turkey).

Moreover, the Committee has pointed out that adequate information is to be provided concerning:

- the number of persons who receive assistance benefits (see most recently Conclusions XIII-2, p. 343, Germany; Addendum to Conclusions XIII-3, p. 72, Luxembourg);

- the existence of a limit to the period of time during which a person can receive public assistance (eg. Conclusions XIII-I, p. 188, Greece);

- the amount of public and private spending on assistance (Conclusions I, p. 66; more recently Conclusions XIII-2, p. 126, Denmark). Where discrepancies between the number of assistance allowance

---

1 According to the Appendix to the Charter, the right to social and medical assistance should be secured to all nationals of Contracting Parties lawfully resident or working regularly within the territory of another Party (see the questions put to Malta in Conclusions XIII-2, p. 344 and to Portugal in Conclusions XIII-3, p. 363).

beneficiaries and the amount of corresponding expenditure are noted, explanations are sought (see Conclusions XIII-2, pp. 125 and 343, Denmark and Germany).

Assessment of compliance

There are a number of cases of non-compliance with this paragraph. Contracting Parties still not complying are:

Greece[1] on two grounds:

a.   there is neither a right to be granted social assistance nor the possibility to invoke such a right before an independent body such as a court (Conclusions XII-1, p. 188 and 189; Conclusions XIII-1, pp. 188 and 189; Conclusions XIII-2, p. 127). (In Greece, social assistance relies upon the provision of funds and services for the needy by a wide variety of bodies including the church, private organisations, the extended family and the state);

b.   there is a six-month residence requirement for obtaining social assistance which applies equally to Greeks (Conclusions XIII-2, p. 127). According to the Committee's consistent case law this condition is inconsistent with the Charter;

Italy:[2] on the ground that there is no guarantee of an entitlement as of right to social assistance with the possibility of an appeal to an independent body such as a court (negative conclusion since the first cycle, latest criticism in Conclusions XIII-2, p. 129);

Luxembourg: on the ground that the guaranteed minimum income (RMG) and specific benefits are restricted to certain categories of the

1 The Committee of Ministers addressed a recommendation on these points to Greece for the first part of the twelfth supervision cycle and the first part of the thirteenth supervision cycle.

2 The Committee of Ministers addressed a recommendation to Italy on this point for the second part of the twelfth supervision cycle, which was renewed for the second part of the thirteenth supervision cycle.

population and cannot alone constitute adequate assistance (Addendum to Conclusions XIII-3, p. 73);

the *United Kingdom* on two grounds:

a. the Social Fund, under which loans are granted to persons receiving social assistance to cover exceptional expenses, does not guarantee granting of assistance as of right, nor does it provide for a right of appeal or a right of review to an independent body (Conclusions XIII-1, p. 190 and XIII-2, p. 132). (The Social Fund replaced the system previously in place for unemployed persons. A person who would have previously been entitled to apply for an increase in weekly benefit or grant may now apply for a "budgeting loan", a "crisis loan" or a "community care grant". Such loans are made at the discretion of the local social officer, depending upon his or her perception of the priority of need or the budget available to the local office);

b. the continuing existence in the Isle of Man of a five-year residence requirement for the receipt of supplementary benefit and of a six-month residence requirement for the receipt of family income supplement, both for United Kingdom nationals and foreigners (Conclusions XIII-1, p. 190).

The Committee's decision is deferred for Iceland, Malta, Portugal, Spain and Turkey. For Iceland the decision was previously negative as there was no right of appeal to an independent body. However, under the Local Authorities Social Services Act. No. 40 of 1991 reforming the organisation of social services, a right of appeal before a Social Services Appeals Committee has been granted. As a result, the Committee deferred its conclusion pending receipt of the information which would enable it to ascertain the independence of this committee (see Conclusions XIII-1, p. 189 and Conclusions XIII-2, p. 128);

Paragraph 2 – Non-discrimination with respect to persons receiving social and medical assistance

Under this paragraph, Contracting Parties undertake:

> "to ensure that persons receiving such assistance shall not, for that reason, suffer from a diminution of their political or social rights".

The Committee noted in the first supervision cycle (see above "General"), that "this provision makes it compulsory for states accepting it to eradicate from their legislation any remnants of social and political discrimination against persons receiving assistance" (Conclusions I, p. 64). It also noted that "the compilers of the Charter were anxious that necessitous persons should not be prevented from exercising their civil and political rights in full or from taking up certain kinds of employment or office. Persons receiving assistance should not be regarded as second-class citizens simply because they are unable to support themselves" (*ibidem*).

Furthermore, "the Committee agreed that this paragraph would be infringed only if discrimination against persons receiving public assistance resulted from an express statutory provision, such as an electoral provision or a provision governing admittance to public service" (Conclusions I, p. 67).

Assessment of compliance

On the whole, all the Contracting Parties which have accepted this provision have been found to comply. Only Ireland was found in breach until 1972, because under the Local Government (Application of Enactment) Order 1898, Article 12[1], a person in receipt of public assistance was not allowed to be a member of a local authority (whose function was to grant public assistance) within a period of twelve months of receipt of assistance benefits.

To verify whether political or social rights of beneficiaries of social assistance are affected, the Committee asks whether any provision guarantees this (see for example Conclusions XIII-3, p. 365, Finland).

---

1 Repealed by the Local Elections Act 1972.

Paragraph 3 – Advice and assistance in case of want

Under this paragraph, the Contracting Parties undertake:

> "to provide that everyone may receive by appropriate public of private services such advice and personal help as may be required to prevent, to remove or to alleviate personal or family want".

As stated by the Committee in the first supervision cycle, "the Contracting Parties must do all they can, in fact, to remove or alleviate want once it has arisen as they must try to prevent want from arising (paragraph 3). Like several other provisions in the Charter paragraph 3 of Article 13 is thus progressive in that it binds the states accepting it to set up an effective system of assistance, but also to ensure that such assistance gradually becomes unnecessary, until it completely disappears – the ultimate aim" (Conclusions I, p. 64).

A delicate problem of interpretation with which the Committee had to deal in the first cycle in connection with this paragraph concerned its field of application *vis-à-vis* that of Article 14 protecting the right to benefit from social welfare services. Although at first sight the two provisions might appear to be overlapping, since the measures referred to in paragraph 3 of Article 13 generally come within the sphere of the social welfare services which are the subject of Article 14, the Committee took the view that in the light of the *travaux préparatoires*, the wording of paragraph 3 of Article 13 and of its context, this provision concerns only advisory services for persons without or liable to be without adequate resources, whereas Article 14 is concerned with social welfare services in general. The Committee felt that the obligation stated in paragraph 3 of Article 13 was much more precise and more restricted than that of Article 14. The point is that although both texts are concerned with the way in which social services are organised, Article 14 is a general provision, while paragraph 3 of Article 13 is specific. The Committee came to the conclusion that the manner in which the Contracting Parties implemented the two provisions needed to be assessed separately. On the basis of this assessment a Contracting Party could be found as complying with Article 14, even though its social services did not meet all the requirements of paragraph 3 of

Article 13. Similarly, compliance with paragraph 3 of Article 13 did not necessarily mean that the requirements of Article 14 were met (Conclusions I, pp. 64 and 65).

In the same cycle the Committee stated that in order to be able to assess compliance with this paragraph, it needed "adequate information on the principal services in its territory of the kind referred to in this paragraph, their functions, and the size of their professional and/or voluntary staffs" (Conclusions I, p. 67; see also Conclusions X-1, p. 118 and XIII-1 p. 191, Greece). It also asks for information on the geographical distribution of social services (see, *inter alia*, Conclusions XIII-3, p. 366 and 367, Portugal and Turkey).

From the reports of Contracting Parties, it appears that advice to help remove or alleviate want could cover such matters as the availability of housing, social benefits and social welfare services, and informing people of their rights and benefits under social security legislation. Advice to prevent future want may include advice on employment and educational opportunities and birth control.

Personal help may take different forms such as home nursing, cleaning help, meals services, day centres or clubs, transport facilities for hospital visits and home help services for the elderly, as well as day nurseries.

Article 13 para. 3 refers to "personal and family want". The family aspect coincides with Article 16 which protects the right of the family to social, legal and economic protection.

The obligation of a Contracting Party is to "provide" advice or help by appropriate "public or private services". It may, therefore, be carried out either by the establishment of public bodies able to give advice or help or by allowing and, if need be, by encouraging private bodies to do so or by a combination of both. The national reports indicate that advice and help is mainly provided through public bodies, although voluntary organisations also play an important role.

Assessment of compliance

Currently there are no cases of non-compliance with this paragraph.

There are, however, five cases of deferral.

Greece: the Committee has adjourned its conclusion pending receipt of information on the numbers of personnel and vacant posts in the regional services of the Ministry of Health Welfare and Social Security entrusted with the provision of advice and assistance, the number of social workers in private bodies, as well as information on the extent to which the 2 000 social workers were engaged in providing advice and assistance in accordance with this provision (Conclusions X-1, p. 118; more recently Conclusions XIII-1, p. 191 and XIII-2, p. 134);

Ireland: the Committee has adjourned its conclusion pending information as to how consultation and personal help services for persons lacking resources are organised and function as well as information on the number of social services staff (Addendum to Conclusions XI-2, p. 41; Conclusions XIII-1, p. 191; Conclusions XIII-2, p. 135);

Luxembourg: the Committee has adjourned its conclusion pending receipt of information on the organisation and functioning of the services and the number of staff assigned to them (Addendum to Conclusions XIII-3, p. 73);

Portugal: the Committee has adjourned its conclusion pending receipt of information on the numbers of staff employed in the centres responsible for providing personal advice and assistance and on whether the centres are located nationwide (Conclusions XIII-3, p. 366);

Turkey: the Committee has adjourned its conclusion pending receipt of comments on the absence of any social services establishment in certain provinces and pending information on the geographical distribution of several offices (Conclusions XIII-1, p. 254 and Conclusions XIII-3, p. 367).

Paragraph 4 – Equal treatment for the nationals of other Contracting Parties with respect to social and medical assistance

According to this paragraph, the Contracting Parties undertake:

> "to apply the provisions referred to in paragraphs 1, 2 and 3 of this Article on an equal footing with their nationals to nationals of other Contracting Parties lawfully within their territories in accordance with their obligations under the European Convention on Social and Medical Assistance".

Appendix to Article 13 para. 4

> "Governments not Parties to the European Convention on Social and Medical Assistance may ratify the Social Charter in respect of this paragraph provided that they grant to nationals of other Contracting Parties a treatment which is in conformity with the provisions of the said Convention".

Commenting on this paragraph in the first supervision cycle the Committee stated that it "is not an autonomous provision, insofar as it merely indicates which persons are to receive protection under the previous three paragraphs. The Contracting Parties are bound, by this paragraph, to guarantee that nationals and aliens receive equal treatment when it comes to social and medical assistance, in accordance with the obligations incumbent upon them under the European Convention on Social and Medical Assistance, signed in Paris on 11 December 1953" (Conclusions I, p. 65).

"In response to one government's observations regarding the category of persons covered by Article 13 para. 4 and regarding the relevance of the principle of reciprocity to certain provisions of the Charter, the Committee felt it necessary to state more completely its interpretation of the scope of this paragraph.

1.   The Committee noted first that the Charter was designed to be

complementary to the European Convention on Human Rights (cf. Preamble). While the Convention covers all persons within the jurisdiction of a Contracting Party, the field of application of the Charter is limited to the nationals of the Contracting Parties: no other restriction is provided by the Charter. Neither instrument has any provisions for reciprocity, either general or specific.

2. Though the Charter permits that states may not accept all its provisions, it is clear from paragraph 1 of the Appendix, that a state has to apply the provisions it has accepted to nationals of all the other states which have ratified the Charter, independently of the fact that these states have not accepted the same provisions. Nevertheless, paragraph 1 of the Appendix is without prejudice, *inter alia,* to the provisions of Article 13 para. 4. It seems therefore necessary to clarify its meaning.

3. In fact, Article 13 para. 4 provides that its paragraphs 1 to 3 should be applied by the states in conformity with the obligations arising under the European Convention on Social and Medical Assistance of 11 December 1953. It is suggested that this provision could give rise to an interpretation according to which the obligations arising under Article 13 para. 4 would apply in regard to the states which have not accepted Article 13 para. 4 only if they are parties to the above Convention. It would follow that the nationals of a state which has not ratified that Convention and which has not accepted Article 13 para. 4 would not be able to benefit from the guarantees included in this provision in the states having accepted it.

4. It is to be observed in this respect that the nature of the reference in this provision of the Charter to the European Convention on Social and Medical Assistance should be considered in the light of the provisions in Part II of the Appendix of the Charter concerning this article. The existence of this provision shows that the ratification of the Charter and the acceptance of Article 13 para. 4 impose an obligation on all such states to grant treatment in conformity with the Convention on Social and Medical Assistance even if they have not ratified this Convention. It follows that the obligations arising from Article 13 para. 4 with respect

to nationals of another state bound by the Charter are not conditional upon the reciprocal application of the 1953 Convention or the acceptance by this state of Article 13 para. 4.

5.   In conclusion, it clearly appears therefore that the reference to this Convention under Article 13 para. 4 of the Charter aims solely at determining the obligations *'ratione materiae'* arising under this article. The phrase 'without prejudice to... Article 13, paragraph 4' in paragraph 1 of the Appendix (which concerns the scope of the Charter in terms of persons protected) serves solely to indicate that the words 'lawfully resident or working regularly within' do not limit the wider scope of application of Article 13 para. 4 which extends to all those 'lawfully within'" (Conclusions VII, pp. 77 and 78).

In other words, the requirement for this paragraph is lawful presence and not residence or place of regular work. Lawful residence would imply the exclusion of those present lawfully for a temporary stay. Conversely, the terms "lawful presence" cover temporary stay in the territory, for example as a tourist (see *inter alia* Conclusions XIII-2, p. 142, Norway; Conclusions XIII-3, p. 367, Finland). Any residence requirement, even applied to nationals, is thus prohibited by the Committee (as this may amount to an indirect discrimination; see Conclusions XIII-2, p. 138, Greece, p. 143 Spain and p. 146, the United Kingdom).

As the Committee recently reiterated (Addendum to Conclusions XIII-3, p. 74), the reference in this paragraph to the 1953 Convention[1] as

---

1 The primary obligation for a Party to that Convention is to ensure that the nationals of other parties to the Convention who are "lawfully present" in its territory and who are "without sufficient resources" are "entitled equally with its own nationals and on the same conditions to social and medical assistance (see Article 1). Under the Convention a contracting party is not entitled to repatriate a national of another party to the Convention because the person concerned is in need of assistance (Art. 6) unless certain conditions are met (Art. 7) (the person concerned has not been "continuously resident" for at least five years if entered before 55 or for at least 10 if entered after 55, he is in a fit state of health to be transported and has no close family or other ties in the state).

clarified in the relevant provision of the Appendix to the Charter, is aimed solely at determining the obligations *ratione materiae* arising under it, including the guarantees of repatriation provided for in Articles 6 and 7 of the Convention.

The Committee, when examining the Danish report in the fourth cycle, stated that it would be quite incompatible with the Charter to repatriate nationals of Contracting Parties to the Charter which had not ratified the Convention (Austria and Cyprus) solely because they were in need (see Conclusions IV, p. 91). This statement was made to clarify the effect of the reference in paragraph 4 of Article 13 to the Convention. In Conclusions V the Committee asked Denmark to take steps to ensure to Austrian and Cypriot nationals a guarantee against repatriation on the sole ground that they were without sufficient resources and in need of assistance.

The Committee has asked for national reports to indicate the number of nationals of other Contracting Parties repatriated for seeking assistance (Denmark, Conclusions XII-1, p. 195) and has wanted to know whether repatriation took place within the limits, under the conditions and according to the arrangements provided for by Articles 6 to 10 of the European Convention on Social and Medical Assistance (see Conclusions XIII-2, p. 137, Denmark; Addendum to Conclusions XIII-3, p. 74, Luxembourg).

The Committee has also asked the Contracting Parties which have accepted paragraph 4 of Article 13 to state whether and how equality of treatment is provided to Finnish nationals lawfully within their territory (as Finland is not bound by the 1953 Convention) and to refugees and stateless persons within their territory (general question posed in Conclusions XII-1, p. 194 and XII-2, p. 186).

Assessment of compliance

France[1] was found as not complying as Cypriot nationals in France were not treated in exactly the same way as French nationals in matters of social and medical assistance (Conclusions VI, p. 91);

The United Kingdom[2] was found as not complying on several grounds:

a. Cypriot nationals were not entitled to free medical assistance if they were visiting the United Kingdom temporarily (Conclusions XII-1, p. 118 and XIII-1, p. 194);

b. in Great Britain and Northern Ireland the regulations implementing the social assistance legislation provided that, except in "urgent cases", persons from abroad temporarily in the United Kingdom were not entitled to receive income support. "Persons from abroad" excluded from its definition the nationals of states which had ratified the European Convention on Social and Medical Assistance. However, as Austria and Cyprus had not ratified that Convention, their nationals could be denied social assistance on an equal footing with United Kingdom nationals (in Conclusions XI-1, p. 134, the Committee asked for confirmation of the situation and in Conclusions XII-1, p. 199, a negative conclusion was reached);

c. six months' residence is required in the Isle of Man for family income supplement and five years for supplementary benefit for both nationals and foreigners. Although in theory there is equality, in reality there is discrimination (negative conclusion since the fifth cycle).

---

1 The situation was remedied by a circular of 10 October 1989 of the French Ministry of Solidarity, Health and Social Welfare, instructing the local and departmental administrative authorities responsible for social welfare to ensure that Cypriot nationals henceforth received equal treatment in this area (Conclusions XI-2, p. 122).

2 The situation was remedied on point a. outside the reference period of the first part of the thirteenth cycle of supervision (see Conclusions XIII-2, p. 145); on point b. by amendment of Regulation 21 of the Income Support (General) Regulations of 1987 entitling all nationals of Contracting Parties to receive social assistance on an equal basis with United Kingdom nationals (Conclusions XIII-I, p. 194). The conclusion is currently deferred.

In the thirteenth cycle "as regards claims for supplementary benefit which were disallowed on the grounds that the applicants failed to satisfy the residence requirements, the Committee noted from the statistics provided that the vast majority of cases concerned nationals of the United Kingdom, not nationals of other Contracting Parties. While the Committee noted that there was equality of treatment in principle, it nevertheless considered that there was a risk of indirect discrimination. The Committee therefore wished to continue receiving information on the number of requests registered and of those rejected, on the grounds that applicants failed to fulfil the residence requirements, as well as on the nationality of applicants" (Conclusions XIII-2, pp. 145 and 146).

Contracting Parties currently found as not complying are:

Greece:[1]

a. "pensions" for those aged over sixty-eight (considered by Greece as a social assistance benefit) are restricted to Greek nationals whereas they should be granted on an equal footing to nationals of other Contracting Parties to the Charter (Conclusions XI-1, p. 133; more recently Conclusions XIII-2, p. 138);

b. Austrian, Cypriot and Finnish nationals (ie. nationals of states which have not ratified the 1953 Convention) are not guaranteed equal treatment in respect of medical assistance, the only exception being the possibility of waiving emergency hospitalisation costs if it is proved that the affected individual cannot pay (the conclusion has been negative since the twelfth cycle: Conclusions XII-1, p. 196 and Conclusions XIII-2, p. 139);

c. the imposition of a residence requirement (of six months) for the granting of social assistance. In cycle XIII-2 the Committee noted that "the six-month residence requirement for obtaining social assistance applied equally to Greeks and to foreigners and that the goal of this

---

1 The Committee of Ministers addressed recommendations to Greece on points a. and c. for the first part of the twelfth supervision cycle and the first part of the thirteenth supervision cycle.

requirement was to verify permanent residence. The Committee considered that this was not compatible with the provisions of the Charter, on the one hand as this requirement was obviously more easily fulfilled by Greeks than by foreigners (creating indirect discrimination) and on the other hand as Article 13 para. 4 of the Charter applied to nationals of Contracting Parties "lawfully within" the territory (Conclusions XIII-2, p. 138);

Malta: there are no provisions affording nationals of all Contracting Parties to the Charter equal treatment in the provision of social and medical assistance (Conclusions XIII-2, p. 349);

Turkey: several social assistance benefits (ie. allowances paid to persons over the age of sixty-five years and to handicapped people in need and the monthly destitution allowance paid by the Directorate of Trusts) are reserved exclusively for Turkish nationals (Conclusions XIII-3, p. 368).

Article 14 – The right to benefit from social welfare services

General

Commenting on this Article in its first Conclusions the Committee stated that as a consequence of the definition of social services as services which use "methods of social work" and "contribute to the welfare and development of both individuals and groups in the community and to their adjustment to the social environment", the scope of Article 14 is "extremely general, in contrast to that of the various articles of the Charter which require states to provide social welfare services with a narrowly specialised objective" (Conclusions I, p. 69).

In view of this the Committee had to resolve the problem of the relationship between Article 14 and Article 13 para. 3 of the Charter, which it had already addressed in connection with the latter provision. It had held that "a state could not be considered as satisfying the undertaking under Article 14 simply because it was fulfilling the obligations deriving from Article 13 para. 3.

As regards the scope of application *ratione personae* of these two Articles, the Committee noted in its general comments that, unlike Article 13 para. 3, which covers only persons who do not have adequate resources of their own, Article 14 applies to a much larger number of beneficiaries. As regards the object of these two provisions, that of Article 13 para. 3 is limited to assistance, whereas Article 14 is wider in scope and includes any action taken to facilitate the development of individuals and their adjustment to society" (*ibidem*).

The difference in the object of the two provisions implies, in the Committee's view that, "beyond a certain level of social development, what the state should do, in order to conform to the provisions of Article 14, is to promote the establishment of services providing advice and individual help rather than to encourage the granting of material assistance. Article 14 may therefore be considered as dynamic in its implications, since the social welfare services for which it provides are designed to keep on increasing and broadening their action" (*ibidem*).

The view that "the scope of Article 14 is broader than that of Article 13 (and particularly Article 13 para. 3) in respect both of beneficiaries and objectives" was reiterated in the eighth cycle on the occasion of the report of a Contracting Party which under Article 14, para. 1, referred to the information supplied under Article 13 (Conclusions VIII p. 170, Iceland; see in the last instance Conclusions XIII-1, p. 372, Turkey).

General comments on Article 14 as a whole were made again by the Committee in its General introduction to Conclusions XII-1. These comments were as follows:

"The Committee recalled the importance of the social services in assisting the more vulnerable sectors of the population to remain a part of the community, limiting the risks of marginalisation or even helping marginalised persons to re-establish ties with the community and the workplace.

Important demographic trends which have put certain groups at greater risk include the ageing of the population and the changes in family structures (higher incidence of divorce, fewer marriages, more single-parent families), leading to concerns as to the protection of the elderly and children. Increased mobility and the reduction of the support available from the 'extended family' are other relevant factors which contribute also to reducing the protection for the disabled. Other vulnerable groups which should be catered for by the social services include ex-prisoners, young persons, women who are the victims of violence, drug and alcohol addicts, migrant workers and their families and refugees.

The Committee therefore first of all wished to stress the importance of the governments' including detailed and updated information on all social services provided for all sectors of the community in their reports under the relevant provisions of the Charter. This was particularly important given the dynamic nature of, especially, Article 14 paragraphs 1 and 2, where in the case of certain Contracting Parties no new information or only very limited information, had been received over more than one cycle of supervision [...]. Furthermore, the Committee particularly asked that future reports indicate the measures being taken to provide services to women, abused children and marginal members of society (those who often fail to qualify for benefits because they no longer have a fixed address, who live in the street or in shelters where available).

At the same time, the Committee noted that a number of initiatives had been taken by the Contracting Parties to address the changing needs with regard to social services. Thus, in Iceland, the United Kingdom and Sweden it noted an increased emphasis on the provision of social welfare services in the community, particularly as regards the elderly, the physically and mentally disabled and children, a policy which would both benefit the clients of such services and the community at large and save on the high costs of institutionalisation. Similarly, in the Netherlands the funds for residential homes for the elderly could now also be used to help elderly people remaining in their own homes, whether or not receiving care. In Denmark, a new service of free personal assistance was being offered to disabled persons at their workplace and, in Greece, the home help programme was decentralised to allow for more appropriate responses tot he needs in different regions.

The Committee, while considering the new initiatives favourably, wished to note that in some instances such a policy also involved an increasing reliance on private organisations and individuals (often voluntary) for the provision of the services, and that care had to be taken to ensure that such services were adequately and fairly provided. Similar considerations could be expressed as regards the increasing encouragement of volunteer work, both through financial and other incentives. These actions are indeed to be welcomed as both increasing community solidarity and the individual's sense of responsibility within the community, but governments must ensure that all categories of persons concerned may benefit from the necessary services, particularly in the poorer communities in the cities or in rural areas.

As a final point, the Committee wished to emphasise the importance of an adequate coverage, geographically and otherwise, of the requirements of the social services, involving sufficient numbers of properly trained social workers and other staff, in order to ensure the effective exercise of the right to social assistance by the whole of the population" (Conclusions XII-1, pp. 38 to 40, General introduction).

Paragraph 1 – Provision or promotion of social welfare services

Under this paragraph, the Contracting Parties undertake:

> "to promote or provide services which, by using methods of social work, would contribute to the welfare and development of both individuals and groups in the community, and to their adjustment to the social environment".

This paragraph may be complied with by the provision of public services or the promotion of private ones.

When examining the first biennial reports of Contracting Parties on this provision, the Committee made it clear that the following information was necessary in order to enable it to assess compliance:

"1.   general measures taken to give effect to the paragraph;

2.   the number of principal social welfare services of the kind referred to in the paragraph;

3.   the functions of those services and the categories of persons for whom they are intended;

4.   the organisation, administration, financing, staff and working methods of the services and their relations with other institutions;

5.   steps taken to promote such services;

6.   whether recourse to such services is compulsory in particular cases;

7.   whether those wishing to use the services are entitled to as of right or whether there is a discretionary power of granting or withholding them." (Conclusions I, p. 70).[1]

The Committee also observed that "it was not enough merely to refer to health services and measures to protect mothers and children, without giving any further details concerning the scope of the social welfare services" (Conclusions I, p. 72, Italy).

Throughout the supervision cycles the Committee has unfailingly drawn the attention of Contracting Parties to the dynamic nature of this provision and the consequent necessity for them to provide for each supervision cycle, updated information on the promotion or provision of welfare services and to produce new elements in order to show that progress is continually being made in implementing this provision (see for example Conclusions III, pp. 71 and 72; Conclusions V, p. 102, Italy; Conclusions XI-2, p. 126 and XII-2, p. 191, France; Conclusions XII-1, p. 200 Denmark and p. 201, Norway; Conclusions XIII-2, p. 352, Germany).

In the third supervision cycle, the Committee, referring to the dynamic nature of this provision, pointed out that information on the number of personnel employed in the various sectors of social services and the amounts allocated to these services should appear in every biennial report (Conclusions III, p. 72).

In assessing compliance with this provision the Committee seeks, *inter alia*, to ensure that social welfare services exist for all categories of individuals likely to have need of them (eg. the mentally ill, the physi-

---

1 These questions were later included in the Form for the Reports for this Article.

cally and mentally handicapped, children, the elderly mothers, young people, unemployed workers, minority groups (gypsies and refugees etc.), the homeless, alcohol and drug addicts, persons in search of housing). It also seeks to ensure that nationals of other Contracting Parties benefit from social services on an equal footing. For instance, in the case of France, the Committee asked for five consecutive cycles whether the right to benefit from the social services was extended to the nationals of other Contracting Parties and in particular whether children and adolescents, mothers and the elderly were admitted on the same basis as nationals to the institutions provided for persons in these categories (see Conclusions V, p. 101 to Conclusions X-2, p. 125).

The Committee welcomes the progress made in expanding or improving the social welfare services provided to individuals and groups. Measures taken with the intention of bringing the decision-making bodies closer to the clients of the services and to reinforce their rights (eg. the enactment in France on 8 January 1986 of the Act on Decentralisation of Social Assistance which, *inter alia*, gave people using the welfare services the right to be heard, with the assistance of a person of their choice, by the Social Assistance Eligibility Committees) were regarded as an improvement to a situation already considered as satisfactory, (Conclusions XI-2, p. 125, France). Support was also expressed for a government's objectives of allowing those in need to remain in the community and to lead independent lives as far as possible and of attempting to reintegrate offenders within the community, thus reducing recidivism (Conclusions XII-1, p. 201, the United Kingdom).

Whilst appreciating the progress made, the Committee shows concern for cases in which governments seem to rely to a significant extent on voluntary organisations for the provision of social welfare services. In such cases the Committee seeks to ensure that in so far as such services take the place of the provision of social services by the government, steps are being taken to ensure that the services are adequately and fairly provided (see for example Conclusions XII-1, pp. 201 and 202, the United Kingdom and Conclusions XII-2, p. 191, Malta).

In the twelfth cycle the Committee noted the establishment in a Contracting Party of a client registration system. As in its view such a system could have disadvantages related to the right to privacy, the Committee asked for information on this register, in particular the information contained therein, who controlled it and who had access to it (Conclusions XII-1, p. 201, the Netherlands).

Assessment of compliance

No Contracting Party has so far been found in breach of paragraph 1 of Article 14.

There are however, two cases of deferral, Finland (first report) and Turkey (second report).

In respect of Finland the Committee wished to have further information on the services made available by the local authorities, particularly on social work, institutional care and family care as well as indications of the organisations and management of these services. It also wished to be informed of staff levels in these areas (Conclusions XIII-3, p. 370).

In respect of Turkey the Committee, after reiterating that the scope of Article 14, in contrast to Article 13 para. 3, "not only covered persons with limited means but a broader group of beneficiaries (see above "General"), asked which were the main social services dealing with all sectors of the population and not only those in need and inquired into the number of staff employed and the amounts spent on these services" (Conclusions XIII-3, p. 372).

Paragraph 2 – Public participation in the establishment and maintenance of social welfare services

Under this paragraph, the Contracting Parties undertake:

> "to encourage the participation of individuals and voluntary or other organisations in the establishment and maintenance of such services".

The Committee made it clear that it could not "judge whether a Contracting State which has accepted this paragraph is really fulfilling its obligations unless the state includes in its two-yearly reports adequate information on the steps it has taken to make possible or encourage participation by individuals, employers and workers' organisations and other organisations[1] in the establishment or maintenance of the services referred to in Article 14" (Conclusions I, p. 71 and Conclusions III, p. 72).

This paragraph, like paragraph 1, has also been characterised as being of a dynamic nature. As a result the Committee often draws the attention of governments to this and asks them to keep updating in each cycle the information as to the encouragement of participation by individuals and voluntary or other groups in the establishment and maintenance of social welfare services (see for example Conclusions III, pp. 72 and 73, Cyprus, Italy, Sweden; Conclusions V, p. 152, Italy; and more recently Conclusions XII-I, p. 203, Norway).

In the fourth supervision cycle the Committee held that the authorities "while rejecting the idea of direct administration of social services by private persons or bodies, nevertheless encourage their participation in the upkeep of these services" and thus that the obligations arising out of this paragraph were fulfilled (Conclusions IV, p. 95, Sweden).

Assessment of compliance

As in the case of paragraph 1, no Contracting Party has ever been found as violating this paragraph. On the contrary, the Committee has noted with satisfaction the measures taken by governments to implement this provision and in particular the award of grants and other assistance to encourage voluntary work in the social services. There are no cases of deferral.

---

1 The Form for the Reports refers to the participation of individuals and charitable organisations and other appropriate organisations.

Article 15 – The right of physically or mentally disabled persons to vocational training, rehabilitation and social resettlement

General

The purpose of Article 15 was explained by the Committee in the first supervision cycle as follows:

"For a long time aid to the handicapped was classed together with aid to the aged; since the second world war aid to handicapped persons has developed on separate lines, under the influence of Anglo-Saxon legislation. Traditional assistance policies are now out of date and in legislation the emphasis regarding this category of persons has shifted to vocational training and rehabilitation, the reintegration within society. The overriding purpose is that such persons shall be enabled to work and be independent. The Charter reflects this trend and after referring to handicapped persons in Articles 9 and 10, raises the right of physically or mentally disabled persons to training, vocational rehabilitation and social resettlement to the level of a separate social right. Such a right is inconceivable in the absence of means for bringing it into effect, and the Charter therefore incorporates some of the provisions already contained in relevant ILO recommendations.[1] Under Article 15, the Contracting Parties undertake to guarantee to disabled persons:

- training facilities, including, where necessary, specialised institutions (paragraph 1);

- that their placing shall be promoted by means of specialised services, sheltered employment and measures to encourage employers to admit physically or mentally disabled persons to employment (paragraph 2)" (Conclusions I, p. 72).

Paragraph 1 – Vocational training arrangements for the disabled

By this paragraph, the Contracting Parties undertake:

> "to take adequate measures for the provision of training facilities, including, where necessary, specialised institutions, public or private".

In order to assess compliance with this paragraph the Committee has made it clear that Contracting Parties should supply information, *inter alia*, on:

- actual steps taken to implement it;

- the type and number of the main specialised institutions providing the appropriate training in the country in question;

- the total number of places available in these institutions;

- the number of persons receiving such training;

- the number of staff engaged in such work;

---

1 Vocational Training (Adults) Recommendation, 1950, No. 88 and Vocational Rehabilitation (Disabled) Recommendation, 1955, No. 99.

- rehabilitation arrangements for disabled persons other than the blind and the deaf and dumb, particularly persons disabled following occupational injuries;

- the criteria by which it is decided to what extent disabled persons are amenable to rehabilitation;

- the way in which vocational training programmes are drawn up in the light of actual employment opportunities;

- the measures taken to adapt rehabilitation methods to the requirements of the labour market;

- the estimated number of disabled persons (in particular the seriously handicapped);

- the number of disabled persons applying for vocational training, rehabilitation or retraining and the number actually trained or rehabilitated during the period of reference; (Conclusions I, p. 72, Conclusions III, p. 74, Conclusions IV, p. 97, Conclusions V, p. 105 and Conclusions XIII-3, p. 179).

The Committee explained that it needed information concerning the criteria used to certify a person as physically or mentally disabled in order "to judge, according to a single standard, what effort the various states were making to provide training and rehabilitation for the disabled" (Conclusions III, p. 74).

One issue for which the Committee has always shown constant concern is the application of the protection afforded under this paragraph to disabled persons nationals of other Contracting Parties to the Charter. Throughout the various cycles of supervision – but more often during the later cycles – the Committee has put specific questions to Contracting Parties with a view to finding out whether disabled foreigners are guaranteed access to vocational training schemes for disabled persons on the same basis as nationals (see for example Conclusions VII, p. 83 France; Conclusions X-1, p. 125, Denmark and Greece; Conclusions XI-1, pp. 137 and 138, Greece; Conclusions XII-1, pp. 206

and 207, Sweden; Conclusions XII-2, p. 195, Germany and pp. 195 and 196, Malta; Conclusions XIII-2, p. 355, Belgium; Conclusions XIII-3, p. 375, Finland and Portugal; see also the general observation under Article 1 para. 4 in Conclusions XII-1, p. 67 and XII-2, p. 57 or above under Article 1 para. 4).

Assessment of compliance

Currently there are no cases of non-compliance with this provision. In the first cycle Ireland and Norway had been found not to be in compliance because the results obtained were insufficient and more efforts needed to be made (Conclusions I, p. 208, Ireland; Conclusions I, p. 73, Norway). Further information led the Committee to change its conclusion in the second cycle. Other countries found not to comply were the United Kingdom and Denmark.

The United Kingdom was found not to comply with the Charter in the seventh cycle of supervision on the ground that the eligibility of physically or mentally disabled nationals of Contracting Parties bound by the Charter for access to the rehabilitation services was governed by passport regulations which constituted discrimination against them, except in the case of EEC nationals who were exempted from those regulations (Conclusions VII, p. 84). This criticism was repeated in the next three cycles. (Conclusions VIII, p. 177; Conclusions IX, p. 91; Conclusions X-1, p. 126). The conclusion was deferred in the eleventh cycle of supervision when the Committee noted that according to the United Kingdom's report the situation was as follows:

– "persons who have lived lawfully in the United Kingdom for more than four years enjoy the same employment rehabilitation rights as British nationals;

– persons who have been residing for less than four years in the United Kingdom and who are still subject to residence and employment restrictions (passport regulations) do not have the same rights as the British but their case is given sympathetic consideration, especially where their rehabilitation is aimed at resettlement in the same work for which they entered the United Kingdom;

- the conditions of admission to employment rehabilitation applicable to foreigners, which the Committee had criticised (knowledge of English, payment of the cost of the course, board and lodging, etc.), apply only to foreigners who go to the United Kingdom *for the purpose* of attending such courses;

- dependent children of foreigners admitted to the United Kingdom once they have reached the age of eighteen, are apparently free from all residence and employment restrictions and may be admitted to rehabilitation courses, even if their parents are still subject to such restrictions" (Conclusions XI-1, pp. 139 and 140).

The conclusion became positive in the twelfth cycle of supervision, when the above situation was confirmed and additional information was given according to which, *inter alia*, the spouses and dependent children of foreigners admitted to the United Kingdom for employment were free of all residence and employment restrictions and could be admitted to rehabilitation courses or any other courses on the same terms as United Kingdom nationals, even if their primary breadwinner was still subject to such restrictions. (Conclusions XII-1, p. 207).

The situation in Denmark was found to be inconsistent with this provision in the eleventh cycle of supervision, on the ground that a residence requirement of two years was imposed on disabled foreigners lawfully residing in Denmark, who were nationals of states bound by the Charter (excluding member states of the European Community and the Nordic states) in order to qualify for vocational training and rehabilitation (Conclusions XI-1, p. 137).

However, in the twelfth cycle of supervision the Committee found that Denmark did comply on the basis that assistance to disabled persons was no longer granted subject to a residence requirement (Conclusions XII-1, p. 204).

Currently there are four cases of deferral; Belgium (Conclusions XIII-2, pp. 354 and 355), Denmark, Finland and Greece (Conclusions XIII-3, p. 179, pp. 374 and 375 and pp. 180 and 181), mainly pending receipt of statistical information and/or information on the access of nationals of other Contracting Parties to vocational training schemes.

Paragraph 2 – Placement arrangements for the disabled

Under this paragraph, the Contracting Parties undertake:

> "to take adequate measures for the placing of disabled persons in employment, such as specialised placing services, facilities for sheltered employment and measures to encourage employers to admit disabled persons to employment".

The Committee has interpreted this paragraph "as covering both physically and mentally handicapped persons. In the Committee's opinion this interpretation follows from a comparison of the expressions used in the English and French texts of this paragraph and the general content of Article 15" (Conclusions I, p. 208).

By reason of this interpretation the Committee was unable in the first cycle of supervision, when examining a national report which was confined to the placing of "the physically handicapped", to decide whether or not the Contracting Party concerned was fulfilling its undertaking under this paragraph or not (Conclusions I, p. 208, Germany).

With a view to assessing compliance with this paragraph the Committee has asked the Contracting Parties to provide adequate information, *inter alia*, on:

- measures taken to ensure the placing of handicapped persons and, where appropriate, to guarantee their employment;

- the approximate number of handicapped persons asking, every year, for sheltered or other employment and those who found jobs;

- the actual number of handicapped persons who found paid employment, through specialised institutions or otherwise, during a certain period;

- steps taken to encourage disabled persons to become self-employed;

- the role which private organisations play in the rehabilitation of disabled persons and the measures taken to coordinate their activities with those of public services;

- measures to encourage employers to employ disabled persons and on the organisation of sheltered employment (Conclusions I, pp. 73 and 74, and Conclusions III, p. 76).

On the last point the Committee, in the earlier supervision cycles, asked Contracting Parties to indicate whether they had legislation making it compulsory for employers to take a certain pèrcentage of disabled persons or to reinstate persons who had become disabled as the result of an accident (Conclusions I, p. 73, Sweden and p. 208, Ireland). However, the Committee has not considered the existence of such legislation to be a prerequisite for compliance. Thus, it found that Sweden fulfilled its obligation under this paragraph even though it did not have such legislation on the ground that "appropriate measures had been taken in accordance with the provisions of this paragraph" (Conclusions II, p. 54; see also Conclusions IV, p. 99, Ireland).

In later supervision cycles the Committee has confined itself to asking about the measures taken to encourage employers to employ disabled persons and has expressed satisfaction at the introduction by Contracting Parties of compulsory recruitment measures and quotas in the public or private sectors, as well as incentives for the recruitment of disabled persons (such as grants to employers, subsidies for ergonomic arrangement of the workplace, reduction in employers' social security contributions).

As in the case of paragraph 1, the Committee has shown particular concern about the application of the measures taken to fulfil the obligations under this paragraph to nationals of other Contracting Parties who, on the basis of the Appendix to the Charter, should enjoy treatment "not less favourable" (see for example Conclusions XI-1, p. 140, Denmark and Greece; Conclusions X-1, p. 128 and Conclusions XI-1, pp. 141 and 142, the United Kingdom; Conclusions XIII-2, p. 357, Belgium and Conclusions XIII-3, p. 378, Portugal).

Assessment of compliance

The only country found as not complying is *Italy*. The Committee first expressed its concern in the seventh supervision cycle about the large number of disabled persons seeking employment. As no evidence was given in subsequent cycles of any progress and as the general reform of the legislation regulating the placement of physically disabled persons which the government had announced since the seventh cycle had still not taken place, the Committee concluded in the thirteenth cycle of supervision that the situation in Italy was not consistent with the Charter (Conclusions XIII-2, p. 222).

There are also four cases of deferral: Belgium (Conclusions XIII-2, pp. 356 and 357), Finland and Portugal (Conclusions XIII-3, pp. 376 to 378) and Luxembourg (Addendum to Conclusions XIII-3, pp. 79 and 80), mainly pending receipt of the statistical information requested and of information on the protection of nationals of other Contracting Parties.

In the revised Charter, the scope of this Article has been extended as compared to that of Article 15 of the Charter, as it no longer applies only to vocational rehabilitation but to the right of persons with disabilities to independent social integration, personal autonomy and participation in the life of the community in general. The words "effective exercise of the right to independence" contained in the introductory sentence to the provision imply, *inter alia*, that disabled persons should have the right to an independent life.

Under this provision Parties must aim to develop a coherent policy for people with disabilities. The provision takes a modern approach to how the protection of the disabled shall be carried out.

The new text reads as follows:

"Article 15 – The right of persons with disabilities to independence, social integration and participation in the life of the community.

With a view to ensuring to persons with disabilities, irrespective of age and the nature and origin of their disabilities, the effective exercise of the right to

---

independence, social integration and participation in the life of the community, the Parties undertake, in particular:

1.   to take the necessary measures to provide persons with disabilities with guidance, education and vocational training in the framework of general schemes wherever possible or, where this is not possible, through specialised bodies, public or private;

2.   to promote their access to employment through all measures tending to encourage employers to hire and keep in employment persons with disabilities in the ordinary working environment and to adjust the working conditions to the needs of the disabled or, where this is not possible by reason of the disability, by arranging for or creating sheltered employment according to the level of disability. In certain cases, such measures may require recourse to specialised placement and support services;

3.   to promote their full social integration and participation in the life of the community in particular through measures, including technical aids, aiming to overcome barriers to communication and mobility and enabling access to transport, housing, cultural activities and leisure.

Article 16 – The right of the family to social, legal and economic protection

General

This provision, which consists of a single paragraph, reads as follows:

> "With a view to ensuring the necessary conditions for the full development of the family, which is a fundamental unit of society, the Contracting Parties undertake to promote the economic, legal and social protection of family life by such means as social and family benefits, fiscal arrangements, provision of family housing, benefits for the newly married, and other appropriate means".

Explaining its understanding of this Article in its very first Conclusions, the Committee stated that it "must be seen in conjunction with a number of other provisions in the Charter, such as Articles 14 and 17, that aim rather to give scope to the individual in our highly developed society, than to remedy a need, as Article 13 does. All these provisions are clearly founded on the idea that, since the industrial revolution and the social upheavals it produced, the modern state has had to take on certain new tasks and, in particular, as provided in Article 16, to create the living conditions necessary to give the family its full scope. The traditional affirmation of the family as the fundamental unit of society is maintained in Article 16, which, however, adds the idea that family welfare cannot henceforth be left to individual effort, as in the liberal epoch. Acceptance of these principles led the authors of Article 16 to lay down in it an obligation to implement a true family policy which was intended to operate in those fields where the needs of families become particularly pressing because of the restricted means they have available to meet them.

In the Committee's opinion a family policy of this sort must take the form of diversified action planned in harmony with and as a supplement to existing arrangements for assistance and social security" (Conclusions I, p. 75).

It is therefore clear that this Article imposes an obligation on Contracting Parties to implement a true family policy covering a number of fields.

The Committee admitted that Article 16 covers a "vast field" and stated that in order to be able to assess whether a Contracting Party complied with it, sufficient information must be provided on the various sectors concerned, in particular on:

- the national system of family benefits, (ie. family allowances intended to ensure permanent financial compensation at least in part for family burdens and occasional benefits intended to give material assistance in certain circumstances);

- alleviation of certain expenses in favour of families (ie. tax relief, special transport rates);

- social and cultural amenities available to families (day-care services for children, consultation services, home-help services, children's holiday homes, family holiday houses, creches, etc.);

- arrangements for the participation of families in the safeguarding of their interests;

- legal protection for the family, particularly in cases of marital disputes;

- provision of family housing, and

- the economic and social situation of families in national terms (Conclusions I, p. 75).

Other issues in respect of which the Committee has asked for information in subsequent supervision cycles are the following:

- the setting up of kindergartens with a view to reducing the number of children per kindergarten;

- various tax brackets, tax concessions for families;

- the composition of families and their economic and social situation;

- the adequacy of housing policy for the needs of families;

- the inhabitants/housing ratio;

- reform of the family law, and

- the proportion of the family income taken up by rent.

In the fourth supervision cycle, in view of the increasing participation of women in the labour market, the Committee underlined "the necessity of providing an adequate number of day-care institutions for children, especially facilities for parents of sick children" (see Conclusions IV, p. 101). This aspect of the protection to be afforded to working parents and their children under Article 16 has subsequently been emphasised on several occasions, *inter alia*, in a general question put to all Contracting Parties in Conclusions XIII-2 (p. 147):

"Given the importance of reconciling family life and professional life, the Committee asked that all states having accepted Article 16 indicate precisely in their following report on this provision the child-minding services available to families, in particular creches, nurseries and after-school and holiday schemes for children."

As far as the legal protection of the family is concerned, the Committee asked to be kept informed of developments in the law concerning the legal status of children, the succession rights of spouses (Conclusions IV, p. 101, Austria), marriage and the solution of marital disputes (Conclusions V, p. 110, Italy).

The Committee has interpreted Article 16 as incorporating the principle of equality of treatment between men and women, in particular equality between spouses. In the fifth supervision cycle it expressed the view that a provision in the United Kingdom legislation according to which "a couple is entitled to the family income supplement only if the man is in full-time work could be considered as incompatible with the principle of equality of treatment between men and women" (Conclusions V, p. 111).[1]

Moreover, in the tenth cycle of supervision the Committee noted with interest the introduction as from 1985 of legislation in the Netherlands "putting an end to the inequality between men and women in personal and family rights and in other domains of law" and of "case law according to which joint parental authority could continue after divorce" (Conclusions X-1, p. 130). It also welcomed the adoption of tax measures establishing tax parity between married and unmarried couples (Conclusions X-2, p. 132, France). The Committee has also noted the efforts made by Contracting Parties to ensure parental equality in the area of family responsibilities, in particular, the fact that parental leave entitlement for either the father or the mother was becoming prevalent in the Scandinavian countries.

Finally it should be pointed out that in the General introduction to its Conclusions XII-1 (p. 30), the Committee, concerned by the situation of large families and of homeless families, "stressed the need to consider family welfare in terms of the right to receive adequate housing and essential services (such as heating and electricity), these being necessary for the welfare and stability of families.

---

1 The situation was remedied by the Social Security Act 1980 which entitled women to receive the family income supplement on the same conditions as men (Conclusions VII, p. 88).

The Committee accordingly noted that the Committee of Ministers of the Council of Europe in its Recommendation No. R (90) 2 of 15 January 1990 on social measures concerning violence within the family (a subject of concern in the General introduction to its previous conclusions) advocated, *inter alia*, the adoption of general preventive measures such as adequate housing and urban policies, social and economic protection for all those caring full-time at home for young children, an elderly parent or a disabled person, and active measures to reconcile family life with working life."

In this context, the Committee also stated that it "considered that all measures to reduce and rearrange working hours to facilitate family life should be encouraged".

Another issue to which the Committee pays special attention is equality of treatment with respect to the protection afforded under Article 16 between nationals of a Contracting Party and those of other Contracting Parties. It has held in particular that a country must grant family benefits to nationals of other Contracting Parties lawfully resident or working regularly within its territory on the same conditions as to its own nationals.

The Committee's case law on this issue, as well as its views on the relationship between Article 16 and Article 12 of the Charter, may be seen clearly from the examination of the situation in Denmark where the granting of family benefits is subject to a qualifying period of residence.

The Committee considered that "the imposition of a qualifying period of residence for eligibility for family benefits could not be justified for the following reasons:

−   firstly, notwithstanding the provisions of the Appendix to Article 12 paragraph 4, no provision authorises the prescription of a qualifying period of residence for entitlement to non-contributory family benefits;

−   secondly, the need to avoid abuses, normally used to justify imposition of a qualifying period of residence, seems inapplicable in this case".

On the basis of this reasoning, the Committee found that Denmark did not comply as ordinary, increased and extra family allowances were granted only if the child or the parent having custody was a Danish national or had been resident in Denmark during the preceding year and special family allowances and youth allowances were granted only if the child or parent having custody was a Danish national or had been resident in Denmark throughout the past three years (Conclusion IX-1, p. 95; see also Conclusions X-1, p. 129).

The Danish Government argued that as family allowances were non-contributory social security benefits, they fell within Article 12 (*lex specialis*) and that Article 16 should be read in conjunction with Article 12 para. 4 in so far as family allowances were concerned. In this case a residence requirement could be imposed, as the Appendix to the latter provision provides that with regard to benefits which are available independently of any insurance contribution, a Contracting Party may require the completion of a prescribed period of residence in respect of nationals of other Contracting Parties.

The Committee did not accept this argument. It emphasised first of all that "nothing proves that the authors of the Charter intended family allowances not to fall within the scope of Article 16 because Article 16 specifically includes 'family benefits' as a means of promoting the welfare of the family. Furthermore, it is possible to satisfy the provisions of Article 12 of the Charter by complying with the conditions for the ratification of ILO Convention No. 102, ie. acceptance of at least three social security branches out of nine. While family benefits constitute one of the nine branches, there is no reason why a State could not comply with Article 12 without providing family benefits. Thus, if a state has accepted Article 16, it has accepted a more specific obligation than that of Article 12, ie. an obligation to protect the family through various measures, including the provision of family benefits. Therefore, while the existence of a family benefits scheme is (with other benefits) a sufficient but not necessary condition for compliance with Article 12, it is a necessary condition for fulfilling Article 16.

Thus it is clear that the authors of the Charter envisaged that family allowances should form part of the family policy provided for under

Article 16. Nevertheless, family allowances are a 'social security' benefit and as such can be viewed in the context of Council of Europe instruments (specifically the 1953 Interim Agreements and the 1964 European Code of Social Security) which allow for a qualifying residence period of up to six months to be imposed in respect of non-contributory (family) allowances in order to prevent abuse" (Conclusions XI-1, pp. 143 and 144).

In the thirteenth cycle the Committee, noting that the "general family allowance", payable to children below the age of eighteen, was paid only in respect of children residing in Denmark, considered that "from a strictly formal point of view the rule was the same for Danish as for foreign nationals. However, the Committee expressed its concern that in practice the circumstances in which family allowances were not payable were more likely to apply to foreign nationals of Contracting Parties to the Charter than to Danish nationals" (Conclusions XIII-1,[1] pp. 198 and 199 and in the last instance Conclusions XIII-2, p. 148).

The same concern about how residence requirements may affect the rights of nationals of other Contracting Parties to the Charter was expressed by the Committee in the case of Germany, where eligibility for child raising allowances was based on lawful residence within the Federal territory, condition also applicable to German nationals (Conclusions XIII-2, pp. 360 and 361).

Finally, it may be noted that in the eleventh supervision cycle the Committee examined the judgment of the European Court of Human Rights (Berrehab case of 26 June 1988) which revealed that the Netherlands had authorised the deportation of a Moroccan national, father of a Dutch child, whose residence permit had expired. In view of the obligation under Article 16 of the Charter to promote the economic, legal and social protection of family life and to ensure the full development of the family which is the "fundamental unit of society", the Committee considered that the deportation order issued by the Netherlands' authorities, by depriving the child of the possibility of receiving visits from

---

1 Dissenting opinion of Mr Fritz Fabricius (Conclusions XIII-1, pp. 275 to 278).

the divorced father, had infringed his right to family life (Conclusions XI-1, pp. 144 and 145, the Netherlands).

The Committee postponed its decision and asked the Government of the Netherlands to inform it of the measures taken to ensure that similar situations did not occur in the future.

In the twelfth supervision cycle the Committee, having been informed that according to Dutch law all judgments of the European Court of Human Rights were given full effect in the law and that as a result appropriate instruction had been given to the police authorities, concluded that the Netherlands satisfied this provision (Conclusions XII-1, p. 213).

Assessment of compliance

On the whole, Contracting Parties have been found to comply with the requirements of Article 16. In the thirteenth cycle the Committee's conclusions were negative for *Germany* and *Malta* as equal treatment is not granted for nationals of other Contracting Partners to the Charter in access to family benefits (Conclusions XIII-2, pp. 360 to 363).

The Committee also reached a negative conclusion in respect of *Turkey*. This was for several reasons, the first of which constituted an interesting development of the case law, in that for the first time a country was found to be in violation of its undertakings under the Charter as only a *small proportion* of families (belonging to privileged categories of workers) received family benefits. The conclusion was also negative as certain provisions of the Civil Code were contrary to the principle of equality between spouses (common property was administered by the husband; the husband was head of the family; it was the husband who chose the couple's dwelling place; the husband could deprive the wife of her legal authority to represent the couple if she abused that authority and in cases of a dispute between the spouses as to the parental authority of the children, the husband had sole parental authority) (Conclusions XIII-3, pp. 381 to 385).

There are also four cases of deferral. Denmark (Conclusions XIII-2, pp. 148 and 149), Iceland (Conclusions XIII-2, p. 150), Italy (Conclusions XIII-2, pp. 152 and 153) and Belgium (Conclusions XIII-2, pp. 359 and 360).

In the revised Charter an Appendix to Article 16 has been included, according to which the protection afforded by the provision also covers single-parent families. This has been done in confirmation of the Committee's case law, but also to show clearly that the protection of mothers covered by Article 17 of the Charter is covered in the revised Charter by Article 16.

Article 17 – The right of mothers and children to social and economic protection

General

This Article, which consists of a single paragraph, reads as follows:

> "With a view to ensuring the effective exercise of the right of mothers and children to social and economic protection, the Contracting Parties will take all appropriate and necessary measures to that end, including the establishment or maintenance of appropriate institutions or services".

A unique feature of the European Social Charter is that its extensive range of economic and social welfare provisions covers not only workers but also persons in other categories. Article 17 covers mothers and children.

Like many other provisions of the Charter, Article 17 is framed in very general terms. As the Committee itself points out this has the advantage of allowing it, in assessing compliance with the Charter, to follow social and economic developments. (Conclusions XIII-2, p. 25).

In the first supervision cycle, referring in particular to the wording of Article 17, the Committee pointed out that it was less precise than that of the principle of "the right of mothers and children to protection" in Part I of the Charter, as Article 17 stipulates only that states shall take all appropriate and necessary measures towards ensuring the right of mothers and children to protection, whereas in paragraph 17 of Part I this right is affirmed "irrespective of marital status and family relations". Moreover, in view of the very general character of Article 17, the Committee made it clear from the very early cycles of supervision that governments should supply adequate information on:

- general arrangements for the social and economic protection of mothers and children;

- economic assistance available to mothers before and after confinement;

- procedures for the establishment of paternity or maternity;

- maintenance arrangements for illegitimate children;

- guardianship, custody, the legitimation and inheritance rights of illegitimate children;

- the protection of unmarried mothers;

- the system of guardianship for orphans;

- the protection of homeless children;

- the measures taken with regard to adoption; and

- the treatment of juvenile delinquents (Conclusions I, p. 77 and Conclusions III, p. 80).

The scope of Article 17 may also be deduced from the long list of detailed questions in the Form for Reports.

No indication is given in the text of the meaning of "children" in terms of age. As already pointed out under Article 7, when distinguishing between Articles 7 and 17 the Committee has taken the view that the latter applies only to children of pre-school age. As, however, the Committee has also held that Article 17 applies to the legal status of children born out of wedlock, it seems that it can apply to adulthood where appropriate.

The obligation of Contracting Parties under this Article is to take "all appropriate and necessary measures". In the first cycle of supervision, the Committee interpreted this as meaning "that the state had to act in pursuance of Article 17 only in so far as the absence of private action rendered state intervention necessary" and concluded that a Contracting Party in which assistance to mothers and children came mainly from private sources, fulfilled its obligation (Conclusions I, p. 77, Italy).

In assessing compliance with Article 17 the Committee has concerned itself mainly with the following issues:

- the protection of single parents;

- the status of the child;

- the protection of young persons in general.

Protection of single parents

The Form for Reports refers to measures for mothers only. These measures cover institutions and services ensuring protection of mothers and children and financial assistance before and after confinement for women not covered by social security systems, as well as medical care or the services of a midwife during confinement (see Questions A and B).

Regarding the protection of unmarried mothers, the Committee made it clear in the third cycle of supervision that "the mere absence of unjust discrimination against unmarried mothers did not amount to 'ensuring the effective exercise of the right of mothers and children to social and economic protection' and considered that special measures were necessary, such as the institution of services of guidance and assistance including financial assistance" (Conclusions III, p. 80).

Even though it is fully aware of the fact that Article 17 covers mothers only, the Committee pointed in the General introduction[1] to Conclusions XIII-2 that "on the evidence of changes in national situations, [it] has progressively added questions to its conclusions regarding other forms of economic protection, such as special single parent allowances, without distinction between fathers and mothers". The Committee states in these Conclusions that "while upholding equality in family relations, it has not exceeded the actual terms of Article 17 which refer to mothers only, and consequently has never adopted a negative conclusion on the grounds that no provision was made for single fathers. However, conscious of the growing number of single fathers supporting children and of the difficulties they face in an area where *de facto* if not *de jure* discrimination against them is frequent, the Committee invariably expresses satisfaction where national legislation prescribes measures on behalf of single parents of either sex and, where only mothers are protected, it raises questions as to the economic and social protection granted to fathers" (Conclusions XIII-2, p. 31).

Commenting on the reports examined during the thirteenth cycle of supervision, the Committee stated that they related chiefly to economic measures: benefits for single persons and higher family benefits for single parents in Ireland; measures to assist one-parent families in Norway; concern expressed over the low income of single parents and the percentage of children living below the poverty line in the United Kingdom. In Spain the measures were of a different kind, taking the form of vocational training for unmarried mothers and leave without pay for childcare purposes available to mothers (not fathers). The Belgian report also mentioned "crisis intervention services" including single mothers' homes designed to house mothers with their children (Conclusions XIII-2, pp. 31 and 32).

---

1 On the occasion of the celebration in 1994 of the International Year of the Family the Committee dedicated the General introduction to Conclusions XIII-2 to the family.

Status of the child

Questions concerning the status of the child have focused on three aspects which, as the Committee itself recognises, have received very unequal treatment both in the national reports and in its own case law (General introduction to Conclusions XIII-2). These issues are:

- establishment of parentage;

- rights of children not born of or within the marriage; and

- protection of orphans and homeless children.

a. *establishment of parentage*

The establishment of parentage concerns the investigation of natural paternity or maternity, legitimation and adoption.

The Committee's interest in the procedure of investigation of natural paternity or maternity focuses on the categories of children who cannot avail themselves of these procedures. It asks for the reasons why some categories cannot benefit from these procedures and the measures taken on their behalf, but makes no appraisal of the procedures as such.

b. *rights of children not born of or within the marriage*

The rights of children not born of or within the marriage relate mainly to liability for their maintenance, their inheritance rights and their general equality of status with children born within the marriage, which reflects the Committee's constant concern over equality between all children.

As in the case of the establishment of parentage, liability for maintenance is usually discussed in first reports and subsequent reports contain little information on the subject. The Committee expresses its satisfaction when the liability for maintenance is the same for all children whether born in or out of wedlock. Thus in the case of Belgium the Committee noted with satisfaction from this state's first report that this was so even for children conceived of incestuous relations (Conclusions XIII-2, p. 34).

The inheritance rights of children born out of wedlock are covered extensively by the case law of the Committee. This case law covers not only the existence of these rights but also equality of rights between children, whether born in or out of wedlock.

As early as the first supervision cycle, when examining the law of inheritance of a Contracting Party in respect of illegitimate children, the Committee considered that the situation "whereby an illegitimate child cannot claim a reasonable share of the inheritance if the will contains no clause in his favour and whereby, if his mother dies intestate, he is entitled to a share of the inheritance only if she leaves no direct legitimate descendant", was not in conformity with the undertaking accepted (Conclusions I, p. 77, the United Kingdom)

Similarly in later cycles, when examining the situation in another Contracting Party, it held that a child born out of wedlock "cannot be regarded as enjoying adequate economic and social protection if he has no claim to inherit the estate of the father whose paternity has been established" (Conclusions IV, p. 104, Austria) and recalled that "this discrimination against illegitimate children, even in the field of succession, conflicts with Article 17 which seeks to guarantee economic and social protection to all children" (Conclusions VI, p. 105).

In the fourth cycle of supervision the Committee considered it necessary, as a result of comments made by the Governmental Committee in its third report and in the light of Opinion No. 71 of the Parliamentary Assembly, to address the question of whether the inheritance of children born out of wedlock fell within the scope of Article 17 which, unlike Article 16, does not explicitly refer to the legal protection of the persons concerned.

It considered that "it was difficult to separate the social and economic protection of mothers and children from the legal provisions governing their situation; objectives of social policy in their regard could not be achieved without taking account of the rights granted to the persons protected and of the duties of those called on to ensure this protection". The Committee further stated that, "generally speaking, it is not possible to disregard the legal position of the mother and her child in establishing the extent of the social and economic protection on which they may call and in assessing the trends within the states in one important sector of social policy which is the very object of Article 17 of the Charter", and concluded that "if there happened to be any measures of legal protection which had no economic and social implications, the Committee would have to ignore them, but it very much doubted that such measures could exist. In any case as regards all the points raised in Conclusions III, in particular the right of succession and the position with regard to its family of a child born out of wedlock, it was quite certain that social considerations were overriding" (Conclusions IV, p. 103).

This position has been maintained by the Committee throughout all subsequent cycles without any diversion. Therefore, cases where the inheritance rights of children born out of wedlock are non-existent or unequal to those of legitimate children prompt negative conclusions (see below).

Even though the Committee's case law on equality between all offspring chiefly relates to inheritance rights, the Committee concerns itself with "general equality of status between all children". As from the third supervision cycle, the Committee stated its position as follows:

"As regards the general legal position of children born out of wedlock, the Committee specified that:

a. while it might not be possible at the present time for such children to be treated before the law in exactly the same way as other children, a state, whose legislation manifestly discriminated against the first group of children, could not be held to satisfy its obligations under Article 17;

b. besides ensuring as near as possible equality of treatment, the state should also take such measures as are necessary and appropriate for the protection of children born out of wedlock, in view of their special needs" (Conclusions III, p. 80).

However, as pointed out by the Committee itself in the above-mentioned General introduction to Conclusions XIII-2 "subsequent social changes now allow the Committee to advocate full equality of all children before the law in every respect". The Committee expressed its satisfaction at the complete absence, in Belgium, of discrimination "between children who enjoy the same rights and owe the same obligations in respect of both parents and of the relatives of the parents and vice versa" (Conclusions XIII-2, pp. 36 and 37).

c. Protection of orphans and homeless children

During the third cycle of supervision, the Committee defined as follows the purpose of protection of homeless children "the basic objective of such arrangements should be to provide such children with the nearest possible approximation to a normal home environment" (Conclusions III, p. 80).

In its General introduction to Conclusions XIII-2 (pp. 37 and 38) the Committee, after noting the fact that none of the reports of Contracting Parties gave any particulars about homeless children, drew the attention of governments to "the *prima facie* severely underprivileged position of these children and to the special care and protection which they must be granted so that their development and well-being are not too seriously impaired". Moreover, the Committee reasserted that "the overriding concern for the protection of homeless children, quite apart from the assurance of economic security, was to provide them with care facilities suiting their needs in human terms" and "that there should be similar concern for orphans, over and above the legal guarantees prescribed for their custody and the administration of their property".

The protection of young persons, in general

Taking account of the necessity to ensure adequate social protection to children, the Committee expressed the wish in the second part of the thirteenth cycle, to reexamine the implementation of Article 17 in the light of the development of national legislations and international conventions. "To this end, it asked all states having accepted Article 17 to provide an update in the next report regarding this provision on the state of their legislation and their application in practice on all areas considered particularly important by the Committee: protection of children against ill-treatment, access of children to civil and criminal courts and protection of young delinquents.

As concerns protection against ill-treatment (including of a sexual nature), the Committee asked for all relevant information on the importance of this problem and the measures taken or planned in order to guarantee children and adolescents the protection to which they are entitled, as well as within their families, including not only preventive but also other measures, together with information about the setting-up and role of the various services responsible for these matters (in particular the social and legal services) and about the regulations governing these services.[1]

As concerns access to civil and criminal courts, the Committee asked if and how the child was ensured representation in court, in particular in cases of conflict with or between the child's parents, custodian or guardian; whether the child could be directly heard in court, and if so, from what age and under which circumstances.

As concerns the protection of young delinquents, other than the elements appearing in Question G of the Form for Reports to which the Committee wished to find more detailed replies (on special institutions and courts), the Committee asked the age at which criminal responsibility was set and the age at which sanctions could be pronounced; the sanctions applied and their forms of enforcement, in particular for custodial sentences; measures of protection, education and health care provided and effectively implemented" (Conclusions XIII-2, p. 157).

---

1 The same question concerning ill-treatment was put to Contracting Parties under paragraph 10 of Article 7 (see above).

Assessment of compliance

Austria was found in breach of Article 17 from the fourth to the tenth cycles (Conclusions IV, p. 104, V, p. 113, VI, p. 105, VII, p. 89, VIII, p. 187, IX-2, p. 89, X-2, p. 135) on the ground of discrimination in respect of inheritance rights against children born out of wedlock. In the eleventh cycle of supervision, the Committee took note of the judgment of the European Court of Human Rights in the Inze case,[1] in which the Court concluded that legislation creating discrimination in the field of inheritance rights between children born within wedlock and children born out of wedlock was contrary to Article 14 of the European Convention on Human Rights, in conjunction with Article 1 of Protocol No. 1 to the Convention. It also noted information to the effect that a new act introduced new rules in the area (Conclusions XI-2, pp. 137 and 138).

The situation was considered remedied in the twelfth cycle of supervision as a result of the introduction of the Right of Succession (Amendment) Act of 1989, BGBI No. 656/1989, which removed discrimination against children born outside marriage in the area of inheritance rights and provided that all children should be treated equally in matters of succession regardless of status of birth (Conclusions XII-2, p. 206).

Other countries criticised in the past but subsequently considered as complying with Article 17 in the light of legislative and other improvements effected are the United Kingdom and Ireland.

The United Kingdom was criticised on the ground that the inheritance rights of illegitimate children under the Inheritance (Family Provision) Act, 1938 as amended, were not adequately protected in the event of "intestate succession" (Conclusions I, p. 77, Conclusions II, p. 37, Conclusions III, p. 82).

The situation was considered as remedied by the Family Law Reform Act of 1969 in Great Britain (Conclusions III, p. 82) and in Northern Ireland (Conclusions V, p. 115) and in the Isle of Man by the 1982 Inheritance Act (Conclusions IX-1, p. 98).

---

1 Inze judgement of 28 October, 1987, Series A No. 126.

Ireland was found to violate Article 17 in the second cycle of supervision on the ground that there were serious gaps and inadequacies in respect of:

- the general legal position of children born out of wedlock, especially with respect to inheritance rights;

- protection of unmarried mothers;

- protection of mothers before and after confinement;

- arrangements for the protection of homeless children (Conclusions II, p. 57).

The negative conclusion was maintained from the third to the tenth cycles, particularly because of the legal status of children born out of wedlock, *inter alia*, with regard to inheritance rights (Conclusions III, pp. 81 and 82; IV, p. 104; V, p. 114; VI pp. 105 and 106; VII, p. 90; VIII, p. 188 and IX-2, p. 90).

In the eleventh cycle, Ireland was found to comply as a result of the enactment of the 1987 Status of Children Act which established equal rights in respect of all children irrespective of whether their parents had married and which, *inter alia,* eliminated legal provisions which discriminated against children born out of wedlock in such areas as guardianship, maintenance and property rights, including inheritance rights (Addendum to Conclusions XI-2, p. 49).

Countries currently found as not complying with Article 17 are:

France: because of the differences in inheritance rights for adulterine children. The situation was first criticised in the thirteenth cycle (Conclusions XIII-2, p. 159) although it had existed since the submission of the first French report. As explained by the Committee, the changes in customs reflected by its case law, which holds any discrimination against children born out of wedlock to be in conflict with Article 17, particularly in issues of inheritance (see, *inter alia*, Conclusions XI-2, pp. 137 and 138) have led it to reconsider the situation.

Malta: on the grounds that the inheritance rights of illegitimate children are inferior to those of legitimate children and of inequalities between children of a first and a second marriage (Conclusions XII-2, p. 207 and 208 and Conclusions XIII-2, p. 365).

There are four cases of deferral: Belgium (Conclusions XIII-2, p. 364), Germany (Conclusions XIII-2, p. 364), Luxembourg (Addendum to Conclusions XIII-3, pp. 83 to 85) and Turkey (Conclusions XIII-3, pp. 389 to 392).

In the revised Charter, the title of Article 17 has been amended to read "The right of children and young persons to social, legal and economic protection" and the Article itself has been amended so as to offer protection for children and young persons outside the context of work and to address the special needs arising from their vulnerability. The protection of mothers is covered by Article 16, which also covers single parents. The word "legal" was added to the title as the Committee's case law has developed to cover the legal aspects of the protection of children.

Article 17 reads as follows:

With a view to ensuring the effective exercise of the right of children and young persons to grow up in an environment which encourages the full development of their personality and of their physical and mental capacities, the Parties undertake, either directly or in co-operation with public and private organisations, to take all appropriate and necessary measures designed:

1.   *a.* to ensure that children and young persons, taking account of the rights and duties of their parents, have the care, the assistance, the education and the training they need, in particular by providing for the establishment or maintenance of institutions and services sufficient and adequate for this purpose;

b. to protect children and young persons against negligence, violence or exploitation;

c. to provide protection and special aid from the state for children and young persons temporarily or definitively deprived of their family's support;

2.   to provide to children and young persons a free primary and secondary education as well as to encourage regular attendance at schools.

Article 18 – The right to engage in a gainful occupation in the territory of other Contracting Parties

General

In the first two supervision cycles the Committee interpreted the field of application of this Article *ratione personae* and defined the scope of its first three paragraphs.

As concerns the personal scope, the Committee takes the view that it applies only to the nationals of the Contracting Parties to the Charter. The full reasoning of the Committee is as follows: "The Committee felt that the guarantees it embodies should be deemed to apply only to nationals of the Contracting Parties bound by the Social Charter. Admittedly, the Appendix to the Charter states that 'the persons covered by Articles 1 to 17 include foreigners only in so far as they are nationals of other Contracting Parties...' and it might be thus concluded that Article 18, and for that matter Article 19, applied to all foreigners. The Committee, however, rejected that argument on the ground that it was clear from the text of Articles 18 and 19 that the provisions applied to nationals of the Contracting Parties only. The Committee also noted that this interpretation of the last-mentioned provisions was supported by the wording of the corresponding paragraphs in the first part of the

Social Charter. It was consequently concluded that the omission of Articles 18 and 19 from the passage quoted above could be explained by the fact that the authors of the passage did not deem it necessary to define the field of application *ratione personae* of the Charter in respect of the two Articles in question on the ground that this was sufficiently clear from their actual wording" (Conclusions I, p. 79).

Article 18 applies not only to wage-earners but also to self-employed persons. It is clear from the *travaux préparatoires* that this category was supposed to be covered by Article 18 and this is how the Committee has proceeded.

As concerns the scope of the provisions of paragraphs 1, 2, and 3 of Article 18 the Committee stated that their very wording gave them "a dynamic character implying an evolution of the provisions and of their application, which should be shown in every biennial report". At the same time, however, the Committee went on to point out that:

"1. the undertakings entered into by virtue of these paragraphs are not concerned with entry into the territories of Contracting Parties but only with the pursuit of a gainful occupation in those territories (see the Appendix[1] to the Charter).

2. A Contracting State cannot be required to report further progress in every report, if the liberal spirit in which the existing rules are applied, the simplicity of formalities and the liberal nature of the regulations are already such that the State in question can be regarded as completely satisfying the undertakings entered into.

...

3. The Committee also pointed out that under paragraph 18 of Part I

---

1 The Appendix to the Charter with regard to Part I, paragraph 18 and Part II, Article 18 para. 1 reads as follows:
"It is understood that these provisions are not concerned with the question of entry into the territories of the Contracting Parties and do not prejudice the provisions of the European Convention on Establishment, signed at Paris on 13th December 1955".

of the Charter 'the nationals of any one of the Contracting Parties have the right to engage in any gainful occupation in the territory of anyone of the others on a footing of equality with nationals of the latter, subject to restrictions based on cogent economic or social reasons'. Article 18 (1-3) must be interpreted in the light of that definition of principle, and it is for the Contracting States to provide evidence, in their biennial reports, of any 'cogent economic or social reasons' to account for the wider or narrower scope of their efforts to meet the commitments contained in Article 18" (Conclusions II, pp. 59 and 60; see the latest reconfirmation in Conclusions XIII-1, p. 262).

Taking into account these considerations, the Committee interpreted the relevant paragraphs of Article 18 as follows:

"1. Any regulation which *de jure* or *de facto* restricts an authorisation to engage in a gainful occupation to a specific post for a specific employer cannot be regarded as satisfactory. To tie an employed person to an enterprise by the threat of being obliged to leave the host country if he/she loses that job, in fact constitutes an infringement of the freedom of the individual such that it cannot be regarded as evidence of 'a spirit of liberality' or of liberal regulations. Moreover, economic or social reasons might justify restricting the employment of aliens to specific types of jobs in certain occupational and geographical sectors, but not the obligation to remain in the employment of a specific enterprise.[1]

2. 'Liberal' regulations should normally make it possible for the foreign worker gradually to have access to activities other than those he was authorised to engage in when entering the host country, and to be perfectly free to do so after a certain period of residence or of activity in his occupation.[2]

3. The letter and spirit of Article 18 mean that the situation of nation-

---

[1] Latest reconfirmation in Conclusions XIII-2 p. 368 in connection with the application of Article 18 para. 1 in Belgium.

[2] Latest reconfirmation in Conclusions XIII-3, p. 400 in connection with the application of paragraph 2 in Turkey.

als of States bound by the Charter should gradually become as far as possible like that of nationals" (Conclusions II, p. 60).

In the light of the above interpretations the Committee concluded that:

"To satisfy the obligations arising from paragraphs 1, 2 and 3 of Article 18, the government of a Contracting Party must establish:

- either that during the period covered by the report, the application of the legislation in force has been liberal and that progress has been made in the direction of simplification and increased liberality with respect to the nationals of other Contracting Parties;

- or else, that the previous situation was already such that no new progress was necessary for the obligations concerned to be regarded as fulfilled" (*ibidem*).

To this end, the Committee specified the information which it considers necessary for assessing compliance with Article 18. A Contracting State should provide the following information:

"1. – According to what criteria are permits for the exercise of a salaried or independent profession in this country granted or refused, *de jure* and *de facto*, to the nationals of other Contracting Parties?

- How many applications were made and how many were granted?

- What is the total number of nationals of Contracting Parties allowed to exercise a professional activity in the country?

- How does that number compare with the number of nationals of countries which are not Contracting Parties?

2. – What exactly and in detail are the formalities necessary for nationals of another Contracting Party to obtain a permit either to take up a salaried or independent professional activity, or to continue an activity already undertaken?

3. – What rights are conferred by the grant of the work permit?

a. What is the position of the beneficiary if he loses his job or ceases his activity during the period of the permit?

b. What is the length of the permit and what is the position of the beneficiary after the expiry of that period? Is he entitled to its renewal? Can he exercise a different professional activity in the same branch of activity or in another branch, in the same geographical are or in another area? Do these rules vary according to the time during which the interested party has resided or worked in the country?

– How do these regulations and practices compare with those applicable to foreigners who are not nationals of other Contracting Parties?

4.   – What economic and social reasons justify the restrictions imposed in the country concerned or the liberty for nationals of other Contracting Parties to exercise a professional activity?" (Conclusions II, pp. 61 and 62).

This information has been consistently requested throughout the various supervision cycles (see for example Conclusions V, p. 118; Conclusions-VIII, p. 197). In addition, the Committee has been keen to ask for information regarding work permit applications submitted from abroad and permit renewal applications by workers already legally in the territory of the state in question.

In the third cycle of supervision the Committee made it clear that "neither restricting a wage-earner or salaried employee who was a national of a Contracting Party to a specific activity under a specific employer, nor systematically refusing a work permit to a foreign national who had entered the territory of another Contracting Party without having obtained a work permit beforehand could be regarded as displaying 'a spirit of liberality' or proceeding from a flexible system of regulations". (Conclusions III, p. 83).

In the fourth cycle of supervision the Committee interpreted further the phrase "restrictions based on cogent and economic reasons" in paragraph 18 of Part I and made it clear "that as long as migrants do not actually enjoy full equality of treatment, the Committee cannot agree to any state evoking the reservation in paragraph 18 of Part I in order to elude its obligations and the effective supervision of their application. The Committee agrees with the Assembly that 'restrictions based on cogent economic and social grounds' apply to 'the introduction of absolute equality..., which is the final aim,' and not to undertakings entered into under Article 18, which entail only liberalising and simplifying existing legislation" (General introduction to Conclusions IV, p. xv).

However, the Committee has acknowledged that "economic or social reasons" may be particularly pressing in times of economic recession such as those experienced by the Contracting Parties in the years reported on (1972-1973) in the fourth cycle of supervision (Conclusions IV, p. 107).

In the case of a Contracting Party which limited for a certain period the issue of work permits to nationals of states with which it had special relations and attributed this to the country's economic situation (the oil crisis), the Committee, whilst accepting that by reason of paragraph 18 of Part I economic grounds could be invoked, stated that it found it hard to accept these arguments as the restrictions affected only a small number of people, ie. the nationals of two Contracting States (Conclusions IV, p. 108, Denmark).

In response to the opinion expressed by a Contracting Party that the liberalisation of regulations required under this paragraph should affect only those foreign workers already in the country, "whilst recalling that the provisions of Article 18 do not cover regulations governing the entry of foreigners to the territory of the Contracting Party, the Committee felt it could not accept an interpretation which would undermine its aim, which is 'to ensure the effective exercise of the right to exercise a gainful activity in the territory of another Contracting Party', by restricting the benefits of liberalisation to only those nationals of other Contracting Parties already in the country.

The Committee considered it necessary to stress that regulations preventing nationals of another Contracting Party who were not in the country from applying for the grant of a work permit (other than a short term permit) owing to the combined effects of the various rules on entry, length of stay, residence and the exercise of a gainful activity would not be in keeping with this provision of the Charter even where regulations governing foreign residents have been liberalised sufficiently in other respects" (Conclusions XIII-1, p. 204, Sweden).

The above case law, according to which restricting the benefits of liberalisation only to nationals of other Contracting Parties already in the country was not acceptable, was recalled in the thirteenth cycle in response to observations made by the Confederation of German Trade Unions, that as a consequence of a new Act (*Gesetz zur Neuregelung des Ausländerrechts*) there would be a tightening of procedures and administrative fees concerning the issue of residence permits (Conclusions XIII-2, pp. 371 and 372, Germany).

Up to the ninth cycle of supervision, the Committee examined compliance with paras. 1, 2 and 3 of Article 18 under one heading instead of separately in accordance with its usual practice.

From the tenth cycle onwards, however, it treated compliance with each of the paragraphs separately. Even though as the Committee itself has admitted it is not easy to distinguish between the scope of the three paragraphs, for reasons of consistency, the approach of presenting the case law separately for each paragraph has been retained. This is also considered to be more useful, as the Charter allows acceptance by Contracting Parties of individual paragraphs.

Nevertheless, in the thirteenth supervision cycle the Committee put a general question to all the Contracting Parties which had accepted paragraphs 1, 2 and/or 3 of Article 18. It requested Contracting Parties "to provide detailed information on any link between residence permits and work permits and on the effect of loss of employment on such permits from the standpoints of national legislation, regulations or practice as well as details on the application of such provisions or practice to nationals of Contracting Parties". This information was considered necessary in view of the fact that the Committee had noted "that in some states, other than in the context of relationships among countries member states of the European Union or party to the Agreement on the

European Economic Area, continuing entitlement to a residence permit was conditional on entitlement to a work permit and that loss of employment might result in loss or non renewal of these permits" (Conclusions XIII-2, p. 168).

Paragraph 1 – Applying existing regulations in a spirit of liberality

By this paragraph, the Contracting Parties undertake:

> "to apply existing regulations in a spirit of liberality".

See also Appendix to the Charter under "General".

Paragraph 1 is concerned with administrative practice rather than legal aspects. The Committee has held the view that a Contracting Party may comply with paragraph 1 even where its legislation on the employment of aliens contains strict rules, provided that these rules allow some administrative discretion and are applied in a liberal spirit. Thus a Contracting Party was found to comply with paragraph 1, even though employment permits were granted for a limited period only and for a specific vacancy and changing jobs required new permission, as in practice a permit for the same job was renewed without difficulty and as after four years in approved employment a foreign worker could apply to be freed from restrictions on work and residence, this application being usually granted (Conclusions III, p. 86, the United Kingdom).

This view was reconfirmed in the fourth cycle, when the Committee found the same Contracting Party as still complying with paragraph 1 despite the imposition of certain restrictions in 1972 for skilled and semi-skilled foreign workers, on the ground that the use made of the law, particularly the new Immigration Act of 1971 "indicated a measure of liberalism". In addition, the number of permits granted compared to those applied for was very high[1] (Conclusions IV, p. 110 and 111, the United Kingdom).

From the case law it appears that:

- a high percentage of successful applications by nationals of Contracting Parties to the Charter for work permits and for renewal of work permits and a low percentage of refusals has been regarded by the Committee as a clear sign that existing regulations are being applied in a spirit of liberality (see for example Conclusions IV, p. 109, Austria; p. 112, Ireland; p. 114, the United Kingdom; Conclusions VII, p. 94, France; Conclusions VIII, p. 194, Germany; p. 197, Ireland; p. 200, the United Kingdom; Conclusions IX-1, p. 101, Sweden; Conclusions XII-1, p. 221, Iceland);

- refusing systematically a work permit to a national of a Contracting Party who has entered the territory of another Contracting Party without having obtained a work permit beforehand cannot be regarded as displaying a spirit of liberality (Conclusions VI, p. 114, Sweden).

In the eighth cycle of supervision the Committee repeated that an appraisal of the application of this provision of the Charter requires updated information for each reference period concerning:

- the number of work permits applied for and the number refused;

- the total number of nationals of Contracting Parties authorised to engage in a gainful occupation;

- how the figures compare with the number for nationals of other

---

1 This did not, however, prevent the Committee from finding this Contracting Party in violation of paragraphs 2 and 3, because the "considerably more stringent restrictions on the issue of work permits to skilled or semiskilled workers, as well as the rule whereby a migrant worker must remain in the same type of employment during the first four years of his residence in the United Kingdom, were still in force and, while not applying to nationals of EEC member states, did affect nationals of some of the Contracting Parties". Thus, there had been no liberalisation of the regulations and formalities during the relevant periods (Conclusions IV, p. 111 and VI, p. 115).

states (Conclusions VIII, p. 197, reconfirmed in Conclusions XII-1, pp. 220 and 221 and Conclusions XII-2, p. 210; more recently Conclusions XIII-1, p. 263, Turkey and Conclusions XIII-2, p. 369, Belgium).

Other information requested by the Committee in order to assess compliance with paragraph 1 concerns the number of applications for residence permits or renewal of residence permits by nationals of other Contracting Parties and the number of such applications refused (Conclusions X-1, p. 138, Greece).

Moreover, the Committee has shown particular interest in whether the existing regulations regarding access to employment of young second generation immigrants and of the spouses of immigrant workers allowed into the country for purposes of family reunion are applied in a spirit of liberality and in this connection asks for information on applications made by these persons and on those refused (Conclusions IX-2, p. 91 and Conclusions X-2, p. 137, Austria).

A statement by a Contracting Party in its report on paragraph 2 of Article 18 that "conditions for granting work permits are now being applied more stringently and, accordingly, the refusal rate is higher than heretofore" was considered "hardly compatible with the obligation 'to apply existing regulations in a spirit of liberality' deriving from paragraph 1 of Article 18 the Charter" (Conclusions X-2, p. 139, Ireland).

Assessment of compliance

There are no cases of non-compliance with paragraph 1 of Article 18. There are, however, four cases of deferral: Belgium (Conclusions XIII-2, pp. 367 to 369), Luxembourg (Addendum to Conclusions XIII-3, pp. 88 and 89), Portugal (Conclusions XIII-3, pp. 398 and 399) and Turkey (Conclusions XIII-3, pp. 399 and 400), which were reached after examination of their first or second reports.

Paragraph 2 – Simplifying existing formalities and reducing dues and taxes

Under this paragraph, the Contracting Parties undertake:

> "to simplify existing formalities and to reduce or abolish chancery dues and other charges payable by foreign workers or their employers"

When explaining, in the Introduction to its first Conclusions, the obligations of Contracting Parties with respect to provisions which it regarded as being of a dynamic character, the Committee included Article 18 para. 2 among the examples of dynamic provisions (see Conclusions I, p. 9). The Committee itself, however, has recognised that there are limits to the potential simplification of formalities and reduction or abolition of charges.[1]

The term "charges" includes charges for work permits or other documents or a tax upon the import of a worker's tools. The imposition of small administrative charges for permits has been held to be consistent with the Charter. Also the requirement of a "deposit" prior to entry, equal to the cost of the worker's return journey and payable only if the country of origin is very far away, has been considered as a sensible precautionary measure and not inconsistent with the Charter (Conclusions IV, pp. 107 and 108, Austria and Addendum to Conclusions XIII-3, pp. 89 to 91, Luxembourg).

The Committee recognised that it is not easy to distinguish clearly between the scope of paragraph 2, which imposes the obligation to "simplify existing formalities", and paragraph 3 of Article 18 which concerns the obligation "to liberalise individually or collectively, regulations governing the employment of foreign workers". This difficulty became apparent when examining compliance with paragraph 2 of a Contracting Party which had not accepted paragraph 3. As the Committee then stated "if these two paragraphs undoubtedly differ, they also

---

1 It was agreed by the Committee of Ministers during the drafting of the Charter that the obligation in the first part of Article 18 para. 2 may be regarded as fulfilled "where existing formalities are already simple" CM (61) 95 revised.

overlap in some respects in that simplification of formalities is normally indicative of a liberalisation of regulations, and conversely the latter is hard to achieve without simplifying the formalities". (Conclusions III, p. 83, Austria).

Moreover, in the ninth cycle of supervision, the Committee stated that regulations governing the employment of foreign workers concerned more particularly paragraph 3 of Article 18, whereas administrative formalities such as the formalities necessary to obtain a work permit or its renewal and the dues to be paid on that occasion concerned paragraph 2 (Conclusions IX-1, p. 102).

Examples of simplification of formalities include:

- the abolition of a visa requirement (Conclusions IX-1, p. 99, Iceland);

- the abolition of all dues and taxes (Conclusions IX-1, p. 100, the Netherlands and Conclusions X-1, p. 140, Sweden);

- replacing the old system of financing by the employers of language courses for immigrant workers by a new system providing for their financing out of public funds (Conclusions X-1, pp. 139 and 140, Sweden);

- the creation of a five-year work permit replacing in certain circumstances the permit formerly renewable annually (Conclusions X-2, p. 142, Spain);

- the possibility of the submission of a request for the renewal of a contract by the employer (previously only the worker could submit such a request) making use of computerised information technology, thus relieving the worker and simplifying the procedure for the employer and the governmental authorities. (Conclusions XII-2, pp. 211 and 212, Germany);

- the repeal of the obligation of employers to report the employment of foreign workers (Conclusions XII-1, p. 224, Sweden);

- the discontinuation of the practice of limiting the initial validity of long-term work permits to a period of twelve months and the issue in their place of permits for up to four years (Conclusions XII-1, p. 225, the United Kingdom).

Regulations and formalities relating to the employment of nationals of other Contracting Parties regarded as rather strict include:

- the need to renew a work permit every year;

- possibility to refuse renewal if there is no shortage of domestic labour;

- requiring a migrant worker who loses his job in the event of illness or unexpected termination of contract for which he is not responsible or because the work is terminated due to unforeseen events, to leave the country (see Conclusions XII-1, p. 223, Iceland).

Assessment of compliance

Contracting Parties currently found as not complying with paragraph 2 are Germany, Greece and Turkey.

Germany was first found to violate paragraph 2 in the ninth cycle of supervision on the ground that the formalities to be completed in connection with applications for or renewal of work permits and residence permits by applicants wishing to exercise an activity as employees remained complex and no measures of simplification had been taken (Conclusions IX-2, p. 92). In the tenth cycle, the Committee rejected the argument of the German Government that the formalities for the employment of foreigners were already sufficiently simple. Referring to the new application form elaborated by the German authorities, the Committee stressed that even though on the face of it the form might have been made more simple, its use could give rise to complications in a number of circumstances, especially since the entire procedure had to be repeated in the event of renewal of the work permit or changes of employment, employer, place of employment or region of employment.

In addition, all the procedures relating to the work permit had to be duplicated by virtually parallel procedures in applying for residence permits; a number of supporting documents had to be attached to the different applications, particularly for members of the immigrant worker's family (Conclusions X-2, p. 141).

The negative conclusion was repeated in the twelfth and the second part of the thirteenth cycles pending receipt of more precise information on the enforcement of a new Act for the New Regulation of the Rights of Foreigners which entered into force on 1 January 1991 (see Conclusions XII-2, pp. 211 and 212 and Conclusions XIII-2, pp. 371 and 372).

Greece[1] was found for the first time as not complying in the thirteenth cycle – second part – because the procedures to be followed by foreigners applying for jobs were complex and no steps had been taken to simplify procedures in respect of nationals of Contracting Parties to the Charter, not members of the European Union and not parties to the Agreement on the European Economic Area.

The procedure for the granting of a residence permit and a work permit is twofold and the work permit is normally valid for only one employer, one place and for a specific period of time. Also the granting or even renewal of a work permit is conditional on the Greek labour market situation (Conclusions XIII-2, pp. 174 and 175).

In the case of *Turkey*, the Committee considers that although the administrative formalities described in the report do not appear to be highly complex as such, the mandatory procedures for the issue and renewal of residence permits are not simple and should be simplified in accordance with the requirements of Article 18 para. 2 (Conclusions XIII-3, pp. 399 and 400).

There are also seven cases of deferral: Belgium (Conclusions XIII-2, pp. 369 to 371), Finland (Conclusions XIII-3, pp. 397 and 398), Iceland

---

1 The Committee of Ministers addressed a recommendation to Greece on this issue for the second part of the thirteenth cycle.

(Conclusions XIII-2, p. 175), Ireland (Conclusions XIII-2, pp. 175 and 176), Luxembourg (Addendum to Conclusions XIII-3, pp. 87 to 89), Portugal (Conclusions XIII-3, pp. 398 and 399) and Spain (Conclusions XIII-2, pp. 177 and 178).

Paragraph 3 – Liberalising regulations

Under this paragraph, the Contracting Parties undertake:

> "to liberalise, individually or collectively, regulations governing the employment of foreign workers".

Paragraph 3 does not require Contracting Parties to immediately bring their legislation up to a particular standard of liberality. It is a dynamic provision, in the sense that it requires continued improvement up to a certain level, after which the obligation is to maintain the *status quo*.

Throughout the various supervision cycles the Committee has identified a number of restrictions which it considers not to be in the spirit of liberality or liberal regulations. Examples of such restrictions are:

– the limitation of a work permit to a specific post for a specific employer (Conclusions II, p. 60; Conclusions III, p. 84, Ireland; Conclusions V, p. 117, Denmark; p. 119, Germany; Conclusions X-I, p. 141, Denmark; Addendum to Conclusions XIII-3, pp. 91 and 92, Luxembourg);

– restrictions preventing workers from changing their job in the first year of employment even with a view to continuing in the same occupation in the same year (Conclusions III, p. 84, Denmark; Addendum to Conclusions XIII-3, pp. 91 and 92, Luxembourg);

– the requirement that work permits be obtained prior to entry into the country (Conclusions V, p. 117, Denmark; Conclusions VI, p. 110, Denmark and p. 114, Sweden, Conclusions X-I, p. 141, Denmark);

- requirement in the case of a change of job of the same formalities as for a first work permit (Conclusions X-2, pp. 140 and 141, Germany);

- a requirement that an alien may not apply for a vacancy if there is a national applicant competent to do the job (Conclusions V, p. 117 and Conclusions VI, p. 110, Denmark and Conclusions VIII, p. 198, Spain);

- the withdrawal of the residence or work permit if the holder loses his or her job while the permit is still valid (Conclusions X-1, p. 141, Denmark);

- a complete ban on the granting of work permits to nationals of other Contracting Parties or to the members of the family of such persons already holding work permits (Conclusions VI, p. 111, France; Conclusions VI, p. 112, Germany);

- geographical restrictions imposed on migrant workers in their choice of residence (Conclusions V, p. 119, Germany);

- the requirement for the granting of residence or work permits of the existence of "essential occupational reasons" (Conclusions XII-1, p. 225, Denmark).

On the whole, restrictions should be relaxed or abolished as the worker's length of employment in the Contracting Party increases (Conclusions II, p. 60).

Developments regarded as positive include:

- more liberal issue of work permits granted to foreigners lawfully residing in a Contracting Party, access to employment facilitated for the spouses of foreign nationals residing in a Contracting Party, provisions governing the renewal of work permits in the event of unemployment (Conclusions VIII, p. 196, France);

- work permits previously renewable annually now issued for five years without any restriction as to occupation or area (Conclusions X-2, p. 143, Spain);

- assimilation of foreign workers with nationals after four years' residence (Conclusions XI-1, p. 154, the United Kingdom);

- possibility in cases of involuntary unemployment to stay in the country for a certain length of time in order to seek new employment, while receiving unemployment benefit (Conclusions IX-1, p. 154, the United Kingdom);

- improvements in access to employment of young people, ie. their entitlement to exemption certificates subject to certain conditions and no work permit requirement for this group before employment contracts were drafted (Conclusions XI-2, p. 140, Austria);

- regularisation of the situation of illegal immigrants (Conclusions XI-2, pp. 141 and 142, Italy).

Questions put in the eleventh supervision cycle to Contracting Parties with a view to assessing compliance with paragraph 3 included the following:

"a. in the case of workers themselves:

- what regulations apply to the renewal of work/residence permits? Must the employer prove that there is no national manpower available? What is the maximum duration of the new permit? After how many years may a worker change his employer/his type of job/his place of residence? In case of involuntary unemployment, is a worker obliged to leave the country or may he seek new employment? After how many years does a foreign worker enjoy the same rights as a national worker with regard to employment?

b. In the case of family members:

- what regulations apply with regard to employment? Does a prospective employer have to prove that there are no national workers able to fill the vacant posts? Are family members bound during a certain time to remain with the same employer/the same type of job or the same area? After how long do they enjoy equal rights with Danish nationals with regard to employment?" (Conclusions XI-1, p. 153).

Assessment of compliance

Contracting States found as not complying with this paragraph are Denmark, Greece, Ireland, and Turkey:

Denmark: the conclusions of the Committee became negative in the thirteenth cycle after having been deferred since the tenth cycle on the ground that the limitations imposed by the Danish regulations for the employment of migrant workers were not in conformity with this provision and no liberalisation took place during the reference period (Conclusions XIII-2, pp. 178 and 179).

In the twelfth cycle of supervision the Committee concluded that there was room for liberalisation of the regulations relating to nationals of Contracting Parties (neither Nordic countries nor members of the European Union). It mentioned in particular that liberalisations could be made in respect of the requirement that there had to be "essential occupational reasons" (meaning in practice that the applicant should have an education or other special skill which could not be acquired in Denmark or that he or she was occupied in a special sector of the labour market) for the granting of residence and work permits and that a recommendation from the local Labour Market Board was needed. It also considered that the regulations relating to the .prolongation and alterations of work permits could be liberalised (Conclusions XII-1, pp. 225 to 227).

Greece was found not to comply with paragraph 3 in the thirteenth cycle – second part – on the ground that no measures had been taken to liberalise the regulations governing the employment of workers from states bound by the Charter not members of the European Union (Conclusions XIII-2, p. 179).

In previous cycles the Committee had found that there was scope for liberalising the highly complex regulations governing the employment of the aforesaid nationals and in particular of the twofold procedure for granting a residence permit and a work permit and the conditions for granting or renewal of work permits (work permit valid for only one employer, one place and for a specific period of time, the granting or renewal of work permits conditional on the Greek labour market situation) (Conclusions XI-1, p. 153, referring to its conclusion under paragraph 2 p. 152, and Conclusions XII-1, p. 227).

Ireland, on the ground that there had been no improvements in the restrictive regulations governing the conditions for granting and renewal of work permits to nationals of Contracting Parties to the Charter who were not members of the European Union (Conclusions XIII-2, pp. 179 and 180). The conclusion has been negative since the third cycle of supervision.

Turkey was found not to comply with paragraph 3 of Article 18 since wage-earners or salaried employees, nationals of a Contracting Party to the Charter, are only allowed to work in a specific activity for a specific employer (Conclusions XIII-3, p. 403).

There are six cases of deferral: Belgium (Conclusions XIII-2, pp. 372 to 374), Iceland (Conclusions XIII-2, p. 179), Luxembourg (Addendum to Conclusions XIII-3, pp. 89 and 90), Portugal (Conclusions XIII-3, pp. 401 and 402), Sweden (Conclusions XIII-2, p. 181) and the United Kingdom (Conclusions XIII-2, pp. 181 and 182).

Paragraph 4 – The right of nationals to leave the country

Under this paragraph, the Contracting Parties:

> "recognise the right of their nationals to leave the country to engage in a gainful occupation"

Any restrictions placed on the right guaranteed in this Article must be justified on the basis of Article 31 of the Charter.[1]

Restrictions examined by the Committee and found in conformity with the Charter include:

- legislation according to which a national will not be allowed a passport if, *inter alia*, it is reasonably suspected that he wishes to avoid a criminal prosecution or sentence or that his residence abroad would endanger national security (Conclusions III, p. 86, Austria).

- restrictions permitted under the Constitution which must not be of a general nature and must be prescribed by law in specific cases, ie. in the event of serious criminal offence, public debt or failure to fulfil military obligations on the part of the person concerned (Conclusions XI-1, p. 154, Greece).

- restrictions imposed by law on the right to leave the country in cases of criminal delinquency, maintenance obligations, debts to the state, bankruptcy, military obligations and security founded on the presumption that the person's departure from the country might permit him to evade his obligations or might jeopardise the security of the Contracting State or allied states (Conclusions VIII, p. 201 and Conclusions IX-1, p. 155, the Netherlands).

- refusal or withdrawal of a travel document if there are "valid suspicions that a person who is by law subject to a prohibition to leave the country under exceptional circumstances will transgress the prohibition". As ascertained, these exceptional circumstances apply only in

---

1 "Article 31 – Restrictions

1. The rights and principles set forth in Part I when effectively realised, and their effective exercise as provided for in Part II, shall not be subject to any restrictions or limitations not specified in those parts, except such as are prescribed by law and are necessary in a democratic society for the protection of the rights and freedoms of others or for the protection of public interest, national security, public health, or morals.

2. The restrictions permitted under this Charter to the rights and obligations set forth herein shall not be applied for any purpose other than that for which they have been prescribed."

the event of war, the threat of war, or similar or related exceptional circumstances and are prescribed in legislation which comes into force if a state of emergency is declared (Conclusions XII-1, pp. 229 and 230, the Netherlands).

- restrictions imposed by law (section 5 of Act No. 33 of 1971 (Emigration) on minors, persons lacking legal capacity, persons serving or due to serve their military service, persons under court supervision during criminal proceedings and prisoners on conditional release (Conclusions XIII-2, p. 183, Spain).

- restriction imposed by the judiciary on an accused person as one of the alternatives to detention on remand (Conclusions XIII-2, p. 374, Belgium).

- regulations concerning the transfer abroad of sums held by a national wishing to engage in a gainful occupation in another state (Conclusions XI-1, p. 155, Iceland).

Assessment of compliance

All the Contracting Parties which have accepted this paragraph have been found to comply, as the restrictions imposed on the right of their nationals to leave the country are considered to be justified under Article 31, since they are prescribed by law and mainly based on grounds of public interest or national security. There are however two cases of deferral: Greece (Conclusions XIII-2, p. 182) and Turkey (Conclusions XIII-3, p. 405).

Article 19 – The right of migrant workers and their families to protection and assistance

General

In the first supervision cycle the Committee defined the scope of Article 19 as follows and interpreted its field of application *ratione personae:*

Scope of the Article

"This Article embodies a series of provisions intended to assist and improve the legal, social and material position of migrant workers and their families.

Its peculiarity consists in its containing certain specific elements which distinguish it from most of the other provisions in Part II of the Charter. In fact it goes beyond merely guaranteeing equality of treatment as between foreign and national workers in the sense that, recognising that migrants are in fact handicapped, it provides for the institution by the Contracting States of measures which are more favourable and more positive in regard to this category of persons than in regard to the states' own nationals.

Such being the case, the Contracting Parties should not limit the fulfilment of their obligations under this Article to ensuring non-discrimination between their own nationals and foreigners but should pursue a positive and continuous course of action. It is in this sense that paragraph 6 stipulates that the Contracting Parties are to '*facilitate* as far as possible the reunion of the family of a foreign worker...'

The application of most of the provisions contained in this Article can also be extended to self-employed workers (cf. paragraph 10 of Article 19), which incidentally represented a new development for international instruments in this field.

Furthermore, each Contracting Party that has accepted the provisions of paragraphs 1, 2, 3, 9 and 10 of this Article is committed to various obligations both towards nationals of other Contracting Parties who are within its territories or wish to come there to work, or who may wish to be accompanied or joined by members of their families and towards its own nationals wishing to proceed abroad for similar reasons" (Conclusions I, p. 81).

In the fifth cycle the Committee returned to the question of the treatment of nationals of other Contracting Parties *vis-à-vis* its own nationals and stated the following:

"In drawing up its conclusions as regards the application of this provision by the states concerned, the Committee found that efforts had been made in several states with a view to ensuring, amongst other things, equality of treatment between nationals and foreign workers in various fields. If, on the one hand, it was pleased to note this development, which had brought about a higher degree of social justice, on the other, it expressed some concern over possible adverse effects resulting from a *strict* application of the principle of equality of treatment in certain areas.

In effect, equality in law does not always and necessarily ensure equality in practice. Hence, additional action becomes necessary owing to the different situation of migrant workers as compared with nationals. This is the case, for example, with measures taken in certain states in connection with allocation of government financed housing for which a period of residence is required, or as regards restrictions which might be imposed on the transfer abroad of the earnings of migrant workers when all residents are subject to restrictions on the export of currencies.

The Committee wished to draw the Contracting Parties' attention to the fact that any measures of this kind, although not specifically intended to limit migrant workers' rights, would in practice operate in this sense and thus constitute a violation of one or more of the provisions of Article 19 of the Charter" (Conclusions V, p. 123).

Field of application

As regards the field of application *ratione personae* of this Article the Committee referred to the comments it had made in respect of Article 18 (see above) which may be summed up as follows: both Articles apply *only* to nationals of the Contracting Parties bound by the Social Charter. Although the Appendix to the Charter states that "the persons covered by Articles 1 to 17 include foreigners only in so far as they are nationals of other Contracting Parties" and it might be thus concluded that Articles 18 and 19, which are not mentioned, apply to all foreigners, the Committee has rejected that argument on the ground that it is clear from the text of these provisions that they apply to nationals of Contracting Parties only. The Committee also observed that this interpretation was supported by the wording of the corresponding paragraphs in the first part of the Social Charter. It consequently concluded that the omission of Articles 18 and 19 from the above-mentioned passage of the Appendix could be explained by the fact that the authors of the passage did not deem it necessary to define the field of application *ratione personae* of the Charter in respect of Articles 18 and 19, this being sufficiently clear from the actual wording (Conclusions I, p. 79).

Paragraph 1 – Free assistance and information services; steps against misleading propaganda relating to emigration and immigration

Under this paragraph, the Contracting Parties undertake:

> "to maintain or to satisfy themselves that there are maintained adequate and free services to assist such workers particularly in obtaining accurate information, and to take all appropriate steps, so far as national laws and regulations permit, against misleading propaganda relating to emigration and immigration".

From the very first supervision cycles the Committee has held that this paragraph imposes on a Contracting Party obligations towards both nationals of other Contracting Parties wishing to enter its territory to take up work (immigrants) and its own nationals wishing to go abroad (emigrants) (Conclusions I, p. 82 and Conclusions II, p. 195). The Committee has repeated this view on several occasions when national reports have referred to measures for the benefit of one group only.

Contracting Parties are required to provide adequate and free services themselves or to "satisfy" themselves that such services are provided privately. Thus for example the Committee noted with interest that in Germany, with state financial assistance, the Confederation of Trade Unions maintained an extensive network of advice centres for all foreign workers on questions of labour law and social insurance (Conclusions IV, p. 114).

"The scope of Article 19 paragraph 1 includes all the services of advice and assistance to migrant workers except those covered by the more specific provisions of paragraphs 2-9 of this Article" (Conclusions IV, p. 114).

The assistance offered to migrant workers should consist of accurate and reliable information, preferably in their own language (Conclusions III, p. 87, Cyprus).

In the first two cycles the Committee held the view that the required services should exist for migration to and from all other Contracting Parties. Thus in response to a remark of a general nature made by the Irish Government that, since immigration to this country by nationals of other Contracting Parties was very low and since virtually all emigration from Ireland was to the United Kingdom, the situation should be assessed according to special criteria, the Committee expressed the opinion that Ireland could not be released "from its obligation to take steps to apply this paragraph with regard to any workers who were nationals of other Contracting Parties and might desire to migrate to Ireland, and particularly with regard to Irish nationals who might wish to migrate to the territory of other Contracting Parties apart from the United Kingdom" (Conclusions I, p. 213).

In the second cycle the Committee re-affirmed that "a Contracting Party should not be released from obligations entered into under the Charter by reasons of the reduced volume of migratory movements affecting it" (Conclusions II, p. 195, Cyprus).

However, in the third cycle, the Committee, "taking into account 1. the small number of immigrants in Ireland and 2. the fact that the large majority of Irish emigrants go to the United Kingdom", considered that the steps which had been taken in Ireland to benefit immigrant workers in its territory warranted the provisional conclusion that this state was fulfilling its undertaking. The Committee nevertheless indicated at the same time that it might revise its position if significant changes in the volume of immigration or in the orientation of the emigration occurred because such changes would imply an obligation to create true services for the aid of immigrants and emigrants (Conclusions III, pp. 87 and 88).

Thus, in assessing compliance, the Committee does examine whether the services offered are appropriate to the prevailing pattern of emigration and immigration. The most recent example is that of Turkey where the Committee, taking into account the small number of immigrants from Contracting Parties to the Charter arriving in this country, considered that the requirements of this provision of the Charter were met. At the same time however the Committee recalled its case law (Conclusions I, p. 213) and insisted on finding information in the next report on the assistance and information services available in Turkey for national workers who wished to migrate to another Contracting Party to the Charter in order to engage in a gainful occupation. In addition the Committee, on the basis of its case law (Conclusions III, p. 88), pointed out that if significant changes in the orientation of immigration occurred, it might revise its position (Conclusions XIII-3, p. 408).

As for emigration, the Committee has underlined the importance of providing emigrants with adequate information about living and working conditions abroad (Conclusions V, p. 125, the United Kingdom and Conclusions X-1, p. 145, Greece).

Another obligation imposed by this paragraph is to take steps to prevent misleading propaganda relating to emigration and immigration. In this context, propaganda means information about employment and other prospects and conditions that might mislead migrant workers. The Committee has indicated that specific legislation on the subject is important and necessary.

In the second cycle the Committee, after recalling the importance it attached to protecting migrants against misleading propaganda, drew the attention of Cyprus to the fact that its legislation, which contained no provision on this question, did not seem to satisfy the Charter (Conclusions II, p. 195).

In the fourth cycle, however, even though in Austria there were no laws or programmes against misleading propaganda concerning immigration comparable to those in respect of emigration, the Committee concluded that this state was complying with this provision since "there was no evidence of dishonest recruitment practices in actual use, and that a pre-entry permit system in itself acted as a disincentive to misleading propaganda" (Conclusions IV, p. 113).

The Committee seeks constantly to ensure that Contracting Parties fulfil their obligation concerning misleading propaganda (see in the last instance Conclusions XIII-3, p. 406, Portugal and p. 407, Turkey).

The words "appropriate steps" imply a certain discretion for Contracting Parties to take existing national patterns of migration into account when determining their exact course of action. The words "so far as national laws and regulations permit" make allowance for constitutional rules or other laws of a Contracting Party protecting freedom of speech but do not "permit laws that substantially limit or undermine the obligation to control misleading propaganda".[1]

Assessment of compliance

There are no cases of non-compliance with this paragraph. In the twelfth supervision cycle, the Committee expressed its satisfaction with developments in several Contracting States.

It noted, *inter alia*, with interest that:

- in the Netherlands a subsidised body, the Netherlands Centre for Foreigners (*Nederlands Centrum voor Buitenlanders*) provided assistance to migrant workers, including information on social security in several languages (Conclusions XII-1, p. 231);

- in Norway the revised version of the book "Immigrant in Norway" would be made available in ten to twelve languages (Conclusions XII-1, p. 231);

- in Sweden a Computerised Knowledge Bank project provided practical and easily available information to placement officers on the skills and aptitudes of foreign workers (Conclusions XII-1, p. 232);

- in Germany there was an increase in the number of counselling centres offering free services to foreign workers and their families (Conclusions XII-2, p. 217);

- in Italy two agencies had been set up by law to take charge of the problems of migrant workers, not nationals of European Community members and their families (Conclusions XII-2, p. 217);

- in Spain the Offences and Sanctions in Social Matters Act provided for sanctions for persons running employment agencies for emigrant workers, spreading incorrect information upon the recruitment of

---

1 David Harris, "The European Social Charter", p. 162.

such workers, charging such workers a fee upon recruitment or abandoning them in a foreign country (Conclusions XII-2, p. 217).

In the thirteenth supervision cycle, the Committee deferred its conclusion under this provision in respect of Belgium (Conclusions XIII-2, p. 376), Greece (Conclusions XIII-2, p. 184), Portugal (Conclusions XIII-3, p. 407) and Turkey (Conclusions XIII-3, p. 408) requesting further information on the national situation in each case.

Paragraph 2 – Measures to facilitate the departure, journey and reception of migrant workers and their families

The Contracting Parties undertake:

> "to adopt appropriate measures within their own jurisdiction to facilitate the departure, journey and reception of such workers and their families and to provide, within their own jurisdiction, appropriate services for health, medical attention and good hygienic conditions during their journey".

This paragraph imposes two distinct obligations, taken in substance from ILO Convention No. 97 (Migration for Employment, Revised).

Furthermore, like paragraph 1, this provision makes obligations for Contracting Parties in respect of both emigrant and immigrant workers.

1. First obligation: to adopt measures to facilitate departure, journey and reception

According to the case law of the Committee, this obligation applies to migrant workers travelling as part of organised emigration and to emigration by individuals (Conclusions I, p. 214).

Satisfaction of this obligation normally involves taking special measures for the benefit of migrant workers, beyond those which are provided for nationals. Only if the general measures taken to facilitate the departure, journey and reception of travellers are of an exceedingly high standard is there no need for special measures (Conclusions III, p. 88).

"Reception must be provided at the time of arrival and the period immediately following, that is to say during the weeks in which immigrant workers and their families find themselves in a particularly difficult position" (Conclusions IV, p. 115; see also Conclusions XIII-3, p. 410, Portugal).

Reception should include not only assistance with regard to placement and integration into the workplace but also assistance in overcoming problems, for example, of short-term accommodation, illness, shortage of money (Conclusions IV, p. 116).

As far as "medical" reception is concerned, the Committee, when examining the Austrian report in the fourth cycle, emphasised "the importance of proper arrangements for medical reception of migrant workers and their families with their interests in mind, in accordance with paragraph 2". It adjourned its conclusion in relation to the situation in Austria where the only arrangements appeared to be a compulsory medical inspection of immigrant workers on arrival, aimed at ensuring that those workers were free from contagious diseases and that only workers who were proved to be in good health were integrated into Austrian life (Conclusions IV, p. 15).

According to the case law of the Committee, the Charter is not violated where a Contracting Party provides no special reception facilities but relies on employers to ensure the social aspects of receiving migrant workers and their families. However, in such cases, the state must be ready to intervene in aid of migrant workers from other Contracting Parties should the employer's or other private arrangements at the point of arrival break down, or where emergencies or special problems arise (Conclusions IV, p. 117, the United Kingdom; Conclusions XIII-3, p. 413, Turkey).

Finally, it should be pointed out that the Committee has stressed the importance it attaches to the social and human aspects of reception and asks that reports not be confined to purely administrative considerations (Conclusions I, p. 83 and Conclusions V, p. 126, France).

2. Second obligation: to provide services for health, medical attention and good hygienic conditions during the journey

In the first cycle the Committee considered that the requirements of paragraph 2 of Article 19 concerning health services, medical attention and hygienic conditions related only to the journeys of migrant workers and/or their families between the countries of origin and of destination. This paragraph did not oblige Contracting Parties to take any such measures either before or after such journeys (Conclusions I, p. 83).

In the fourth cycle the Committee, reviewing its interpretation of paragraph 2, concluded that its second obligation "related to migrant workers and their families travelling either collectively or under the public or private arrangements for collective recruitments and that Contracting Parties obviously could not provide such services for their own travel arrangements; however, in that case the need for reception facilities would be all the greater" (Conclusions IV, p. 115).

In assessing compliance with this paragraph the Committee seems to have taken into account, as in the case of paragraph 1, the actual patterns of emigration and immigration between the Contracting Parties for employment purposes. The lower the level of immigration and emigration, the less is expected of Contracting Parties. For example in the fifth cycle the Committee concluded that Cyprus complied with this provision since "the very small volume and the specific pattern of emigration and immigration affecting other Contracting Parties bound by the Charter made it unnecessary to take any special measures of the kind required by paragraph 2" (Conclusions V, p. 126).

The Committee has also considered various measures promoting the social and cultural integration of migrant workers and their families, these being clearly important under this provision (Conclusions V, p. 25). Especially relevant are language classes for migrants (Conclusions XIII-2, p. 189).

There are no cases of non-compliance with this provision. However, the Committee has recently deferred its conclusion in respect of Belgium (Conclusions XIII-2, p. 376), Finland (Conclusions XIII-3, p. 409), Greece (Conclusions XIII-2, p. 184), Luxembourg (Addendum to Conclusions XIII-3, pp. 91 and 92), Portugal (Conclusions XIII-3, pp. 409 and 410) and Turkey (Conclusions XIII-3, p. 410), pending receipt of further information.

Paragraph 3 – Co-operation between social services in emigration and immigration countries

Under this paragraph, the Contracting Parties undertake:

> "to promote cooperation, as appropriate, between social services, public and private, in emigration and immigration countries".

From the case law of the Committee it appears that the "social services" referred to in this paragraph cannot be restricted to employment services but include all public or private organisations which facilitate the life of emigrants and their families, their adjustment to their new environment and their relations with members of their families who remain in their country of origin (Conclusions III, p. 91, Ireland). Germany, for example, was found to comply because of an arrangement whereby German organisations responsible for assisting foreign workers, which are private, sent social workers to countries from which migrant workers come to establish and develop contacts with public authorities and private organisations there (Conclusions I, p. 215).

The Committee has expressly stated that this provision does not extend to questions of social security (Conclusions VIII, p. 207).

The words "as appropriate" should be understood as applying not to the undertaking as such but to the ways of implementing it, cooperation being organised "as appropriate" between either public services or between private services, or between both of them, depending on the structure of the social services in the countries concerned. The Committee took this position when rejecting an argument of the Irish Government to the effect that the word "as appropriate" left each government free to decide whether or not cooperation should be established (Conclusions III, pp. 90 and 91).

The existence of cooperation between public or private social services and those in the other countries only in the case of group recruitment is not sufficient (Conclusions III, p. 91, Norway).

A claim that cooperation between the services concerned is outside the Government's control is not pertinent to the undertaking entered into by virtue of this provision of the Charter (Conclusions IV, pp. 118 and 119, the United Kingdom and Conclusions IX-1, p. 106, the Netherlands).[1]

Where systematic cooperation does not exist, it is necessary to provide information on forms of unsystematic cooperation adapted to individual circumstances, even through private agencies (see Conclusions IV, p. 118, and Conclusions VII, p. 101, Norway).

As in the case of the previous two paragraphs, in assessing compliance with this provision the Committee takes into account existing patterns of migration. Cyprus, for example, was found in the fourth cycle to comply on the basis of proof of cooperation with the United Kingdom. The Committee observed that cooperation existed between the social services and "was suited to the present migration trend relating to the island" (Conclusions IV, p. 118; see also Conclusions XIII-2, p. 191, Ireland).

In the eighth cycle the Committee pointed out that the aim of this paragraph was to ensure that appropriate cooperation was established between the public or private social services of the emigration and

---

1 In the eleventh cycle the Committee concluded that the Netherlands complied, in the light of information supplied by the Dutch Government according to which numerous organisations such as Caritas International, Cura Migratorum, the *Nederland Centrum voor Volksontwikkeling* and International Social Service establish contacts with corresponding organisations in migrant workers' countries of origin to solve problems of a social and family nature that might arise.

immigration countries, so as to help to solve the personal and family problems which migrant workers and their families might encounter (Conclusions VIII, p. 206, Ireland; in the last instance Conclusions XIII-3, pp. 410 and 411, Finland and Portugal).

Common situations in which such cooperation would be useful would be that of the migrant worker who leaves his family at home and fails to send back money or needs to be contacted for some other family reason, or the case of a migrant worker who has returned home and has to recover unpaid wages or otherwise needs to settle pending affairs in the state in which he was employed.

Assessment of compliance

There are no cases of non-compliance. However, in five cases the Committee has deferred its conclusion: Belgium (Conclusions XIII-2, pp. 377 and 378), Finland (Conclusions XIII-3, pp. 410 and 411), Luxembourg (Addendum to Conclusions XIII-3, p. 92), Norway (Conclusions XIII-2, p. 191) and Portugal (Conclusions XIII-3, p. 411).

Paragraph 4 – Treatment of migrant workers not less favourable than that of nationals in respect of employment, trade union rights and accommodation

Under this paragraph, the Contracting Parties undertake:

> "to secure for such workers lawfully within their territories, in so far as such matters are regulated by law or regulations or are subject to the control of administrative authorities, treatment not less favourable than that of their own nationals in respect of the following matters:
>
> a. remuneration and other employment and working conditions,
>
> b. membership of trade unions and enjoyment of the benefits of collective bargaining,
>
> c. accommodation."

This paragraph is modelled closely upon ILO Convention No. 97 (Migration for Employment, Revised, 1949).[1]

The Contracting Parties' undertaking under this paragraph extends to nationals of other Contracting Parties "lawfully within their territories". Workers are lawfully "within" a state's territory if they have entered that territory in accordance with its laws and if their continued presence is in accordance with them.

Considering the scope of the provisions of paragraph 4, the Committee has held that "it is not enough for a government to prove that no discrimination exists in law alone but that it is obliged to prove in addition that no discrimination is practised in fact, or to inform the supervisory organs of the practical measures taken to remedy it" (Conclusions III, p. 92, referring also to Conclusions II, p. 68).

In the fourth supervision cycle the Committee made an introductory statement under this paragraph, which stressed that "the obligation deriving from this paragraph to grant the migrant worker equality of treatment in respect of employment is increasing in importance and poses particular problems in a period when most Contracting Parties are suffering from economic recession" and called upon the countries concerned to "take specific action to avoid discrimination to the extent that an increase of the level of unemployment is likely to have a particular impact on this category of workers" (Conclusions IV, p. 119).

---

1 Article 6 para. 1 a. of this Convention reads as follows:

"1. Each Member for which this Convention is in force undertakes to apply, without discrimination in respect of nationality, race religion or sex; to immigrants lawfully within its territory, treatment no less favourable than that which it applies to its own nationals in respect of the following matters:

a. in so far as such matters are regulated by law or regulations, or are subject to the control of administrative authorities

i. remuneration including family allowances where these form part of remuneration, hours of work, overtime arrangements, holidays with pay, restrictions on home work, minimum age of employment, apprenticeship and training; women's work and the work of young persons;

ii. membership of trade unions and enjoyment of the benefits of collective bargaining;

iii. accommodation;

....."

The words "in so far as such matters are regulated by law or regulations or are subject to the control of administrative authorities"[1] do not, according to the case law of the Committee, impose on Contracting Parties an obligation to regulate the matters in question by legislation or regulations or to subject them to the control of administrative authorities. Therefore a state which does not cover these matters by legislation or subjects them to the control of administrative authorities cannot be regarded as failing to comply with this paragraph (Conclusions II, p. 67). What is required is that the laws of a Contracting Party must not discriminate and that its officials must not do so either in the exercise of any discretion that they may have in law.

In assessing compliance with this paragraph, the Committee, as in the case of the previous paragraphs of Article 19, takes into account the pattern of migration. However, the Committee has expressly stated that any discriminatory practice against migrants will violate the Charter, even if the number of persons affected is small (Conclusions V, p. 129, Cyprus and p. 130, Italy).

a.   Equal treatment in respect of remuneration and other employment and working conditions

"Remuneration and other employment and working conditions" has been interpreted to include "pay, training in the course of employment and promotion" (Conclusions III, p. 92) "removal or settling in allowance" granted to workers changing jobs or taking up employment (Conclusions III, p. 94) "all vocational training" (Conclusions VII, p. 103). Thus the United Kingdom was found in the seventh cycle not to comply with this paragraph because of the imposition of restrictions on migrant workers' access to training under the Training Opportunities Scheme.

---

1 During the *travaux préparatoires*, a proposal by the workers' delegates at the Tripartite Conference (December 1958) to replace the words "are subject to the control of administrative authorities" by the words "by collective agreements" was opposed by a government representative (the United Kingdom) on the ground that the former had been inserted to cover matters such as the allocation of housing by local authorities (see CE/Soc/TrPr. (70) 20, p. 26).

In the eighth cycle the Committee stated that the non accessibility of migrant workers to posts in the civil service was not incompatible with the Charter. (Conclusions VIII, p. 208, Norway). This was owing to security reasons and reference could be made to Article 31.

b. Membership of trade unions and enjoyment of the benefits of collective bargaining

The Committee found in the sixth cycle that France did not comply with this paragraph because of the restrictions on foreign workers in the exercise of certain administrative and managerial functions in trade unions under the Labour Code. These restrictions were incompatible with the Charter in as much as they applied to the nationals of states bound by the Charter.[1] In the thirteenth cycle, the Committee found that Turkey infringed the Charter because of restrictions in national law as regards membership of trade unions (Conclusions XIII-3, p. 418, see below "Assessment of compliance").

c. Equal treatment in respect of accommodation

From the first cycle the Committee has expressed the view that accommodation is a matter of "prime importance", affecting the situation of the migrant worker and his family (Conclusions I, p. 84).

Situations criticised by the Committee include:

– allocation of grants to migrant workers in Germany for the construction of family houses only if they had been carrying on an occupational activity in the country concerned for at least two years (Conclusions I, p. 215).[2]

---

1 Situation remedied by Act No. 82-915 of 28 October 1982 amending the Labour Code (these restrictions were also considered incompatible with Article 5; see under this Article).

2 This criticism was withdrawn in the second cycle on ascertaining that the general measures to promote housing applied to foreign workers on absolutely equal terms with nationals and a special programme of assistance had been adopted to encourage building of accommodation for migrant workers and their families (Conclusions II, p. 67).

–   the existence of restrictions (birth or length of residence) for access to subsidised housing in Northern Ireland for nationals of Contracting Parties outside the European Union (Conclusions VIII, p. 210).[1]

According to the case law of the Committee, paragraph 4 is concerned not only with the allocation of public housing but also with access to private housing.

A restriction in law upon the acquisition of accommodation by a migrant worker would be contrary to paragraph 4 of Article 19 (Conclusions IV, p. 121). The same applies to discrimination in the eligibility requirements for housing assistance measures such as loans or other housing allowances (Conclusions III, p. 92).

Measures designed to restrict the freedom of migrant workers to choose their place of residence in certain areas with a high alien population would also be contrary to paragraph 4 (Conclusions VI, p. 121).[2]

The Committee's view that, in effect, equality in law does not always and necessarily ensure equality in practice, and that to avoid direct discrimination additional action becomes necessary owing to the different situation of migrant workers as compared with nationals (see above under "general"), has been applied in relation to housing and especially the imposition of residence requirements for access to social housing. This may be clearly observed in the case of Norway.

"The Committee noted with interest the contents of the Norwegian report, particularly the contention that the residence requirements for low-cost housing applicable in many municipalities in Norway do not infringe Article 19 para. 4 because they apply to Norwegian and foreign nationals alike. As stated in its previous conclusions, the Committee stressed that the Charter requires that the migrant worker receive treat-

---

1 This criticism was withdrawn in the tenth cycle: the Committee noted that incoming workers in Northern Ireland had special treatment as regards subsidised housing, as such persons were granted priority over any other person (Conclusions X-1, p. 148).

2 In the Contracting Party concerned (Germany), these measures ceased to apply in June 1977.

ment "not less favourable" than that of nationals. Where a Norwegian municipality imposes a residence requirement, it is easier for Norwegians to fulfil that requirement in the town in which they normally live, creating a 'de facto' less favourable situation for a foreigner. While a Norwegian is in a comparable situation if he wishes to move to another town, by definition a migrant worker cannot prove residence in any Norwegian town. These residence requirements, therefore, while formally providing for equality of treatment, create an inequality of treatment in substance and are therefore not in keeping with the provisions of the Charter" (Conclusions XI-1, pp. 159 and 160).

Nevertheless, the Committee requests facts in order to ascertain that there is really a case for claims of indirect discrimination (also termed de facto discrimination) (Conclusion XII-1, p. 234, Norway and XIII-2, p. 195, Spain).

The Norwegian situation served as the basis for developing this case law, but it is not an isolated case (see Conclusions XIII-2, pp. 193, Italy, 195, Spain and 197, the United Kingdom). The growing number of cases which potentially could be contrary to the Charter led the Committee to ask, in the General introduction to Conclusions XIII-2, "all states which have accepted Article 19 para. 4 to look closely at their housing legislation and report on all conditions of eligibility for housing whose application to nationals and to foreigners may differ" (Conclusions XIII-2, p. 50; see also Fourth report on certain provisions of the Charter which have not been accepted, pp. 21 to 24).

Assessment of compliance

Contracting Parties currently found not to comply with this paragraph are:

Germany: the provisions of the Employment Protection (National Service) Act, which guarantees the employment of persons who are obliged to return to their own country to perform military service, do not apply to foreign workers, nationals of Contracting Parties not members of the European Union, with the effect that there is no equality of treatment for these persons in this matter (Conclusions XIII-2, p. 380);

Italy: in some regions there is no equality of treatment as regards access to public authority housing for foreigners nationals of Contracting Parties to the Charter (Conclusions XIII-2, p. 193);

Portugal: under domestic law only nationals are entitled to apply for local authority housing (Conclusions XIII-3, p. 418);

Turkey: there are restrictions in legislation on the right of foreign workers, nationals of Contracting Parties to the Charter, to become founding members of a trade union (Conclusions XIII-3, p. 418).

Moreover the Committee's conclusion is deferred in the case of Belgium (Conclusions XIII-2, pp. 377 and 378), Luxembourg (Addendum to Conclusions XIII-3, p. 93), Norway (Conclusions XIII-2, p. 194), Spain (Conclusions XIII-2, pp. 194 and 195) and the United Kingdom (Conclusions XIII-2, p. 197) pending receipt of additional information/ clarification, mostly on issues concerning equality of treatment with regard to housing of foreign workers, nationals of Contracting Parties to the Charter.

Finally it may be noted that in respect of Norway and Spain, the Committee's conclusions were negative until the eleventh cycle (as from the sixth cycle in respect of Norway and the ninth cycle in respect of Spain).

The Committee found that Norway failed to comply on the ground that the residence requirements for low-cost housing applicable in many municipalities in Norway infringed on paragraph 4, despite the fact that these requirements applied to Norwegians and foreign nationals alike (see above and Conclusions XI-1, pp. 159 and 160). The Committee also questioned the requirements applying to foreigners for access to low-cost housing for purposes of family reunion (ten years' residence, five years' marriage and first generation migrant status).

Spain was found not to comply since in the Balearic Islands "public promotion housing" was allocated only to Spanish nationals. The Committee did not accept the Spanish Government's argument that the number of foreign workers not entitled to subsidised housing was very limited as the foreigners living there were mainly pensioners or tourists (Conclusions XI-2, p. 147).

In the twelfth cycle, the Committee reiterated its negative conclusion in respect of Spain, but noted with satisfaction the intention of the local authorities of the Balearic Islands to change the regulations (Conclusions XII-2, p. 222).

In subsequent cycles the Committee adjourned its conclusion for both countries pending receipt of information concerning residence requirements for access to housing in practice (Conclusions XIII-1, pp. 207 and 208, Norway and Conclusions XIII-2, pp. 194 to 196, Norway and Spain).

Paragraph 5 – Treatment of migrant workers not less favourable that than of nationals in respect of employment taxes, dues and contributions

Under this paragraph, the Contracting Parties undertake:

> "to secure for such workers lawfully within their territories treatment not less favourable than that of their own nationals with regard to employment taxes, dues or contributions payable in respect of employed persons".

This provision does not seem to have caused many difficulties for Contracting Parties which have accepted it. This may be due to the fact that taxation and social security contributions are not based on nationality.

In the seventh supervision cycle Sweden was found not to comply with this paragraph since, under the system of financing language instruction for migrant workers, an employer had an obligation, when engaging a migrant worker still unconversant with the Swedish language, to pay a considerable amount for the purpose of financing his language instruction. The Committee believed that this state of affairs could create *de facto* discrimination against migrant workers, in that an employer seeking the service of a worker has a financial incentive to opt for a national in order to reduce employment costs and this would result in violation of the Charter (Conclusions VII, p. 104).[1]

In the tenth supervision cycle the Committee noted that taxpayers in Germany, whether German or aliens, could claim a tax rebate for each dependent child resident in Germany. If the child was not resident in the country, the rebate was not granted, but the taxpayer could claim a rebate for essential expenses for the support and vocational training of the child.

Although the Committee accepted that there was *de jure* equal treatment between nationals and aliens in respect of paragraph 5, it expressed its concern about the possibility of *de facto* discrimination, since aliens were proportionally more affected than Germans by the tax situation with regard to children resident abroad and asked whether the rebates for maintenance and occupational training of children residing abroad were identical in conditions and amounts to those granted in respect of children resident in Germany (Conclusions X-2, pp. 148 and 149; see also Conclusions XI-2, pp. 148 and 149).

In the twelfth supervision cycle, the Committee was informed that the taxation legislation had changed as from 1988 and taxation exemptions (reduction in taxation) were granted for all dependent children, whether in vocational training or education, and whether in Germany or not. However, this reduction was one or two-thirds less when the child was resident in a country where the cost of living was lower than in Germany. In view of this information the Committee reached a positive conclusion, but asked for which Contracting Parties such difference in rates of reduction existed and the level of reductions in each case (Conclusions XII-2, p. 223; see also Conclusions XIII-2, pp. 381 and 382).

In the same supervision cycle the Committee found that the granting of tax-free travel expenses in the United Kingdom to temporary workers by

---

1 Situation remedied by an Act of 1986 which abolished the employer's obligation to finance language courses for migrant workers in his employment.

their employer was a positive discrimination and thus compatible with the Charter (Conclusions XII-1, p. 237).

Assessment of compliance

There are no cases of non-compliance.

However, the Committee has deferred its conclusion in respect of Italy pending receipt of clarifications concerning the nature and financing of a fund set up in 1986 within the National Social Welfare Institute to finance the return journey to the country of origin of migrant workers, not European Union nationals, unable to meet the cost (Conclusions XI-2, pp. 149 and 150; Conclusions XII-2, p. 223 and Conclusions XIII-2, pp. 198 and 199).

Paragraph 6 – Family reunion

The Contracting Parties undertake:

> "to facilitate as far as possible the reunion of the family of a foreign worker permitted to establish himself in the territory"[1].

Appendix to Article 19 para. 6:

> "For the purpose of this provision, the term "a family of a foreign worker" is understood to mean at least his wife and dependent children under the age of 21 years".

In the fourth cycle, "the Committee considered that the term 'worker' as used in the Charter applied equally to female workers except in cases where the context demands a different interpretation. Consequently the

---

1 Paragraph 6 of Article 19 goes beyond ILO Convention No. 97 of 1949 which does not cover family reunion. ILO Convention No. 143 of 1975, however, provides that "a Party may take all necessary measures to facilitate the reunification of the families of all migrant workers legally residing in its territory".

definition of the family of a migrant worker appearing in the Appendix of the Charter includes the children (but not the husband) of a female worker" (Conclusions IV, p. 124).

Applying this interpretation the Committee found that the restrictions in a Contracting Party on husbands rejoining their wives were compatible with the Charter by reason of the wording of the Appendix to para. 6. At the same time, however, it expressed the opinion that, if such restrictions had the effect of preventing a married female worker from bringing in her dependent children, *prima facie*, they were contrary to the Charter (Conclusions IV, p. 127).[1]

From the first two cycles, the Committee established that in order to facilitate the reunion of migrant workers' families, a Contracting Party must not only eliminate any legal obstacle preventing the members of a migrant worker's family from joining him, but also introduce appropriate practical administrative and social measures, particularly with regard to housing (Conclusions I, p. 85 and Conclusions II, p. 197).

In response to a request made by the government of one of the Contracting Parties in the course of the third cycle of supervision, the Committee confirmed its previous ruling that paragraph 6 "indeed appears to oblige a state which accepts it to take special steps to aid foreign workers to find accommodation, unless conditions on the housing market are such that no steps are necessary" (Conclusions III, p. 94).

In the fourth cycle, the Committee had occasion to reaffirm this point. The Austrian Government had argued that the issue of housing and accommodation for migrant workers fell completely within Article 19 para. 4 (which it had not accepted) and therefore could not be raised under paragraph 6. The Committee rejected this argument, stating that "because of the fundamental importance of adequate housing for family reunion, Article 19 para. 6 obliges states to take practical measures of

---

1 In the next cycle, the Committee noted that there were in fact no restrictions, directly or indirectly preventing a married woman, the national of another Contracting Party, working in the United Kingdom, who was the breadwinner of the family, from being joined by her dependent children (Conclusions V, p. 136).

some kind to assist migrant workers in obtaining accommodation; *de jure* equality in access to housing being a means, among others for carrying out this obligation" (Conclusions IV, p. 125). The Committee also rejected in a later cycle the view that special action in favour of migrant workers in the field of family housing would discriminate against the state's own nationals (Conclusions VI, p. 126, the United Kingdom).

The application of paragraph 6 of Article 19 has raised many problems in a number of Contracting Parties. The fact that these problems, most of which were identified as early as the first supervision cycle, continued to remain unresolved cycle after cycle, led the Committee in the eighth cycle to state more clearly the context of this provision as follows:

"The aim of paragraph 6 is to oblige states to create the conditions which make family reunion possible. The extent of the effort of each state is made conditional, by this provision, on the objective possibilities which shape its action in this sense.

Therefore, as paragraph 6 provides for the obligation to 'facilitate as far as possible the reunion...', it should not be interpreted in the sense that it permits the adoption of restrictions likely to deprive this obligation of its content.

The Appendix to the Charter completes this rule by defining the terms 'family of a foreign worker' as meaning 'at least his wife and dependent children under the age of 21 years'. In this respect, the Committee underlined that given the very terms of this Appendix, it should by no means be interpreted as permitting the establishment under the form of a general rule, of an age limit lower than 21 years. But since the persons concerned must also be 'dependent' on the migrant worker, in accordance with the said Appendix, those fulfilling the age condition could be deprived of the right to family reunion in the case where it is established that they are no longer dependent on the migrant worker.

The concept of 'dependent' persons should be understood, under this provision of the Charter, as being that of persons who depend, for their existence, on their family, in particular because of economic reasons or, at the case may be, for such reasons as continuation of education without remuneration or for reasons of health.

Given the above considerations, the Committee moreover thought that the principle of family reunion is but an aspect of the recognition in the Charter (Article 16) of the obligation of states to ensure social, legal and economic protection of the family which is regarded as 'the fundamental unit of society'. Consequently, the application of Article 19 para. 6 should in any case take account of the need to fulfil this obligation" (Conclusions VIII, pp. 211 and 212).

The situation in Contracting Parties concerning the maximum age of dependent children up to which family reunion must be facilitated differs. Some set no such age limit, whereas others, whose number has increased in recent years, set an age limit lower than that specified in the Appendix to the Charter.

In response to questions and in some cases criticism by the Committee, some Contracting Parties stated that in practice all dependent children of migrant workers are admitted, whereas others have claimed that in practice they give favourable consideration to requests for family reunion submitted by children of migrant workers, nationals of Contracting Parties, up to the age specified in the Charter.

As a result, in assessing compliance with Article 19 para. 6, the Committee has in more recent cycles – this can be seen more clearly from the eleventh cycle onwards – qualified its earlier position to take fuller account of practice. Thus the Committee has stated clearly that in the absence of a statutory right to family reunion, statistical information must be furnished in each cycle of supervision on the number of applications for family reunion on behalf of children of migrant workers, nationals of the Contracting Parties under the age of twenty-one, and on the number of residence permits granted (Conclusions XII-1, pp. 239 and 240, Sweden; see also Conclusions XIII-2, p. 200, Austria). The same statistical information is also required for children aged between the limit fixed and twenty-one, where the established age limit for family reunion remains lower than twenty-one (Conclusions XIII-2, pp. 204 and 205, the United Kingdom and Conclusions XIII-3, p. 418, Portugal).

Depending on the information furnished, the Committee may conclude that there is no infringement of Article 19 para. 6 even where the age fixed by law is not in keeping with the Charter in view of the fact that the situation in practice is in compliance: thus comparable legislation may also provoke a negative conclusion or a deferral.

Where the maximum age fixed by a state for family reunion is under twenty-one, the Committee exercises some caution as children of migrant workers who are over the age stipulated by national legislation may be deterred from submitting an application for entry to that state for purposes of family reunion (see below, under "Assessment of compliance", the case of the United Kingdom).

As regards the admission of sick members of a migrant worker's family, the Committee has stated that refusal to admit such persons except in exceptional cases and for social and humanitarian reasons would not be compatible with paragraph 6 (Conclusions V, p. 134, France). Similarly, no general prohibition should prevent family reunion in cases of physical or mental illness. Individual cases should be examined exclusively from the medical, family, social and humanitarian viewpoints, with due consideration of any other special circumstances (Conclusions X-1, p. 151, the Netherlands; in the latest instance Conclusions XIII-3, p. 417, Finland).

Refusal should be confined to the quarantinable and other diseases specified in the WHO international rules (Conclusions VII, p. 104, Cyprus).

Family reunion should not be refused on grounds of health unless the illness is likely to endanger public health or possibly public interest (Conclusions X-1, p. 150, Greece).

Assessment of compliance

Much criticism has been exercised by the Committee in relation to the application of this provision. Thus, for instance, the Committee criticised the United Kingdom over many cycles for its restriction on family re-union in the case of migrants working as domestic servants (first raised in Conclusions I, p. 85) and ancillary staff resident in hospitals (first raised in Conclusions V, p. 136). The United Kingdom argued that as work permits for domestic service were never issued to a person with dependents, except in the case of a married couple being employed together, the issue of family reunion would only arise where individuals concealed their true family circumstances. In such cases, paragraph 6 would not apply. The Committee considered that this argument would be valid in cases of deception, but not where the migrant entered employment as a domestic servant and subsequently married or had children (Conclusions III, p. 97). This issue was finally solved when the Committee learned that work permits had not been delivered to these workers since 1 January 1980 (Conclusions IX-1, p. 110 and Conclusions X-I, p. 152).

The existence of a rule according to which sick or disabled members of a migrant worker's family may be denied entry has often attracted criticism from the Committee.

In the third cycle, Austria was criticised on the ground that the power to exclude a family member of a migrant worker because of a contagious disease was too general (Conclusions III, p. 95). In the sixth cycle, the Committee sought clarification from France over the implications in practice of the power to deny a sick person entry to the country on the basis that their illness could endanger public order or public safety. The Committee was eventually satisfied in the tenth cycle (Conclusions X-2, p. 152).

In the eighth cycle, the Committee found that the Netherlands failed to comply with this provision as it was possible to bar family members from entering the country if they suffered from certain forms of mental illness (Conclusions VIII, p. 214). The Committee did not consider such ill-nesses as falling within the scope of the "public interest" restriction provided for in Article 31 of the Charter.

In the eleventh cycle, the Committee criticised the general prohibition in Greece by Section 4 1. of Act No. 4310/29 concerning the Status, Entry and Residence of Foreigners of access to Greek territory of members of migrant workers' family suffering from mental illness or infectious diseases (Conclusions XI-1, p. 162). Despite Greece's insistence that this provision would only be applied if the illness in question were to endanger public health, the criticism was reiterated in the twelfth cycle on the ground that the act was too general in its scope (Conclusions XII-I, p. 238).

The requirement of residence of the migrant worker for a long period before family reunion is permitted is incompatible with paragraph 6.

In the first cycle Germany was found in breach of this provision since under the existing regulations permission for members of the family to join a migrant worker could be given only if the migrant had been living in Germany for three years (Conclusions I, p. 69).[1]

Another issue which had often been criticised is the age limit for admission of the dependent children of a migrant worker.

In the United Kingdom the normal age for admission for family reunion was eighteen with the exception of unmarried and fully dependent daughters, for whom the maximum age was twenty-one, on condition that the whole family was settled in the country. As this fell short of the general rule that all dependent children under twenty-one should be admitted, the United Kingdom was found not to comply from the seventh to the eleventh cycle (Conclusions VII, p. 106, VIII p. 216, XI p. 152, and XI p. 164).[2]

On the basis of information supplied by the United Kingdom that in compassionate cases consideration would be given to admitting sons

---

1 In the fourth cycle of supervision the Committee asked for explanations why it was not possible to have a less unfavourable rule than three years' residence and in the sixth cycle it appeared that the Committee could accept the one year working period, which apparently was the normal practice despite the legal requirement of three years' residence, as in line with paragraph 6, if the practice was transposed into law.

2 The situation was remedied by the enactment in 1991 of Act No. 1975. A person may be prohibited from entry if he or she endangers public health, the decision being taken by the Minister of Health in accordance with information from WHO (Conclusions XIII-1, p. 209).

aged eighteen to twenty-one and that there was a right of appeal, the Committee, in line with its new approach (see above), adjourned its conclusion in the twelfth cycle pending receipt of statistical information on applications from this group (Conclusion XII-1, p. 240). In parts one and two of the thirteenth cycle, the Committee was able to confirm that during the relevant reference period there had been no violation of this provision as no applications had been received. However, in view of the continuing absence of applications for residence the Committee asked to what extent the young people concerned and their families were informed of the possibility of benefiting from family reunion (Conclusions XIII-2, p. 205).

The Committee criticised Norway[1] for making suitable housing a prerequisite for family reunion whilst at the same time preventing the worker from applying for family housing as long as he was living alone in the country (Conclusions IV, p. 126 and Conclusions V, p. 136).

Four Contracting Parties are currently found as not complying with Article 19 para. 6: Austria, Belgium, Germany and Greece.

Austria: there is no statutory right to family reunion for young persons aged nineteen to twenty-one and no information has been provided on the number of applications for family reunion by young persons in this age group which have been granted or rejected (see in the last instance Conclusions XIII-2, p. 200).

Belgium (first report): the restrictions placed upon family reunion by the Act of 15 December 1980 on entry, residence, establishment and removal of aliens limit its scope so much that they cannot be considered compatible with the undertaking entered into under Article 19 para. 6: the established age limit for children to be eligible for family reunion is eighteen years, except in the case of the children of nationals of member

---

1 The Norwegian Alien's Act abolished the prerequisite of suitable housing (Conclusions XI-I, p. 163). The Committee however expressed its concern about the situation in practice since a migrant worker must wait ten years for access to subsidised housing which does not facilitate his family reunion (see conclusions under Article 19 para. 4). The position of the Committee is reserved (see cases of deferral below).

states of the European Union and, on certain conditions, the dependent disabled children of a foreign worker; in cases where a foreign national of a non-member state of the European Union has been joined by a member of his family in the context of family reunion, the other members of his family may join him only during the course of the year in which the first reunification has taken place and the following calendar year and it is impossible for an alien who has himself been admitted for family reunion to invoke the right of reunion for his own family. Other issues have given rise to questions posed by the Committee, such as a cohabitation requirement laid down for the family reunion of the spouse and children or the housing situation of immigrants (Conclusions XIII-2, pp. 382 to 384).

Germany: the Committee criticises the age limit for the entry of the children of migrant workers from countries outside the European Union, which is sixteen years. Furthermore, family reunion is not allowed in the case of young people with only one parent resident in Germany, and the spouses of second generation foreigners are allowed in only if the latter has been resident in Germany for at least eight years and has been married for at least one year (Conclusions XI-2, p. 151 and Conclusions XII-2,[1] p. 225). The Committee has sustained its criticism of Germany, despite the entry into force of the new Foreign Nationals Act, which has improved the situation on several issues, as the above restrictions (except the last one) remain (Conclusions XIII-2, p. 385).

Greece: the conclusion is negative as for foreign workers' children aged between eighteen and twenty-one years the granting of a residence permit may be dependent upon evidence indicating that they have sufficient means of subsistence. The Committee asked which criteria are used by the authorities to determine "sufficient means of subsistence" and wished to know what provision is made for those persons over eighteen who are disabled and dependent upon their family, having no "private" means of support. It also asked the number of children aged

---

1 The Committee of Ministers addressed a recommendation to Germany for the second part of the twelfth cycle.

eighteen to twenty-one who were refused entry (Conclusions XIII-1, p. 209; in the last instance, Conclusions XIII-2, p. 201).

The conclusion is deferred in respect of nine Contracting Parties: Finland, Italy, Luxembourg, Norway, Portugal, Spain, Sweden, Turkey and the United Kingdom pending receipt of additional information (see Conclusions XIII-2 and XIII-3):

Finland (first report): information was asked on measures to assist migrant workers in obtaining accommodation suitable for their families; since, in the case of nationals of states not parties to the Agreement on the European Economic Area, family members include dependent children between eighteen and twenty-one years and living in the family, the Committee has asked to learn the number of applications for and refusals of family reunion for children in this age group not living in a foreign workers's family; it has also requested a list of illnesses that may justify a refusal of family reunion for nationals of states not parties to the Agreement, the number of refusals of applications for family reunion on health grounds, and the illnesses concerned (Conclusions XIII-3, pp. 416 to 418);

Italy: information was sought on the interpretation and application of the condition according to which a worker applying for family reunion is required to have suitable accommodation and an adequate income; statistics were requested on applications on behalf of children of nationals of Contracting Parties between the ages of eighteen and twenty-one years, wishing to be reunited with their father or mother and to settle in Italy (a Circular of 1992 restricted the right to family reunion to children under the age of eighteen) (Conclusions XIII-2, pp. 201 and 202);

Luxembourg: as there were restrictions on the admission of children between eighteen and twenty-one years for nationals of states outside the European Union or the European Economic Area, the Committee has asked the legal basis of the restrictions and requested statistics on the number of applications made for family reunion, the number accepted and refused; it has also requested information on refusals of entry on grounds of health and other grounds, particularly in respect of nationals of Contracting Parties not member states of the European Union or parties to the Agreement on the European Economic Area (Addendum to Conclusions XIII-3, pp. 94 to 96);

Norway: the Committee has repeated its request for information about the conditions applying to migrant workers in respect of access to low-cost housing for purposes of family reunion (Conclusions XIII-1, pp. 209 and 210; in the last instance Conclusions XIII-2, p. 203);

Portugal: as the age limit for children entitled to family reunion is eighteen years, except in respect of the children of citizens of the European Union, the Committee has asked to be informed of the number of applications accepted and rejected for children between the ages of eighteen and twenty-one years; it has also requested information on the housing situation of immigrants (Conclusions XIII-3, pp. 418 and 419);

Spain: the Committee asked a number of questions, *inter alia*, on the conditions laid down for the issuing of residence permits to members of the migrants workers's family, the period of validity of residence permits issued for the purpose of family reunion, the numbers of applications submitted for the purpose of family reunion by nationals of Contracting Parties and the numbers of rejections and the grounds for refusal, the diseases which would justify the refusal of family reunion on grounds of public health or safety or public interest (Conclusions XII-2, pp. 226 to 228; in the last instance Conclusions XIII-2, p. 203);

Sweden: the Committee has asked for information on the number of applications for residence permits submitted by young people aged between eighteen and twenty-one, children of nationals of the Contracting Parties (particularly nationals of Cyprus, Malta and Turkey) and the number of those granted and rejected (Conclusions XIII-2, pp. 203 and 204);

Turkey: the Committee asked for a description of the measures taken or envisaged with a view to ensuring that the migrant worker and his family were not discriminated against in law or in practice as regards accommodation; it also asked whether a member of the family having contracted a contagious disease during his stay was granted medical care and if not, whether he or she was liable to expulsion for this reason (Conclusions XIII-3, p. 419);

For the United Kingdom, see above.

In the revised Charter, the appendix to Article 19 para. 6 reads as follows:

"For the purpose of applying this provision, the term 'family of a foreign worker' is understood to mean at least the worker's spouse and unmarried children, as long as the latter are considered to be minors by the receiving state and are dependent on the migrant worker."

Paragraph 7 – Treatment of migrant workers not less favourable than that of nationals in respect of legal proceedings

Under this paragraph, the Contracting Parties undertake to:

"secure for such workers lawfully within their territories treatment not less favourable than that of their own nationals in respect of legal proceedings relating to matters referred to in this Article".

According to this undertaking, migrant workers must be allowed access to courts and tribunals, to lawyers and to legal aid on the same conditions as nationals of the Contracting Party in whose territory they are lawfully. (Conclusions I, p. 86).

In the first supervision cycle the Committee stated that it could not judge whether a Contracting Party satisfied this provision unless it gave adequate information as to whether the forms of legal assistance available to necessitous nationals (exemption from costs, or their payment or part payment from public funds) were also available to migrant workers and their families (Conclusions I, p. 86).

The Committee also made it clear that the undertaking to secure equal treatment for migrant workers[1] in relation to its own nationals must extend to legal proceedings relating to all the matters covered by Article 19 (ie. pay, working conditions, housing, trade union rights, taxes) and that it is insufficient for a state to guarantee it only in some fields, for example criminal law and the law concerning contracts of employment (Conclusions I, p. 217).

There is no requirement of domicile in another Contracting Party in order to benefit from this provision; the text requires only lawful presence within a state's territory (Conclusions VII, p. 108).

The Committee has often questioned Contracting Parties about migrant workers being forced to pay any special security or deposit during legal proceedings which would not be imposed on nationals.[2] In the tenth cycle, it found that Section 534 of the Spanish Civil Procedure Act, which provides for the application of the "*cautio judicatum solvi*" to aliens on condition of reciprocity, was inconsistent with the Charter for this reason (Conclusions X-2, p. 153). However, as the areas covered by Article 19 para. 7 (the right to work and the right to accommodation) are not governed by the above-mentioned Section 534 but by special regulations which do not provide for any legal guarantee for aliens, the Committee "observed that no national of a Contracting State of the Charter could be required, in Spain, to pay the '*cautio judicatum solvi*' in any of the areas covered by Article 19, and that Spain had consequently met its obligation under paragraph 7 of that Article" (Conclusions XI-2, p. 152).

---

1 In his book "The European Social Charter" (p. 180), David Harris expresses the view that even though the text refers only to "workers", it can probably be taken to require that equal rights be accorded also to members of their families in so far as any legal proceedings in which they might be involved (eg. in respect of their admission to the country) come within Article 19.

2 A number of international treaties, such as the 1954 Hague Convention on Civil Procedure and the European Convention on Establishment, provide that securities for costs may not be demanded from nationals of signatory states who take legal proceedings in another signatory state. Not all Contracting Parties to the Charter have ratified these treaties.

Assessment of compliance

Contracting Parties found as not complying are:

Belgium: plaintiffs, nationals of Contracting Parties not bound by the 1954 Hague Convention on Civil Procedure are required to pay security for costs (*cautio judicatum solvi*) at the request of a Belgian defending lawyer (Conclusions XIII-2, pp. 385 to 387);

Luxembourg: domestic law restricts legal aid to nationals only (Addendum to Conclusions XIII-3, p. 96).

The Committee's conclusion is deferred for Portugal (first report) and Turkey (second report) (Conclusions XIII-3, pp. 420 and 421).

Paragraph 8 – Security against expulsion

Under this paragraph,[1] the Contracting Parties undertake:

> "to secure that such workers lawfully residing within their territories are not expelled unless they endanger national security or offend against public interest or morality".

Paragraph 8 applies only to migrant workers who are "lawfully residing within the territory of a Contracting Party". The Committee has interpreted this as meaning workers "in possession of all papers legally required by the country of residence for regular residence, including if need be, a residence permit and a work permit" (Conclusions II, p. 197). In view of this interpretation, the Committee has expressed the view that a person who loses his work permit because he loses his job loses also the protection of paragraph 8 if, as a result, he is no longer entitled to reside in the territory of the Contracting Party.

---

1 This provision is similar to Article 3 para. 1 of the European Convention on Establishment 1955. The Convention covers, however, the expulsion of the nationals of other Contracting Parties generally, whereas paragraph 8 of Article 19 deals only with the expulsion of migrant workers.

On the basis of this interpretation the Committee has held that a Contracting Party which obliges a worker to leave its territory when he loses the job for which he has been granted a work permit and therefore is no longer entitled to reside there, is not infringing paragraph 8, even though the situation causes concern because it allows employers to exert intolerable pressure on the migrant worker (Conclusions II, p. 198, Cyprus).

The Committee has underlined "the limitative nature" of the list of reasons for expulsion as it appears in Article 19 para. 8 and stated that it "would lead it to consider as contrary to the Charter an expulsion based exclusively on health reasons (Conclusions V, p. 138)" (Second report on certain provisions of the Charter which have not been accepted, p. 18).

In the above-mentioned Conclusions, the Committee indicated that a threat to "public health" could not be considered as included in the concept of "public interest" and would not justify expulsion except in the case of a refusal to undergo appropriate treatment (Conclusions V, p. 138, Germany and more recently Conclusions XIII-3, p. 421, Finland and p. 423, Portugal; see also below "Assessment of compliance").

The Committee has stressed, moreover, that Article 19 para. 8 and Article 13 para. 4 (see above under this provision) are complementary. "In view of the reference made by the latter provision to the European Convention on Social and Medical Assistance of 1953, the Charter thus protects also foreigners lawfully residing on the territory of a Contracting Party against the possibility of expulsion due to their being in need or to their bad state of health. This protection completes that provided by paragraph 8 of Article 19, which protects these persons against expulsion unless they endanger national security or offend against public interest or morality" (Second report on certain provisions of the Charter which have not been accepted, p. 18).

According to the case law of the Committee, to fulfil its obligations under this paragraph a Contracting Party "must not only have laws excluding in principle any possibility of expelling workers who are legally resident in its territory unless they endanger national security or offend against public order or morality, but must in addition provide suitable guarantees against the possibility of arbitrary decisions in this matter" (Conclusions I, p. 86). In particular, a Contracting Party must grant migrant workers a right of appeal to a "court or other independent body" against an expulsion order. The Committee has stressed repeatedly that this is so even in cases where national security, public interest or morality are at stake (Conclusions IV, pp. 129 and 130; Conclusions V, pp. 137 to 139; Conclusions VI, p. 128; Conclusions VII, p. 109; Conclusions XII-1, p. 242; Conclusions XIII-1, p. 211; Conclusions XIII-2, p. 207; see also Second report on certain provisions of the Charter which have not been accepted, p. 18).

However, the Committee has never insisted that such appeals have suspensive effect on the order of deportation.

Assessment of compliance

In the past, Cyprus and Germany were found not to comply with this paragraph:

Cyprus:[1] on the ground that migrant workers could be deported under the Aliens and Immigration Law, *inter alia*, if they were destitute, if they were for any reason unable to take care of themselves or if they were considered to be an "undesirable person" (Conclusions III, p. 97; Conclusions IV, p. 128; Conclusions V, p. 137).

Germany:[2] since its laws and regulations provided that migrant workers who were found to have, or suspected of having, certain diseases

---

[1] Situation remedied by the Aliens and Immigration (Amending) Law 54/1976 which prohibited the expulsion of migrant workers unless they endangered national security or offended against the public interest or morality. (Conclusions VI, p. 126).

[2] In the eighth supervision cycle, the Committee concluded that Germany could be regarded on the whole as complying after taking into account the statement of the German Government that health is not normally a reason for expulsion and that this measure is taken only in exceptional cases where the worker refuses to undergo medical treatment and represents a threat for public health (Conclusions VIII, pp. 218 and 219). The Committee asked to be kept informed of cases of expulsion on grounds of health.

(epidemic diseases subject to notification or contagious venereal diseases) could be expelled if "special protective measures did not suffice, in such cases to prevent the health of third parties from being endangered" (Conclusions V, p. 138; Conclusions VI, pp. 127 and 128; Conclusions VII, p. 109).

The Committee did not accept the arguments of Germany that the protection of the health of third parties was a "public health" measure aiming to avoid a threat to "public interest", a concept appearing in paragraph 8. The Committee "could not accept such assimilation of quite distinct concepts. Article 19 para. 8 provided for exceptions to the prescribed rule only where the person concerned 'endangered national security or offended against public interest or morality'; the concept of a threat to 'public health', which had not been added here as in the case of other provisions, was one which could not be considered in terms of the Social Charter as included in the concept of 'public interest' and which in any event, would not justify expulsion except in the case of a refusal to undergo appropriate treatment" (Conclusions V, p. 138; see also Conclusions VI, p. 127). More recently, however, the Committee has sought confirmation for each period of reference that no deportations are ordered in Germany on the ground that the person refuses treatment for a serious illness (Conclusions XII-2, p. 229 and Conclusions XIII-2, p. 388).

Contracting Parties still not complying are:

Greece:[1] even though expulsion was only permitted for acts which offended against public order, which was in conformity with the Charter, there was no right of appeal to an independent body against a decision of expulsion taken by an act of government. The Committee did not consider as a satisfactory remedy the fact that the person issuing an expulsion order may be subjected to disciplinary and penal sanctions if the order is contrary to the Constitution or the law or that the state may be held responsible for the order under civil law (Conclusions XII-1,

---

1 The Committee of Ministers addressed a recommendation to Greece for the first part of the thirteenth supervision cycle.

p. 242; criticism reiterated in Conclusions XIII-1, p. 211 and Conclusions XIII-2, p. 206).

Ireland:[1] nationals of Contracting Parties to the Charter, neither member states of the European Union nor bound by the European Convention on Establishment of 1955 (currently Cyprus and Malta) have no recourse to an independent authority against expulsion (situation constantly criticised since the fourth supervision cycle: Conclusions IV, p. 129; see in the last instance Conclusions XIII-2, pp. 206 and 207).

Sweden:[2] There was no provision for appeal to an independent body in the event of deportation for reasons of national security. The law on suppression of terrorism, which gave the authorities considerable freedom of action and tended to restrict the guarantees given to the persons concerned, had been largely incorporated in the legislation on aliens. While recognising the need to take action against terrorists, even when the latter exploited the privileges conferred on migrant workers to justify their presence in the country's territory, the Committee considered that migrant workers as a whole should not suffer from anti-terrorist measures and that for this purpose the decisions of the administration should be subject to an appeal before an independent body, to prevent any abuses (Conclusions V, p. 139)

The Committee did not accept the argument of the Swedish Government that a deportation order on grounds of national security could not be made unless based on cogent evidence and that a decision could be reviewed if necessary. It insisted on a right of appeal to an independent body (Conclusions VII, p. 109). Neither did the Committee accept the opinion that the judicial hearing preceding government's decisions was an adequate guarantee of aliens' rights (Conclusions XI-1, p. 167).

---

1 The Committee of Ministers addressed a recommendation to Ireland for the first part of the thirteenth supervision cycle, which was renewed for the second part of the thirteenth cycle.

2 The Committee of Ministers addressed a recommendation to Sweden for the first part of the thirteenth supervision cycle, which was renewed for the second part of the thirteenth cycle.

In the third part of the thirteenth cycle, the Committee renewed its negative conclusion, since the new 1991 Act on the control of foreigners stipulated that a deportation order against a foreigner suspected of engaging in terrorist activities was "an act of state" which was not subject to appeal or to the jurisdiction of the Courts. The Committee asked, however, to be informed for each period of reference whether this statutory rule, which was contrary to the Charter, had in practice infringed the rights of migrant workers, nationals of the Contracting Parties to the Charter or their families (Conclusions XIII-2, p. 208).

the *United Kingdom:* There is no right of appeal to a court or any other independent body against an order of the competent Secretary of State to deport a foreign worker lawfully resident on grounds of national security or for political reasons, or relations between the United Kingdom and other countries and therefore no guarantee against arbitrary decisions in such cases (criticism made since the fifth cycle and reiterated in all subsequent cycles: Conclusions V, p. 139; see in the last instance Conclusions XIII-2, p. 209).

The Committee does not consider as adequate the procedure whereby a person subject to a deportation order may make representations to the Secretary of State's panel of three advisers (or to the former directly) because even though the panel's advice may be persuasive, it is in no way legally binding on the Secretary of State (see Conclusions XI-1, p. 167, Conclusions XII-1, p. 243 and Conclusions XIII-2, p. 209).

Turkey: Turkish law permits expulsions on health grounds and nationals of Contracting Parties were expelled for this reason during the reference period. (second report – Conclusions XIII-3, p. 426).

The Committee's conclusions is deferred for Belgium (first report – Conclusions XIII-2, pp. 387 and 388), Finland (first report – Conclusions XIII-3, pp. 421 and 422), Luxembourg (Addendum to Conclusions XIII-3, p. 97) and Spain (Conclusions XIII-2, pp. 207 and 208).

Paragraph 9 – transfer of earnings and savings

Under this paragraph, the Contracting Parties undertake:

> "to permit, within legal limits, the transfer of such parts of the earnings and savings of such workers as they may desire".

In the first cycle the Committee "felt it necessary to scrutinise the intended scope of the words 'within legal limits' which, if taken literally, would deprive the paragraph of any real meaning. It considered that this restriction, while authorising some limit on what might be transferred for currency reasons, could not be understood as permitting a state which had accepted paragraph 9 to place any obstacle in the way of transferring a reasonable amount of earnings and savings, having regard to the situation of the migrant and his family" (Conclusions I, p. 86).

The following have been found as compatible with the requirements of this paragraph:

a. arrangements whereby a migrant worker temporarily resident in a Contracting Party is entitled to transfer to his country of origin any amount of money up to the total of his net earnings, provided he has paid his income tax and deducted "reasonable" current expenses, whereas a migrant worker who notifies his intention to live in that Contracting Party permanently becomes subject in principle to the same restrictions as any resident of that Party. In this case, however, any transfer he might wish to make to his home country to continue payment of certain family obligations such as the education of his children, will be given consideration (Conclusions I, p. 87, the United Kingdom);

b. a situation wherein banks may, upon application by foreigners temporarily resident in a Contracting Party, transfer their earnings provided that:

- the applicant has been living in the country for at least a month;

- total transfers in any period of twelve months do not exceed 50% of the applicant's earning during that period;

– the savings are transferred to the applicant's country of origin.

Any transfer above these limits is allowed for frontier, seasonal and other non-resident workers provided that it is made to the recipient's country of residence (Conclusions I, pp. 218 and 219, Ireland);

c. regulations providing for assessment, in the case of final departure, of a migrant worker's fiscal transactions, taking into account the amounts transferred by the worker during the time of his residence in the Contracting State concerned, aimed at facilitating verification of declared income in order to prevent tax avoidance (Conclusions XII-1, pp. 241 and 242 and Conclusions XIII-1, p. 212).

Furthermore, from the examination of the situation in a Contracting Party it appears that the existence of a rule, under which transfers of money to countries other than the country of origin are not permitted, would still be compatible with this provision provided certain exceptions are possible eg. for the payment of maintenance and payments to dependants and other similar expenses for which an immigrant worker may be liable (Conclusions IX-1, p. 111 and X-1, p. 155, Sweden).

As regards equality of treatment with nationals, the Committee stated in the fourth cycle, reacting to a statement made in the report of a Contracting Party that the nationals of other Contracting Parties were treated equally with nationals, that this provision implied that if substantial restrictions were imposed on the transfer of money abroad by citizens of a state, more generous arrangements should be made for foreign migrants on the state's territory (Conclusions IV, p. 131, Italy).

In order to assess compliance the Committee asks:

– whether there are any restrictions to the right of workers to transfer their earnings, either whilst they reside or when they leave the territory of the Contracting Party concerned;

– if so, the extent of such restrictions;

– whether transfers can be made to countries other than the country of origin;

– whether self-employed migrant workers can transfer their earnings and savings in the same way as employed migrant workers.

On the whole, the application of this provision poses no problems to Contracting Parties which do not impose any restrictions on the right of migrant workers to transfer earnings or savings less deductions of tax, social security contributions and the amount necessary for their subsistence outside their territory.

Assessment of compliance

There are no cases of non-compliance with this provision. The Committee has deferred its conclusion in respect of Turkey, pending receipt of further information (Conclusions XIII-3, p. 428).

Paragraph 10[1] – Extension of protection and assistance to self-employed migrants

Under this paragraph, the Contracting Parties undertake:

> "to extend the protection and assistance provided for in this Article to self-employed migrants in so far as such measures apply".[2]

In the first supervision cycle, the Committee stated that as this provision related solely to extending the protection and assistance embodied in the other paragraphs of Article 19 to the self-employed, it is important that its comments should be considered not in isolation, but together with those made under each of the other paragraphs of Article 19. Hence any statement that a particular state has fulfilled its obligations deriving from paragraph 10 is valid only in so far as the Committee has been able to reach a similar conclusion in respect of the other paragraphs also (Conclusions I, p. 87).

---

1 It goes beyond the ILO Migration for Employment Convention (Revised) 1949 No. 97, which applies to employed persons only.

2 The only measure which would seem not to apply is that in Article 19 para. 4a. concerning "remuneration and other working conditions".

In the third cycle, while taking note of the fact that in a Contracting Party there was no legislation which discriminated against the self-employed, the Committee called attention to its case law (Conclusions I, p. 81) to the effect that "Article 19 imposes on governments not merely the obligation to prevent discrimination between migrant and national self-employed workers, but also requires continuous positive action designed to give migrants equivalent protection to that enjoyed by other workers" (Conclusions III, p. 99, Italy).

In the fourth cycle, the Committee recalled that "paragraph 10 implies not only equality in law between salaried workers and independent workers but provides as well for positive and specific measures for the latter category" (Conclusions IV, p. 131, Norway).

In the ninth cycle (second part) the Committee pointed out that "by virtue of this provision, certain paragraphs of Article 19, relating, for instance, to free assistance services, family reunion, equal treatment as regards taxation, dues, access to courts, housing, etc. must also be applied to self-employed migrant workers and their families" (Conclusions IX-2, p. 102, France; see in this connection the previous footnote).

The Committee's conclusion under Article 19 para. 10 is generally that a Contracting Party complies with this provision of the Charter to the extent that it complies with the other paragraphs of Article 19 (see above or Conclusions I, p. 87; more recently, Conclusions XIII-3, p. 425, Portugal).

However, such a conclusion implies that the same legislation applies to salaried and independent migrant workers; when it is not the case, the Committee's conclusion under paragraph 10 of Article 19 does not refer to the other paragraphs of this Article. Thus, for instance, having noted that in a Contracting Party self-employed migrant workers enjoyed only the facilities provided under paragraph 6 of Article 19, the Committee was obliged to conclude that this state did not fulfil the undertaking deriving from paragraph 10 of this Article (Conclusions I, p. 88, Norway; see also Conclusions VIII, p. 221, where the Committee, noting that "no difference exists between the rights which self-employed immigrants enjoy and those which other migrant workers enjoy under paragraphs 1-9 of Article 19", adopted the same, positive conclusion under Article 19 para. 10 as under the other nine paragraphs).

Assessment of compliance

There are no cases of non-compliance.

The Committee has however adjourned its conclusion in respect of Turkey and sought more information, as foreigners are apparently excluded from self-employment and forbidden to practice certain professions which would attract self-employed migrant workers (Conclusions XIII-1, p. 273, first report and Conclusions XIII-3, p. 425, second report).

In the revised Charter, the following two new paragraphs have been added to Article 19:

"With a view to ensuring the effective exercise of the right of migrant workers and their families to protection and assistance in the territory of any other Party, the Parties undertake:

...

11. to promote and facilitate the teaching of the national language of the receiving state or, if there are several, one of these languages, to migrant workers and members of their families;

12. to promote and facilitate, as far as practicable, the teaching of the migrant worker's mother tongue to the children of the migrant worker."

Appendix I

System of supervision of the application of the European Social Charter

A system of international supervision has been established to monitor the effective implementation of the various provisions of the Charter by the Contracting Parties (Articles 21 to 29 of the Charter). It is based on the examination of the national reports which the states bound by the Charter submit at regular intervals; these reports review each state's application of the provisions it has accepted.[1] The Protocol amending the European Social Charter, opened for signature on 21 October 1991 in Turin, modified this system of supervision. Currently ratified by ten states (Austria, Cyprus, Finland, France, Italy, Malta, the Netherlands, Norway, Portugal and Sweden) and signed by five other Contracting Parties, the protocol will enter into force when it has been ratified by all the Contracting Parties to the Charter. However, in compliance with the final resolution of the Turin Ministerial Conference during which it was opened for signature and the decision taken by the Committee of Ministers on 11 December 1991, the provisions of the Amending Protocol are applied "before its entry into force, in so far as the text of the Charter will allow".

The control mechanism presently functions as follows:

---

1 See, in appendix 1, Article 20 of the Charter concerning undertakings.

- firstly, analysis of reports – which are public – falls to the *Committee of Independent Experts*. The Committee is composed of nine Experts elected by the Committee of Minister for a period of six years, assisted by an observer from the ILO. It assesses from a legal standpoint the compliance of national law, regulations and practice with the obligations arising from the Charter. Its assessments take the form of "conclusions"; these are "positive" if the Committee finds the situation in conformity with the Charter, "negative" if it considers that the situation is not – or not entirely – in compliance with the requirements of the Charter, and the Committee adjourns its conclusion if it does not possess all the necessary information. When a new issue arises which concerns all the Contracting parties, or when the Committee decides to examine a question in more depth and wishes to obtain information on national situations in this area, it asks a "general question" on a precise provision.

The adopted decisions are collected in a volume of "Conclusions", which is public;

- then the *Governmental Committee*, composed of representatives of the Contracting Parties and observers from the European social partners, prepares the Committee of Ministers' decisions. In particular, in the light of the conclusions of the Committee of Independent Experts, it selects, on the basis of social, economic and other policy considerations the situations which should, in its view, be the subject of recommendations to each Contracting Party concerned. The result of this work is a "Report to the Committee of Ministers";

- finally, on the basis of the Governmental Committee's report, the *Committee of Ministers* adopts a resolution on the whole of the supervision cycle and individual recommendations addressed to the Contracting Parties concerned.

Furthermore, in conformity with the Turin Protocol and following an exchange of letters between the President of the Parliamentary Assembly and the Chairman of the Committee of Ministers in September 1992, the *Parliamentary Assembly* decided to abstain from communicating its views on a particular set of conclusions and to organise periodical social policy debates on the basis of the conclusions of the Committee of Independent Experts (Directive No. 482 of 7 October 1992).

Until 1992, the control procedure took place every two years with regard to each Contracting Party. With a view to ensuring that the work of the competent bodies was organised on a more rational basis, in 1981 the Contracting Parties were divided into two groups, subject to supervision in alternate years. Following a decision of the Ministers' Deputies (17 September 1992), the periodicity of the national reports was changed. According to the system then adopted, which was introduced for a trial period of four years, all the Contracting Parties, with the exception of those states having recently ratified the Charter as well as Germany (which did not accept the system), report each year on certain selected Articles of the Charter.

In September 1996, the Committee of Ministers decided on a new system for the presentation of national reports. According to the new system all the Contracting Parties will submit a report for the same reference period and on the same provisions. They have to report on the hard core every second year and on the non-hard core provisions every fourth year. The Contracting Parties have a choice as to whether they wish to submit yearly reports or reports every second year. The first reports under the new system will be submitted in June 1997.

The Additional Protocol providing for a system of collective complaints

This Protocol was adopted by the Committee of Ministers in June 1995. It was opened for signature on 9 November 1995. Its aim is to increase the efficiency of the supervisory machinery of the Social Charter, by providing that in addition to the current procedure of examination of governmental reports, collective complaints against alleged violations of the Charter may be dealt with.

Who is entitled to submit complaints?

- international non-governmental organisations of employers and workers participating in the work of the Governmental Committee under Article 27 para. 2 of the Charter;

- other international non-governmental organisations having consultative status with the Council of Europe, included for this purpose on a special list drawn up by the Governmental Committee;

- the national employers' and workers' associations of the Contracting Party concerned.

In addition, each state may, by a declaration to the Secretary General, allow national non-governmental organisations to file complaints against it.

What is the procedure?

Collective complaints are examined by the Committee which must first of all assess their admissibility according to certain criteria listed in the Protocol, which should be specified in its rules of procedure. Following this and after having collected information from the initiator of the complaint, from the State concerned, from the other Contracting Parties to the Charter and from the social partners, the Committee draws up a report to the Committee of Ministers containing its conclusions as to whether or not the Contracting Party in question has ensured the satisfactory application of the provision of the Charter referred to in the complaint.

The Committee of Ministers must then adopt either a recommendation addressed to the Contracting Party in question if the Committee finds that the Charter has not been applied satisfactorily, or a resolution if application is found to be satisfactory.

The Protocol has been ratified by one state (Cyprus) and signed by seven others (Belgium, Denmark, Finland, France, Italy, Portugal and Sweden) and will enter into force after its ratification by five Contracting Parties to the Charter.

Appendix II

Membership of the Committee of Independent Experts

Date of (first) election			Terms of office
1966:	Mr Arena	(Italian)	1966-1967
	Mr Armbruster	(German)	1966-1972
			1973-1976
	Mr Bull	(Norwegian)	1966-1972
			1972-1978
			1978-1984
			1984-1990
	Mr Busuttil	(Maltese)	1966-1972
	Mr Geary	(Irish)	1966-1972
	Mr Kahn-Freund	(British)	1966-1972
	Mr Laroque	(French)	1966-1970
			1970-1976
1967:	Mr Parrillo	(Italian)	1967-1970
1970:	Mr Strasser	(Austrian)	1970-1973
1972:	Mr Kojanec	(Italian)	1972-1978
			1978-1984
			1984-1990
			1990-1996

Date of (first) election			Terms of office
	Mr Loizou	(Cypriot)	1972-1978
			1978-1984
	Mr Troclet	(Belgian)	1972-1978
	Mr Zanetti	(Swiss)	1972-1978
			1978-1984
1976:	Mr Fabricius	(German)	1976-1982
			1982-1988
			1988-1994
	Mr Morgan	(British)	1976-1980
1978:	Mr De Gaay Fortman	(Dutch)	1978-1984
			1984-1990
1980:	Mr James	(British)	1980-1982
1982:	Mr Laurent	(French)	1982-1988
1984:	Mr Ohlinger	(Austrian)	1984-1990
	Mr Vida Soria	(Spanish)	1984-1990
			1990-1996
1988:	Mrs Grévisse	(French)	1988-1994
			1994-2000
1990:	Mrs Billum Stegard	(Swedish)	1990-1996
	Mr Harris	(British)	1990-1996
	Mr Jaspers	(Dutch)	1990-1996
1994:	Mr Birk	(German)	1994-2000
	Mr Grillberger	(Austrian)	1994-2000
	Mr Mikkola	(Finnish)	1994-2000
1996:	Mr Akillioglu	(Turkish)	1996-2002
	Mr Aliprantis	(Greek)	1996-2002
	Mr Bruto Da Costa	(Portuguese)	1996-2002
	Mr Evju	(Norwegian)	1996-2002
	Mrs Jamoulle	(Belgian)	1996-2002

Appendix III : Table showing details of acceptance of the various provisions of the European Social Charter and of the Additional Protocol of 1988.

	accepted		not accepted

Provision of the Charter	Austria	Belgium	Cyprus	Denmark	Finland	France	Germany	Greece	Iceland
Article 1 (1)	✓	✓	✓	✓	✓	✓	✓	✓	✓
Article 1 (2)	✓	✓	✓	✓	✓	✓	✓	✓	✓
Article 1 (3)	✓	✓	✓	✓	✓	✓	✓	✓	✓
Article 1 (4)	✓	✓	✓	✓	✓	✓	✓	✓	✓
Article 2 (1)		✓	✓		✓	✓	✓	✓	✓
Article 2 (2)	✓	✓		✓	✓	✓	✓	✓	
Article 2 (3)	✓	✓	✓	✓	✓	✓	✓	✓	✓
Article 2 (4)	✓	✓			✓	✓	✓	✓	
Article 2 (5)	✓	✓	✓	✓	✓	✓	✓	✓	✓
Article 3 (1)	✓	✓	✓	✓		✓	✓	✓	✓
Article 3 (2)	✓	✓	✓	✓		✓	✓	✓	✓
Article 3 (3)	✓	✓	✓	✓	✓	✓	✓	✓	✓
Article 4 (1)	✓	✓		✓		✓	✓	✓	✓
Article 4 (2)	✓	✓		✓	✓	✓	✓	✓	✓
Article 4 (3)	✓	✓		✓	✓	✓	✓	✓	✓
Article 4 (4)		✓	✓	✓	✓	✓		✓	✓
Article 4 (5)	✓	✓			✓	✓	✓	✓	✓
Article 5	✓	✓	✓	✓	✓	✓	✓		✓

Ireland	Italy	Luxem-bourg	Malta	Nether-lands'	Norway	Portugal	Spain	Sweden	Turkey	United Kingdom

accepted (shaded) — not accepted (white)

Provision of the Charter	Austria	Belgium	Cyprus	Denmark	Finland	France	Germany	Greece	Iceland
Article 6 (1)	accepted	accepted	accepted	accepted	accepted	accepted	accepted		accepted
Article 6 (2)	accepted	accepted	accepted	accepted	accepted	accepted	accepted		accepted
Article 6 (3)	accepted	accepted	accepted	accepted	accepted	accepted	accepted	accepted	accepted
Article 6 (4)		accepted	accepted	accepted	accepted	accepted	accepted		accepted
Article 7 (1)		accepted	accepted		accepted	accepted		accepted	
Article 7 (2)	accepted	accepted		accepted	accepted	accepted		accepted	accepted
Article 7 (3)	accepted	accepted	accepted		accepted	accepted	accepted	accepted	
Article 7 (4)	accepted		accepted		accepted	accepted	accepted	accepted	
Article 7 (5)	accepted	accepted		accepted	accepted	accepted	accepted	accepted	
Article 7 (6)		accepted				accepted	accepted	accepted	
Article 7 (7)	accepted	accepted	accepted		accepted	accepted	accepted	accepted	
Article 7 (8)	accepted	accepted			accepted	accepted	accepted		
Article 7 (9)	accepted	accepted				accepted	accepted	accepted	
Article 7 (10)	accepted	accepted			accepted	accepted	accepted	accepted	
Article 8 (1)	accepted	accepted	accepted	accepted		accepted	accepted	accepted	
Article 8 (2)	accepted	accepted	accepted		accepted	accepted		accepted	
Article 8 (3)	accepted	accepted				accepted	accepted	accepted	
Article 8 (4)	accepted	accepted				accepted	accepted	accepted	

Ireland	Italy	Luxem-bourg	Malta	Nether-lands	Norway	Portugal	Spain	Sweden	Turkey	United Kingdom
								1			

1. Spain has not been bound by sub-paragraph *b* of this provision since 5 June 1991.

Legend: shaded cell = accepted; empty cell = not accepted.

Provision of the Charter	Austria	Belgium	Cyprus	Denmark	Finland	France	Germany	Greece	Iceland
Article 9	accepted	accepted	accepted	accepted	accepted	accepted	accepted	accepted	
Article 10 (1)	accepted	accepted		accepted	accepted	accepted	accepted	accepted	
Article 10 (2)	accepted	accepted		accepted	accepted	accepted	accepted	accepted	
Article 10 (3)	accepted	accepted		accepted	accepted	accepted	accepted	accepted	
Article 10 (4)	accepted	accepted		accepted	accepted	accepted		accepted	
Article 11 (1)	accepted	accepted		accepted	accepted	accepted	accepted	accepted	accepted
Article 11 (2)	accepted	accepted	accepted	accepted	accepted	accepted	accepted	accepted	accepted
Article 11 (3)	accepted	accepted	accepted	accepted	accepted	accepted	accepted	accepted	accepted
Article 12 (1)	accepted	accepted	accepted	accepted	accepted	accepted	accepted	accepted	accepted
Article 12 (2)	accepted	accepted	accepted	accepted	accepted	accepted	accepted	accepted	accepted
Article 12 (3)	accepted	accepted	accepted	accepted	accepted	accepted	accepted	accepted	accepted
Article 12 (4)	accepted	accepted	accepted	accepted	accepted	accepted	accepted	accepted	accepted
Article 13 (1)	accepted	accepted		accepted	accepted	accepted	accepted	accepted	accepted
Article 13 (2)	accepted	accepted		accepted	accepted	accepted	accepted	accepted	accepted
Article 13 (3)	accepted	accepted		accepted	accepted	accepted	accepted	accepted	accepted
Article 13 (4)	accepted	accepted		accepted	accepted	accepted	accepted	accepted	accepted
Article 14 (1)	accepted	accepted	accepted	accepted	accepted	accepted	accepted	accepted	accepted
Article 14 (2)	accepted	accepted	accepted	accepted	accepted	accepted	accepted	accepted	accepted

Ireland	Italy	Luxem-bourg	Malta	Nether-lands	Norway	Portugal	Spain	Sweden	Turkey	United Kingdom
			1							

1. Only the provisions of paragraph 4.*a* and *d* have been accepted.

accepted   not accepted

Provision of the Charter	Austria	Belgium	Cyprus	Denmark	Finland	France	Germany	Greece	Iceland
Article 15 (1)	accepted	accepted	accepted	accepted	accepted	accepted	accepted	accepted	accepted
Article 15 (2)	accepted	accepted	accepted	accepted	accepted	accepted	accepted	accepted	accepted
Article 16	accepted	accepted	not accepted	accepted	accepted	accepted	accepted	accepted	accepted
Article 17	accepted	accepted	not accepted	accepted	accepted	accepted	accepted	accepted	accepted
Article 18 (1)	accepted	accepted	not accepted	accepted	accepted	accepted	accepted	accepted	accepted
Article 18 (2)	accepted	accepted	not accepted	accepted	accepted	accepted	accepted	accepted	accepted
Article 18 (3)	not accepted	accepted	accepted	accepted	accepted	accepted	accepted	accepted	accepted
Article 18 (4)	accepted	accepted	accepted	accepted	accepted	accepted	accepted	accepted	accepted
Article 19 (1)	accepted	accepted	not accepted	not accepted	accepted	accepted	accepted	accepted	not accepted
Article 19 (2)	accepted	accepted	accepted	not accepted	accepted	accepted	accepted	accepted	not accepted
Article 19 (3)	accepted	accepted	accepted	not accepted	accepted	accepted	accepted	accepted	not accepted
Article 19 (4)	not accepted	accepted	accepted	accepted	accepted	accepted	accepted	accepted	accepted
Article 19 (5)	accepted	accepted	accepted	accepted	accepted	accepted	accepted	accepted	accepted
Article 19 (6)	accepted	accepted	accepted	not accepted	accepted	accepted	accepted	accepted	not accepted
Article 19 (7)	accepted	accepted	accepted	not accepted	accepted	accepted	accepted	accepted	not accepted
Article 19 (8)	accepted	accepted	accepted	not accepted	accepted	accepted	accepted	accepted	not accepted
Article 19 (9)	accepted	accepted	accepted	not accepted	accepted	accepted	accepted	accepted	not accepted
Article 19 (10)	not accepted	accepted	accepted	not accepted	not accepted	accepted	accepted	accepted	not accepted

Ireland	Italy	Luxem-bourg	Malta	Nether-lands	Norway	Portugal	Spain	Sweden	Turkey	United Kingdom

| | accepted | | | not accepted | | |

Provision of the Protocol	Denmark	Finland	Italy	Nether-lands[1]	Norway	Sweden
Article 1	accepted	accepted	accepted	accepted	accepted	accepted
Article 2	accepted	accepted	accepted	accepted	accepted	accepted
Article 3	accepted	accepted	accepted	accepted	accepted	accepted
Article 4	accepted	accepted	accepted	not accepted	accepted	accepted

Index

European Court of Human Rights, 117, 118, 120, 355, 356, 368.

European Union, 41, 42, 193, 247, 273, 274, 311, 312, 377, 384, 388, 389, 409, 410, 414, 422-424, 431.

Expulsion, 113, 425, 427-432.

F

Fair remuneration, 15, 75, 185, 203, 206.

Family benefits, 300, 311, 312, 349, 350, 353, 354, 356, 362.

Family business, 191, 199.

Family housing, 349, 351, 416, 421.

Family policy, 350, 354.

Family reunion, 266, 380, 411, 414-424, 436.

Father, 228, 352, 355, 356, 362, 364, 423.

Finland, 19, 26, 27, 34, 37, 38, 42, 46, 49, 53, 54, 60, 61, 82, 86, 147, 148, 159, 161, 184, 208, 213, 215, 238, 257, 263, 270, 274, 278, 280, 281, 290, 291, 293, 302, 308-311, 314, 319, 325, 326, 337, 342, 343, 346, 384, 403, 405, 418, 423, 428, 432, 439, 442.

Forced labour, 21-23, 28.

Foreign workers, 20, 106, 137, 224, 275, 278, 376, 378, 381, 382, 385, 387, 394, 396, 399, 403, 408, 410, 411, 415, 422, 423.

France, 19, 20, 23, 24, 45, 47, 79, 83, 84, 98, 106, 111, 121, 127, 138, 149, 155, 157, 179, 181-183, 188, 189, 191, 199, 204, 211, 233, 234, 243, 246, 248, 263, 265, 268, 271, 275, 276, 289, 292, 299, 307, 309, 311, 316, 327, 335, 336, 341, 352, 369, 379, 386, 402, 408, 418, 419, 436, 439, 442.

Free employment services, 35-38.

Freedom of association, 21, 110, 112, 114, 116, 120, 132, 136, 137, 140, 141, 153, 155, 157, 170-172, 174.

Freedom to join trade unions, 115, 116, 121.

G

Germany, 22, 31, 34, 42, 48, 53, 83, 89-91, 128, 138, 146, 150, 164-167, 169, 170, 174, 183, 194, 208, 216, 232, 243, 265-268, 270, 274, 275, 289, 294, 308, 311, 316, 317, 335, 342, 344, 355, 356, 370, 377, 379, 382, 383, 385, 386, 396, 399, 403, 408-410, 413, 420-422, 428-430, 441.

Governmental Committee, 9, 12, 364, 440, 441.

Greece, 19, 20, 24-27, 33, 34, 37-39, 41, 50, 68, 71, 79, 83, 90, 97, 99, 103, 191, 199, 215, 224, 225, 231, 233, 238, 239, 246, 248, 251, 252, 259, 262, 269, 272, 273, 279, 280, 314-317, 321, 322, 325, 328, 333, 341, 343, 345, 380, 383, 384, 388, 390, 391, 398, 400, 403, 418-422, 430.

U

V

W

Y

Imprimé en France. JOUVE, 18, rue St Denis, 75001 PARIS
N° 243414H. Dépôt légal : Avril 1997